THE
BUS
STOPS
HERE

THE
BUS
STOPS
HERE

A Study of
School Desegregation
in Three Cities

by Anna Holden

AGATHON PRESS, INC., NEW YORK

Distributed by

SCHOCKEN BOOKS, NEW YORK

For information address:
Agathon Press, Inc.
150 Fifth Avenue
New York, N.Y. 10011

Trade distribution by:
Schocken Books Inc.
200 Madison Avenue
New York, N.Y. 10016

Printed in the United States

Library of Congress Cataloging in Publication Data

Holden, Anna.
   The bus stops here; a study of school desegregation
   in three cities.

Bibliography: p.
      1. School integration—Charlottesville, Va.
      2. School integration—Providence.
      3. School integration—Sacramento, Calif.
         I. Title.
LA381.C45H64   370.19'342   72-95964
ISBN 0–87586–038–9

Contents

Introduction and Acknowledgments

THIS study originated in 1968, when the concept of establishing racial balance in the schools was just beginning to penetrate at the local level and desegregation was being carried out mainly on a one-way basis, by busing minority pupils to predominantly white schools. Two of the districts studied, Charlottesville, Virginia, and Providence, Rhode Island, were then groping their way toward racial balance, primarily because of local pressures, and both had instituted some desegregation of black as well as white schools. The third district, the Sacramento City Unified School District, Sacramento, California, was resisting both racial balance and two-way desegregation when field work for this project began, although the California State Board of Education had adopted new regulations that included guidelines for racial balance in local districts. Only early in 1972, when this research was ending, did the Sacramento district show signs of beginning to implement state racial balance requirements in its desegregation plans.

Pressures on local school systems to desegregate through a districtwide racial balance approach have increased considerably since 1969, as has the demand for two-way desegregation—the busing of whites as well as minorities and the simultaneous integration of both minority and white-dominated schools. Indeed, it is the prominence of these two trends in the current desegregation thrust that has created the heightened controversy over busing. While most of the data presented here predate the present busing debate, the experiences of these three districts foreshadow the current conflict, documenting the problems and issues that have prompted the courts, state departments and boards of education, and state legislatures to specify that desegregation be defined in terms of racial balance and carried out with the movement of white as well as minority children.

The bulk of the research for this project was carried out under a contract to the U. S. Commission on Civil Rights, in 1969 and 1970, in an attempt to illustrate some of the positive accomplishments and problems of small and medium-sized school systems that had undertaken substantial pupil desegregation. Following its major study *Racial Isolation in the Public Schools* (1967), the

Commission was interested in reporting in greater detail on how desegregation had come about in specific school systems in different parts of the country and how desegregation had worked in these districts once it was put into practice. Pointing out some of the lessons of successful desegregation for other local school districts was a chief concern of the Commission. The Commission contracted with the author and the Center for Urban Education to examine three school districts that had made important gains in ending racial separation in their schools in the mid-1960s: Charlottesville, Virginia; Providence, Rhode Island; and the Sacramento (California) City Unified School District. While the Commission funded the initial research, that agency is in no way responsible for the ideas or conclusions in this report.

Specific school districts selected for study by Commission staff were picked in consultation with the author on the basis of a number of factors, including geographic spread, forces precipitating desegregation, ethnic composition, the relative ease or difficulty with which desegregation had taken place, and the kind of community setting. Having narrowed down the choice to a few school districts, there was an attempt to secure as much variety as possible among these variables. There were several other, more specific criteria used in choosing the sample districts. To broaden the scope and make the study as realistic as possible, at least one system among those picked was to have an ethnic group other than blacks involved in desegregation; at least one was to have experienced opposition to desegregation from a significant segment of the minority community; and at least one was to have achieved desegregation only with the greatest of difficulties. In addition, school districts where studies were recently completed or where outside evaluations were known to be in process were avoided. In balancing all these considerations the three districts included in this report were finally chosen.

Most of the data were collected in the winter and spring of 1969 during field trips of approximately three weeks' duration to each of the districts. Field work included interviews with school district administrators, board members, principals, teachers, community leaders active in desegregation, parents, and students. School district records, organizational files, and newspaper accounts were examined. Local studies, reports, and position papers on desegregation were collected, and copies of court decisions, citizen complaints, public hearings, and legislation bearing on desegregation were studied. The Washington, D.C. files of the Office for Civil Rights, U.S. Department of Health,

Education and Welfare (HEW), and of the Division of Equal Educational Opportunities, U.S. Office of Education, were checked for information on all three districts. Where pertinent, other U.S. Office of Education program files were also examined. In California and Rhode Island, where state policy and action affected the sample districts, state agency sources were consulted. Published articles on desegregation in all three districts were searched out. In short, every effort was made to bring together as much information as could be found on the course and direction of desegregation in these districts.

After completion of the original research, the study was updated in late 1971 and early 1972 by examining newspapers from the districts available in the Library of Congress and other published sources. Appropriate HEW and U. S. Office of Education files were rechecked and new proposals for desegregation in these districts were obtained. A limited number of telephone interviews with community leaders and/or school district officials were conducted and 1970 census information, where available, was substituted for 1960 reports. The data on Providence was brought up through October 1971; Charlottesville, through November 1971; and Sacramento, through February 1972. Because of lack of funding for more extensive research, no other work following up on the 1969 research could be done.

The final report is more comprehensive and covers a longer period of time than originally contemplated. The research process itself has highlighted important facets of the school desegregation struggle: (1) the search for equal educational opportunity on the part of minorities is long-term and continues; (2) although important, the desegregation of pupils is only one aspect of the total quest for equality in education; and (3) the past history of race and education is so intertwined with present developments that it is difficult to separate the two and see a beginning or an end to racial problems in the schools. Yet the break with the past must be made. Racial inequality in education must end and the schools must learn, however painful the lesson, to serve black and Mexican children and the children of other ethnic minorities. Desegregation is essential to equality in education, as far as the author is concerned, and it was with this hope that the report was written—that other school districts grappling with problems of racial integration might benefit from the experiences of these districts.

I would like to thank, first of all, the many black, white, and chicano community leaders, parents, interested citizens, and students in each of the three cities who agreed to interviews for this study and generously shared their knowledge and concerns about school desegregation. I cannot list them all individually, but I would like to name those who were especially helpful in loaning personal or organizational files, locating hard-to-find background reports, and suggesting important sources to round out my understanding of the process of desegregation in their districts. They include:

Charlottesville, Virginia—Mrs. Fred Landess, President, PTA Council, 1967–1969; and Mrs. Daniel Mohler, President, PTA Council, 1965–1967.

Providence, Rhode Island—Charles Bakst, Education Writer, *Providence Journal-Bulletin;* Reverend Raymond E. Gibson, Chairman, Rhode Island State Advisory Committee to the U. S. Commission on Civil Rights; Dr. Myron Lieberman, formerly Professor of Education and Director of Education Research, Rhode Island College; Mrs. John Rollins, Chairman, Committee to Eliminate Racism in the Public Schools; Mrs. Kenneth W. Stanley, President, Providence Council of PTA's; Mrs. Stanley Summer, President, League of Women Voters of Providence, Rhode Island; and James N. Williams, Executive Director, Urban League of Rhode Island.

Sacramento, California—Mrs. Herbert Cortez, former Chairman, Community Education Advisory Committee on Compensatory Education; Adolph Moskovitz, Board of Education; Ples A. Griffin, Acting Director, Bureau of Intergroup Relations, California State Department of Education; and Dr. Leonard D. Cain, Jr., sociologist and former staff member, Sacramento State College.

I am particularly grateful to Dr. Harold W. Pfautz, Department of Sociology and Anthropology, Brown University, for allowing me to read his own unpublished study of school desegregation in Providence and for sharing his analyses of racial enrollment in the Providence schools, prepared for the Urban League of Rhode Island.

The cooperation of school personnel in the three cities was crucial to the study. I would like to thank Superintendent of Schools Edward W. Rushton, Charlottesville; Acting Superintendent Louis Kramer, Providence; and Superintendent Paul B. Salmon, Sacramento, for making it possible to interview teachers, principals, and other staff and to explore relevant files in their central administration offices. In Charlottesville, Assistant Superintendent William C. Berry; Director of Secondary Education Thomas L. Varner; Administrative Assistant and Clerk of the Board Booker T. Reaves; and Mrs. Betty B. Glass, Secretary to the Superintendent, were of great assistance in furnishing me with background information and reports. In Providence, Coordinating Principal Thomas J. McDonald; former Coordinating Principal Mary K. Joyce; Miss Mary C. O'Brien, Principal, Martin Luther King School; and Miss Gertrude Coleman, Director of Elementary Education, reviewed their own experiences with desegregation in depth and loaned me much material. In Sacramento, Dr. Donald E. Hall, Assistant Superintendent, Planning and Research Office, secured for me numbers of planning and research documents bearing on the district's desegregation projects. Dr. Ervin Jackson, Assistant to the Superintendent, Intergroup Relations Services, and Richard D. Whinnery, Program Specialist, Social Science, also made many other pertinent clippings, memos, and reports available to me.

Miss Joanne Williams, Research Assistant for the project, conducted most of the interviews in the black community in the three cities, researched most of the school district and agency files in each of the districts, and searched out many of the published sources on the three cities.

Mrs. Bernice Wright of Washington, D.C. worked far beyond the call of duty in typing most of the early drafts of this report.

The U. S. Commission on Civil Rights funded this study under Contract CCR 68-39, opened their files on the three cities to me, and were helpful in other ways.

I am indebted to the Center for Urban Education for making it possible to carry out this project under Center auspices. I would particularly like to thank James Elsbery, Ruth Dropkin, and others at the Center who gave this study their wholehearted support.

PART 1

Charlottesville, Virginia: A Southern City's Struggle to Achieve Racial Balance

Foreword

COMPLETE desegregation of the Charlottesville public schools was accomplished over a period of 12 years extending from 1955 to 1967. Throughout this period, the school board ran the gamut of reactions and approaches, from massive resistance to busing. By 1967, when the last white elementary school was desegregated, the board had accepted an informal racial balance policy that was partially incorporated in a policy resolution concerning the building of new high school facilities. The purpose of the board's racial balance policy, which was not fully spelled out in writing at the time of this study, is to distribute blacks throughout all schools, limiting the concentration in any one school to 40 percent of the total student enrollment.

The struggle for total desegregation in Charlottesville can be roughly divided into four phases: (1) massive resistance to desegregation, 1955–1959; (2) token desegregation under court order, 1959–1964; (3) major desegregation of junior high schools and elementary schools, 1965–1967; and (4) major desegregation of Lane High School, 1967–1969. With the desegregation of Lane High School, all of Charlottesville's regular schools were completely desegregated.

This report summarizes major developments in each of the four phases of desegregation, including the teacher and staff desegregation that took place along with pupil desegregation. The last section points up some of the current—and unresolved—racial issues before the school district, even though physical desegregation of the schools has for all practical purposes been achieved.

1

Community Background

Location. The city of Charlottesville is located in central Virginia near the point where the rolling countryside of the Upper Piedmont meets the Blue Ridge Mountains. The city itself is

3

in the hilly terrain of the Upper Piedmont, about 21 miles from the Shenandoah Valley and Shenandoah National Park. In the geographic center of Albemarle County, Charlottesville is 70 miles west of Richmond, Virginia's state capital, and 115 miles southwest of Washington, D.C. Easy access to these two major urban and governmental centers is important to developments in both the white and black communities of Charlottesville.

Early History and Famous Residents. Albemarle County was settled in the 1730s by English colonists who migrated westward from the Tidewater area of Virginia. Among Albemarle's first pioneers were two men whose sons became prominent in the American Revolution and early American history—John Henry, the father of Patrick Henry, and Peter Jefferson, the father of Thomas Jefferson. Both Henry and Jefferson received or bought large land grants and were living in Albemarle County by 1737. The county itself was established in 1744, and in 1761 Charlottesville was created as the county seat. In 1762 Charlottesville was officially recognized as a town and named for Queen Charlotte, wife of King George III of England.

Albemarle County was a center of revolution and democratic thought prior to and during the American Revolution In addition to supplying Revolutionary leadership, 4,000 Revolutionary prisoners of war captured in Saratoga were quartered in Charlottesville in 1777. In 1781 British troops raided Charlottesville, hoping to capture Thomas Jefferson and other Revolutionary Virginia state officials who had fled to Charlottesville when Richmond fell.

Besides its well-known Revolutionary leaders, two native sons of Albemarle County are among the country's most famous explorers and conquerors of the Northwest Territory. Meriwether Lewis of the Lewis and Clark expedition was born in Albemarle County, as was General George Rogers Clark, the older brother of Meriwether Lewis' partner, William Clark, and a famed Indian fighter in early conflicts with native Americans of the Northwest. Another prominent early resident of Albemarle County, though not a native, was James Monroe, fifth President of the United States. A good friend of Jefferson's, Monroe made his home on the outskirts of present-day Charlottesville in a plantation adjacent to Jefferson's.

"Jefferson's County." Of all the well-known and outstanding early citizens of Albemarle County, Thomas Jefferson was the most influential in local affairs and left the most lasting mark on the city of Charlottesville. A lifelong resident of Albemarle, Jefferson represented the area in the Virginia House of Burgesses before becoming Governor of Virginia and President of the United States. Following his two terms as President of the United States, Jefferson returned to Albemarle County to found and charter the University of Virginia, which is located physically in the city of Charlottesville but is technically a part of Albemarle County. Jefferson was the first rector of the University, designed its original buildings and grounds, and implemented his own philosophy of education in its initial courses of study. The central institution in Charlottesville, the University is not only the mainstay of the city's economy, but also plays an important role in social and cultural developments in the city.

A visitor to Charlottesville is immediately impressed with many reminders of the past, but particularly with the emphasis on Jefferson and his heritage. Some of the stress on Jefferson is, of course, part and parcel of the local tourist business, which is based in large measure on the relics Jefferson left behind—his self-designed plantation home, Monticello; Ash Lawn, the house Jefferson planned for his good friend James Monroe; and the Rotunda, Serpentine Wall, and gardens created by Jefferson at the University of Virginia. Beyond this, one feels that Jefferson the plantation owner and Jefferson the slaveholder still casts a shadow over Charlottesville and that whites who keep the Jefferson image alive are to varying degrees paying homage to a way of life that is gone in its purest form, but that still survives, transformed, in the 20th century. It is this aspect of the lingering presence of Jefferson that adult blacks allude to when they joke that "Jefferson still lives" in Charlottesville. Young blacks see Jefferson as a symbol of slavery and have on occasion been openly hostile to the local practice of putting pictures of Jefferson in municipal buildings. In a series of confrontations between black youth leaders and city officials in 1969, for instance, young Charlottesville blacks protested pictures of Thomas Jefferson, "who owned many slaves,"* appearing on the walls of their recreation center while they were denied the opportunity to put up pictures of black heroes who meant something to them. Similarly, University of Virginia students demonstrated at Mr. Jefferson's school early in 1969, equating the 150th anniversary of the University with "150 years of racism."

---

*To keep references to a minimum, the sources of quotations from interviews collected for this study are not cited. Published sources only are cited. References appear at the end of each section and are numbered consecutively throughout the section.

Population Trends. Population figures alone tell much about overall racial patterns in Charlottesville and Albemarle County, with early census reports documenting the degree to which the area was actually rooted in the plantation-slavery system. Albemarle County, for instance, was nearly half black (46 percent) in 1790, and nearly all the black people were slaves—there were only 171 free blacks in the county, while 5,579 blacks were slaves. The Charlottesville-Albemarle area remained nearly half black through the Civil War and Reconstruction until about 1890, when the proportion of blacks began to decline. Since 1890, the percentage of blacks in the total population of both the city and county has decreased steadily. The black population of the city of Charlottesville dropped from 45 percent in 1890 to 15 percent in 1970; Albemarle County's black population was down to 13 percent of the total when the 1970 census was taken. The actual number of blacks in Charlottesville has increased little by little with each decade, but the white population has grown at a faster rate, making up a larger proportion of the city's inhabitants with each census count.

While the black population of Charlottesville-Albemarle traces its origins back to slavery, the white people of the area have traditionally been Anglo-Saxon and Protestant since the early days of settlement. At no time in the city's history has there been a significant influx of immigrants from any Catholic country or from other parts of the world with different ethnic or religious backgrounds. For all practical purposes, blacks and white Anglo-Saxon Protestants have historically made up the two racial groups in Charlottesville, and for many decades, both populations have been almost exclusively American-born. In 1960, for example, only 2 percent of the total population of Charlottesville was made up of foreign-born whites.

In 1970, Charlottesville's total population was 38,880, an increase of 9,453 over the number of people living there in 1960. The white population of the city was 32,711, or 84 percent of the total, reflecting an increase of 8,881 since 1960. A total of 5,884 blacks lived in the city in 1970, only 187 more than the 5,597 blacks who resided in Charlottesville in 1960. The percentage of blacks in the total population dropped from 19 percent in 1960 to 15 percent in 1970. The large increase of whites over blacks was due at least partly to the annexation of two suburban residential areas to Charlottesville in 1963 and 1968. Together these annexations changed the city's land area from 6.4 to 10.4 square miles. It should be noted that because of special legislation, the University of Virginia is officially part of Albemarle County, and the University's student population is not counted in the city of Charlottesville's population.

Albemarle County's population, exclusive of Charlottesville, was 37,780 in 1970, just slightly under the city count. The county is 100 percent rural, apart from the city of Charlottesville, and—probably because of the two annexations mentioned above—is as a whole growing at a slower rate than the city. Albemarle County's black population, which is a little smaller in numbers than Charlottesville's, increased by 439 from 1960 to 1970. There were 32,591 whites (86 percent) in Albemarle County in 1970 and 5,045 blacks (13 percent). It is interesting that the black population of Albemarle grew between 1960 and 1970. The number of blacks in the county decreased between the 1950 and 1960 censuses.

Charlottesville's Economy. As suggested earlier, Charlottesville has a substantial tourist business consisting of visitors to historic shrines in the area and to scenic parks and parkways in the nearby Blue Ridge Mountains. Over a million people per year visit Jefferson's home, Monticello; the Blue Ridge Parkway, which is only 20 miles away, annually attracts more than eight million visitors—more than any other U. S. national park. Many tourists combine a trip to the Blue Ridge Parkway or the Skyline Drive, also in the vicinity, with a visit to Jefferson's and Monroe's homes and a tour of the old buildings and gardens at the University of Virginia. Visitors to Charlottesville buy in the stores, eat in the restaurants, and frequently use overnight hotel and motel accommodations.

In addition to the tourist trade, Charlottesville also serves as a retail, banking, and shopping area for Albemarle County and the surrounding area. The city's retail sales alone amount to roughly $85 million per year. There is some diversified light industry in both Charlottesville and Albemarle County, including several plants producing electronics and communications equipment and several food processing and textile plants. The combined payrolls of all manufacturing plants in the city and county total about $65 million annually. The largest single industrial plant in the county is Morton Frozen Foods, which employs about 1,500 persons.

A regional office of the U. S. Department of Health, Education and Welfare (HEW) has been important to Charlottesville's economy for the past 12 years. This one HEW office employs a total of 457 persons, bringing a payroll of about $5.5 million into the city each year. Much to the distress of Charlottesville's civic leaders, President Nixon announced in the spring of 1969 that the HEW regional office would be moved to Philadelphia by 1970. Immediate protests and appeals were unsuccessful in changing plans to relocate this office. Local pleas fell on deaf ears, in spite of the fact that a new $2 million office building to house the HEW offices was constructed in Charlottesville in 1966, and the traditionally Democratic Charlottesville city government went Republican in 1968. Democrats, it should be noted, regained control of City Council and the Mayor's Office in 1970.

University of Virginia as an Employer. Although the sources of income and employment discussed above are important, Charlottesville's largest single employer and the mainstay of the city's economy is the University of Virginia. Though the University's student body is comparatively small, consisting of about 9,000 students, the University staff, including nonprofessional employees, totaled 5,500 in the spring of 1969. Certain divisions of the University, such as University Hospital, hire many Charlottesville residents in nonacademic as well as academic positions.

The University's role as the city's chief employer was highly visible in the winter and spring of 1969, when a broad-based "Coalition Committee" of campus student organizations launched a general campaign against the University's "racist" and "discriminatory" policies and practices. In January 1969, a number of influential campus leaders and organizations decided to celebrate the school's 150th anniversary with a "continuing series of demonstrations . . . until we see evidence of genuine intention to redress ancient grievances by positive action."[1] Student demands included a "living wage" for nonacademic employees at the lowest pay scale and the right of all University employees to organize unions, bargain collectively, and strike for higher wages. The University Student Council, some individual faculty members, and a group of six chaplains serving University students, endorsed these demands. Student spokesmen said, moreover, that the University sets wage standards for the area, since it is by far the largest employer. The six ministers supporting the student protest pointed out that the University's minimum wage of $52 for a 40-hour week for nonacademic staff was inadequate. The chaplains also stated that the University "could become a potent force through its economic power" in changing substandard slum living conditions in the area.[2] Although the student protest yielded some gains in areas affecting campus issues, such as enrollment of black students and the hiring of more black faculty, the demand for higher wages and the right of employees to organize unions made no headway. As a state institution, the University follows a minimum wage scale established for state employment and apparently comes under legislation that prohibits state employees from forming unions. Students took their cause from the campus to the Governor of Virginia, but were unsuccessful in securing his support for legislation he said was necessary to make the two major economic changes they sought.

It should be noted here that the 1969 student demonstrations marked a turning point in University of Virginia campus politics and a willingness on the part of students to involve themselves in both community and other popular student protest issues. Made up largely of "white upper middle class male urbanites from well-educated families,"[3] the University of Virginia student body bypassed the various civil rights demonstrations of the early and mid-1960s, stayed away from local community political issues, and kept out of the activist anti-war movement until 1969. In addition to uncorking the bottle of student protest, one of the significant results of the 1969 150th anniversary demonstrations was an official student-faculty review of University admissions and employment practices that called for recruitment and welcome of black students, two black admissions officers at a professional level, creation of a new dean to develop and retain a more broadly based student body, and more economic aid opportunities for students. A black assistant dean of admissions was appointed in the fall of 1969, and black enrollment at the undergraduate level increased slightly for the 1969–70 school year.

Jobs and Income, Black and White.   The central employment issue raised in the 1969 University of Virginia student protest was that the good paying professional positions at the school were held by whites, while blacks were hired in the lower paying, menial jobs such as maids, orderlies, and janitors. This sharp distinction between the economic conditions of blacks and whites in Charlottesville has persisted for many decades, showing up clearly in the 1960 census. In 1960, 71 percent of the men in the black work force in the city of Charlottesville were working at unskilled or semi-skilled jobs; 43 percent were employed as service workers. Only 11 percent of the men in the black work force were in skilled jobs in 1960 and only 5 percent in professional or managerial positions. By contrast, 57 percent of the white men working in 1960 were in white collar jobs, with 37 percent holding professional and managerial positions. Only one-fifth of the white working men were in unskilled or semi-skilled jobs.

The differences between the kinds of jobs held by black and white women are just as drastic. Also, white women as a group were working at higher job categories than black men. In 1960, 69 percent of the white women working in Charlottesville were employed in white collar jobs; 27 percent of all working white women held professional or managerial positions; 34 percent of the employed white women were doing some kind of clerical work; and only about one-fourth held semi-skilled or unskilled jobs. While white women were overwhelmingly working in white collar positions, 77 percent of the black women in the labor force in Charlottesville in 1960 were in unskilled or semi-skilled jobs. The largest number of them—43 percent of all working black women—were in the most unstable and unprotected of all jobs, doing domestic work in private homes. Only 11 percent of all employed black women were in white collar jobs in 1960, with 9 percent of the total in this category holding down professional and technical positions.

As might be expected from the different kinds of jobs held by blacks and whites, there is a wide gulf between the income levels of the two groups. Seven-tenths of Charlottesville's black families were earning less than $4,000 per year in 1960, while 72 percent of white families were earning more than $4,000. Of all white families, 26 percent had incomes above $8,000 per year in 1960, whereas only 4 percent of Charlottesville's black families earned more than $8,000 in 1960. Median family income for whites was $5,584 in 1960; for blacks, $3,046.

Although there has been some change in racial employment patterns in Charlottesville since 1960, employment discrimination and lack of employment opportunities remain one of the chief complaints of the black community. The University of Virginia, for example, employed only one full-time black faculty member during the 1969–70 school year. A local bank that employed a total of 144 persons in 1969 hired seven black people, with only one of these working in a non-menial job as a teller. Charlottesville's black leaders have become increasingly frustrated over the employment situation, particularly the failure of federal, state, and local governments to take steps to end discrimination in hiring. Lack of federal action on employment complaints filed with the Equal Employment Opportunity Commission has embittered key leaders in the National Association for the Advancement of Colored People (NAACP), and an editorial in the local black weekly, the *Charlottesville-Albemarle Tribune*, pointed out in October 1969 that "Negro inclusion in local and state agencies in categories beyond that of domestics is just above nil." The editorial suggested that black voters keep this in mind when voting at the polls in November.[4] Black unemployment is generally at least twice as high as white unemployment and there is wide agreement that the longstanding pattern of blacks moving away from the Charlottesville area stems from poor employment opportunities in the city.

Charlottesville's "Ghetto Slums."   Another major demand of the 1969 University of Virginia student Coalition Committee to the University was "to consider . . . the ghetto slums provided by Charlottesville for its black citizens and the consistent refusal of the University to involve itself in the larger community."[5]

For the most part, blacks and whites in Charlottesville live in physically and socially separate communities, with few meaningful bridges between. There are a few older streets in the city where blacks and whites are still mixed and a few professional blacks live in newer "white" areas. But the bulk of the housing is segregated, with the majority of blacks concentrated in the older, downtown section of Charlottesville. The black community, in fact, forms an arc around the central business area, halfway circling it on the western and southern fringes of the downtown shopping district. A report by James W. Barksdale noted that black housing areas of the city are "near the railroads and in the low-lying regions near the center of town." There has been no change in the basic pattern in the past 20 years, although the space available to blacks has shrunk considerably. Two trends already in progress at the time of the Barksdale study have accelerated since 1949: (1) a "shut out" of blacks from traditionally black blocks with the encroachment of business, public buildings, and industry into what were predominantly black residential neighborhoods and (2) a "hemming in" of existing black areas by expansion of white businesses and residences on nearly all sides.[6]

There is now fairly wide recognition, from the mayor down, that the amount of land available to blacks for residences has grown progressively smaller as urban renewal and other building programs have taken over formerly black residential blocks without making new housing available. Vinegar Hill, a vacant, 13-acre plot of land in the middle of downtown Charlottesville, is a good example of this trend. Site of some of the worst slum housing in Charlottesville, Vinegar Hill was leveled some time ago for an urban renewal project. The site has remained empty, while court suits and conflicts over land use proceed. Projected plans provide that only part of the Vinegar Hill tract will eventually be used for housing. Similarly, a 50-acre urban renewal project currently planned for the southern fringe of the downtown business district will displace many black families and a few white families. This urban renewal plan includes a low-rent public housing project and a neighborhood facilities building, but will also convert residential property to light industrial use. Another controversial aspect of this and other proposed low-rent public housing projects planned by the Charlottesville Redevelopment and Housing Authority is the placing of all of these low-rent projects in existing ghetto areas. Three sites for low-rent housing selected by the Housing Authority in 1968 were challenged in court by the NAACP because of their location in predominantly black neighborhoods. The NAACP has also opposed the "narrow" approach of the Housing Authority in considering high-density rental projects only.

When the 1960 census was taken, 74 percent of white Charlottesville's housing units were sound, with all plumbing facilities. In the black community, however, almost the reverse was true: only 37 percent of the housing units occupied by blacks were sound, with all plumbing. Over half the housing units in which blacks lived (54 percent) were deteriorating or dilapidated; over one-third had no shower or bathtub at all, or these facilities were shared; and one-fifth lacked toilets or shared a toilet. Four-fifths (82 percent) of the housing units blacks occupied in 1960 were built before 1940. To remedy this situation, only one public housing project, Westhaven, was built in Charlottesville in the 1960s. This project, with 126 units, is located in a black neighborhood and has been occupied almost exclusively by blacks since it opened.

Charlottesville's shortage of decent, low-cost housing for blacks reached a crisis in the winter of 1969, following the eviction of 13 black tenants from substandard housing condemned for code violations. Although the apartments lacked most indoor plumbing and central heating, had sagging floors, and had walls that did not always meet the floors, the tenants fought eviction on the grounds that they could not find other housing at a price they could afford to pay. These tenants and a number of other black citizens demanded immediate action to solve the housing problem. Many blacks and some whites criticized city officials for not building more low-cost housing units, for failing to pass a fair housing law, and for initiating urban renewal projects that absorb black residences without guaranteeing blacks the opportunity to buy in other areas. The city fathers were reminded that the Vinegar Hill tract still stood vacant in the center of the city.

Black Segregation and White Power. In addition to the segregation and lack of opportunity in housing and employment, all public facilities and institutions in Charlottesville were traditionally segregated. This pattern of separation did not begin to break down until the 1950s and the early 1960s, when the federal courts outlawed segregation at the University of Virginia and in the public schools, and when community pressure, plus the 1964 Civil Rights Act, opened up lunch counter service and access to other public accommodations. While segregation in public institutions and facilities is slowly breaking down, local power and decision-making are still concentrated in the hands of whites, who have been both resistant and reluctant to change where the status of blacks is concerned. The Charlottesville City Council, for instance, was all white until 1970, when one black councilman was elected. Public boards and commissions, such as the Housing Authority, the school board, and the City Planning Commission, now have only token black representation, which has come about since the early 1960s. The first black man was appointed to the Charlottesville Housing Authority in 1961, for example, and the first black person—the same man, incidentally—was put on the City Planning Commission in 1969.

White control of local governmental and quasi-governmental bodies has meant that blacks have had to fight for civil and economic rights largely from outside the local political system, using the federal courts, complaints to federal agencies, and whatever pressure from governmental or civil rights sources they could bring to bear. The present generation of black adult leaders has fought segregation primarily through the NAACP, relying heavily on court suits handled by state NAACP lawyers based in Richmond, since there are no black lawyers in Charlottesville. The NAACP was for many years the only civil rights organization in Charlottesville, but in 1969 there was a Charlottesville-Albemarle Chapter of the Virginia Council on Human Relations, a Charlottesville-Albemarle Fair Housing Committee, and a chapter of the National Welfare Rights Organization was in the process of organizing. The mayor also set up an advisory biracial Human Relations Committee in 1968 that accomplished little and was to be replaced by a permanent commission, also advisory.

Even with the addition of newer organizations, the NAACP was still the major civil rights organization when this study was done. More militant groups such as the Student Nonviolent Coordinating Committee (SNCC) and the Congress of Racial Equality (CORE) never got a foothold in Charlottesville in the 1960s.

Although Charlottesville's adults have fought segregation and racial injustice primarily through the courts and the NAACP, Charlottesville's black youth, in contrast to their elders, are attracted to "black power" and demonstrations. Charlottesville's black young people were not organized in a formal way or affiliated with any national organizations in the late 1960s, but they were marching, staging walkouts, and engaging in direct confrontations with the agents of power and authority in the community. The contrast between the older and younger generation of black leaders vis-à-vis white power shows up dramatically in the school situation, where black high school students assumed completely different tactics from those of their elders in challenging racism and discrimination within the schools, following desegregation.

2
Charlottesville Public Schools

Early Beginning. Public schools in the city of Charlottesville were initially a part of the Albemarle County public school system, which dates back to 1870. The first public elementary school in Charlottesville opened in 1871 and the first public high school, 1890. Although county and city schools were initially in one district, a gradual separation of the Charlottesville and Albemarle schools took place between 1880 and 1892. By 1892, the Charlottesville schools were completely independent of the Albemarle County schools, with a separate board of education and a separate superintendent for each system. Although the two systems cooperate in many undertakings, and the merging of the two systems again is under consideration, Charlottesville and Albemarle County have maintained separate boards of education and separate superintendents since before the turn of the century.

Present School District and Schools. The Charlottesville Public Schools are currently organized to serve the city population, with the school district boundaries coinciding with the city limits. Although county areas recently annexed to the city became a part of the Charlottesville school district when brought into the city, there are three Albemarle County schools located physically within the city of Charlottesville. These schools serve county residents only, and two are found in Charlottesville's ghetto area, where black county children were taught prior to desegregation. Because of this unique situation, Albemarle County now buses white and black children to these schools, as it buses nearly all of the 7,000 pupils enrolled in the county system.

During the 1968–69 school year, the Charlottesville public schools enrolled a total of 6,739 pupils in grades 1–12. A little over one-fifth (22 percent) of these children were black. A total of 1,543 school children in the Charlottesville public schools in 1968–69 were classified as members of minority groups: 1,530 black, nine Spanish, two Oriental, and two American Indian.

When field work for this study was carried out in the winter of 1968–69, the Charlottesville school district operated a total of 11 schools: six elementary schools, two junior high schools, one high school, and one special education center. Five of the city's elementary schools included grades 1–5, with all children in the city attending a Sixth Grade Center located in the Jefferson Elementary School. A Special Education Center at McGuffey School also served children on a citywide basis. McGuffey School housed children in the age group for grades 1–9 who were mentally retarded but educable, or who were considered to be too severely handicapped educationally to keep up in a regular classroom.

Beginning in September 1969, half-day kindergartens were added to schools with primary units, and a new lower elementary school was opened during the 1969–70 school year. The addition of the kindergartens and the new school were part of an overall plan of July 1967 to gradually convert to a K-4-4-4 grade organization, with the timing of specific changes geared to the availability of additional facilities. Middle schools with grades 5–8 will replace existing junior high schools when new high school facilities are built. The board is slowly moving ahead with this reorganization plan, but implementation has been complicated by the possibility of merger of the city-county governments, which was defeated by a referendum vote of March 1970, but is still a long-range possibility in the eyes of many people. Merger of the two school districts, regardless of the fusion of city and county governments, has also been discussed. With the possibility of some kind of merger pending, there has been a certain amount of reluctance to go ahead with major building programs.

School Board. The school board for the Charlottesville public schools is composed of seven members appointed by the City Council for three-year terms. Board terms are staggered, with as many as three members appointed some years. In 1969 all members of the board were men, six white and one black. The Reverend Henry B. Mitchell, the one black board member, was appointed in June 1968. He replaced Raymond I. Bell, the first black board member, appointed in 1965.

Although it is legally possible for school board members to serve consecutive terms, the board has experienced a fairly high turnover in membership in the past few years. Since the mid-1960s this turnover has been related to two factors: City Council decisions not to reappoint incumbent board members and board members themselves declining to be reappointed. The last few years have been difficult and demanding, with major controversies over the replacement of a school superintendent, completion of desegregation of the public schools, racial unrest in the schools, and lack of consensus over badly needed high school facilities. The Council put new men in all board vacancies in 1966, after the superintendent was replaced, and again in 1969. Two board members whose terms expired in 1969 refused reappointment, and the Council declined to reappoint the third man whose term was up, a board member who had criticized the Council for cutting the school board's budget and failing to support a bond issue for two new high schools. The Council's failure to reappoint this board member brought accusations that he was "being purged" and opened up public discussion over the basic question of board independence under an appointive system.[7] The Council's 1969 appointments also touched off a wave of protest over token black representation, as all 1969 appointees were white men. Community demands for more black board representation will be discussed later in this report.

Peabody Report and Recommendations. A major study of the Charlottesville public schools carried out by the George Peabody College for Teachers during the 1966–67 school year had already spotlighted two problems that surfaced with the City Council's 1969 appointments: lack of community-wide representation on the school board and the board's dependence on the City Council because of the appointive nature of the seats. The Peabody report, entitled *Charlottesville, Virginia Public Schools,* noted the total absence of women on the school board and the fact that the board included only one black person. "Scrupulous attention" to broadening representation of the total community was recommended. The Peabody study also favored a change to an elected board, so that good schools in the community would not be dependent on the city administration "for wise appointments and adequate support."[8]

In the area of personnel problems and practices, the Peabody report found a high turnover of teachers and principals, with a great many relatively inexperienced persons in both teaching and administrative jobs. During the 1966–67 school year, for example, 57 percent of the professional staff was made up of individuals in their first or second year of employment in the system. This situation, which is partly related to the number of University of Virginia wives and graduate students employed, creates serious problems. The report found that elementary principals, for example, were generally unable to help teachers with instructional and pupil guidance problems because of their own newness and inexperience. There were also two somewhat distinct groups of teachers and administrators, because of the contrast between the young, University-connected teachers who often come from outside the region, and the older teachers and professionals who are a stable part of the Charlottesville community and have considerable experience in the local schools. Higher salaries, continuing contracts, scheduled salary increments during the first three years of service, and larger financial incentives for advanced graduate training were suggested as ways of attracting and holding a more experienced professional staff. Salaries have been raised since the Peabody report, but in 1969 some people in the community still felt that Charlottesville's pay was not competitive. Although not brought out in the Peabody report, it should also be noted that there is a distinct contrast between black and white professionals in the Charlottesville schools, as far as stability, identity with the community, and length of service in the system are concerned. The problems of high turnover, lack of local ties, and temporary service apply to young white rather than black teachers. Black teachers tend to be long-term residents of the community and generally stay in the school system on a permanent basis.

The Peabody report also recommended: (1) addition of a free kindergarten grade to all elementary schools with primary units, now established; (2) conversion to a middle school plan with 4-4-4 grade organization, adopted in principle and slowly way; (3) a discontinuation of the Special Education Center at McGuffey School; (4) a building program, including new facilities at the elementary and high school levels, currently in progress; (5) provision of free basic textbooks for all students; (6) complete revision of the social studies curriculum; (7) a vocational education center to be owned and operated jointly with the Albemarle school system; and (8) complete merger with the Albemarle County schools as soon as this is feasible. These and other recommendations of the Peabody study which affect desegregation and racial problems in the schools will be discussed more fully at appropriate points throughout this report.

Financing of Charlottesville Schools. The bulk of the funds for Charlottesville's public schools come from local tax sources, with no more than one-third or one-fourth of the operating budget being derived from state and/or federal funds in any given year. During the 1968–69 school year, for example, fully 73 percent of the operating budget of $4,120,153 came from local tax funds; 26 percent came from state sources; and only about 1 percent came from other sources, including federal funds. About two-thirds (63 percent) of the 1969–70 budget was drawn from local tax sources.

In addition to the federal funds reflected in what is called the operating budget, the school system has in the last few years received additional federal monies for special projects financed under legislation such as the Elementary and Secondary Education Act (ESEA) and Title IV of the Civil Rights Act. During the 1967–68 school year, for instance, the Charlottesville schools received approximately $103,000 under Title I ESEA for a language skills project, about $15,000 under Title II ESEA for supplementary library materials, and $25,000 for a learning disabilities program conducted jointly with Albemarle County under Title III ESEA. A Head Start program funded by the Office of Economic Opportunity (OEO) has been carried out for several years, with OEO contributing about $35,000, or 80 percent, of the budget for this program. In 1968 the Charlottesville schools also received a grant of approximately $21,000 under Title IV of the Civil Rights Act for a technical assistance program in desegregation. The amount of federal funds obtained for these projects is not particularly large, but the school system is definitely interested in receiving the money and hopes to increase the number of such projects in the future. Another recommendation of the Peabody report was that the Charlottesville schools seek more federal funds.

With the bulk of the school system's funds coming from local sources and with the present legal provisions for establishing the annual budget, the City Council makes crucial decisions on adequate funding of the schools. Each year, under Virginia law, the school board must submit to the City Council by April 1 a proposed operating budget for the next fiscal year. The Council first approves the budget and then levies the local school tax to provide the required money. The board must go back to the Council during the year for approval of any expenditures not established in the adopted budget. The City Council also plays a crucial role in the financing of school capital outlay projects, since Council approval is necessary to initiate bond elections for major building programs. As an alternative to holding a bond election, Council can, if it chooses, finance school building from the city's capital improvement fund. In either case, Council backing is necessary to launch a school building project. The Peabody report concluded that many of the educational deficiencies of the school district are directly or indirectly related to inadequate financial support, although Charlottesville citizens have the ability to provide more money for the schools. The Peabody team recommended special state legislation that would permit the school board to submit a proposed budget and tax levy to a referendum vote in the event that the City Council failed to adopt a proposed budget. There has been no such action to help free the district from financial dependence on the Council and there is generally much haggling and negotiation between the school board and the Council over proposed budgets and building projects, with the Council insisting on cuts and revisions that many feel are not in the best interests of the schools.

Segregated Schools and Black Education. Until 1959, public schools in the city of Charlottesville were completely segregated, with all white children assigned to "white" schools and all black children placed in "black" schools. Residential location did not enter into the picture; the schools were racially separate as a matter of state law and policy. Children living in scattered black pocket areas out from the center of town attended Jefferson Elementary School in the heart of the black community, as did black children on the western edge of the ghetto who were closer to Venable, a white elementary school. Furthermore, the separation extended to all facets and phases of school life—teachers and principals were appointed to schools on a racial basis, teachers' meetings were segregated, intramural and inter-school student activities were organized separately, and the board of education and the central administrative staff of the school system were all white.

For many years prior to desegregation, *all* black children in the city attended Jefferson School, built in 1924 in the central downtown area, just west of the shopping district. The Jefferson School is only a few short blocks away from McGuffey School, which was traditionally white, in spite of its close proximity to the black community. Although backed up to the black community, McGuffey served whites living northeast of the school. Jefferson and McGuffey are on either side of Vinegar Hill, which contained some of the worst black housing in the city before urban renewal bulldozed all of the buildings. All of the Vinegar Hill children went to Jefferson, however, even when that school was seriously overcrowded. Initially, Jefferson was an elementary school, but was later expanded to include high school grades. Before Jefferson offered any high school courses, black youth desiring more than a grade school education were forced to attend schools outside the city. A 57-year-old native of Charlottesville interviewed for the study told of living with relatives in Washington, D.C. to attend high school although the "white" high school was within a few blocks of his home.

Separate and Unequal.   In 1949, five years before the U. S. Supreme Court outlawed public school segregation, James W. Barksdale, a Phelps Stokes Fellow at the University of Virginia, investigated and compared black and white public education conditions in the city of Charlottesville. His report stated, "Plain observation is enough to prove that Negro education facilities in Charlottesville are not today equal to those of whites."[9] There were three public elementary schools and one high school for whites in Charlottesville when Barksdale made his study, while black educational facilities consisted of two buildings at the Jefferson School—one for the elementary grades and one for the high school.

Barksdale found that "the Negro public school system had been operating under overcrowded conditions and with inadequate facilities for many years" and that classrooms for black elementary grades were "drastically overcrowded." His comparison of black and white high school facilities indicated that "many high school facilities which are found in Lane High School [for whites] are lacking in Jefferson High School." Barksdale reported that Jefferson High School offered one less grade than Lane High School, was deficient in home economics and vocational shop facilities, and had an inadequate gymnasium with no showers. The Jefferson auditorium was used as a classroom at this time and had inadequate stage space. Barksdale also noted the school did not have a hospital or clinic room. Blacks eligible for training benefits under the G.I. Bill of Rights were then taking International Correspondence School Courses at night in Jefferson. Instructors were there to help them, but were not teaching any courses. Barksdale concluded that the combined Jefferson School was an overstrained physical plant where limited facilities were overworked, that teachers were overloaded, and that there were "grossly unfavorable classroom and learning conditions for pupils."[10]

In spite of the unfavorable conditions at the Jefferson School, Barksdale found that the percentage of black students enrolled in high school in Charlottesville was higher than it was in other cities throughout Virginia. He was also impressed with the number of young blacks in Charlottesville who attended college. He said that blacks in the city realized "that the young Negro's best chances for full employment and economic and social advancement lie in his securing a college education."[11]

In 1951, after six years of negotiation, planning, and the passing of a special enabling act by the state legislature, Charlottesville and Albemarle County opened a new joint high school for black city and county students. This school, the Jackson P. Burley High School, was operated by the two systems on a segregated basis between 1951 and 1967. Burley is physically located in the Charlottesville black community, about seven blocks from Jefferson and about five blocks from Lane, the one all-white high school in the city prior to desegregation. Although a "white" school, Lane was built in the center of the black community, across from Vinegar Hill in 1941. Black citizens in Charlottesville still complain that black housing was torn down to construct Lane, although their children were not permitted to attend. The advent of Burley improved high school conditions for blacks but the school was not as oriented toward college preparatory courses as Lane. Burley offered more vocational training courses than Lane, fewer English and foreign language classes and about the same number of commercial subjects. The 1967 Peabody report stated that 20 to 25 percent of Burley's graduates attended college, in comparison to 60 to 70 percent of Lane's.

3
Massive Resistance
to Desegregation: 1955–1959

NAACP Challenges School Segregation. In June 1955, following the U. S. Supreme Court's May 31 order implementing the 1954 school desegregation decision, the Virginia NAACP announced a statewide policy regarding school desegregation. Local branches were to petition their school boards, wait a reasonable period of time, and then go to court if nothing was done to comply with the Supreme Court's ruling.

In keeping with state NAACP policy, on October 6, 1955, Oliver W. Hill, a Richmond NAACP attorney representing 44 black children enrolled in segregated schools in Charlottesville, petitioned the city school board "to take immediate steps to reorganize the public schools under your jurisdiction so that children may attend them without regard to their race or color." A week after the desegregation petition was filed, the board replied that it had previously formed itself into a committee on the whole to study the problem of segregation. The board stated further:

> It was not the intent of the Supreme Court's decision . . . to disrupt a system of public education. Therefore, the problem confronting the board is to find a solution which will conform to the law and be acceptable to parents and taxpayers who use and support the public schools.[12]

When no action on desegregation resulted, the NAACP inquired by letter as to the board's plans. The board replied that it could not end segregation as requested at that time. George R. Ferguson, President of the Charlottesville NAACP branch at that time commented in an interview for this study that whenever blacks in the city ask for something, the psychology of the power structure is always to refuse. He said that their thinking is, "Don't give it and they'll forget it."

With the school board's refusal to formulate a plan for desegregation of the Charlottesville schools, the local NAACP branch brought suit in the federal courts. Charlottesville had one of the largest NAACP branches in the state at that time, with about 1,500 members. The NAACP was the only civil rights organization in the city in 1955, and included many local black teachers in its membership.

On July 12, 1956, U. S. District Judge John Paul issued an

order, effective September 1956, restraining the school board from any and all action that would deny admission of any child to any public school on the basis of race or color. Judge Paul's order in the Charlottesville case was the first in Virginia to instruct a local school board to begin complying with the Supreme Court's school decision by a specific time. His decision was immediately appealed and enforcement of his order was stayed pending action by the U. S. Court of Appeals for the Fourth Circuit. Judge Paul's order was upheld in the Circuit Court, December 31, 1956. The board then appealed the Circuit Court's ruling to the U. S. Supreme Court. With the decision under appeal, Judge Paul's order remained unenforced and the schools continued on a segregated basis. It was not until July 8, 1958, after all appeal possibilities had been exhausted, that Judge Paul's order became effective and the school board adopted its first plan for racial desegregation of the schools.

Charlottesville and the State "Massive Resistance" Program. In 1954, shortly after the U. S. Supreme Court's decision on school segregation was first announced, Virginia's Governor, Thomas B. Stanley, stated he contemplated "no precipitate action" but would call together representatives of state and local governments to "work toward a plan which will be acceptable to our citizens and in keeping with the edict of the Court."[13] The Gray Commission, which Governor Stanley subsequently convened, recommended a series of new laws that would permit a certain degree of minimum desegregation under local option, but also make it possible for local boards to avoid major desegregation through pupil assignment practices and public grants for private school tuition.

Governor Stanley seemed to be supporting the Gray Commission's approach up until the summer of 1956, when U. S. District Courts in both Charlottesville and Arlington County, Virginia, ordered desegregation of the public schools by a fixed date. Calling a special session of the legislature in August 1956, Governor Stanley then backed a more drastic approach that came to be known as Virginia's "massive resistance" program. The key "massive resistance" legislation adopted in that special session denied state funds to desegregated schools, made funds cut off from desegregated schools available for private school the payment of the wages and salaries of school personnel, gave the governor the authority to close schools that desegregated, and established a State Pupil Placement Board with full jurisdiction over school assignments for all pupils in Virginia. A *Nation* reporter, commenting on the Charlottesville and Virginia school situation in the late summer of 1956, stated that Virginia legislators who adopted the "massive resistance" program feared that "certain communities" such as Charlottesville "might go quietly ahead and accept the law of the land,"[14] without state intervention. The University of Virginia, following its initial acceptance of a black student under court order in 1950, had admitted about a dozen graduate students for fall 1956. A biracial Human Relations Council had formed to support desegregation in Charlottesville, and the City Council was said to favor a minimum of desegregation rather than close the public schools.

In the two-year period following Charlottesville's first court order to desegregate, support for massive resistance built up. Few Charlottesville citizens protested against massive resistance, and vocal segregationists "virtually pre-empted the field of opinion-making."[15] While there was strong support for any form of resistance among county political leaders, Charlottesville leadership was divided between advocates of massive resistance and segregationists who wanted to maintain local options for handling the school integration issue.

In the spring and summer of 1958, an atmosphere of crisis developed. It was clear by this time that no further legal delay of desegregation was possible and that Judge Paul's order would be enforced in September. It was equally clear that the schools would be closed under state massive resistance legislation if desegregated. Johan Galtung, a Norwegian sociologist who studied the Charlottesville situation over a period of two years, identified the spring and summer of 1958 as the "time of greatest tension in the community."[16] Opinions polarized and there was virtually no communication between people of opposing points of view. City officials and a few leading citizens met once with the local NAACP during this period to ask the organization to drop its fight for Negro admissions to Lane High School to keep the school from closing. The NAACP refused. This is the only occasion in 12 years of school desegregation where city officials requested a discussion with NAACP leaders. White organizations and white leadership did not want to become publicly involved in the issue, even though continuation of the public schools was at stake.

Developments in the Venable School community illustrate the division of opinion over integration, plus the reluctance of whites to "stand up and be counted" in favor of desegregation. The Venable Elementary School Parent-Teacher Association (PTA) decided to poll its members in May 1958 to determine what real opposition to the closing of schools existed. Each of the 49 families with children to be enrolled in Venable for the 1958–59 session was sent a questionnaire and asked to choose between the two options the PTA considered the realistic choices available: (1) some measure of integration or (2) a closed Venable Public School. Responses were returned unsigned. The results of this poll indicated that 58 percent of the 305 families responding preferred "some measure of integration," while 42 percent chose "a closed Venable Public School." Following the PTA poll, an independent group of Venable parents with segregationist sympathies conducted a second poll. Questionnaires sent out in the second poll were numbered and parents were told to sign their responses. The second poll asked parents first to state a preference for "integrated" or "segregated" schools and then to choose between "integrated schools" or "segregated private schools" supported by tuition grants, in the event desegregation took place. Fourteen of the 200 families responding to this poll stated in response to the first question that they preferred integrated schools; 186 chose segregated schools. In the event desegregation took place, 179 said they preferred "segregated private schools" supported by tuition grants. After the second poll was taken, the Executive Board of the Venable PTA released a public statement expressing their opinion that segregated public schools were no longer a realistic choice and that "the best interests of the people of Virginia require the continuation of public schools."[17] The citywide PTA Council did not take any action on the pending school closing issue.

Venable and Lane Schools Closed. With a federal court order to desegregate by September 1958, the school board adopted its first "desegregation" plan July 8, 1958. This plan, which was submitted to the court for approval, relied on a combination of several techniques for continuing the existing pattern of segregation in the schools. Elementary attendance zones based on the broad outlines of racial residential patterns were established, with children automatically transferred out of their home zone if they were in the minority from a racial standpoint. All other transfers had to be requested and approved by the board. A black child living in a predominantly white school zone, for example, would be automatically transferred to Jefferson or Burley and would have to apply for a transfer back to the school in his home attendance area. All transfer applicants were to be tested, interviewed, and screened by a special five-man committee. Blacks involved in the Charlottesville school case boycotted the special tests and challenged the plan in court. On September 13, Judge Paul approved only part of the board's plan and ordered 10 black students admitted to Venable Elementary School and two admitted to Lane High School. The school board appealed this order but was unable to block its implementation.

"Massive resistance" became a reality in the fall of 1958. All the public schools except Lane and Venable opened on schedule in September. On September 19, Governor J. Lindsay Almond took jurisdiction over Lane and Venable under the provisions of state legislation and issued orders not to open them. The Charlottesville City Council and school board announced this action jointly and advised parents "to make the best private arrangements possible concerning the schooling of their children during this period of uncertainty."[18] Charlottesville thus became, as one school administrator expressed it, "a model of intransigence for the state."

After the governor closed Lane and Venable, two white groups that had been formulating preliminary plans moved into action. The group that had spearheaded the Venable PTA poll, composed primarily of housewives from that community, organized temporary, emergency classes that they agreed to abandon when the public schools reopened. This group, formally organized as the Parents Committee for Emergency Schooling, was prepared to accept desegregated public schools, if no other alternative form of public education were available. They sought out space in private homes and were known informally as the "basement mothers" or "emergency mothers." The Parents Committee set up classes for 340 of Venable's pupils—the majority of children enrolled in the school.

The second group, the Charlottesville Education Foundation, established classes for 182 displaced Venable pupils. This organization was an outgrowth of the second Venable poll and was dominated by segregationists who intended to maintain private schools on a permanent basis to avoid desegregation in the public schools. This group obtained a large house and expected to support their schools on a long-term basis from state tuition grants available under the massive resistance legislation.

Financing and securing teachers for the emergency schools was considerably simplified by a City Council-school board decision to continue the contracts of all Lane and Venable teachers. With their salaries assured by the city, Venable teachers agreed to volunteer for the emergency schools and split up between the schools sponsored by the two groups. Lane High School teachers, on the other hand, agreed to volunteer their services only under stipulated conditions: that they would work as a single unit; that they as a faculty would maintain control of the education program; and that a satisfactory plan for implementing one high school program would be worked out between the two emergency school groups and the Lane faculty. Because of the united front presented by the Lane teachers, the two parents' groups were forced to work out a joint high school plan. The cooperative high school program agreed upon by all parties was set up on a temporary basis in churches and other buildings throughout the city and enrolled 872 of the 1,080 pupils expected at Lane that fall. According to several people interviewed for this study the stand of the Lane teachers considerably weakened the development of the Charlottesville Education Foundation's high school program.

Altogether, a total of 1,735 white children were affected by the Lane-Venable closing. In addition to the 1,384 pupils taught in the emergency schools, 179 attended other public schools or established private schools; the rest were not accounted for.

Black children assigned to Lane and Venable schools and their parents were under a good deal of pressure during this period, as many whites felt that the black litigants were responsible for denying an education to the white children. George R. Ferguson, a parent of one of the Lane applicants, as well as president of the Charlottesville NAACP branch, said that many attempts were made to get him to withdraw his daughter from the suit. Many whites also resented the fact that the NAACP challenged use of public funds to pay teachers in the emergency schools. When Judge Paul ruled that public funds could not be used to pay the teachers if black children were refused admission, parents of black children in the suit were approached to enroll in the emergency schools. School officials, on the other hand, wanted these children to attend the city's all-black schools, which continued to operate. Parents involved in the suit rejected all these alternatives, reasoning that acceptance of either the emergency schools or the segregated schools might weaken their case. At the insistence of their parents, black children admitted to Lane and Venable by Judge Paul were tutored in the school board offices.

Initially, there was little public or organized protest over Charlottesville's school closing and little public activity aimed at reopening the schools. A group called the Committee for Public Education formed to try to keep the schools open, but this organization was unsuccessful in getting the City Council to petition the governor to return the schools to local control. Paul M. Gaston and Thomas T. Hammond, two University of Virginia historians who studied the early phases of desegregation, felt that the faith many persons placed in the mayor was partly responsible for the failure of citizens to protest these school closings. In his inaugural address, which took place as the fall crisis was building up, Mayor Thomas J. Michie expressed respect for the courts and a determination to preserve the public school system. He also made it clear that violence and mob action would not be tolerated. The mayor and others were confident that the massive resistance legislation would be struck down quickly by the courts, freeing the local school system to resume public education.[19]

Collapse of Massive Resistance. The tide of public opinion throughout the state of Virginia turned sharply against massive resistance in October and November of 1958, after school closings took effect in several Virginia communities. This was true in Charlottesville, where the schools were closed with very little outcry from the city's leaders and officials. The *Charlottesville Daily Progress,* then edited by a member of the Charlottesville school board, joined other white papers in the state in opposing masssive resistance in the fall of 1958. Charlottesville businessmen, who had left the school issue to the politicians prior to the time the schools were closed, now acted to get them reopened. Following the shift in public opinion, the Virginia Supreme Court of Appeals and a three-judge federal court in Norfolk issued simultaneous rulings on January 19, 1959, that declared Virginia's key massive resistance laws unconstitutional.

After the January 19 rulings, local action was taken to reopen the Charlottesville schools. The Charlottesville school board voted January 26 to reopen Lane and Venable, desegregating the schools as required by court order. The board requested a delay of desegregation until September 1959, however, so that a plan could be prepared. The board assured the court that the 12 black children already assigned to Lane and Venable would be tutored during the second semester of the year, pending implementation of a desegregation plan. The City Council adopted a unanimous resolution on January 27 endorsing the school board's action and favoring a "minimum of integration" rather than closed public schools. On January 30, 1959, Fourth Circuit Court of Appeals Judge Simon Sobeloff granted Charlottesville's delay, declaring the board's vote to go ahead with desegregation "an historic event." "For the first time," Judge

Sobeloff stated, "a town in Virginia has set the pace by saying, 'We're through with resistance.'"[20]

Lane and Venable reopened on a segregated basis in February 1959, with black students assigned to the two schools being tutored the rest of the year in the school board offices. Olivia Ferguson, one of the black students in the suit, completed her high school work that year and was given a certificate saying she had graduated "from the public schools of Charlottesville." The board first attempted to give her a diploma from Burley, the all-black city-county high school, but her father refused to accept it. Although the court had assigned her to Lane High School, the board would not give her a Lane diploma.

4
Token Desegregation
Under Court Order: 1959–1964

Charlottesville's Pupil Assignment Plan. On February 18, 1959, as black and white children began their last semester in officially segregated schools, the Charlottesville school board adopted a new plan for desegregation and nondiscrimination, but controlled the impact by keeping most whites and most blacks in segregated schools. The two key elements in the 1959 desegregation plan were (1) the establishment of geographic elementary school zones that followed racial residential concentrations and (2) giving wide latitude to the superintendent in making pupil assignments to individual schools.

Six elementary school zones were set up and "in general" children in these areas were to attend the grade school in their zone. (See Figure 1.) The superintendent was empowered to assign any student outside his district, however, when the pupil or parent requested a transfer and the superintendent found that reassignment was "consistent with the best academic interest of the pupil" and would not violate a maximum pupil-teacher ratio set for elementary classrooms. No zones were established for high school pupils. The superintendent was to make assignments based on pupil and parental preferences, a maximum pupil-teacher ratio, "convenience of attendance," and academic qualifications. The plan stipulated that any pupil or his parent might ask for a transfer, and that in granting transfers the superintendent should take into account residence, academic qualifications, the student's "personal desires," the need for particular courses, enrollment, available teaching personnel, physical facilities, and "other lawful and objective considerations." The superintendent could require a transfer applicant to take "any standard academic or achievement test" when he considered the applicant's school record "not sufficient" to determine whether a transfer would be in a student's best academic interests. The plan prohibited discrimination in administering the transfer assignments and stated that any further administrative procedures adopted by the superintendent to carry out the plan were to be published in advance and applicable to white and Negro pupils alike.[21]

The Charlottesville pupil assignment plan paralleled the new state strategy for desegregation, which was to limit school desegregation as much as possible while avoiding outright resistance. Immediately after the massive resistance statutes were ruled unconstitutional in January 1959, the Virginia legislature repealed the state's compulsory attendance law. Two months later the legislature passed new laws providing for "freedom of choice" and "local option" in dealing with school desegregation. The basic intent of this legislation was to permit pupils to avoid desegregation in the public schools by attending private schools or segregated public schools outside their district. All references to desegregation and race were removed from the provisions for state tuition grants, to make "freedom of choice" possible. Any child attending any accredited school, public or private, outside his own public school district could obtain a tuition grant, without any restriction as to economic need or prior enrollment in a private school.

Beginning March 1, 1960, local school districts not under court order had the option of handling their own pupil assignment plans or remaining under the jurisdiction of the state Pupil Placement Board. Other legislation in the state "freedom of choice" package permitted local school districts to provide transportation to nonsectarian private schools and allowed tax benefits to private schools that had previously been limited to public schools.

Application of Pupil Assignment Plan. Under Charlottesville's new desegregation plan the Jefferson School zone was drawn to encompass the bulk of the black school population. It also took in some white children living in the Jefferson area and missed some black children living in other zones, such as Venable. (See Figure 1.) There were no provisions in the official plan for automatic transfer of children on the basis of racial minority

Figure 1. *Elementary School Zones, Charlottesville, Virginia, 1959*

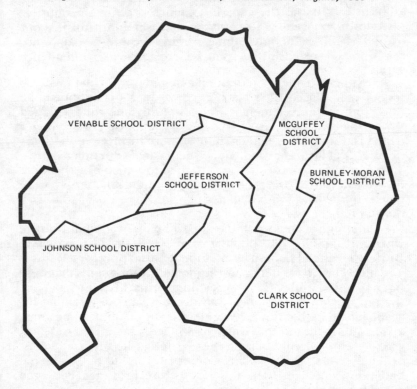

status in a zone, but from 1959 to 1961 the superintendent automatically transferred white children in the Jefferson attendance area to white school zones without transfer requests. The superintendent also automatically assigned blacks living in white zones to Jefferson. If these black students wished to attend the school in their own residential zone, they had to make a written application to the superintendent and be considered for a "transfer." It was the superintendent's practice to routinely turn down applications from blacks who asked for transfers out of Jefferson, although whites—even those who did not apply—were freely shifted from Jefferson to other attendance areas.

The superintendent's first pupil assignments for the 1959–60 school year placed nine black children in Venable, but none in the other white elementary schools. Only one child assigned to Venable was not a party to the desegregation suit or a younger child in a family where other children were involved in the court case. This child was a resident of the Venable attendance area. Two of the elementary children assigned to Venable by the court the previous year were now ready for high school and were placed in the black high school, since they lived closer to Burley than to Lane.

At the high school level, the superintendent's initial practice was to assign all white pupils to Lane and all black pupils to Burley. To attend Lane, a black student must apply for a transfer and meet certain residence and academic requirements that were not applied to whites. The black student must live closer to Lane than to Burley, for instance, and demonstrate on tests that his academic and scholastic achievement equipped him to perform adequately in the grade to which he applied. "Emotional stability" was also considered. Utilizing these criteria, the superintendent assigned three black students to Lane in the fall of 1959. One had been placed in Lane the year before by Judge Paul; the other two students were not involved in the court case.

Desegregation Begins.   When the schools finally began desegregation, the peak of community tension had passed. Many whites had accepted the fact that desegregation was inevitable and were willing to go along with the minimal approach adopted by the school board. A few hoped for more than resigned acceptance, but were disappointed. Mrs. Sarah Patton Boyle, a University faculty wife and one of the few whites who had supported desegregation actively and publicly, later wrote:

As September 1959 moved closer, I tried to tell myself that there was yet time to make of integration something more than grim necessity. I hoped until after the day our local schools opened that a statement from a small group of parents and teachers, or a delegation of them, would publicly welcome the Negro children who would soon be so lonely in our midst. As the first day of school came and went, this last sick little hope quietly died.[22]

There was no public welcome, but there were no disturbances. Mayor Michie issued a proclamation that law and order would be maintained and gave instructions to the police chief to tolerate no violence. Reporters and photographers were on hand at Lane and Venable where only a few persons observed in parked automobiles. A teacher on the Venable staff in 1959 recalled that everything went smoothly and there was no overt trouble or tension in the beginning of the year.

The nine black students assigned to Venable were spread out over the elementary grades. There was one first grader; three second graders; one third grader; one fourth grader; and three seventh graders. A black student who attended Venable in 1959 as a seventh grade transfer student said that there was no name-calling and he could not remember "ever being in a fight or feeling any tension." He said, "There weren't really enough Negroes to have any trouble." A party to the NAACP suit, this young man had completed his first five elementary grades in Jefferson and was tutored in the school board office during the 1958–59 school year. He found the Venable kids "curious" and said that he had some "semi-friends." Another black student, who attended Venable in 1959 as a first grader and completed elementary school there, said, "There didn't seem to be any difference between the black and white kids at Venable," and there were no fights then.

Not all of the children entering Venable had such positive experiences, however. One young man who began at Venable as a first grader in 1959 could not remember much about that first year, except that the white children "called him names" and he "felt dumb." He recalled being called "nigger" and fights over name-calling. He completed elementary school in Venable, but felt the school staff "favored the white kids." He was kept back in the first grade, but does not know why. Later he was friendly with some of the kids he met at Venable, and is still friendly with them. Another student who began at Venable in 1959 as a seventh grader dropped out of school and was taught at home the rest of the year by a teacher supplied by the school board. This child was referred to the Children's Service Center for psychiatric treatment. The next year he attended Burley High School.

Similarly, there were no overt incidents at Lane with the initial desegregation. The three black high school students admitted to Lane did satisfactory academic work. School social and athletic activities continued but the black students did not participate. None of the three black students who first attended Lane were available for interviews when field work for this study took place.

There was no official preparation of pupils or teachers for desegregation, but according to a teacher in Venable in 1959, the Venable staff engaged in much informal discussion during the period they were teaching in the "basements." She said that the teachers were aware the schools would be desegregated and the most resistant joined "the other group," the private elementary school started by the Charlottesville Education Foundation. She felt that the unofficial discussions carried on at this time helped to prepare the "basement" teachers for desegregation. In the early phases of the court suit, the NAACP sponsored a parents' and children's workshop in the summer, expecting desegregation in the fall. Students who were pioneers in desegregation efforts in other communities were brought in, along with adult experts in the field of desegregation. Some of the children who participated in this workshop eventually went to desegregated schools, but the impact was minimized by the time lag. This workshop was also fairly well limited to the black community. Mrs. Boyle, quoted earlier, was the only white parent to register, although several other white persons attended some of the sessions or participated in other ways.

When desegregation was a few weeks underway and it was clear that the schools were continuing to function in a calm and orderly fashion, there was a psychological release in the white community. Mrs. Boyle described this reaction among whites as follows:

The first week came and went without disaster—or even difficulties—then the second. About the middle of the third week, a sigh of relief went up from the community that you could almost hear. As tangibly as the dark cloud had settled down in the summer of 1954, I felt it lift. The heavy air became mountain fresh. The sun sparkled on still waters.[23]

With desegregation and the advent of pupil tuition grants, Lane's enrollment was down 27 percent; Venable's student population dropped off 25 percent. School district figures show the following drop in enrollment in the two schools between 1957, the last "normal" school year, and 1959:

	Pupil Enrollment		
School Year	Venable	Lane	Total
1957–58	600	1,025	1,625
1958–59	552	881	1,433
1959–60	450	750	1,200

The superintendent estimated that one-tenth of the "normal" total public school enrollment were attending private schools during the 1959–60 school year.

The majority of the students who dropped out of the public schools with the first year of desegregation enrolled in two schools opened on a permanent basis by the Charlottesville Education Foundation (CEF). The Charlottesville Superintendent of Schools reported processing a total of 611 tuition grants in the fall of 1959 under the state "freedom of choice" program, with 463 of these paid to city students attending the two new CEF schools. An additional 148 grants went to Charlottesville children attending established private schools. In 1959 Charlottesville students receiving tuition grants made up nearly the entire enrollment in the CEF schools. Robert E. Lee Elementary School enrolled approximately 200 pupils in September 1959; Rock Hill Academy, the CEF high school, enrolled about 300 students. Each Charlottesville student attending private schools under the tuition grant program in 1959–60 received $234.43, the equivalent of the cost of per pupil education in the public schools. The state paid $78.55 of each grant and the city paid $155.88.

NAACP Challenges Pupil Assignment Plan. During the first three years of desegregation the NAACP was constantly in court challenging both the provisions and application of the pupil assignment plan. NAACP legal action began in the summer of 1960, after the board announced pupil assignments for the coming school year. Specifically, the NAACP opposed: (1) white elementary children in the Jefferson zone being automatically transferred out of that attendance area; (2) the superintendent's practice of routinely denying transfers out to black children living in the Jefferson attendance area; (3) black children being assigned to Jefferson although they lived in white school attendance areas; (4) the use of tests to determine whether black children would be admitted to white schools; (5) the granting

of elementary transfers to any child on the grounds that his
race was in the minority in his zone of residence; and (6) the
application of residential and academic requirements for black
pupils applying to Lane High School, while all white children
were admitted without any restriction.

In the course of the litigation it became clear that the school
board was not administering the pupil assignment plan on a
nondiscriminatory basis and that the board's policy was one of
avoiding "compulsory desegregation." The board admitted
openly in court that transfers were granted on the principle
that "no pupil should be compelled to attend against his will
a school occupied entirely or predominantly by pupils of the
opposite race."[24] Initially, the federal courts accepted this principle. The U. S. Court of Appeals for the Fourth Circuit held
April 14, 1961, for instance, that the assignment plan itself was
not unconstitutional or discriminatory. The Court found that
the plan was not applied evenly to white and black children,
however, and warned the Charlottesville school board that violation of the rights of black children could not be continued.

As a result of the U. S. Court of Appeals' criticism of the
administration of the desegregation plan, some changes in the
handling of pupil assignments were made, beginning with the
1961–62 school year. The board said it would now assign children
by residence, and sent all children attending schools outside
their zone letters stating that they were tentatively assigned to
these schools but must fill out a transfer form in order to remain
away from their zone of residence. Blacks living in the Jefferson
zone were denied transfers out and the board continued to accept racial minority status in a district as a valid reason for
transfer. With these "new" transfer procedures, all 149 white
pupils living in the Jefferson attendance zone transferred out of
this zone in the fall of 1961. Approximately 50 black elementary
pupils residing in predominantly white districts transferred to
Jefferson. At the high school level, the board continued to use
residence requirements and academic tests to screen black students applying for Lane, although the Circuit Court had
indicated these practices were discriminatory. On December 18,
1961, the federal District Court ordered the board to drop both
the residence criteria and academic tests required of black applicants to Lane. The Board continued to administer academic
tests to black applicants after this ruling.

On September 17, 1962, the U. S. Court of Appeals for the
Fourth Circuit found that there had been little change in the
Charlottesville schools since the period when the schools were

officially segregated. The Court also stated that "little progress in the integration of schools may be expected" if the board continues with the same policy. The Court ruled the elementary pupil assignment plan "invalid" and threw out all high school screening procedures, commenting, "The discrimination involved is too clear to require discussion." Judge Clement F. Haynsworth, Jr., President Nixon's 1971 nominee to the U. S. Supreme Court, was one of two judges on the Fourth Circuit Court dissenting from the majority opinion. In his dissenting opinion, Judge Haynsworth defended the board's practice of allowing children to transfer on the basis of racial minority status in an attendance area as a justifiable interim measure. He felt this practice was valid for the sake of the "unwilling minorities" who cannot adjust to schools or classes in which all others are of the opposite race.[25] When the decision was appealed, the U. S. Supreme Court refused to stay the Circuit Court's order or review the case.

With enforcement of the Circuit Court's September 1962 order, there were 31 black students in Venable and 26 in Lane. The Court also ordered the admission of four black children to Johnson Elementary School in 1962, opening up a third desegregated school to black pupils. A few more black students entered these three schools in 1963, but the court's 1962 order had little effect on the basic pattern of school segregation in Charlottesville. (See Table 1.)

Table 1 — Assignment of Black Students to White Charlottesville Public Schools Under Pupil Assignment Desegregation Plan and Court Supervision, September 1959 to September 1963

	1959	1960	1961	1962	1963
Elementary Schools					
Burnley-Moran	0	0	0	0	0
Clark	0	0	0	0	0
Greenbrier	*	*	*	0	0
Johnson	0	0	0	4	12
McGuffey	0	0	0	0	0
Venable	9	13	20	31	58
High School					
Lane	3	7	16	26	42
TOTAL	12	20	36	61	112

*Not built at this time.

Source: Charlottesville Public Schools, "Outline of Charlottesville School Integration Case" (December 2, 1963), pp. 2–3.

Black Students in White Schools. Two studies of school
desegregation during the period of court-enforced tokenism
comment on the participation and adjustment of black pupils
in the desegregated but overwhelmingly white schools.

Professor Edward A. Mearns, Jr., University of Virginia Law
School, found in the 1961–62 school year that lunchrooms,
assemblies, and school-sponsored clubs in the desegregated
schools were open to all students and that the band at Lane
High School included blacks. Athletics at Lane were still segregated, however, and dances and social activities at Lane were
banned by the superintendent in 1961 when it was feared black
students would attend. Professor Mearns noted that there had
been no "major incidents" involving black students at Lane or
Venable and that academically the students "ranged from the
top to the bottom of their classes."[26]

In the fall of 1962, two University of Virginia history professors, Paul M. Gaston and Thomas T. Hammond, surveyed 44
black students who had attended Lane and Venable up to September 1962. Gaston and Hammond sent questionnaires to all
children who had actually attended these schools, plus their parents. Thirty-six of the 44 families responded. The results of
the survey indicated that parents' and students' overall experiences with desegregation were positive, in terms of prevailing
standards, concerns, and expectations.

The majority of the students returning questionnaires
reported that a school official or a student offered moral support
during the first days at school; that white students were friendly;
that they were never afraid; that a greater variety of courses
was offered in the white schools and equipment was more
adequate; and that they felt they were included in classroom
participation just as often as they made themselves available.
None of the students characterized their fellow white students
as hostile, none reported encountering violence, and all reported
that the teachers were friendly and helpful. Over half (54 percent) of the black students participating in the survey had met
some unpleasant treatment, mostly limited to name-calling. The
students' responses indicated that the incidence of name-calling
diminished between 1959 and 1962; only one instance of name-
calling was reported in 1962. Although the majority of these
students felt participation in extracurricular activities was
allowed, few actually took part. Among the 36 students, four
participated in band, none in the concert choir, four were in
"treble choir," and none were in athletics. Nearly half of the
students (46 percent) had experienced feelings of anxiety or

tension, with those who enrolled in the first year of desegregation reporting that they had had feelings of anxiety or tension more often than those who had enrolled in white schools more recently. Gaston and Hammond did not ask the students about their participation in school social activities, which were then reinstated at Lane by PTA request, with the PTA assuming responsibility for Lane's dances.

Nearly all of the parents (96 percent) responding to the Gaston-Hammond questionnaires felt that desegregation had gone smoothly. The majority of the parents said that their children had greater motivation to learn; that the homework seemed more massive and difficult; and that their children appeared to miss nothing from the old school and had made friends among the white students. The majority of the parents also reported they had participated in conferences with the teachers and had attended PTA meetings.

Black and white students' current recollections of that period suggest there were more problems than black participants would discuss publicly in 1962. A white high school girl who entered Venable in 1960 as a third grade transfer student from another city remembers that none of the children would play with a black girl in the school or hold hands with her during games. The black child left Venable. Similarly, several black girls who transferred to Venable in 1961 and 1962 recall being "ignored by the white kids," spit on, called names, and sneered at; white children also whispered behind their backs. One of these black girls was put in Venable as a third grader under a 1961 court order. She said that her grades dropped as she wasn't used to the environment of a majority of white kids. The whites "just didn't say anything to her at first." Another girl who transferred to Venable in 1962 as a seventh grader, also under court order, said that the boys were more friendly than the girls and would sometimes sit beside her, although the girls would not. Another seventh grade black transfer student recalled that the teachers "tried to make you feel small" by telling the black students, "You haven't had the background." She said that everyone smiled at first, but there were some minor instances of unfriendly behavior on the part of white children.

Acceptance of Token Desegregation by Whites. By 1962 the pattern of token desegregation established in Charlottesville was fairly well accepted by whites. The Gaston-Hammond report noted, for example, that no white child dropped out of the Johnson Elementary School when it was desegregated by court order in the fall of 1962. Although this court order was appealed, the chairman of the school board indicated that he felt the appeal was a waste of money and effort. Public school enrollment was back to the pre-massive-resistance level by 1962 and that fall the City Council adopted a compulsory municipal school attendance law. The Virginia State compulsory attendance law, repealed during the massive resistance campaign, was not restored until 1968. Gaston and Hammond also reported in 1962, that some white parents had gone beyond mere acceptance of desegregation and welcomed it as a valuable experience for their children. Others felt that the time had come to base long-range planning for the schools on the recognition that desegregation was a fact of school life. Gaston and Hammond stated in December 1962:

> Many parents, no longer fearful of desegregation, criticize the board for what they consider to be lack of board leadership in school problems. They maintain that school decisions based primarily on racial considerations frequently interfere with constructive planning . . . and greater educational gains will be made by accepting it [desegregation] rather than by seeking further useless means of resisting it.[27]

Role of State Tuition Grant Program. For whites who did not want to accept desegregation, the state tuition grant program and the two schools established by the Charlottesville Education Foundation initially provided an almost cost-free escape. State law establishing the tuition grants gave localities several alternatives in fixing the size of the grants awarded in their districts. The Charlottesville City Council annually set tuition grants at the cost of education per pupil in the public schools, increasing the size of the grants as the cost of public education grew. Each year, in turn, the CEF set tuition in its own schools at $15 above the announced size of the tuition grants. Local advocates of "freedom of choice" boasted that their operating costs were no higher than those of the public schools. Since the majority of the pupils attending the CEF schools were getting tuition grants, local and state tax monies were in effect subsidizing most of the operating costs of these "private" schools. In 1960, for example, 524 of the 637 pupils enrolled in the CEF elementary and high schools were receiving tuition grants. Even in 1962, after many pupils had returned to the public schools, 488 of the approximately 700 pupils in the CEF schools were under the tuition program. Between 1959 and 1964, 526 to as many as 761 Charlottesville public school age children received tuition

Table 2 — Tuition Grants Issued by Charlottesville Public Schools
1959—1968*

Number of Tuition Grants by Year	School			
	Robert E. Lee (Elem.)	Rock Hill Academy (H.S.)	Other Private Schools	Total
1959	161	299	66	526
1960	165	359	146	670
1961	157	338	133	628
1962	159	329	122	610
1963	172	328	261	761
1964	166	238	206	610
1966†	94	81	145	320
1967	104	90	152	346
1968	116	104	137	357

*Tuition grants were paid on a semester basis each year; where the total number of grants fluctuated by semester, the higher figure is reported. The 1959 figure reflects grants made by December 10, as breakdowns by school for grants made later in the year were not available.

†1965 data not available.

Source: Charlottesville Public Schools.

grants each year, with the majority of these grants going to pupils attending the CEF schools. (See Table 2.) During this period, the district was paying for at least one tuition grant for every ten children enrolled in the public schools; in some years the ratio was even higher, with the district awarding one tuition grant for every seven children in the public schools.

The constitutionality of the tuition grant program was not initially challenged in Charlottesville, although suits were filed in other parts of Virginia and there was some local criticism of public funds being channelled into private institutions. The League of Women Voters, for instance, spoke out publicly against the tuition grant program, as did Professor Hardy C. Dillard of the University of Virginia Law School. Many felt that the CEF school served a useful purpose, however, by draining off from the public schools whites who were most hostile to desegregation. There were also several vocal and influential advocates of "freedom of choice" in the community, including Chester Babcock, a member of the school board and editor of the *Daily Progress*. Babcock defended the tuition grants primarily on the basis of the "freedom of choice" in education they offered, avoiding a position based on racial grounds. One of the major spokes-

men for "freedom of choice" on a statewide basis, Leon Dure,
also lived in the Charlottesville area. Babcock and Dure were
said to have persuaded many local people to support the
"freedom of choice" program.

With the size of the tuition grants tied to the growing cost
of per pupil education, Charlottesville spent an increasing
amount each year on the tuition program. The size of each
grant was $234.44 in 1959; by the 1961–62 school year the grants
had grown to $312.39 each. Since the state's contribution was
fixed at a rate of $150 per high school student and $125 per
elementary school student after the program got underway, the
city paid a larger proportion of the grants as the size went up.
For example, the total cost of tuition grants issued in Charlottesville for the 1960–61 school year was $185,082.34. The state
paid $93,332.82 of this cost; the city, $91,749.52. The next year,
the total cost of the grants increased to $193,294.60. The state
reimbursed the district for $87,327.25 of this amount and the
city bore an expense of $105,267.35. By the 1963–64 school
year, the peak of the program as far as the number of tuition
grants issued, the annual cost of the program had climbed to
$227,529.90, with Charlottesville's share of this amounting to
$120,554.90.

As the tuition grant program continued, it was not only
more costly to the taxpayers of Charlottesville, but was used
more extensively by pupils in established private schools that
many would have attended in any case. The majority of the
grants continued to go to students in the two CEF schools, but
beginning in 1963, from one-third to 45 percent of the local
tuition grants went to pupils in private schools other than the
two CEF-sponsored schools. Children benefiting from the grant
program attended private academies, boarding schools, and
military schools in New England,New York, Pennsylvania, the
middle Atlantic states, and Florida, including exclusive schools
such as Phillips Exeter Academy. This was possible because the
1958 amendments to the tuition grant legislation removed all
references to race or desegregation. Parents seeking tuition
grants were not asked to justify their selection of schools or give
any reason for not wanting to attend the public schools.

There was, however, a sharp drop in the number of Char-
lottesville pupils receiving tuition grants after 1964. In 1964, the
U.S. Supreme Court ruled that the tuition grant program in
Prince Edward County was unconstitutional. Although the
Prince Edward ruling did not strike down the tuition grant pro-
gram in other parts of Virginia, the number of grants issued in

Charlottesville dropped drastically after this ruling. (See Table 2.) Grants to pupils attending the two Charlottesville CEF schools continued, but on a reduced basis.

The tuition grant program was finally ended by court order at the end of the 1968–69 school year. On February 11, 1969, a three-judge federal court ruled the entire Virginia state tuition grant program unconstitutional. This decision resulted from a suit filed by the NAACP that challenged the payments to 10 schools in the state, including the two Charlottesville CEF schools. The NAACP sought reimbursement of public tax monies paid to these schools after the 1965–66 school year, but lost this part of the suit. The court permitted tuition grants to continue through the 1968–69 school year, but ordered them eliminated thereafter. At the time of the ruling, officials of the two Charlottesville CEF schools estimated that approximately 35 to 40 percent of their total operating costs were paid by the tuition grants. The press reported that a total of $20 million had been paid out in tuition grants in Virginia in the 10-year period the program existed. There was no effort to save the tuition grants after the February 1969 ruling. The governor announced that the ruling would not be appealed.

5
Major Desegregation of Junior High Schools and Elementary Schools: 1965–1967

New School Facilities and Desegregation. With the return of most students to the public school system by 1962 and the annexation of a portion of the county, effective January 1963, Charlottesville was faced with the need for new school facilities. A new elementary school, the Greenbrier School, was opened in the fall of 1962 in the suburban county area being annexed to the city. This school, which opened on an all-white basis, solved the problem of facilities for elementary children in the annexation area. But what about the high school pupils? Lane was built to accommodate 900 to 1,000 students, and its fall

1962 enrollment was about 1,200. With the newly annexed territory, 1,400 students were expected for the 1963–64 school year.

In the spring of 1962, a special committee of the board recommended that a new high school be built for the northwestern part of the city. If geographic attendance zones were set up, a school located in this area would become a white school, leaving Lane with a mixed student population. Lane's enrollment would also include the southeast part of Charlottesville where segregationist sentiment is strong among whites. While this proposal was still in the early stages of discussion it became clear that a bond referendum, which was necessary for this large a project, would probably be defeated by a combination of black and white voters whose children would remain in the Lane area. The proposal for a new high school was dropped and early in December 1962 the special committee recommended shifting to a junior high school system, building three schools for grades 7–9 and retaining Lane as a senior high school.

Although the Charlottesville schools were supposedly desegregated, the committee's proposal called for two completely new schools "on sites located as strategically as possible," with the third junior high school built in conjunction with the county on the site of Burley High School. The Albemarle County Board of Supervisors soon announced the county would cooperate. Although the NAACP immediately protested the proposal, by January 21, 1963, both the Board of Supervisors and the Charlottesville City Council had approved the junior high school building program and authorized the school boards of both districts to go ahead with plans for the joint black junior high school at the Burley site. The NAACP filed suit to prevent the construction of segregated junior high school facilities on April 26, 1963. Following the NAACP suit, plans for the junior high school at Burley were shelved and the city held a bond election to build two junior high schools. The NAACP supported this bond issue, which passed. The NAACP branch also resumed efforts about this time to get a black person appointed to the school board. The black community had been pressing for representation on the board unsuccessfully since at least the early 1950s.

When the NAACP leaders inquired about racial policy in the new junior high schools, they were told that the present "freedom of choice" plan would continue, with Jefferson students being given the choice of continuing the seventh grade at that school or attending one of the two new junior high schools. Burley was to continue accepting city students who chose to go there in grades 8 and 9 as well as in the high school grades. The district had adopted a "freedom of choice" policy after the court had ruled out its pupil assignment plan in 1962, which abandoned geographic zoning and placed the burden of responsibility for desegregation completely on the black parent and child. "Freedom of choice" had resulted in little additional desegregation.

The NAACP next asked that all city students be automatically assigned to one of the new junior high schools and that an "adequate and meaningful desegregation plan be drawn up for all other schools," including the desegregation of school personnel. The board was informed that the NAACP would fight the new junior high school assignment plan "in every legal way, including the use of publicity and litigation."[28] In May 1964, the NAACP presented petitions to the school superintendent with 306 signatures asking for an end to racial segregation in the public schools, including an end to discrimination against black administrative personnel, teachers, and clerical and custodial employees.

Concern for the new junior high schools extended beyond the black community. A local Community Relations Committee headed by a white banker met with the school board in March 1964 to request that "the same rules should apply to white and Negro children" at the time the new junior high schools were opened.[29] The board agreed to consider this proposal, but subsequently informed the Committee it would continue the seventh grade at Jefferson, giving children there the option of transferring to the new junior high schools. Chester R. Babcock, editor of the *Daily Progress* and chairman of the school board, wrote the chairman of the Community Relations Committee:

> It has been our experience that a large number of Negro graduates of our elementary schools—substantially more than half of them—prefer to enter Burley High School rather than Lane. *We believe that taking the seventh grade at Jefferson will facilitate the transition from sixth grade in the elementary system to eighth grade at Burley for those pupils.*[30] (Emphasis added.)

Blacks Exercise "Freedom of Choice."   With passage of the 1964 Civil Rights Act, support for complete desegregation of schools gained momentum. An informal, biracial coalition of several key organizations and individuals began working together to secure major desegregation of the city's schools, concentrating

first on the new junior high schools, which were scheduled to
open in the fall of 1965. Representatives of the NAACP, the
Virginia Council on Human Relations, and the Education Committee of the Citizens Democratic Council, and the Reverend
Henry B. Mitchell of Trinity Episcopal Church made up this
coalition. Reverend Mitchell, a black minister later appointed
to the school board, was one of the litigants in the school suit
that desegregated Lane and Venable. The group first met with
the Superintendent of Schools to try to secure a commitment
to assign all students in grades 7–9 to the new junior high schools.
When the board persisted in maintaining "freedom of choice,"
members of the coalition began contacting black parents to talk
with them about their "choice."

When sixth grade parents were polled as to their choice of
schools for the 1965–66 school year, all except 30 of the 113
black children in the sixth grade at Jefferson School chose to
attend the new junior high schools. The school board held a
special meeting to discuss the Jefferson situation February 22,
1965, but before this meeting, the Citizens Democratic Council
adopted a resolution asking the school board to assign all junior
high school pupils to the new junior high schools. Speaking
before the Council in support of this resolution, Dr. Richard
C. Boden, chairman of the Education Committee of the Citizens
Democratic Council, said that the pattern in Charlottesville had
been the same since 1956, with the school board taking no initiative to provide desegregated education. The school board voted
at its February 22 meeting to drop the seventh grade at Jefferson,
but did not specify which school or schools the children would
attend. Dr. Boden and others continued to press the board for
a definite commitment that the Jefferson children would be
assigned to the new junior high schools on a nondiscriminatory
basis. The board continued to deliberate on the proposal,
although it had passed a resolution at the February 22 meeting
stating that it would comply with the new U. S. Department
of Health, Education and Welfare (HEW) regulations concerning
nondiscrimination in federally assisted programs.

The coalition next filed a complaint of noncompliance with
the 1964 Civil Rights Act with the Equal Educational Opportunity
Program of the U. S. Office of Education, the agency in HEW
which then administered compliance with Title VI of the Civil
Rights Act in the public schools. In addition to filing the complaint the coalition also organized a massive "freedom of choice"
campaign among blacks currently sending their children to the
remaining elementary grades in the Jefferson School. Interracial

teams went door to door in the black community urging parents to transfer their children to all-white and predominantly white schools. The teams gave parents a transfer form to fill out. Canvassers found black parents "eager" to transfer, and by May 20, 1965, approximately half of the pupils who had been attending the Jefferson School submitted transfer forms to the school board office. In addition, about 100 black students then enrolled in Burley High School had filled out forms requesting transfers to Lane.

"Freedom of Choice" Revisited. The school board met May 20, 1965, to adopt a formal statement of policy and a plan for compliance with the 1964 Civil Rights Act. This action was taken following a letter from a staff member of the Equal Educational Opportunities Program (EEOP) stating that the board's February 22 resolution and material sent with the resolution was not sufficient for EEOP to pass judgment on Charlottesville's desegregation plan. The April 1965 school desegregation "Guidelines," the first adopted by HEW, required school districts under a desegregation court order to submit a breakdown of the racial distribution of pupils and teachers by school and other compliance data, along with their court order. In addition, the "Guidelines" stated clearly that a court order to desegregate would establish eligibility for federal funds only if it required elimination of the dual system. In accordance with these "Guidelines" Charlottesville drew up a fuller statement of its plan for desegregation, which was passed at the May 20 meeting.

The board's May 20 statement reaffirmed the existing "freedom of choice" policy whereby any child might elect to attend any formerly white or formerly black school in the system. This "freedom of choice" was to continue at all levels, except that seventh graders would choose "either of the two junior high schools which will be operated on a fully desegregated basis." Eighth and ninth graders, however, could still attend the all-black Burley High School, and Burley was to continue serving city school children in grades 10–12. At the elementary level, the Jefferson School was to continue; preference would be given to "those children living nearest the school" in the event "freedom of choice" transfers would cause overcrowding. Ignoring the transfer forms already submitted, the district announced that it would soon distribute "freedom of selection" transfer forms. When the May 20 statement was released to the press, school board chairman Chester R. Babcock said it would "open the way for the continued payment of federal funds the school system is entitled to." [31]

Since the ad hoc coalition had heard nothing from its initial complaint to HEW filed in March, the group again wrote EEOP, reviewing its unsuccessful efforts to exercise "freedom of choice" and criticizing the board's May 20 statement of policy. The letter noted the distribution of new transfer forms, the new provision that children living closest to a school would have first preference in the event of "overcrowding," the lack of publicity for the "freedom of choice" plan for the past three years, the continuation of Burley High School, and the failure of the board to assign black teachers to formerly white schools on a nondiscriminatory basis. The coalition explained that the desegregation of school staff, mentioned in the May 20 statement, consisted of two black teachers being assigned to each of the two new junior high schools. The letter said that the signers would not object to a plan for geographic zones at the elementary level, if this were "strictly and fairly enforced." Copies of the letter were sent to Vice President Hubert H. Humphrey and James M. Quigley, an Assistant Secretary of HEW who served as the Secretary's coordinator and liaison for enforcement of Title VI. On June 23, 1965, David Seeley, EEOP Director, wrote the concerned groups that the regulation governing HEW's civil rights compliance program provided "in effect" that his office "would not attempt to interfere" in school districts where a federal court had taken jurisdiction in a desegregation case. He noted, however, that EEOP would look further into the Charlottesville situation if the school district was not abiding by the court order. By the time Seeley responded to Charlottesville's complaint, EEOP had adopted a practice of keeping "hands off" districts under court order and routinely accepted any court order submitted as evidence of compliance with Title VI, a practice protested by the major national civil rights organizations.

"Freedom of Choice" Abolished for Elementary Schools. The new set of "freedom of choice" transfer forms circulated by the board after its May 20 policy statement resulted in an even higher number of children transferring out of the Jefferson School. When compilation of these transfer forms indicated that only 327 pupils would attend Jefferson the following year, the board again reconsidered its policy. Jefferson had enrolled 817 students in the 1964–65 year.

On June 30, the board voted to abolish "freedom of choice" at the elementary level, substituting a geographic zoning plan. The new plan provided for the elimination of Jefferson as an elementary school, established new attendance lines for all other elementary schools, and prohibited transfers across district lines. (See Figure 2.) At the same time, the superintendent announced that the Jefferson building would be used to house the two new junior high schools the following year, as construction of the new plants was behind schedule. The new policy did not affect "freedom of choice" at grade 8 and above; black secondary students already enrolled in Burley would remain there, if they had not submitted transfer forms by June 24. In reporting the new elementary desegregation plan the next day, the *Daily Progress* stated that the board had consulted both the City Council and HEW officials in working out the plan.

Another major gain for civil rights in the schools took place about the same time "freedom of choice" in the elementary schools was abandoned. The City Council's school board appointments in the summer of 1965 included Charlottesville's first black board member, Raymond Lee Bell, a 38-year-old undertaker. This appointment was the culmination of at least 15 years of effort on the part of the NAACP and other groups in the black community.

Junior High School Desegregation Begins. Major desegregation of Charlottesville's junior high schools took place in the fall of 1965, with the beginning of the junior high school program. All black and white seventh graders attended the desegregated schools, which operated on double sessions in the Jefferson building, pending completion of the new plants. Although black eighth and ninth graders could elect to attend Burley, most transferred to the new schools. Enrollment figures show that only 15 eighth graders and 29 ninth graders from the city of Charlottesville attended Burley High School during the 1965–66 school year. Thus only 44 black junior high school pupils were in segregated schools, in contrast to the 269 enrolled in segregated schools the year before. To put it another way, 85 percent of the black children at the junior high school level who were enrolled in Jefferson and Burley in the 1964–65 school year attended desegregated schools in 1965–66.

A separate faculty and administrative staff manned each session of the junior high schools in Jefferson, with students supposedly enrolling in the Buford or Walker session, depending on the section of town in which they lived. Buford was to serve South Charlottesville; Walker, the northern part of town. Little attention was paid to attendance areas, however, and many students enrolled in the morning or afternoon sessions on the basis

Figure 2. *Elementary School Zones, Charlottesville, Virginia, 1965*

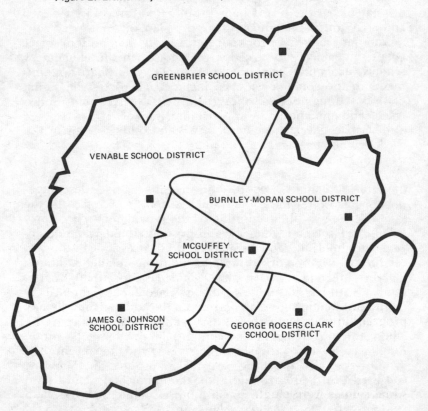

of personal preference as to time. Buford's enrollment totaled 699; Walker's 779. Again, there was little defection from the public schools as a result of the new school desegregation. The combined enrollment of Buford, Walker and Burley in grades 7–9 totaled 1,422 regular students, only five students less than the total number in these grades the previous year.

For the first time, whites were attending a school that had been identified as a black school under the segregated system. John E. Huegel, the first principal of Buford Junior High School, said that "the problem" in desegregating the junior high schools "came the summer before, from [white] parents reluctant to send their child to a Negro school." "The real problem," he said, "was that parents had fears about the cleanliness of the building." They asked to come and see the school. Finding Jefferson clean and in good condition pacified them to some extent.

Black teachers were also assigned to teach white children for the first time. At the junior high school level, Buford was assigned one black teacher; Walker was assigned three. Huegel said that the black teacher assigned to Buford did a competent job of teaching, but "sat back and did not project" and "did not participate" in faculty committees and discussion on a voluntary basis. Similarly, he did not involve himself in any of the school's social activities. In order to "draw him out," Huegel made a special effort to place this teacher on committees and to see that he took part in school activities. There was very little planning for junior high school desegregation, but Huegel said that the Buford faculty worked hard to find materials that were suitable for students at different achievement levels and to bring the black students "up to academic standard."

The two junior high sessions opened with a non-graded basic program in both mathematics and science for grades 7 and 8. The mathematics program consisted of six levels of instruction ranging from basic arithmetic to algebra readiness, with an option for advanced eighth graders to take algebra. The science course consisted of 18 progressive levels of instruction. English and social studies were taught along more conventional lines, with students grouped for these classes primarily on the basis of achievement. There were four levels of English instruction for each grade, with the lowest level serving students whose reading skills were more than two years below "normal." Social studies classes were grouped in three achievement levels. No attempt was made to group students in other classes.

Staff in the two schools experienced some problems in implementing the non-graded courses and also found that the initial grouping procedures were not satisfactory, partly because of desegregation. Buford's principal from 1965 to 1968 said, for example, that the grouping of pupils by achievement in the English classes did not work and they had to "regroup." In order to help black students who could not keep up with the program as set up, class sizes at Buford were lowered, separate and district teaching materials for each level were selected and a new system of teacher evaluation was developed to place pupils at the proper level in reading groups and in subject areas, such as math. This new teacher evaluation was based on a complete review of the child's record and in many cases included talks with the child. By 1968–69, all ungraded classes at Walker Junior High School except one math course had been dropped. The principal said that he personally favored fewer levels of instruction and felt that counteracting the proliferation of grouping had created more opportunity for youngsters of different races to be together. The numerous levels of instruction in math and science with the non-graded program apparently caused more de facto segregation than ability grouping at several levels. "If you have many levels," he said, "you will end up in de facto segregation—more Negroes at the bottom and fewer at the top." The principal noted that there was still some de facto segregation in classes such as reading, where more black students were deficient. He also pointed out that there were only a few blacks in some courses for college-bound students, such as geometry, Latin, and algebra.

Increased Desegregation in Elementary Schools. With the closing of Jefferson as an elementary school and with the new elementary attendance zones adopted in the summer of 1965, Clark and Burnley-Moran received black students for the first time and McGuffey shifted to a predominantly black school. The new attendance lines brought both the Clark and Burnley-Moran boundaries closer into the center of town, giving each a slice of the area formerly served by Jefferson. Burnley-Moran also got most of the white population that had previously attended McGuffey, and with the elimination of the Jefferson elementary zone, McGuffey's new attendance area encompassed the central core of the old Jefferson district. McGuffey had enrolled a few black students for the first time in 1964 under "freedom of choice," but had remained overwhelmingly white. In the fall of 1965, with the new boundaries, the NAACP estimated that McGuffey's black enrollment was over 90 percent. Jefferson's black principal, Booker T. Reaves, was made principal of the McGuffey School. What happened, in effect, was that a great deal of the old Jefferson School was transferred to McGuffey. The rezoning of elementary schools had no effect on Greenbrier's racial composition; this school was now the one all-white elementary school in the district.

In early September 1965, Drewary Brown, president of the Charlottesville NAACP branch, wrote the school board to protest "the deplorable situation that has developed at the McGuffey School." He demanded that the situation be "corrected immediately," and put the NAACP on record as opposing any school in the future having more than a 50 percent black population.[32] The school board chairman replied that it "would not be possible to adopt an assignment plan . . . which would insure that all schools would have less than a 50 percent Negro enrollment." She explained that the current plan "caused the least disruption to the total education program and also pointed out that for the first time, white students were required to be in the minority in one school.[33] She was referring to McGuffey School, which retained a few white pupils under the new attendance lines.

Elementary Teachers Desegregated. While there were only limited gains in the desegregation of pupils in the fall of 1965, elementary teachers in the regular schools were completely desegregated. With the phasing out of Jefferson as an elementary school, the staff was distributed among the other elementary schools, with each school, including Greenbrier, receiving from three to six teachers. One black teacher was also made an itinerant teacher. (See Table 3.)

There was no particular preparation of elementary teachers for desegregation, but then-Superintendent of Schools George Tramontin had instituted two changes prior to 1965 that helped pave the way for staff desegregation. A native of Michigan and a newcomer to the South, Tramontin came to Charlottesville in 1960 as Assistant Superintendent for Curriculum and Instruction. By the 1961–62 school year, Tramontin was holding citywide teachers meetings on a desegregated basis, calling together all sixth grade teachers, all high school teachers, all librarians, and so forth. Tramontin also instituted a system of teacher rotation, which involved occasional assignment of teachers to other schools in the system so that they could observe conditions and methods outside their own particular schools. As a part of this rotation, white teachers were assigned to black schools. Initially, some white teachers stayed home "sick" the first day they were assigned to a black school. The teachers

Table 3 — Distribution of Professional Staff in Charlottesville Public Schools by Race, 1964—1968

W=White B=Black	1964-65		1965-66		1966-67		1967-68		1968-69	
SCHOOL	W	B	W	B	W	B	W	B	W	B
Elementary										
Burnley-Moran	28	0	24	5	23	5	23	5	23	4
Clark	26	0	21	5	22	5	22	6	26	5
Greenbrier	18	0	15	3	15	3	16	3	16	3
Jefferson†	0	38	*	*	17	5	22	4	20	5
Johnson	29	0	23	5	25	6	28	5	27	5
McGuffey	10	0	12	6	*	*	*	*	*	*
Venable	27	0	24	4	22	5	24	7	20	8
Junior High										
Buford	*	*	31	1	32	4	38	5	34	8
Walker	*	*	33	3	38	5	30	9	34	7
High School										
Burley	0	40	0	38	6	25	*	*	*	*
Lane	75	0	53	0	56	2	63	5	63	9
Other										
Children's Rehabilitation Center & University Hospital	3	0	3	0	4	0	5	0	6	0
Itinerant	8	0	12	1	16	1	13	2	14	2
Special Ed. Center	*	*	*	*	16	2	18	1	15	3
TOTAL	224	78	251	71	292	68	302	52	298	59

* Not applicable; school not in operation.

† Jefferson became a sixth grade center in 1966-67.

Source: Charlottesville Public Schools, Director of Personnel.

generally accepted their second assignment, however, and complaints ceased as they became accustomed to the desegregated rotation.

Tramontin was a controversial superintendent for several reasons, including the fact that major strides in pupil and staff desegregation were made during his tenure. Tramontin became Superintendent of Schools for Charlottesville in 1963 and presided over both junior high school desegregation and the first major departure from tokenism at the elementary level. Many people in the community felt that he was personally responsible for these changes, and some of his actions were resented. It was said, for instance, that he irritated many whites by sitting with the black plaintiffs during federal court proceedings on Charlottesville's desegregation case. Others opposed Tramontin for other reasons, particularly his efforts to get rid of Lane's principal of many years and other entrenched staff members. Tramontin was asked to leave the school system at the end of the 1965–66 school year, and was replaced by Dr. Edward W. Rushton, who had been Superintendent of Schools in Roanoke, Virginia.

Dr. Rushton is an older man, with an active interest in intercultural teaching exchange. He has brought exchange teachers to Charlottesville from Germany and other countries, was President of the Association for the Advancement of International Education from 1967–1969, and is a consultant to the U. S. State Department and its Overseas Schools Advisory Council. Dr. Rushton's interest in international intercultural relations, which takes up a great deal of his time and sometimes causes long absences from Charlottesville, is rather irritating to key adults and students concerned with local racial problems, as they feel he has little interest in intercultural relations at home.

Major Desegregation of Elementary Schools, 1966. Major desegregation of Charlottesville's elementary schools finally took place in the fall of 1966. With the new junior high schools ready for occupancy, the Jefferson building was free once more and was needed to accommodate the growing elementary school population. There was community sentiment against going back to Jefferson as a regular elementary school, however, and the NAACP had already protested the predominantly black enrollment at McGuffey. After a "packed" board meeting on proposed new elementary zones that many elements of the community opposed, the board established Jefferson as a Sixth Grade Center beginning September 1966, and set up new attendance lines for grades 1–5 in all remaining schools except McGuffey. McGuffey was discontinued as a regular elementary school and converted to a Special Education Center. With the new zones, Greenbrier retained its old boundaries and its white upper-middle class population, but the other five elementary schools were rezoned on a vector basis. Attendance boundaries were brought into the center of the city so that each school included a section of the black population. Although there was some modification of the 1966 zone lines in the next two years, these boundaries remained essentially the same through the 1968–69 school year. (See Figure 3.)

After 11 years of petitions, court suits, massive resistance, and tokenism, major desegregation of the elementary schools was finally achieved. For the first time, there was no predominantly black regular elementary school in the center of the black community and five of the city's six elementary schools had substantial numbers of black students enrolled. No racial enrollment records were maintained by the school board in 1966, but the distribution of the resident school population in these attendance areas was approximately the same as in 1967, when the board began keeping racial records again. The black population was thus approximately 25 percent in Burnley-Moran; 11 percent in Clark; 0 percent in Greenbrier; 23 percent in Johnson; and 40 percent in Venable. Jefferson, with a citywide sixth grade population, was approximately 24 percent black.

Although Charlottesville was past the point of school closings and massive withdrawals from the public schools, there was an undercurrent of "rumbling and grumbling," particularly with regard to the Sixth Grade Center at Jefferson. Mrs. Pauline Garrett, a staff member of Burley High School, was appointed principal of Jefferson. Mrs. Garrett was the first black principal to head a predominantly white school in Charlottesville and the first black principal to have a predominantly white staff. Jefferson reopened as a Sixth Grade Center with 17 white and five black teachers. Booker Reaves, formerly principal of Jefferson and McGuffey, was moved to the central administration offices as an administrative assistant and clerk of the board. This assignment brought the first black person into Charlottesville's central school offices, but was considered a demotion by the black community, as the position was viewed as one without the authority and responsibility of a principal.

There was, according to Mrs. Garrett, some negative feeling in both the white and black communities when Jefferson shifted to a citywide sixth grade school. Another Jefferson staff member

Figure 3. *Elementary School Zones, Charlottesville, Virginia, 1968–69*

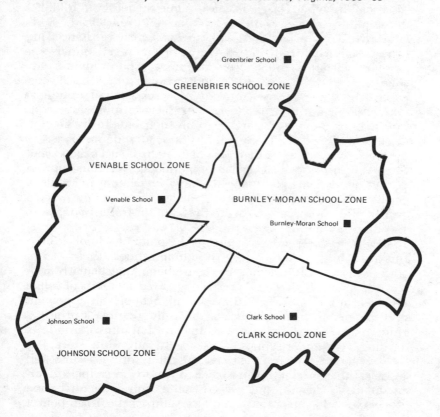

said that some whites were "apprehensive" about sending their
children to a formerly black school and came to look at the
building. She also said some whites objected to the fact that
their children would have to walk through a black neighborhood
to get to Jefferson. The school district did not provide transportation to Jefferson and much of the initial griping among whites
focused on the transportation problem rather than the race issue.
A white faculty member felt that some of the early dissatisfaction
among some white parents might also be traced to the fact that
their children had black teachers. These objections did not
develop into an open community issue, however, and the Sixth
Grade Center was launched without incidents or massive withdrawals. Mrs. Garrett said that only six or seven pupils who
were initially enrolled in Jefferson transferred to Robert E. Lee
Elementary. Mrs. Garrett attributed the smooth transition
within the school to the "attitude of the staff," which was to
take into account the "past history of the school situation." She
says that many problems are "circumvented due to the attitude
of the staff." A black teacher felt that some staff members are
afraid to open up and discuss problems across racial lines, however, and this same teacher had experienced reluctance on the
part of some white parents to discuss their children's academic
problems with a black teacher.

Although there were no acute problems at Jefferson that surfaced as community issues, the school was reorganized after its
first year to meet some of the needs of the students and try
out a teaching approach that the administration had in mind
for middle schools later on. A modified team teaching program
was set up, with two teachers being paired to teach the same
children in large blocks of time roughly equivalent to morning
and afternoon sessions. One teacher was assigned a group of
students in the morning—for example, for English, social studies,
reading, writing, spelling, and a special interest subject such
as French or music. In the afternoon, the second teacher would
instruct the same children in a block of subjects including science,
mathematics, health, and physical education. One of the two
teachers would supervise the children during the lunch period.
Youngsters were placed in a group for block instruction according to a combination of test scores, teacher recommendations,
and interest, with children electing special subjects such as French
being placed in the same block where this language was taught,
for example. This new organization cut down on movement
in the school and made for a quieter school that was more condu-
cive to work in the eyes of the administration.

With the reorganization, three general levels of ability grouping were established—high, high-average, and a combination of average and below-average pupils. Different readers were used in teaching each of the three groups. This grouping set up a kind of elite group of students at the top, with only a few black students, but the high-average ability level was more integrated and the average-below average classes were well mixed. Average and below average pupils were combined into one level to accomplish more classroom desegregation, as the majority of black children were in the lower achievement groups. A remedial reading program for about 80 pupils was also set up during the second year that Jefferson was used as a Sixth Grade Center, utilizing a language skills teacher based in Venable. The teacher worked in both schools on a part-time basis. The remedial reading program was deemed necessary because some pupils were reading below a fourth grade level. Use of typewriters was introduced as part of the remedial reading effort and the librarian at Jefferson helped find high-interest material the children could handle. The librarian is generally buying more books on African culture and famous Negroes since desegregation and puts up displays marking events that are important to blacks, such as the anniversary of Martin Luther King's assassination.

According to one staff member, there were some discipline problems at Jefferson the first year when grouping for instruction was more homogeneous and black "slow learners," many of them overage for their grade level, were clustered together in the lower ability groups. This same staff member said that each year there are more black children in the high ability group coming up from the lower elementary grades, but it will be a long time before the distribution of children by achievement level is the same for both races. Several Jefferson staff members —black and white—stated that black students were on the whole more poorly motivated than their white counterparts and two commented that the black pupils do not always get what the white children get, "an initial thrust from parents to produce good grades." A third thought that the fact that the black children "were not fully socially absorbed . . . could have some bearing on their achievement." "We have a lot of slum kids . . ." as one of the Jefferson staff put it:

It is very hard for them to adjust to the mores of the white middle class. It is hard for other people to adjust to them. Their ideas of discipline, their work habits are so different. They don't relate in the same way. . . . That's the crux of the whole matter.

Jefferson staff said that black and white children are fairly well integrated in school activities, although they have few out-of-school contacts across racial lines. One faculty member told of a couple of white children now at Jefferson who would not sit at the table with black children in the lower elementary grades three years ago at another school. "The children met again in Jefferson," she said. "Things are different now. They accept it [desegregation]." A teacher observed that the black children "would scatter" during the 1967–68 school year, but in the 1968–69 term, with "black power," black students were "more clannish" and were sitting together more. He had established a seating chart to spread out the black students in his class. It should also be noted that during the 1967–68 school year an activity program was sponsored at Jefferson to give the children more opportunity to get together and give them an outlet in working on something that interested them. Children picked chess or checkers, or an art, sewing, drama, science, "charm," or shop project and spent an alloted period of time on the activity chosen once per week. These activities were integrated and parents helped as resource persons. The principal felt the activity program had a positive effect on desegregation in the classroom, but did not think it was necessary to repeat it in the 1968–69 school year.

Although the Jefferson Sixth Grade Center is generally considered successful as a school, and some consider it a better transition to junior high school than a regular elementary school sixth grade, the Jefferson Center will be phased out with the advent of middle schools and a K-4-4-4 grade organization. According to present plans, Jefferson will be abandoned as a regular school and converted to a central warehouse and maintenance shop. This use of Jefferson was recommended by the Peabody Report and will take place when the building program permits the change to middle schools.

Impact of Major Desegregation on Venable. Venable School was most affected by the first year of major desegregation in the elementary schools. Close to the University of Virginia, in an older, established neighborhood of professional families, including University faculty, Venable was traditionally "the school" in Charlottesville at the elementary level. Venable had enjoyed a "choice" reputation for many years and had provided a satisfactory public education to many children who could have attended private schools. Some affluent county residents paid tuition to send their children to Venable. There was a kind of parent interest in Venable not present in other schools and a history of parents going to the board, demanding things—and getting them. As one school administrator summed it up, the "power structure" lives in the Venable community. Because of its academic standing and prestige, Venable was especially attractive to the nearby black population. In the earliest phases of desegregation, Venable was the target school in court suits. It was the elementary school most sought after by blacks during the period of pupil assignment and "freedom of choice."

With the elimination of a central ghetto school in the downtown area and the new attendance zones, Venable's black population more than doubled. The principal of Venable during the 1968–69 school year said that there were 60 to 100 black children in the school in the last phases of "freedom of choice" and that the number jumped to about 220 to 230 with the beginning of the 1966–67 school year. The percentage of blacks rose from about 10 percent to about 40 percent in the space of two years. The white elementary age population in Venable was declining because of the aging of settled families, but the main shift in ratios came from the sudden influx of more black students. The change in Venable's black population was qualitative as well as quantitative, although the increase in numbers and proportions was important to many white parents. In the earlier period of desegregation, Venable had attracted and received children from the relatively better off segments of the black community. With the new zone lines, however, Venable "caught" the black children from the Westhaven public housing project who had previously attended Jefferson and then McGuffey. The entrance of the lower income black population into Venable was the crux of many of the problems that developed during the 1966–67 school year, as there were class as well as racial and educational differences between the children.

There were, first of all, differences between the two school populations resulting from the widely different educational opportunities and approaches. Jefferson had been overcrowded and lacking in new equipment for many years. The philosophy at Jefferson, which was carried over to McGuffey, was to keep the children in a grade until they mastered the material. There were many overage children in the group transferred to Venable in 1966, including some who had repeated some grades two or three times. The presence of large black boys in classes with small white children was upsetting to some parents and apparently upset some teachers. Emphasis on heterogeneous grouping during the early stages of major desegregation accentuated the problem of age spread. For example, a white primary child in Venable said that he liked school but "there was a giant in his class." The "giant" turned out to be a 12-year-old black pupil who had reading difficulties and was getting special help with some of the younger children. Discipline had been more rigid in the black schools, and some of the children overreacted to the new situation where there was a more permissive atmosphere. The black children from lower income families often played rougher than the white middle-class children and were more accustomed to reacting physically rather than verbally to adverse situations. The black children were also more likely to group together and gang up on a white child. A white child, on the other hand, might be friendly with a black child in school but have nothing to do with him outside of school.

The mere presence of large numbers of black children created problems for some white parents, who became convinced that the school was predominantly black. Parents would visit a classroom with 10 or 12 black children out of a total of 28 and come away with the impression that there were more black than white children in the class. Another situational factor disturbed white parents and contributed to the impression that the school was predominantly black. Many of the black children left home at 7 or 7:30 when their parents went to work. They arrived at Venable around 8 o'clock and played in the yard, since they were not allowed to enter the building or classrooms. When the white children arrived around 8:40 the school yard would be full of black kids running around and playing, and in some instances, scuffling. White parents driving their children to school would see a whole yard full of active black kids and conclude the school was predominantly black.

As the 1966–67 year progressed, the white Venable parents became more and more dissatisfied. There were numerous reports and rumors circulating among white parents to the effect that black children were crawling around on the floors and out of control in the Venable classrooms, and that black pupils were roaming around the halls, using obscene language, fighting, stealing, and bullying and extorting money from white children. Average scores for the entire school on statewide achievement tests dropped that year. An active PTA leader said that she tried unsuccessfully throughout the year to get both the PTA and the principal to bring parents together to discuss the situation. She and others said that the principal would not give parents the racial enrollment of the school or discuss the problem with them. Even parents whose children had a good teacher and a good classroom situation became upset by the panic that was developing. Whites began pulling their children out of school and sending them to private schools and moved or talked of moving to the Greenbrier zone where there were no black children. By the end of the year, the proportion of blacks in the school had risen to about 45 percent and enrollment was down from the previous fall. Hovey S. Dabney, a Venable parent and a member of the school board, said that parents were coming to him in "droves" to tell him that they were going to place their children in private schools or move out of the area. Real estate interests were telling whites not to buy in the Venable community. A 48 percent black school population was predicted for the fall of 1967, and whites were beginning to feel they were "losing the school" and something must be done to "save Venable." Blacks, on the other hand, were pleased that their children were in a good school and were not alarmed by their substantial numbers in Venable.

In June 1967, school board member Dabney called a meeting between the superintendent and 20 to 25 white Venable parents. Parents aired their concerns and made it clear that they would stay in Venable on the condition that something was done to end what they saw as "chaos" in the school. Dabney proposed busing some of the black Venable children to Greenbrier. This would relieve the pressure of numbers in Venable and at the same time put blacks in Greenbrier, which was becoming the haven for whites who wanted to escape desegregation. The parents who attended the meeting were divided as to solutions and some opposed the idea of busing.

Venable's principal and the superintendent were already working on a proposal for a "model school" plan for Venable, which they hoped to finance under Title I of the Elementary and Secondary Education Act (ESEA). After the meeting with Venable parents, the superintendent's office began developing a series of plans that might be used in modifying the Venable situation, including a plan for busing children to Greenbrier. Real estate people with interests in the Venable area backed the busing idea. On August 17 the school board approved a plan for establishing a model school program in Venable and busing approximately 51 children to Greenbrier.

Greenbrier Busing.   Fifty-five children from the Venable zone were bused to Greenbrier School in the fall of 1967 as part of the total attack on Venable. Children selected for Greenbrier were drawn from a small geographic area which included but was not restricted to the Westhaven public housing project. A small area was used so that all children could be picked up and deposited at one spot. There was an effort to keep families together, rather than splitting children between Venable and Greenbrier, and classroom space at Greenbrier was also a consideration. Greenbrier had the highest pupil-teacher ratio in the city at that time. Families who were candidates for busing were approached by a black teacher well known in the community and asked to participate voluntarily. Although not stated officially, one of the key features of the busing plan was to get some of the housing project children out of Venable.

On the community level, an immediate problem was financing the busing. The district had not provided any transportation prior to 1967, even for handicapped children, who were bused by a private welfare agency. There were sufficient surplus funds available from the 1966–67 school year, but there was no item in the budget for busing. In order to transfer unexpended funds or appropriate new monies, the City Council had to approve the use of funds for busing. The Council refused the board's request for funds several times, forcing the board to seek financing from other sources. Virginia State Department of Education officials were approached concerning Title I ESEA money, but they indicated ESEA funds could not be approved for busing unless the board could demonstrate the children would get better educational opportunities in Greenbrier than in Venable. With the new model school plan in Venable, this avenue seemed closed. The projected cost per child was set at $50 and some black parents indicated they were able to pay this amount when Council failed to appropriate the money. The issue was discussed publicly in terms of transporting "culturally deprived" children, however, with no mention of the ability of some families to take care of their own expenses. This upset some of the black parents. Meanwhile, community opposition to the use of district funds for busing developed, particularly among parents with children in the Jefferson Sixth Grade Center who had to provide their own transportation. In October 1967, petitions for and against the Greenbrier busing were presented to the City Council. Ninety-nine Greenbrier parents signed a petition supporting the school board on the issue while 455 parents located in Greenbrier, Johnson, Burnley-Moran, and Clark attendance areas signed a statement protesting the use of public funds for transportation between elementary schools, except for special education. After much uncertainty over funds, the board ultimately raised the money from private sources, including contributions from the parents of bused children.

The Greenbrier busing was undertaken primarily to alter conditions in Venable, with almost no time allowed for planning and almost no special resources made available to Greenbrier. The Greenbrier principal knew about the busing approximately three weeks before school opened. With classroom space already tight, the busing placed more third graders in Greenbrier than could be accommodated in self-contained classrooms. Team teaching was therefore introduced in one of the larger classrooms, with three teachers assigned to 73 children. Team teaching was dropped the second year of busing, when three portable classrooms were added to Greenbrier School. Since some of the bused children were eligible for Title I services, the Greenbrier principal was able to call upon the part-time help of a home-visiting teacher paid for with Title I funds for liaison with parents. Other than this, no Title I help was available.

According to the principal, the children bused to Greenbrier were as quiet as mice at first and there was a fairly long "honeymoon period." He felt that some of the black parents saw the busing as a "chance for a step forward in civil rights and may have overprepared the children, expecting harrassments that did not arrive." At the same time, a "fairly large number" of white parents worked with their children, orienting them positively. Some teachers asked particular students to help acquaint the new students with the building. The total result was that the early period of busing passed with outward smoothness but inward restraint. As the principal put it, "The worst fears were not realized . . . But it was not such a good start that everyone went home happy. Nor was it so bad that everyone went home unhappy."

Greenbrier was working toward an ungraded primary unit when the busing began, but had adopted a non-graded program in reading only. After the first year of some team teaching, all pupils were in self-contained classrooms, grouped heterogeneously. Black children were well spread throughout the school, being initially selected to fit into classrooms that could absorb them. The principal said that busing not only caused an increase in class size, but also brought a wider range of pupils into the classroom. Although Greenbrier has some low income white families in its resident population, the majority of the children are from higher socioeconomic status families. Many of the bused children lacked advantages common to most of the resident children, such as travel, many books in the home, and a wide range of exposure to community activities and facilities. Teachers found it necessary to do more individualized work with pupils after desegregation and needed to utilize more material designed for students at lower achievement levels. Because of the differences in the resident and new pupils, the school began providing more field trips and outside experiences in the lower grades, and placing more emphasis on oral language and development of readiness for reading after desegregation. Greenbrier also began using the Bank Street Readers and similar series as supplementary texts and has made a conscious effort to get more black-oriented material in the library. Although the principal felt that he and the Greenbrier teachers were doing everything they could to strengthen the children with limited home experiences and poor academic backgrounds, he was also aware that their resources in this area were limited. He personally felt that some of the bused children would probably be better off in Venable due to the Title I program there.

According to the principal, two areas of differences created problems of acceptance for the bused children as desegregation evolved past the "honeymoon stage"—academic achievement and physical aggression. Academic achievement is heavily stressed among whites in the Greenbrier School and is often the criterion for success. Apart from racial differences, the fact that a black child is relatively less successful in school might condition his acceptance. "In some instances," the principal stated, "it is difficult to determine if a child is not accepted because he is black or because he is not an acceptable student." Although Greenbrier has not experienced anything like the reaction of white parents in Venable, the fact that the bused children are "more prone to solve their problems through overt physical aggression" has also led to some problems of acceptance by the resident community. This has not been a widespread problem, but individual white parents have complained that their children are being "picked on" by black children. "A bully is a bully," the principal said, "but perception of a bully's actions might be different if the bully were white or black." Complaints of black children "picking on" or bullying white children are handled on an individual basis. On a school level, the principal has tried to provide more activities where black children can succeed and interact with the resident children in nonacademic activities. More plays have been put on through the Student Cooperative Association, and black children participate in the school Safety Patrol and in an after-school YMCA sports program. In the case of the "Y" program, fees for participation have sometimes been reduced or eliminated to make participation possible. Resident parents, school staff, and adult leaders have helped with transportation for after-school activities where necessary. Few black children participate in these after-school activities, however.

The principal has had some difficulty in communicating with parents of the bused children, but has gotten help in this area from the black Title I home-visiting teacher. In some cases, parents cannot be reached by telephone because they are working during the school day. In other instances, he senses "parents don't feel free to be open with me." "I am 'they'," as he put it. This is not simply a racial matter, as he has run into the same problem in schools with lower economic status whites.

Although the City Council refused to appropriate money for the Greenbrier busing the first year, it did approve funds for busing in the 1968–69 school budget, after obtaining a written statement from the board on its busing policy. The board did not mention race in this statement, but said that it would undertake transportation of pupils "to the degree necessary" where the board felt "an imbalance of any sort hampered the best educational functioning of a school." Although at least one councilman tried to press the board for more specific criteria for busing, the board declined to define any specific percentage of "Negroes or of culturally deprived children that would put a school in line for busing."[34] Several community leaders, including a board member, felt that the Venable experience had established the fact that the white community would not tolerate more than a 40 percent black population in a school.

A white parent in the Greenbrier area said that people there who were against desegregation complained about the city providing busing for some children, but not all children. Desegregation was behind this, she felt, but they wouldn't come out and say they were against desegregation. "The real racists have gone underground," she commented. "The problems are not solved, but the vicious talk is over." This parent noted that whites in the area who cannot accept desegregation move out into the country or put their children in private schools. There is no mass exodus, but Greenbrier's enrollment was 445 students in September 1968, compared with 458 in September 1967, even with the addition of 55 black children. This same mother noted the broad range of teachers' reactions at Greenbrier. She knew of one older white teacher who "couldn't take it" and had retired early after the first year of desegregation, while another white teacher of 30 years' tenure said that the first year of desegregation at Greenbrier was her most difficult year, but also the "most rewarding." While this parent felt most parents and staff were going along with desegregation, she regretted a lack of warmth and a real welcome when blacks first arrived. "It would have been good," she said, "if [the black children] were really made to feel we were *glad* they were there." A black mother with an older son who was one of the early black students enrolled in Lane, said that her fourth grade son, who was attending Greenbrier, had always been in integrated schools and as far as she knew did not have any trouble at Greenbrier. She commented that he was "picking up different mannerisms . . . a little more refined" than her other children. A white citywide PTA leader agreed that vocal "agitation" over the Greenbrier busing focused on the transportation rather than the race issue. Whites throughout town were most resistant to busing at first, she said, but after about six months, they "were glad Greenbrier is getting it, too."

Venable Model School Program.   Venable opened the 1967–68 school year with a new principal, 80 children fewer than the previous year and a 41 percent black population. Fifty-five of the 80 children who did not return to Venable were, of course, bused to Greenbrier. The new principal, Dallas Crowe, announced the racial composition of the school to parents at the first PTA meeting and admitted that the school "had problems." He also told parents about the model school program being implemented and expressed his own confidence that "we can work it out." Mr. Crowe appealed to parents to come to him or to Venable teachers "who can do something to solve these problems," instead of talking to neighbors or someone at the shopping center. A white mother active in the Venable PTA said that the contrast between the 1966 and 1967 school years was "like the difference between night and day."

The Venable model school program brought in several new special resource teachers and services and also stepped up some existing programs. A part of the model school program was financed under Title I and intended for the benefit of low income children in the school. Title I resources and services included: (1) an oral language teacher to work with small groups of primary children in enlarging their vocabularies and orienting them to that part of their vocabulary that was suitable for school use; (2) a half-time home-school liaison worker to make contact with families regarding children's absences, illnesses, and other problems; and (3) three aides to assist primary teachers with clerical tasks, audiovisual equipment and supervision of children. A learning disabilities resource teacher for all grades was hired with funds available through Title III ESEA. This teacher was to work with emotionally disturbed children on a crisis basis and help classroom teachers learn techniques for managing these children. Other new personnel added to Venable under the model school program included: (1) a full-time guidance counselor to work with behavior and discipline problems; conduct group guidance activities on personal behavior, grooming, hygiene, and study habits; and coordinate parent-teacher conferences, psychological testing, and special school services; (2) a reading resource teacher to do intensive work with children in the upper elementary grades two to three years behind in reading skills; and (3) a primary "helping teacher" to assist the regular classroom teachers in planning teaching units, selecting meaningful material for children, and arranging field trips. A black woman with many years experience in the local system was chosen as the new guidance counselor. The new "helping teacher" had taught in Venable a number of years and had spent the summer of 1967 developing curriculum materials for "disadvantaged" children in connection with a Title I project.

In addition, the model school "package" included the services of the school psychologist one full day per week; help from University of Virginia consultants in several fields; an intern teacher for the primary grades; additional in-service training for Venable teachers; and three teacher aides, to be financed from local school funds. The reduction of the school population freed several classrooms for specialized use by the reading resource teacher, the oral language teacher, and the learning disabilities teacher. Another aspect of the model school program was the reduction of the pupil-teacher ratio from 24 pupils per teacher to 22 pupils per teacher.

The cost of the Venable model school program for the 1967–68 school year was estimated at $57,000 to $62,000, with $35,000 to $40,000 of the money coming from federal sources, primarily Title I and Title III ESEA. About $22,000 of the projected cost was to come from local sources. After the first year of the program, a full time "crisis teacher" with a classroom of her own was added to work with emotionally disturbed children who needed to leave their regular classroom. The learning disabilities program was also expanded to function on a citywide basis, but was still housed at Venable. More teacher aides were also added in the 1968–69 school year.

Staff of the Consultative Resources Center at the University of Virginia discussed problems in the area of interracial communication and race relations at Venable's 1967 preschool conferences. The Consultative Resources Center is established through a grant under Title IV of the 1964 Civil Rights Act to give technical assistance on desegregation to local school districts in the Charlottesville vicinity. Two Center staff members met with Venable teachers to sensitize them to prejudiced and derogatory terminology they might be using and help them become aware of individual personal prejudice. A similar meeting was held later in the fall. Crowe felt that these sessions with Center staff enabled some of the teachers to talk more freely to each other and to face up to racial problems within the school. Prior to these meetings, the staff had almost completely avoided discussion of race relations in Venable. Each teacher was given a copy of a handbook by Dr. James H. Bash, Director of the Consultative Resources Center, *Effective Teaching in the Desegregated School.*[35]

The preschool conferences were also used to introduce teachers to a series of changes in school organization and administration that were to be made in addition to the model school program. Traditionally, Venable had been run like a miniature high school, with children changing classes for specialized department work as far down as the primary grades. Classrooms for all grades were scattered over the three-story building. In 1967 all primary children were put in self-contained classrooms and the specialized departmental work in the upper elementary grades was reduced, so that children received most of their instruction in self-contained classrooms. Classrooms for each of the primary and upper elementary grades were clustered together in a particular part of the building. Venable was also opened earlier in the morning and children were permitted to come inside before school officially started. Teachers were to report to their classrooms 15 minutes before the teaching day began to supervise the children and assist them in getting organized for the day. Teachers were also asked to eat lunch with their classes and more teachers were placed on yard duty during recess. Schedules were set up so that teachers and/or aides would supervise the children at all times. Beginning that fall, all classrooms were locked when not in use. After two years, Crowe felt that these measures had reduced disorder and confusion in the halls, given the children a more stable classroom environment, permitted more flexibility in teaching, and diminished the fears of white parents for the safety of their children.

One of the key problems in 1966 was the number of children with a history of grade failure who were overage for their grade placement. In the fall of 1967, about 25 of these children were advanced one or two grades, with the understanding between the principal, the teachers, and the children that the children would get special help and would be free at all times to come to the office to discuss any problem that might develop. The children were not "just put in classes." Crowe explained to each child that he was being placed with children he should be with and that he would get additional help. "We communicated that somebody cared," Crowe stated, "and that we saw things there for them to do." Teachers were alerted to potential problems and special materials and assistance with reading problems were made available. Another 18 children who were overage for their grade placement were transferred to the Sixth Grade Center at Jefferson and one child was transferred to a junior high school. All children promoted in this fashion in 1967 were black.

Other changes introduced at Venable included the use of supplementary texts with pictures of blacks, such as the Bank Street and Detroit Readers; the use of the more culture-free tests of ability and achievement where it is possible to select tests independently of state requirements; and attempts to "balance" classrooms racially, so that there is a 50 percent white population in each classroom wherever possible.

Attempts to balance Venable's classrooms have cut into other grouping practices and are generally more successful in the upper elementary grades where there are more white pupils. Since major desegregation, the first grade at Venable has been predominantly black. All Venable pupils are classified by five ability levels, based on test scores and other evaluations. In grades 1–3, children are grouped for classroom instruction mainly on the basis of their ability level, with some "borrowing" from adjacent ability groups to achieve better racial balance. The fourth grade is grouped heterogeneously and grade 5 uses homogeneous grouping for placement in the self-contained classrooms and heterogeneous grouping for specialized departmental work. At all grade levels, homogeneous grouping tends to result in a concentration of black pupils at the lower ability levels, few blacks in upper levels, and a good mix of blacks and whites in the middle. This is particularly true in the primary grades, where more blacks are enrolled. In the first grade, for example, there is one all-black classroom; one predominantly black classroom; one that is exactly half white and half black; and two that are almost evenly divided between black and white, but have one or two more white than black children.

Impact of the Venable Program.   At the end of the first year
of the model school program, Venable's principal could report
to the school board that the percentage of children attending
school daily was a little higher than it had been previously and
that average scores for the school on achievement tests given
as part of the state program in grades two and four had been
brought up. Crowe also told the board that a group of first
grade Venable pupils tutored after school by the Westminister
Church Tutorial Program raised their median I.Q. test scores
from 88 to 97 during the school year. This tutorial program
is sponsored and administered independently of the school, but
is planned and carried out with the cooperation of Venable staff.
These children, he stated, are suffering from social, rather than
mental, retardation. Crowe said, furthermore, that the total Venable program had generated "an enthusiasm for school" and
had brought about changes in attitude and behavior, especially
among children who had been discipline problems in the past.
He pointed out that changes in the children's attitudes took
place

> particularly where they had perhaps some physical problem which
> had gone unnoticed up to this point or where we were able to secure
> helpers and they were able to feel concretely that there was interest
> in them personally by the staff, by the teacher, by everyone else
> at the school. They began to present a new face to us. *Perhaps because
> we presented a new face to them.*[36] (Emphasis added.)

Changes instituted at Venable, combined with the Greenbrier
busing, succeeded in holding many whites in the school and
in checking a large-scale exodus of whites from the Venable
area. Venable's enrollment dropped off a total of about 80 children in the first few years of major desegregation but stabilized
at a little under 500 between 1967 and 1969. (See Table 4.)
The black population leveled off at around 40 percent, with
the busing program and a higher enrollment of transient white
children in the upper elementary grades living in the area
because of an army training project at the University of Virginia.
On a long-term basis, Venable's declining white population is
crucial to maintaining racial balance.

While Venable's immediate and critical problems were under
control in 1969, there were still some adjustments to be made
between black and white teachers and children. A black staff
member at Venable noted the overall loss of prestige black
teachers suffered with desegregation and the hesitancy of many
to assert themselves after being placed in predominantly white

schools. She said that Venable had "grown into frankness" between black and white staff since major desegregation, but the atmosphere was still not completely free. Although the principal feels that relationships between the children are generally pretty good, Crowe acknowledges continuing problems of adjustment between black and white pupils. Some of these problems stem from class as well as racial differences, some from the segregated nature of the surrounding community. Black children from low income families are more likely to react to situations physically and, in some instances, "gang up" on a white child to "get him" for something that happened earlier. While there is emphasis in school on all children participating in all activities, there is little association between the children outside of school, in their homes, in scout activities, or in recreation. The black children are aware of the discrepancy between school and after-school association and are sensitive to paternalistic attitudes held by some well-intentioned whites. Black children sometimes rebuff overtures of friendship from white children for this reason and the white child may then become negative, not understanding the cause of the black child's behavior. Some white parents complain because their children are in predominantly black classrooms, and there are sometimes racial tensions in the school, particularly when black/white student confrontations are taking place at the high school level. The principal said that black children sometimes make negative remarks about whites, usually on the playground or in more relaxed classroom situations. If a child says something to the effect that "white people don't care about me," Mr. Crowe always picks up on the statement and asks the child about the whites in Venable who are there working with him. He thinks this helps to break down stereotyped thinking about race.

On balance, there is general community satisfaction with the Venable situation, however, and a feeling that solutions to problems there are well underway. At a January 1969 session on the 1969–70 budget, a newly organized group called Parents and Friends of Children with Learning Disabilities asked that resource rooms similar to the one in operation at Venable be placed in all elementary schools in the city.

Creation of Special Education Center. As part of the overall plan for major desegregation in 1966, McGuffey School was converted to a Special Education Center. The stated purpose of McGuffey School is to bring together under one roof as many of the city's special education programs as possible, particularly classes for the educable mentally retarded. In addition to the mentally retarded, McGuffey has a number of educationally retarded children, mainly black, and is also said to include other black pupils who are considered poor risks for desegregated schools because of behavior problems. An administrator in the school system said that McGuffey was set up at the time the schools went into major elementary desegregation "because many kids came into desegregation with psychological problems or they couldn't cope with the academic program." A crash testing program identified those children considered most in need of remedial work or other special attention. These children were transferred from the regular schools to McGuffey with the permission of their parents. This same administrator said that McGuffey was initially thought of as a stop-gap measure and it was expected that most of these children would be returned to the regular schools after some remedial education. In 1969 long-range plans still called for moving special education classes into the regular schools, when classroom space became available. Meanwhile, around 200 children per year, two-thirds of them black, attended school at the McGuffey Special Education Center. (See Table 4.)

Continuation of the McGuffey Special Education Center was not an overt public issue in the black community up to the time this study was done. Some administrators feared that segregation in McGuffey would become a public issue, but McGuffey was actually a continuing source of embarrassment to the school system because of criticism it has received in professional educational circles. The 1967 Peabody Report noted the number of educationally rather than mentally retarded children in the McGuffey Center and recommended strongly that these children be returned to the regular classroom and provided with supplemental and remedial help. The Peabody Report was also critical of the qualifications of staff, the curriculum, and the limited equipment available to teachers at McGuffey. A Virginia state official, the Chief of Mental Retardation for the Division of State Planning and Community Affairs, stated at a public meeting in the spring of 1969 that the Charlottesville schools "have some of the poorest services for the mentally retarded and the mentally ill that can be found. . . ." She singled out the McGuffey Center for specific criticism, stating that in earlier visits to the city she "saw children running wild in the halls" in McGuffey, while she "had expected to see a model program."[37] There were no immediate plans to discontinue the center at McGuffey School in 1969 when this study was made; in fact, that spring the

Table 4 – Racial Distribution of Pupils in Charlottesville Public Schools, October 1967 and October 1968

| | | 1967 Enrollment | | | | | 1968 Enrollment | | | |
| | | White | | Black | | | White | | Black | |
	Total	Number	Percent	Number	Percent	Total*	Number	Percent	Number	Percent
Elementary Schools										
Burnley-Moran	653	488	75	165	25	678	495	73	183	27
Clark	659	587	89	72	11	692	615	89	77	11
Greenbrier	455	400	88	55	12	447	390	87	55	12
Jefferson†	523	398	76	125	24	524	426	81	97	19
Johnson	797	614	77	183	23	823	626	76	195	24
McGuffy‡	205	71	35	134	65	199	65	33	134	67
Venable	494	289	59	205	41	490	291	59	199	41
Junior High Schools										
Buford	714	569	80	145	20	700	565	81	132	19
Walker	805	632	79	173	21	860	674	78	184	21
High School										
Lane	1,333	1,068	80	265	20	1,326	1,049	79	274	21
TOTAL	6,638	5,116	77	1,522	23	6,739	5,196	77	1,530	22

*Total enrollment figures for the 1968–69 school year include 13 pupils of Indian, Oriental and Spanish backgrounds.

†Sixth Grade Center.

‡Special Education Center.

Source: Charlottesville Public Schools, Director of Federal Programs.

administration was considering a work-study plan for the older children in McGuffey, who had formerly participated in pre-vocational training at Burley High School, prior to changes in that school with the desegregation. McGuffey was set up for children in grades 1–9, but has students who are as old as 18. A black principal was appointed to McGuffey in 1968, giving Charlottesville its second black principal since major desegregation.

Elementary School Building and Racial Balance. In November 1968, the NAACP branch filed suit in the federal district court, attempting to block the building of three new public housing projects in predominantly black southside neighborhoods. The school board was also named in the suit, since the board

> has not expressed opposition to the proposed housing project; neither has the school board devised and published a plan to prevent the racial segregation of children in one or more public schools which will be attended by residents of the said projects in their immediate vicinity.[38]

At the time this suit was filed, a new elementary school on the south side of town, not far from the proposed location of one of the housing projects was under construction. This new southside school, now called the Jackson-Via School, was planned by the board in executive session and opposed by a minority of board members because of the fact that the site would surely cause segregation problems. The NAACP suit did not attempt to block construction of the Jackson-Via School, but asked that the board be restrained from erecting further schools in the vicinity of the proposed projects until the court could approve a plan to prevent racial segregation in such schools. In answering the suit, the board denied that the concentration of black children in the proposed housing projects would result in segregated schools. The board stated that it located schools "in accordance with the areas of residence of the children" and "is in no wise using racial criteria in making decisions as to the location of its public schools."[39]

Before the NAACP suit came to trial, the board revised elementary attendance zones for the 1969–70 school year to take into account the new Jackson-Via School and the enlargement of the Greenbrier School. The new zones, which were adopted March 19, 1969, extend the attendance boundaries of all elementary schools, including Greenbrier and Jackson-Via, into the center of the city. (See Figure 4.) These new zones eliminated the need for busing to Greenbrier and distributed blacks more evenly in all of the city's elementary schools. Black enrollment for the 1969–70 school year was projected as follows: Burnley-Moran, 23 percent; Clark, 16 percent; Greenbrier, 20 percent; Jackson-Via, 19 percent; Johnson, 16 percent; and Venable, 37 percent. Board member Dr. Robert R. Humphris, who opposed the new attendance lines, called it an "injustice" to send children from the center city to Greenbrier. "I believe they are at a definite disadvantage when forced to compete with children from a higher economic level," he said. A black board member, the Reverend Henry B. Mitchell, who supported the new zones, stated that the neighborhood school concept had existed only for whites in the past. He said he opposed the neighborhood school concept "until I or any other black man can buy a house anywhere in this city." Board member A. J. Kessler, who also supported the new attendance zones said that the idea of returning to the neighborhood school concept was desirable "in the same way we'd like to return to a lot of other things no longer present in our society."[40]

The new Jackson-Via School, which was to open in the 1970–71 school year, was the first in the city to be named jointly for a black and a white. Mrs. Nannie Cox Jackson, who taught more than 40 years in Albemarle County, spent many years in the Jefferson School, first at the primary and then at the secondary level. Mrs. Via, also a veteran of over 40 years in the local school system, was principal of both the Johnson and Venable schools and has published three children's books and numerous magazine articles. Children assigned to Jackson-Via for the 1969–70 school year were to be housed temporarily in Clark and Johnson until Jackson-Via could open.

The new zone lines should stabilize elementary enrollment for a few years at least, preventing the many shifts between schools that some children were caught in between 1965 and 1969. Transfers due to zone changes were not restricted to black children, but bore most heavily on them, particularly those in the Westhaven public housing project and its vicinity. With the several changes in zone lines affecting that area, the busing to Greenbrier, and the automatic transfer to Jefferson for the sixth grade, some of these children could have attended as many as five schools in their first six grades.

Figure 4. *Elementary School Zones, Charlottesville, Virginia 1969—70*

6
Major Desegregation of
Lane High School

Decline of Burley High School. The decision to assign all seventh graders to the new junior high schools beginning with the fall of 1965 sounded the death knell for Charlottesville's sponsorship of Burley High School. Burley had been operated jointly by the city and the county since 1951, with a few more county than city students enrolled and the two districts contributing to the operating cost. Each school district owned a 50 percent interest in the Burley plant. There was a sharp drop in all city students attending Burley after the 1965–66 school year although black pupils in grades 8–12 could elect Burley. The number of Charlottesville pupils attending Burley dropped from 410 in 1964, to 242 in 1965, to 151 in 1966. Decreased enrollment at Burley brought a cutback in faculty members. Between 1964 and 1966, Burley's faculty dropped from 42 to 31. County enrollment began falling off too, after 1965, when Albemarle adopted a "freedom of choice" desegregation plan. The main drop in Burley's enrollment in this period, however, came from the cutoff of seventh graders feeding in from Charlottesville schools.

Shortly after school opened in the fall of 1965, George C. Tramontin, Charlottesville School Superintendent, initiated a discussion with the county concerning termination of Burley as a joint city-county facility. The Charlottesville school board had not at that time set a definite date for ending its support of Burley, but there was some consideration of terminating city students at Burley at the end of that school year. A long period of joint city-county discussion and negotiation about Burley's future followed, however. Albemarle County was behind Charlottesville in school desegregation when the city first initiated talks about pulling out of Burley, but the county came under increasing pressure to desegregate in 1965 and 1966. As both districts realized Burley must be discontinued as an all-black school in the near future, debate centered on possibilities for conversion of the Burley plant. The Peabody study recommended development of a joint city-county vocational center at Burley or complete acquisition of Burley by the city for use as a K–4 elementary school. Both these possibilities were explored in depth.

As debate over Burley's future proceeded, the uncertainty

had serious ramifications for the staff. After 1965, faculty left
Burley voluntarily, as well as because of cutbacks, with some
teachers moving into city and county schools that were desegregated. A report, "Where the Faculty Went," in the *Burley Bulletin*, November 1966, traced the whereabouts of 15 staff members
"displaced" in the past few years. These Burley teachers had
relocated as follows: Lane High School, 1; Charlottesville Junior
High Schools, 6; Jefferson Sixth Grade Center, 1; Albemarle
High School, 1; other Virginia school systems, 4; and graduate
study, 2. Recruiting new staff was difficult. In November 1966,
when the Southern Association of Colleges and Schools dropped
its double standard for accrediting black and white schools, Burley was removed from the list of "approved schools" for "major
deficiencies." Two teachers lacked a bachelor's degree from an
approved institution and five were teaching subjects they were
not certified to teach. In spite of the deficiencies, the average
cost to the city for each child in daily attendance at Burley was
now far greater than the average cost for each child at Lane.
In September 1965, for example, the annual cost to the Charlottesville Public Schools for the average child in daily attendance at Burley was $694.51, while the cost at Lane was $426.80.
   Early in December 1966, following the announcement that
Burley was dropped from the list of secondary schools approved
by the Southern Association of Colleges and Schools, a group
of black citizens protested Burley's continuation. Eugene Williams, former president of the Charlottesville NAACP,
threatened to reopen the suit he had filed to end segregation
in Burley in 1963. Williams stated, "A padlock ought to be put
on Burley tomorrow morning." Randolph White, editor of the
Charlottesville-Albemarle Tribune, the area's black weekly newspaper, stated that his son graduated from Howard University
only after he hired a University of Virginia professor "to teach
him something he should have had at Burley.[41] The Charlottesville school board was then in the midst of negotiations to secure
dismissal of the two major suits against segregation at Burley
and Jefferson. At its next meeting, the board voted not to continue participation in the operation of Burley after the end of
the 1966–67 school year. After informing the court of its plan
for withdrawal of all students from Burley and testifying to the
use of Jefferson as a completely desegregated school, the board
got both cases dismissed March 1, 1967.
   Burley was terminated as a high school in the fall of 1967, but
a final decision as to its disposition was not reached until April
1968. In the midst of the debate over Burley's future use, the

county began renting the city's half of Burley on a temporary basis, using the building as an annex to Jack Jouett Junior High School. The school was designated Jack Jouett Annex, but the old name, Jackson P. Burley, was left over the door. In April 1968, the county finally bought Charlottesville's interest in Burley at a price of $700,000. The county's purchase was made after a city-county study committee opposed the idea of a joint vocational center at Burley and after the school board showed no really keen interest in buying Burley. At one point during the negotiations over Burley, the county offered to sell all three of its schools in Charlottesville to the city for $2,800,000. The board turned down this offer. Two of these schools, Burley and Rose Hill Elementary, are located in the middle of Charlottesville's black ghetto. The third, McIntire, is located a little northeast of the city's black population. The county now buses whites into all three schools. The city's decision to sell its half of Burley was questioned by many, particularly in the black community. The Burley plant was in good condition and during the debate Burley was described by the Charlottesville city manager as the best-constructed school in the city. Burley is located on a 17-acre campus that some considered too valuable a piece of property for the city to let go regardless of the building. There was a feeling in the black community that the school board did not want to take on another formerly black school that whites would have to attend on a desegregated basis.

When Burley was discontinued as a high school, the city and county school districts agreed to retain and reassign all faculty and staff members employed at Burley prior to the 1966–67 school year. Twenty teachers and administrators were divided equally between the two systems, with each district assuming responsibility for placing 10 Burley staff members. Charlottesville assigned three Burley teachers to Lane; five to the junior high schools; and two to the Jefferson Sixth Grade Center. Although all the Burley staff retained professional classifications and teaching jobs, some were downgraded in terms of position and responsibility, and some were placed with children at a different age level than they were accustomed to teaching. Burley's assistant principal, for example, who had been in the local school system 33 years, was assigned to teach mathematics and science in the Jefferson Sixth Grade Center. He had never taught elementary children. One of Burley's coaches was placed in a junior high school where he teaches physical education. On the county side, Burley's principal was put in the administrative offices of the Albemarle schools. The failure of both school systems to place principals and assistant principals in jobs with comparable responsibility and prestige in desegregated schools has been a major issue with the black community, particularly in view of the high turnover in administrative positions among whites. Burley teachers hired for the 1966–67 school year who were let go were not an issue, as they had been hired without a commitment beyond the year.

Impact of Burley Closing on Lane Student Body. With the closing of Burley High School, about 80 students in grades 10–12 were transferred to Lane. The black population of Lane more than doubled in the fall of 1967 with the addition of the Burley students, plus an increasing number of black students from the city's junior high schools. Lane had had 122 black students in 1966; there were now 265. In spite of the increase, black pupils at Lane made up only 20 percent of the school's enrollment in 1967. In 1966 blacks made up 10 percent of Lane's student body. (See Table 5.)

In addition to the increase in numbers, the 1967 influx of Burley students introduced a new element in Lane's black population. Under the pupil assignment plan and "freedom of choice," a *highly* select and then a *fairly* select black student population had attended Lane. Lane's curriculum is heavily weighted with college preparatory courses, and the first black students, particularly, were highly motivated and academically oriented and entered Lane for compelling educational reasons. They accepted conditions there because of the better educational opportunities.

Table 5 — Lane High School Enrollment by Race, 1964–1968

Year	Total Enrollment	White Number	White Percent	Black Number	Black Percent
1964-65	1682	1619	96	63†	4
1965-66*	1052	996	95	56†	5
1966-67	1175	1053	90	122†	10
1967-68	1333	1068	80	265	20
1968-69	1326	1052	79	274	21

*The drop in total enrollment is due to the fact that Lane became a three-year high school in 1965 with the switch to a junior high school program; prior to this Lane enrolled grades 8–12.

†Based on count of black students' pictures in Lane yearbook, "Chain."

Source: Charlottesville Public Schools, Annual Enrollment charts and Director of Research and Development.

The growing number of these students was followed by black students coming up from the desegregated junior high schools, who were also more or less attuned to desegregation. The Burley students transferred to Lane in 1967 were, however, the "hold-outs" against desegregation; they preferred a black school under "freedom of choice" and had no desire to attend Lane. Much to the consternation of white school officials, some of these Burley students openly stated that Lane should have been closed and all white students put in Burley. Furthermore, the closing of Burley overlapped with two other trends that affected black-white relations in Lane—the return of more segregationist whites to the public schools with the cutback in tuition grants, and the rise of race consciousness and militancy among all black students.

There was no planning or thinking through of the merger of the Lane and Burley student populations, although a Lane student leader tried unsuccessfully to get an orientation program set up the previous year. There was no discussion of the incoming Burley students in preschool teacher's conferences, for example, and no procedures were worked out to give Burley students representation or leadership positions in Lane's student body. All Burley students were put through the usual "sophomore orientation" as though they were ordinary new underclassmen. "There was not even the basic courtesy of extending a welcome when a block of students comes in," one teacher stated. Burley's leaders, the student body, and class officers "were all dumped into Lane and vanished." Since county Burley students were assigned to Albemarle High School, friends were separated.

A black student who graduated at the end of the 1967–68 school year, contrasted her first three years at Lane with the last two, when there were more black students. During the first three years, she found "a policy of friendliness in school" but white students "wouldn't speak to you on the street." Black and white students sat together in classes and some got together on homework. This girl was a good student and felt that the friendliness of whites was "mainly for homework reasons." In her last two years at Lane, particularly after the Burley students came in, there was more grouping together of blacks in the classroom and in the lunch room. She said the Burley influx brought in more "block kids." The "block kids" were more vocal and outspoken than the black students who had been in Lane previously and "grouped together more." This student attended Lane a total of five years, as she began in the eighth grade, when Lane enrolled grades 8–12, before the junior high school program was instituted.

With more black students and a more militant posture on the part of the school's black students, tensions began to surface. A student leader said that as the 1967–68 year went by, friction grew between the Lane and Burley senior class students. There was name-calling and there were fights between some black and white students, and there were also more student-teacher confrontations. Both white students and white teachers referred to black students as "boy," "nigra," "nigger," and "you people." Teachers would make remarks like, "You people don't do anything to help yourselves." One black student said that she had three teachers she considered "unfair" who would not call on her in class. One day she "just stood up" and spoke in one of these classes. The teacher was "stunned." The president of the Lane student government, the Student Cooperative Association, pointed out that the prejudice of the Lane teachers and students was the same "but the teachers are in a different position." He spoke of the "callousness" and insensitivity of white teachers toward black students. He related, for example, an incident that occurred shortly after the news of Martin Luther King's assassination reached school. A white study hall teacher reprimanded several black students who were discussing King's murder in subdued voices, including one girl who was crying. The teacher told them to "be quiet," adding, "The world has to go on." The teacher was "taken aback" when one of the students told her it was "no big thing" for them to be talking under the circumstances. Students complained particularly about the teachers who had been at Lane for some time. One student leader said that after three years in the system, a teacher's mind was "closed." A Lane teacher stated the faculty was divided between those "who felt the Negroes were not getting a good deal and those who stopped facing life in 1947 and wanted Lane to be pre-1954."

Discipline imposed on black students was a major issue. Black students said that they were suspected whenever anything happened. If there was a "ruckus" in the hall, the teacher would "look for a black person." If the teacher looked out in the hall and saw a white student, it was "right," but if the teacher saw a black student it was, "Where is your pass?" One student said that whenever a theft was reported, the black students were the first to be questioned and their lockers were searched frequently. There was an incident where a white teacher slapped a black student. Some of Lane's teachers were concerned about "harsher penalties given to black than to white students." A young white teacher thought the administration overreacted in disciplinary situations because of fears of "the black students getting out of control."

Another problem black students faced was that there was "no favorite teacher to go to." There were only five black teachers in Lane the first year of major desegregation and most of these were in nonacademic subjects such as business education and vocational training. Among both black and white faculty, black students felt they could trust only two or three teachers. The majority of teachers did not understand their needs and problems, they said, or would not "stick their necks out." This included Lane's black teachers, who were "scared" and "didn't do anything." A black social studies teacher who had taught at Burley 16 years was demoted after four months of teaching at Lane and reassigned as a library assistant in various elementary schools in the city. The board claimed that this teacher was deficient and unable to handle her classes, but the teacher said she was harassed by white students who called her by her first name and walked out of her class. With the backing of the NAACP, she filed a suit against the board when her contract was not renewed. As far as their counselors were concerned, black students found Lane's white counselors of little help. Black students said the counselors did not know anything about black colleges and did nothing to prod the black students or make them aware of opportunities for scholarships and financial help. They said only a small percentage of Lane's black graduates planned to go on to college and that these would have gone without any help from or stimulation by counselors.

The Lane administration contributed to the school's racial problems, rather than leading toward a solution. The principal, W. I. Nickels, was an older man who had been in both the school system and Lane a number of years. A board member questioned whether Nickels was able to cope with the situation "physically and emotionally,"[42] and a student leader classified the principal as "almost a racist." According to students, Nickels was rarely seen and was generally unavailable to black students—"especially if we had some definite proposals," a black student leader noted. One of the assistant principals "ran the school" and "would automatically write out a suspension slip" for a black student sent to the office "no matter what the trouble was." He tape-recorded all conversations. Police were called in and stationed in the halls to prevent incidents. An Usher's Board was also formed to help "keep things cool, especially during the lunch hour." Four black students were appointed from faculty recommendations to help in the cafeteria and monitor the halls and rest rooms. According to the black student leader, the administration "thought that the black Usher Board members would be especially hard [on black students]."

When there was "trouble" at school, white parents would hear about it through telephone calls from their children or from other parents and would go to Lane or call to check on their children, sometimes taking them out of school. A white mother who telephoned Lane one day when she heard "the students were completely in chaos" said that there was "bedlam" in the principal's office. She heard later that there were two groups of kids lined up on each side of the hall, with whites on one side and blacks joined by a few whites on the other side. There was "a yelling siege and a few blows." This mother was not afraid for her son's safety, but wanted him to leave the school if there was any danger of his being arrested.

With racial tensions and problems mounting, Lane's principal decided to try to improve participation in school activities. All Lane's extracurricular activities and school events were already open to all students, but there was little involvement on the part of many black students, except in sports, where blacks were well accepted. Black athletes were heavily represented on the basketball and football teams, were stars in the games, and many black students attended sports events. Otherwise, only a few token blacks took part in any school affairs, often the same people. Typically, there were no blacks on the debating teams or on the varsity cheerleading squad, and only one to three blacks on the student newspaper, in plays, in the band, attending school club meetings, and elected to class offices. To try to remedy this situation, 30 new clubs were formed and school time was set aside once a week for meetings. A drastic increase in participation by whites resulted. The clubs were a major source of irritation to black students, moreover, as they did not feel accepted and welcome and were "turned off" by the "cold reception" they got.

Concerned students suggested a joint student-faculty committee on human relations, which was formed about March 1968. About this time, Jed Orkin, a white student, was elected president of the student council on a platform that included doing something about the school's racial problems. Orkin and a few other sensitive students and teachers could see that "ignorance and bigotry on the part of whites were backing the black man into a corner."

Lane Student Walkouts. There were two student walkouts in response to racial conditions in Lane, one at the end of the 1967–68 school year and another in the fall of 1968. Both walkouts raised similar issues, but the first walkout was more successful for two reasons—the number and organization of the students involved and greater community support.

The first Lane walkout took place Monday, May 13, 1968, after a racial incident in which a group of white students attacked a black Lane student returning home from a school function. Six white students in a car threw a bottle at the young man as he ·was walking home from a senior class carnival at 1 A.M. Saturday. The student's ankle was cut and he was treated at University Hospital and released. Over the weekend, rumors as to his injury and condition spread. Feelings among Lane's black students were running high. Fearing an outburst of violence at school, a group of student leaders met fellow students at the door Monday morning, asking them to leave school for a meeting at Trinity Episcopal Church. About 200 students, black and white, gathered at Trinity Church and spent the morning discussing the underlying causes of racial problems at Lane. The Reverend Henry B. Mitchell, rector of the church, met with the students. Some parents sat in on the meeting, but it was a student-led meeting. The majority of students participating were black, but from 10 to 25 percent of the group was white. A biracial committee was elected to represent the boycotting students.

Students meeting at the church drew up a list of grievances which they attempted to present to Lane's principal. When he was "too busy" to meet with them, the students took their concerns to School Superintendent Rushton, who talked with them and promised a formal reply in a week. The students' demands to the superintendent included: (1) Negro history courses; (2) a Negro guidance counselor; (3) remedial reading and speech programs; (4) fair and proportionate teacher employment; (5) voting machines at all elections and biracial election officials; (6) improved student-teacher relations; (7) qualified personnel on the staff to deal with racial situations; and (8) orientation for students and teachers. The demand for voting machines grew out of a dispute over a cheerleaders election in which black candidates ran but were not elected. Black students questioned the counting of votes. Boycotting students returned to Lane Tuesday with the statement that they would remain there "only if reasonable measures were taken."

The superintendent's reply to the students indicated that the

grievances were for the most part legitimate. Dr. Rushton said
that the administration was already working on several of the
concerns raised by the walkout, and promised to do what he
could in the other areas. He noted the need to secure additional
funds before remedial reading and speech courses could be set
up or a black counselor hired. The superintendent's formal reply
to the student demands was at first received negatively, as students were not convinced that he would actually act in a few
key areas. After a second meeting with a small student-faculty
committee, student leaders felt that they had gotten "five and
one-half out of our seven points" and agreed to stay in school.
The eighth demand for qualified personnel to deal with racial
situations dropped out early in the discussions. Students were
dissatisfied with Rushton's promise to seek additional funds to
implement a remedial reading and speech program and his
failure to make a firm commitment to add a black guidance
counselor.

 There was a great deal of support for the students in the
black community and some whites also recognized the legitimacy
of the students' demands. A parent who sat in on the meeting
at Trinity Church wrote the superintendent:

> It was quite apparent to me that the Negro students at Lane do
> not feel a part of the school. I also realize that though the social
> activities and clubs are open to Negroes, more could be done to
> invite and encourage Negroes to join these activities. . . . More is
> needed to create an atmosphere of harmony, rather than hostility.
> I am aware that we all possess some prejudice. But in the case
> of the Lane teachers, this prejudice is so great that it hinders their
> quality of teaching, to say the least of the sour atmosphere between
> faculty and students . . .[43]

Several days after the walkout, the Lane student-faculty human
relations steering committee unanimously endorsed the students'
demands.

 Resolution of the Lane crisis was left in the hands of the
superintendent. Students participating in the walkout were given
unexcused absences for Monday, although those students who
left school in the next few days because of fear of violence were
excused. A plainclothesman was stationed in the school and
teachers were given special assignments to monitor the halls
and rest rooms before and after school and during class changes.
Additional city police surveillance of the Lane grounds was
requested. The superintendent requested background information on key students in the walkout from Lane teachers and

counselors and found that a broad cross section of students participated, as far as grades, cooperativeness, attitudes toward school, disciplinary history, and behavior in class were concerned. The top leadership of the walkout included students who had been at Lane all through high school, as well as Burley transfers.

Implementation of Walkout Demands. Lane opened in the fall of 1968 with several visible signs that the administration was following through on student demands. There was a black guidance counselor, a course in black history, a black remedial reading teacher, a black journalism teacher and a black study hall supervisor. Lane had also made arrangements with the Consultative Resources Center at the University of Virginia to do a survey of student attitudes and meet with faculty for training in race relations. Lane's old principal was "kicked upstairs" to the central administration and replaced by a younger man, formerly principal of Buford Junior High School.

Although some changes were taking place, concerned students and some of the young, liberal faculty members were not satisfied with the way in which the administration was carrying out the students' demands. The new black guidance counselor, for example, was an older woman transferred from one of the junior high schools. No new black person had been hired and student leaders said that she was too old, did not have much information on black colleges and "doesn't really know what we want."

Students also reacted negatively to the new black history course, a TV program entitled "Americans from Africa: A History." One day per week all students in the 11th grade American history class looked at this program, broadcast over WCVW, an educational station in Richmond. The "teacher" in this lecture series is Dr. Edgar A. Toppin, a black history teacher at Virginia State University. Dr. Toppin's weekly presentation did not always fit in with material currently being studied by the class and both black and white students found him "boring." The telecast, which was prepared for college level students, took most of the class hour, leaving about ten minutes for discussion. Students complained that the teachers did not know enough about black history, skipped discussion, and "do not make an effort to teach on their own." Because the program was built into the 11th grade history course, other students were left out. The administration had initially made arrangements to use Dr. Toppin's program for in-service training for history teachers, but later decided to add it to all 11th grade classes and make it available on an optional basis to junior high school eighth grade history classes. The junior high school pupils reacted to Dr. Toppin even more negatively than high school students, nicknaming him "Dr. Sominex." By mid-year, there was fairly general agreement that Dr. Toppin's course was not working out satisfactorily. An administration staff member said it would be dropped at the end of the year, and the regular history teachers would incorporate black history into the U. S. history course. Mr. Thomas Varner, Director of Secondary Education, admitted that most teachers had "difficulty" teaching black history as they were not familiar with the material and sources.

In order to help the teachers improve their knowledge of black history, reference material on blacks was made available to all eighth grade and 11th grade history and social studies teachers at the beginning of the 1968–69 school year. Varner arranged a display of Negro history materials available in the various school libraries, listed these items for the teachers, and ordered individual copies of books which teachers requested for their classrooms and personal use. The school district spent about $1,600 on material for classroom teachers—an average of $100 per teacher. This material was paid for from the district's In-Service Training Fund, as was the Toppin TV course. After the school year started, Varner purchased about $2,000 worth of black history material for Lane and the two junior high schools, including several sets of filmstrips. Even with this additional library and teacher reference material, the chairman of the Lane history department requested $2,000 for black history and multiethnic materials for the 1969–70 school year.

Some literature on the black experience, primarily a paperback collection, was made available to the Lane English department after the walkout. Teacher use of this material was optional and several young teachers complained that not enough copies of most books were available. They also noted the material was "heavily censored" and that requests for new curriculum guides incorporating material on blacks were ignored. A "Language Arts Guide" prepared by Lane faculty in 1969 supports this claim. Among other things, the Language Arts Guide listed books other than basal texts available in large enough numbers to be assigned to an entire class. Not one publication written by or about blacks in America was among the reading selections available in classroom "sets" in any of the different level English courses taught at Lane. Books by black authors such as James Baldwin, Martin Luther King, Arna Bontemps, Langston Hughes, and Richard Wright were on lists of suggested supplementary reading but could not be assigned to an entire class, as the school owned only one or a few copies. Writers such as Malcolm X and Eldridge Cleaver do not appear on any of the lists. The Director of Secondary Education stated that they "would get a reaction from whites if they went too far" in their selection of supplementary material on blacks.

In the area of in-service training for faculty, staff members of the Consultative Resources Center at the University of Virginia were called in to meet with Lane faculty immediately after the spring 1968 walkout. Center members dwelt primarily on often-used terms that offend blacks, such as "boy," "you people," and incorrect versions of "Negro," such as "nigra" and "nigger." Several faculty members said that a negative remark about the Virginia Education Association made by a Center Staff member alienated many teachers who needed to hear the University members. In the fall, Consultative Resources Center staff again met with Lane faculty to present the results of a survey of student attitudes. The survey itself reinforced student complaints, as it showed: (1) black students do not feel there are enough opportunities to gain recognition in school activities; (2) black students feel that the faculty openly discriminates against them; (3) black students feel strongly and white students agree moderately that the study of black history and culture is important for all students; and (4) all students agree there is much discrimination against black students by other students. Several teachers noted that the survey findings were presented in such a complex statistical fashion that many staff members found it difficult to comprehend the results. This limited the impact of the survey.

An in-service training seminar for Lane and junior high school English and social studies teachers, held later in the year, was a complete fiasco, as far as Lane's racial problems were concerned. The course was sponsored jointly by the district and the Consultative Resources Center, supposedly to help teachers develop discussion techniques and approaches that would enable them to work more effectively with "disadvantaged" children at "low learning levels." In Charlottesville, "disadvantaged" is generally the code word for "black." The class was actually a routine Junior Great Books Basic Leadership Training Course taught by a staff member of the Great Books Foundation's Baltimore office. The course, as one teacher described it, was "oriented toward women who have time in the daytime to read more." Teachers participating in the seminar read selections from Aristotle, Sophocles, Plato, Xenophon, and other classic authors featured in the Junior Great Books series and took part in drills and discussion on how to bring out and interpret points covered in the readings. A Lane teacher said that discussion at the last session about the intended purpose of the course brought out the fact that the Great Books leader flown in from Baltimore did not know the course was supposed to be anything other than a routine Great Books leaders' course. "We were told," this teacher stated, "the purpose was to recognize the differences between different levels of learning, black and white, and to learn how to work with this. . . . The people who took it did not learn anything to help the problem it was supposed to help with." The cost of the Great Books instructor and teachers' tuition was paid for by the Consultative Resource Center under a grant from Title IV of the Civil Rights Act. The district paid the cost of substitutes for teachers attending. As a result of the training, the Charlottesville Public Schools were able to offer a Great Books discussion course for junior high school students in the summer of 1969.

As another followup to student demands, Lane set up a remedial reading center in the fall of 1968. A black reading specialist from Virginia Union University was employed as the sole reading teacher. While students enrolled in the reading program raised their reading levels throughout the year—some drastically—only a limited number of students could be accommodated. Using recommendations from English teachers, the center selected for instruction 53 students who were reading at least two grade levels below average. Thirty-four of these students were reading at sixth and seventh grade levels in January 1969. By the end of the year, 27 of the 53 students had raised their reading level at least two years; 15 were reading at or above grade level; and one had progressed five grade levels in four months. In addition to these 53 students, who got intensive help, an additional 27 students referred by other departments received some assistance. Both teachers and students at Lane stated that more remedial courses were needed.

Student-Staff Confrontations, 1968–69. With the graduation of some of the prominent figures in the spring 1968 walkout, leadership among black activist students was assumed by more aggressive, black-power-oriented youth. These students were willing to charge individual faculty and staff with being racists on a personal basis, and began these personal confrontations with the opening of school in the fall of 1968. At an orientation assembly, for example, there were noisy groups of students, black and white. The principal singled out a group of blacks and asked for quiet. The students raised their fists in a black power salute and there was a scream. The principal told a new white teacher to come down and remove the student causing trouble. The teacher replied that he doubted he could tell which one as "they all look alike." This remark incensed some of the black students and they later confronted the teacher in the hall and called him a "honkey." This teacher said he was "put on the list" to be "despised, hated and glared at." He was later involved in another confrontation with a black student over a makeup test. This girl called him a "racist pig" and requested a transfer to another teacher's class. According to this teacher, the black students involved in these confrontations were "not problems in class" but would "gang around the doorway" after class, "make slurs," "break rules in the lunch room," and create problems in the halls. They were involved in confrontations with white students as well as with teachers. Some white students claimed that the black students were allowed to get away with things they would never be allowed to do; that the teachers would take more from black students than they would take from whites because they were afraid of repercussions. White students said, for instance, that the black militants were not reprimanded when they did such things as make noise during tests. Some white students felt that the principal was afraid of the black students and made concessions to them for this reason.

Lane's racial problems came to a head again around the beginning of November 1968, after a black student who struck a white assistant principal in a confrontation in the hall was expelled. On November 4, the Monday morning following this expulsion, about 150 black students gathered in the auditorium and asked for a meeting with the principal. In addition to expressing anger over the expulsion, the students demanded more black teachers, an expanded black history course, and fairer treatment from white teachers. The new Lane principal, John E. Huegel, refused to talk with the entire group at that time, but said he would meet with a small delegation the next day. The students were told to go to class or leave the building. About 75 students walked out and the rest returned to class. No formal protest meeting followed, nor was any organization formed to back the demands, although a group of black students later met with the principal. Only a few white students, including the president of the student government, Jed Orkin, supported the walkout. Although publicity and community discussion focused on the problems of Burley students adjusting to Lane, the key leaders again included students who had come up through the desegregated schools, as well as Burley transfers.

Three of the black walkout leaders were suspended from school indefinitely the following Thursday for allegedly beating up a white student at a football game October 4, a month before. The "indefinite suspensions" were tantamount to expulsion and took place on the word of the complaining white student. The students were in effect expelled without a hearing, questioning of any witnesses, or contact with their parents. The night before the tardy accusation was made, about 100 white students and 25 to 30 white parents had gathered in a parking lot in an outlying shopping center to discuss Lane's racial problems. The open-air meeting had begun in the afternoon with members of the Lane Motorcycle Club, a group one teacher described as a "junior KKK." Lane's assistant principal and athletic director, Willie Barnett, a target of many complaints by black students, was present and told the press that the meeting was a reaction to incidents at school. Barnett said that the students are "tired of their education being interrupted."[44] A delegation of five of these white students met with the Lane principal the next morning. The following morning the white student who said he was beaten in October made his complaint for the first time. Because of Barnett's participation in the shopping center gathering, blacks took the expulsions to be more or less officially rigged by the Lane administration.

The second walkout generated a mixed reaction in the black community, but many protested the expulsions, which were initially upheld by the school board. The mother of one of the expelled students filed a complaint of discrimination with the HEW Regional Office for Civil Rights in Charlottesville, a division of the HEW agency-wide office for enforcing Title VI, which replaced separate programs within HEW in 1966. A predominantly black delegation of Lane students, including the three suspended indefinitely, appeared at the next school board meeting to defend the expelled students and object to the numerous suspensions of black students at Lane. Larry Fortune, a black student leader not identified with the militant group, told the board that there had been eight suspensions of black students in one week, plus the three students suspended "indefinitely." Parents of the three students were also at the board meeting to plead their case for reinstatement. The black students maintained that a non-student was responsible for the October 4 fight at the football game and said this person had so informed the Lane principal. An inquiry into the beating conducted by the HEW Regional Office for Civil Rights concluded that there were no reliable witnesses to the incident, that such extreme punishment as indefinite suspension was unusual in the history of Lane High School, and that there were no existing procedures for the students to be readmitted.

Following community pressure on the board, the three students suspended in the beating incident were readmitted to Lane. A fourth student, expelled for striking Assistant Principal David Garrett, was tried and convicted of assault in court, served a jail sentence, and was kept out of school for the rest of the year.

The HEW Regional Office's handling of the student complaint filed in connection with this incident illustrates the inadequacy of the various federal agencies in enforcing civil rights violations and the reason why Charlottesville's black leaders have become so disillusioned with the federal government on civil rights issues. Staff of the Regional Office for Civil Rights (OCR) wanted to act on the Lane expulsion case but were told by the overall director of the Charlottesville Regional HEW Office that they would have to obtain permission from the Justice Department to do so because the district was "under court order." OCR staff knew the court order had been dismissed a year and a half before, but their records did not contain an official notice to this effect. When the Regional OCR asked the Justice Department for clearance to act on the case, OCR received permission to investigate the "validity" of the complaint only. Fortunately for the students involved, the complaint was resolved by the board without intervention from either HEW or the Justice Department. An OCR staff member said that they had had similar problems with establishing jurisdiction after dismissal of court suits throughout the region. The OCR staff would know from reading the newspaper that a suit was dismissed, but could not act because there was no official record of the dismissal in the appropriate bureaucrats' files.

Surface Calm, but a Widening Gulf Between the Races. A major effort of Lane's new principal, John E. Huegel, was to try to calm Lane down and stabilize the internal school situation. Several teachers said that, in contrast to the previous principal, Mr. Huegel assumed leadership in faculty meetings and "at every seeming breach," he or someone from the administration would "rush in and sew everything up." They said that faculty members were still divided between "yeas" and "nays" on the race issue, but were no longer permitted to "flounder." They found the principal's willingness to move into a situation quickly and make what they considered a positive effort to deal with it a great improvement.

In his posture vis-à-vis black militants, Lane's new principal focused on shifting the arena of struggle away from the school and bringing the most militant students under control. He told the students their complaints should go through the "proper channels"—that is, that their parents should take their grievances to school board meetings. He did not support their position, which was that they did not want to get their parents involved. While he refused to discuss school racial complaints with the black militants on a group basis, he talked with these students individually. He felt that about ten of the most militant students were "operating as a gang" and "doing their best to disrupt school." He tried to break up the "group action," by discussing with them the importance of their acting as individuals. In addition, he took a firm stand with those blacks he considered "troublemakers," making it clear he would suspend them if he considered it necessary. In a further measure related to student control, all in-school club meetings were banned, supposedly because black militants were wandering around the halls during the activity period. The black students themselves claimed that the principal banned all clubs because most blacks were attending the Afro-American Culture Club, which was interracial, but predominantly black. This was the only club attracting a large number of black students. Black student leaders said that the principal was "afraid of black power" and that the administration was upset because all the blacks were "getting together."

In addition to efforts to unify the faculty and bring the most militant students under control, Mr. Huegel also searched for courses—other than a black history course—that would meet special needs of black students. Lane instituted a home economics class for male students during the 1968–69 school year, for instance, as a result of conferences between the principal and some of the militant students. The all-black home economics course for males included "soul" cooking, table setting, and etiquette, plus sewing and tailoring. In the winter of 1969, some of the students were planning to make dashikis for their sewing projects. Lane already offered a course in general office procedures for low ability students that had a two-thirds black enrollment, and a second course of this type, combining typing and office machines, was planned for the 1969–70 school year. Mr. Huegel feels that the "typical academic program" does not "suit" many of the black students, although they do not necessarily want a vocational program. With its emphasis on college preparatory courses in most of its curriculum, Lane has little to offer the student who is not college-bound. In addition to expanding courses for the pupil not planning to enter college, Mr. Huegel is also interested in bringing in teaching materials for students at different ability levels, as he did at Buford.

Grouping by ability level is not widespread at Lane, but English classes are grouped into three ability, or achievement, levels, plus an Honors section which "skims the cream off Level 1." The Honors and Level 1 sections tend to be all white or almost all white, while Level 3 classes tend to be half black and half white, or predominantly black. There are also some special classes in math and science for "slow children," but other courses are not grouped and a weak student who insists can enroll in any class over the advice of his counselor. English teachers who have tried on their own to reorient their Level 3 classes toward the interests and problems of black pupils have had the freedom to do so, but have been handicapped by a lack of material available on a classroom basis.

Having eliminated the one student activity other than sports in which large numbers of black students participated—the Afro-American Culture Club—the Lane administration approved several student proposals during the winter of 1968–69 designed to involve more black students in school affairs. The basis of representation in the student government constitution was changed so that more blacks would have a chance to be elected, and academic requirements for participation in activities such as student government and cheerleading were lowered to allow more blacks to qualify. Two black cheerleaders were chosen for the 1969–70 school year, after student election of cheerleaders was replaced with selection by a committee of students, Lane physical education teachers, and teachers from Walker and Buford Junior High schools. A few outstanding black students continued to participate in school "establishment" activities, such as Usher's Board, National Honor Society, the drama club, and student government, but "the same old problems are still there."[45]

There were no further major racial confrontations during the 1968–69 school year, but black student leaders continued to complain of racial tensions, the cold atmosphere, lack of enough remedial courses, prejudging of black students by teachers, emphasis on punishing black students, a forcing of white standards on blacks, and the low number of black teachers. These complaints came from "moderate" as well as from militant black students. Larry Fortune, a black Lane student who militants criticized for cooperating with whites, stated in a community panel discussion on Lane, February 1, 1969, that about two-thirds of the black students would go back to Burley if they could, "not because we're separatists, we want integration, but because some of us can't take it." "I try to be liberal-minded," Fortune said, "I try to say 'White man, come be my friend,' but then [I] hear him say as I walk down the corridor, 'Look at that nigger go.'"[46]

A young black woman, one of two black Lane teachers to resign in mid-year for personal reasons, noted a "backing off" on both sides. She said: "Blacks are withdrawing mainly because they [feel] unwelcome. Whites are withdrawing because they don't know how to react to the blacks' new militant attitude." Two of the black militants, expelled from Lane in the fall of 1968 and later reinstated, seemed to be completely alienated from whites as a result of their experiences. They had lost confidence in the administration and felt that the teaching staff did not want blacks at Lane. One of these young men had attended integrated schools all his life and recalled no "difference between the black and white kids at Venable" when he was one of the few black students there, or any name-calling or racial incidents "at Venable." He now believes black students have nothing "in common" with white students, that white students "don't really want you around anyway." He said black students going into a newly desegregated school should "be cautious of the white man" and not join any committees as "you just get tricked up and get into trouble that way." The young black teacher quoted earlier thought that the black students "could be more courteous," but also felt teachers could "try and understand what the black student is going through . . . why the black student is militant and belligerent."

A white student leader who continued to support black students' complaints, despite a "shunning" from white students, stated that the situation was "deteriorating" in the middle of the 1968–69 school year because there were "no signs from anywhere" of any progress or interest from the administration or the majority of white teachers and white students. He noted the superintendent was away on an extended foreign trip, progress reports on implementation of student demands had been discontinued without an explanation, and most whites were no longer willing to involve themselves in efforts to try to solve the problems. He said that only about 300 Lane students—200 black and 100 white—really cared what happened and were willing to try to struggle with the problem. The rest were "content to be upset," becoming outraged by the walkouts and the use of the black power salute, but "not concerned with the root of the problems, with the why, the reasons." He pointed out that a Unity Weekend, sponsored by a biracial group of concerned students in January 1969 to help resolve school tensions and promote understanding, drew only a small proportion of Lane's students. This student observed that everyone was interested at first, but that a great deal of tension and apathy had developed and that whites, who "don't expect anything good from the black man," would pick on a minor point in a program, or a small incident such as use of the black power salute by a black speaker, as a rationalization for staying out of the situation. Lane brought in several black speakers during the 1968–69 school year in an effort to "balance out" presentations at assembly programs. At one of these assemblies held in connection with the Unity Weekend, a black woman from Danville, Virginia, raised her fist in the black power salute. This upset some white students who felt their rights were being violated.

None of the reform measures instituted at Lane remedied the toughest problem, the failure of many white staff and students to accept blacks. "Integration," the white student leader quoted earlier stated, "cannot mean 'come over and be white,' which is what the whites expect. We won't get anywhere until we get rid of that attitude. . . . Both ways are beautiful and can go on together."

Dilemma over New High School Facilities. In addition to racial attitudes, one of the key ingredients in the Lane situation is the fact that the school is seriously overcrowded, without adequate classroom and lunch room facilities. Lane was built to accommodate 900 to 1,000 students; the cafeteria seats 300. With Lane's enrollment of over 1,300 for the past few years, some Lane classes have met in the nearby Jefferson School. Beginning with the 1969–70 school year, three mobile classroom units were to be utilized. Congestion in the halls and lunch room has contributed to racial problems and incidents. "The kids are waiting for something to happen so that they can fight back," one white mother stated. Jed Orkin, president of Lane's Student Cooperative Association in 1968–69 said, "The biggest reason the school is so tense right now is the overcrowding."[47]

In the summer of 1969, the school district began drawing up plans for a single new high school, after a two-year effort to build two new high schools was defeated in a bond election

April 22, 1969. Many factors contributed to the defeat of the two-high-school bond proposal, including the implications of two high schools for racial and economic segregation. The two-high-school proposal originated with the 1967 Peabody Report, which recommended conversion of Lane to a middle school and the construction of new high schools located in the northeast and southwest parts of the city. The board reached agreement on the two-high-school plan July 27, 1967, only after the proposed locations of the schools had been stricken from the proposal and the resolution to build two schools was amended to state that zone lines would be set to provide racial and cultural balance "as nearly as practical." The proposed new high schools were to be four-year schools, with Lane and the two existing junior high schools becoming middle schools for grades 5–8.

Following adoption of the two-high-school proposal, the board spent nearly two years reexamining and restudying the issue, because of opposition from various quarters. The City Council and many of the downtown businessmen favored one centrally located high school throughout the debate and discussion. When the board finally selected sites for the schools, they were to be in the northeast and southwest, as originally recommended by the Peabody Report. Some blacks and pro-integration forces objected to these locations, as the northeast site would serve a predominantly white population, while the southwest site was located near a large concentration of blacks in the vicinity of the proposed public housing projects being challenged in court by the NAACP. Lower income whites in the south part of the city assumed they would be desegregated, while more affluent whites in the northern part would be in a predominantly white school.

When the bond issue on the proposed schools came to a vote, black leaders were divided on the referendum. The Reverend Henry Mitchell, a school board member, supported the bond election, as did Eugene Williams, a past president of the Charlottesville NAACP branch and a litigant in the Burley suit. The current president of the NAACP, James Fisher, favored the bond issue, but also felt the city should buy Burley back from the county and use this school as well. The bond issue, in fact, rallied other support in the black community for the city's buying Burley and possibly combining Burley with Lane as one large, central downtown high school.

The two-high-school proposal was defeated in April 1969 by 66 votes, with a light turnout in the black community contributing to the defeat. The votes of property owners in the two precincts with most of the city's black voters were fairly evenly split for and against the two high schools. Post-election analysis listed the fear of economic and racial imbalance among both black and white voters as one of the reasons the bond issue was voted down.

With the defeat of the two-high-school proposal, board members began making plans for a single new high school, which is to be built in northwest Charlottesville. Architects contacted to design the school estimated that September 1973 would be the earliest possible date for opening the new school, assuming the city approved plans and financed it. Meanwhile, Superintendent Rushton anticipated having to use more mobile units, split shifts, a six-day week, or a trimester program to accommodate the increasing numbers of students who would attend Lane before the new high school is completed. A bond issue on the proposed high school was to be voted on in June 1970.

With completion of the new high school, the way should be clear for conversion to a K-4-4-4 grade organization plan. The overall plan adopted by the board earlier called for teaching the four senior high school grades in the new high school; dividing grades 5–8 between Lane, Buford, and Walker; converting all regular elementary schools to grades K–4; and abandoning the Jefferson School as a Sixth Grade Center.

7
Continuing Racial Issues in the Schools: 1969–1970

Black School Board Representation. On July 21, 1969, after the City Council's new appointments to the school board were announced, members of the Charlottesville Society of Friends organized a series of confrontations with the Council over their failure to add more black representatives to the Board. The Quaker Action Group first challenged councilmen to discuss the issue at regular meetings throughout the summer, and then held a silent vigil on the steps of city hall and a three-day round-the-clock fast and demonstration in Lee Park in support of their proposal. The Quaker group also asked for a biracial student school board, a fair housing law, an ombudsman to handle citizen complaints and grievances, and a permanent "committee of unity" representing people in the city concerned with social change. There was no immediate, official response to these requests from the Council, but individual members reacted. Mayor G. A. Vogt stated that the next year when school board vacancies would be open, "we will appoint the two best men, black or white."[48] Another councilman said that the Council selects men for the school board "who have experience and temperance in the community . . . men who have no bones to pick."[49] Although the Quaker group and participants in their demonstrations were predominantly white, their proposals gained support in the black community. Their demands, in fact, included some measures such as a fair housing law that had already been before the Council and the community for some time. At one of the Council meetings where the Quakers raised discussion of their proposals, a black teacher employed in Fairfax County said that he left Charlottesville because of "inadequacies in the city school system." In the course of the dialogue at the Council meeting over the Quakers' proposals, one Councilman defended the progress Charlottesville had made, recalling a race relations committee set up in 1963 when blacks could not receive service in local restaurants and motels. Mayor Vogt said he would "like to know from the black people what to do."[50] Responding to these two themes, school board member Reverend Mitchell stated:

I for one am not proud of all the accomplishments in the community. . . . They came 100 years too late. These so-called achievements came only after great pressure had been exerted. We want an understanding council who will tackle the problems aggressively. I am mad when I think of the progress we could have made and we've dragged our feet. It really burns me up when somebody says look what we've done. . . . Anytime in 1969 when someone asks what the black man wants, he's not with it. We want what everyone else wants.[51]

While Council did not act on the Quaker proposals, a new advisory resource specialist on desegregation for the Charlottesville Public Schools stated early in September 1969 that he would set up a biracial board of student representatives as part of his work. This specialist was employed in connection with a grant under Title IV of the Civil Rights Act that Charlottesville received for the 1968–69 school year. Funds for an advisory specialist on desegregation constituted the main contribution of the grant, which was not implemented in 1968–69 because the "right person" for the job could not be found. The new specialist, a black hired for the 1969–70 school year, had previously been a guidance counselor in Richmond, Virginia. The grant was set up under the supervision of Lane's former principal W. I. Nickels, now Director of Research and Program Development for the central administration offices. Stated objectives of the proposed program were numerous, including developing a training program to improve the ability of school personnel to deal with problems related to desegregation, counseling teachers, developing an activity program in which the "disadvantaged" student would become involved, identifying educational deficiencies of the disadvantaged student, developing programs and materials to meet the needs of disadvantaged students, and surveying the problems involved in completely integrated schools. How effective a new person could be in a one-year project of this nature is, of course, the first question to come to mind.

Racism in the Schools. Employment of the new advisory desegregation specialist was timely, as the Charlottesville NAACP branch charged the school board in mid-September 1969 with "not integrating a physically desegregated school system." James Fisher, NAACP branch president, also told the board that "racism still pervades the operation of the school system" and "the most acute problem has to do with the treatment of black students by some faculty members." Fisher accused the board of discriminating in the hiring of black teachers and administrators and not consulting black professionals in the system or giving them a say in how the schools are run. He singled out the Lane faculty for particular criticism and also suggested that Superintendent Rushton be replaced "with an administrator who has demonstrated his commitment to the establishment of a school system with an atmosphere in which all pupils can learn to the best of their abilities." Fisher called for the "removal from the school system of all teachers and administrators who persist in racial slurs and discriminatory action against black students and teachers."[52] Reverend Mitchell called the statement a "serious presentation" and asked the rest of the board to "face up to the problems mentioned here tonight and effect a change in this school system."[53] The board promised to study the matter, giving no immediate response.

The NAACP statement followed on the heels of late summer publicity concerning a racial outbreak at Walker Junior High School that took place at the end of the 1968–69 school year. Although the Lane situation dominated public discussion during that year, several community leaders were aware of racial tensions and problems in other schools. Field work for this study indicated there were racial problems smouldering at Walker Junior High School. Black students at Walker complained of arbitrary discipline and continual frustration in their efforts to express racial pride and awareness through dress, Afro hair styles, and black oriented activities in the school. A group of black Walker students said, for example, that if a conflict between a white and black student arose, the white student's word would be taken. They said that black students were frequently suspended for several days for reasons which they felt were not justified. They felt that the principal was not equally fair to black and white students and that the white teachers "mark" black students automatically as troublemakers although most of the black students are "quiet." These students said there was open racial conflict between black and white students at Walker, with name-calling and quite a few fights. Blacks had been refused permission to organize a "black power" club and were not permitted to wear Afro hair styles, dashikis, or pendants, although white students were allowed to wear long hair, "hippie" beads, and peace symbols. The day of Martin Luther King's funeral, for instance, some black students wanted to wear African dress in tribute to King, but were threatened with suspension. They said that they felt stifled at Walker and were looking forward to attending Lane. A white school board member told of taking his daughter to her first dance at Walker and being somewhat "taken back" when blacks "hooked together" in the middle of the dance floor and started yelling "black power." White students then did the same thing, hooking each other and yelling "white power." It might be added, James Brown's song "Say It Loud, I'm Black and I'm Proud" was popular among black kids during the 1968–69 school year, and tended to inspire blacks to raise their fists or make some kind of black power demonstration on the dance floor. Blacks at Lane, for example, rallied to the dance floor and gave the black power salute when "Black and Proud" was played at the Unity Weekend dance, although this was frowned on by the administration.

Walker's principal for the 1968–69 school year said that there were "no more interracial differences than other differences between students." The assistant principal said that the school had not had over five fights between fall and mid-January and that these were not racial. According to the principal, Walker had a larger percentage of black students who tended toward "separatism" during the 1968–69 school year than previously and these were concentrated in the seventh grade. The principal said that he was careful to see that Negroes had the opportunity to participate in all school activities and that black students were represented in all clubs, the student newspaper, and student government offices. He said that participation in sports was very high among black students and there were black students in the National Honor Society. Blacks received scholastic awards. Although he did not acknowledge any racial problems among students, the principal said there had been a "certain lack of communication" between white and Negro teachers the previous year, at the time additional black teachers were assigned to Walker from Burley. He had arranged a series of in-service meetings through the Consultative Resources Center at the University of Virginia and felt that the series of small discussion groups set up during the 1967–68 and 1968–69 school years helped develop a "healthy dialogue between the two races" at the faculty level.

On June 10, 1969, there were two racial clashes between black and white Walker students on the school grounds and on a special school bus operated by the local transit system. Nine Walker students were tried in Juvenile Court afterwards on charges such as assault, assault and battery, and disorderly conduct. Press reports described the fracas as an attack of black students on white, and a Walker student testified at the trial that there had been racial disturbances before and after school and in the cafeteria all year that had gotten worse toward the end of the year. A new white principal and a black assistant principal were appointed for the 1969–70 school year. The new assistant principal came from Louisa, Virginia, where he had been an instructor of agricultural education for the previous 17 years. Even with a new administration at Walker, the school opened in the fall of 1969 with a racial incident. Shortly after the term began, a 13-year-old black student was told to leave school when he refused to remove a "black power" neckpiece. The student claimed that the principal attacked him while trying to force him to leave school and pressed these charges in court. When tried, the principal was found innocent of the charge of assault. The judge who heard the case stated he would back "to the hilt" school administrators who bar students from wearing racial emblems.[54]

The school board responded on November 20, 1969, to the NAACP's charges of continued racism in the schools and discrimination in hiring. The board adopted a formal policy statement that banned racial discrimination on the part of students, teachers, and members of the administration and pledged the board to work for "maximum participation" of all students in extracurricular activities and all teachers in professional activities. The board also agreed to try to increase the number of black teachers and administrators "in each discipline and in each school" and to sponsor programs "to promote harmonious relations between individuals of different races, creeds and national origins."

The school board also defended the "considerable progress" being made "toward a school system that is desegregated in fact as well as in name." Specific evidence of the board's progress mentioned in the statement included: (1) the addition of 15 new black professionals in the 1969–70 school year, bringing the total number employed by the system up to 68, or 17 percent of all the professional staff; (2) race relations dialogues currently being carried on with principals, teachers, and students through the Title IV grant for the Advisory Resource Specialist in Desegregation; and (3) a new policy of the board adopted August 21 as a guide for student control, the purpose of this policy being to reserve suspension as a final resort after other measures such as the services of teachers, psychologists, counselors, and parents were brought to bear. The statement pointed out that membership on the following official and quasi-official bodies is biracial: the Superintendent's Advisory Council, which is made up of teachers and which works on teacher problems; the Administrative Council, composed of central office staff, principals, and supervisory personnel who advise the Superintendent on overall policies and procedures; several citywide curriculum committees set up to recommend textbooks and curriculum guides and to assist in planning in-service opportunities; and the Charlottesville Education Association, whose committees are selected on a biracial basis. The board also noted its "conscious and deliberate efforts . . . to incorporate multi-ethnic studies in English and social studies" and "specific revisions" made in social studies in grades 7, 8, and 11 "to give a more accurate content of Negro contributions to American history."

Need for Textbook Reform. Textbooks adopted at the state level are at the heart of the problem of the treatment of race and black history in social studies. Social studies and history

textbooks have not been a prominent public issue in Charlottesville, but have concerned parents, teachers, students, and
administrators who feel that reform in this area should
accompany desegregation. Most criticism regarding textbooks
focuses on the two state-prescribed Virginia history books in
use in grades 7 and 11 as part of the social studies curriculum.
Written and published under the supervision of a special commission created by the General Assembly of Virginia in 1950, these
two textbooks have generated continued protest from Virginia
educators and historians, as well as from statewide civil rights
and human relations groups. In 1965, for example, the
Virginian-Pilot found that half of a group of 18 directors of
instruction and school superintendents in local districts contacted
by the newspaper believed the two Virginia history textbooks
were slanted to some degree. The *Virginian-Pilot* chose a cross-
section of local school systems for the survey and reported that
the most objections to the books came from urban areas. A staff
member of the central administration in the Charlottesville Public
Schools described the seventh grade text, *Virginia: History, Government, Geography*,[55] as "ridiculous," and a parent interviewed
for this study called the book "dreadful." She said that her
daughter's seventh grade teacher had refused to use the book,
telling the students it was "just a bunch of baloney." A PTA
leader stated that the seventh grade teachers generally "have no
patience" with the book and "supplement it heavily," bringing in
a great deal of U.S. history and downplaying material in the
prescribed book.

Written to present the "Virginia point of view," the two state
history textbooks glorify and romanticize the Virginia "cavalier"
past, giving a sugarcoated version of slavery and race relations
in the state's history. The seventh grade text, generally considered the worse of the two books, states, for instance:

> Life among the Negroes of Virginia in slavery times was generally
> happy. The Negroes went about in a cheerful manner making a
> living for themselves and for those for whom they worked.[56]

President Lincoln is pictured as threatening "to invade Virginia
and use force to interfere with the state's own affairs," and the
book claims that Virginia slaves "paid little attention" and "were
not worried by the furious arguments going on between North-
erners and Southerners over what should be done with them."[57]
The companion piece to the seventh grade text, *Cavalier Commonwealth*, required for social studies and government classes
at the high school level, says that "the slave enjoyed what we

might call comprehensive social security" and that during Colo-
nial times blacks

> lacked the basic incentives to exert themselves and to work effi-
> ciently . . . most Negroes did not learn well the more skilled types
> of labor—carpentry, bricklaying, nail making, tanning, weaving, and
> so on.[58]

Cavalier Commonwealth describes race relations in the period
between the Civil War and 1900 as "friendly" and "about as
cordial as it had been in the days of slavery." Blacks who migrated
to cities during this period were said to be "imitating the white
people." This text also states that black tenant farmers of this
era "sometimes missed the social life that had been provided
by the old plantation."[59]

Authors of both the junior high and high school texts have
stated publicly that the Virginia History and Government Textbook Commission, which engaged them to write the books,
changed their original presentation of slavery and other race-
related developments in Virginia's history, such as the disen-
franchisement of blacks in the 1900s. In some cases, their original
discussion was altered by leaving out paragraphs or an entire
section of a manuscript that gave the "dark side" of the record.
Other criticisms of the textbooks have centered on the overall
conservative political point of view, lack of material on
nationalities of Virginia settlers other than the English, emphasis
on governors' biographies in presenting the state's history,
unrealistic analysis of modern Virginia politics and government,
and too little information on recent developments in the state.

Anticipating a new state adoption of social studies textbooks
in 1971, the Charlottesville PTA Council passed a resolution
on February 11, 1970, objecting to the seventh grade Virginia
history book and requesting a completely new history for grade
7. Their stand was based on three criticisms of the present text:
(1) poor coverage of events of the 20th Century; (2) inadequate
discussion of the participation of blacks in the growth of Virginia,
particularly the interpretation of the master-slave relationship
during slavery, and of the role of Negroes in contemporary
Virginia history; and (3) overestimation of the influence of Virginia upon the growth of the nation. This resolution was sent to
the State Board of Education, the governor, state legislators
from the Charlottesville area, and the local school board. The
Charlottesville School Board adopted a similar resolution, requesting a new seventh grade textbook to replace the current
one in February 1970.

Although the two Virginia history textbooks are the worst in use in the system from the standpoint of black history and racial bias, they are not the only basic textbooks with shortcomings in this area. After the first Lane student walkout, where the demand for black history at the high school level was a major issue, the central administration staff began "doctoring" the American history textbook used in the eighth grade to improve the black history content. A committee of staff members, including the Director of Secondary Education and history teachers from the two junior high schools, went through the basic textbook, *One Nation Indivisible,* in the summer of 1968, locating places where information on blacks could be added, appropriate supplementary material could be recommended, and biased statements and interpretations should be counteracted. Mimeographed inserts were then prepared and stapled to all teachers' copies of the textbook, so that instructors would have access to supplementary information on black history and know precisely where it fit in. Altogether 22 mimeographed inserts were placed in the first two-thirds of the eighth grade history text.

Most of the material inserted in *One Nation Indivisible* contains supplementary information on the participation and contributions of blacks from the early period of exploration of America through Reconstruction. For example, a statement placed at the top of page 185, where the War of 1812 is discussed, notes:

Captain Oliver Perry praised the courage of Negroes who served under him during the naval battles of Lake Erie, especially that of John Johnson, who was killed in action.

Similar inserts contain information about black heroes and troops who fought in other battles and other wars. Some of the slips stapled to the book summarize the accomplishments of black explorers, scientists, and inventors. A few of the inserts attempt to correct biased interpretations and conclusions in the text. The textbook states, for instance, that "politics was a complete mystery to many former slaves" who, during Reconstruction, "looked to white people to tell them what to do" and were used by carpetbaggers.[60] An insert stapled to this page points out that the qualifications of blacks elected to public office during Reconstruction "were comparable to those of the average white persons elected from the same areas at the same time" and goes on to say:

Despite the common notion otherwise, Negroes in Congress rendered valuable service, not only in the areas of civil rights and education, but also in working for local improvements such as new public buildings and appropriations for rivers and harbors.

Blacks elected to "significant public positions" in Mississippi, Louisiana, and South Carolina are listed. Unfortunately, there are only a few such "corrective" inserts. Although the text is one of the new "integrated" editions with some pictures of black leaders and a photograph of the March on Washington and a black Peace Corps volunteer, there are still biases in the treatment of historical events involving blacks and other minorities. The "doctoring" process was limited to black history and did not extend to other minorities such as the American Indian, whose past is also misrepresented. The account of the Seminole Wars and U. S. attempts to move the Florida Seminole Indians to the West, for example, is greatly distorted.

The committee that worked on the junior high school history text in the summer of 1968 had intended to "doctor" the high school U. S. history text also, but did not have time to work on that book. The Director of Secondary Education, who supervised the task of preparing the inserts, admitted that the job went slowly because he and other whites working on the project were not familiar with black history sources. Inserting black history materials in the regular textbook is viewed as a stopgap measure, until the state adoption list includes texts that are more accurate and bias-free. In most subjects—Virginia history being an exception—the state maintains a multiple adoption list from which local school districts select a basic text. Though newer editions of some basal texts now on the state adoption list contain pictures of blacks, the state textbook commission has been criticized for selecting the "segregated" edition where publishing companies offer dual editions of basal texts. Most of the multiethnic texts and materials now in use in the Charlottesville schools are supplementary to the basal text, which means that they are obtained and used at the discretion of individual principals and teachers. The district allows wide choice in the area of supplementary materials, but selects one basal text for each subject, which must necessarily be drawn from the state adoption list. Reform in the selection of textbooks must therefore come from the state level.

8
Summary and Conclusions

Evolution in Nature of Segregation. Traditional southern *de jure* segregation, required by Virginia law and buttressed by local policy, ended officially in Charlottesville in 1959 with enforcement of a federal court order admitting black pupils to formerly white schools. While the court's action initiated some token desegregation, traditional *de jure* segregation was replaced by a new pattern of separation based on gerrymandered attendance areas, racially oriented transfer policies, and a "freedom of choice" policy putting the burden of desegregation on the black community. This new, northern-type segregation was accompanied by a nondiscrimination policy and was carried out in connection with "desegregation" plans. It proved to be almost as effective as the old, southern-style segregation in keeping the majority of black and white pupils in separate schools.

Title VI of the 1964 Civil Rights Act Responsible for Major Desegregation. After years of litigation, token desegregation plans, and the rise of a new, northern-type pattern of separate schools, Title VI of the Civil Rights Act of 1964 was finally responsible for moving the district into major desegregation. Prior to the passage of Title VI, the federal courts actually helped maintain segregation by approving plans that fostered tokenism and kept the dual system intact. With the passage of Title VI and new federal standards for desegregation, the district responded to citizen pressure to abandon predominantly black schools and assign blacks to schools which were mainly attended by whites. Making sure that the district qualified for federal funds under Title VI seemed to be one of the main factors that finally motivated broad scale desegregation.

Community Enforces Title VI. Pressures to enforce Title VI of the Civil Rights Act came primarily from the community, rather than from officials of the federal government. Concerned citizens got little direct support from HEW's civil rights staff when they complained of the continuation of segregated schools in Charlottesville, but they were able to use the threat of federal funds being cut off to secure plans for further desegregation at the local level. Because district officials were convinced Title VI would be enforced and the flow of federal funds

111

would be affected, Title VI was an effective tool in the hands of community leaders.

Black Leadership Crucial to Desegregation. Most of the actions that brought about desegregation came from the black community, specifically the NAACP, which was responsible for initiating and sustaining the long campaign that gradually brought about full desegregation. The NAACP relied primarily on court suits in the early phases of its attack on school segregation, but after passage of the Civil Rights Act, supplemented court suits with other tactics, such as complaints to HEW, petitions, and a massive transfer effort designed to force the closing of separate black schools. There was almost no active white support for desegregation until about 1965, when predominantly white human relations and political organizations joined black groups and leaders in an ad hoc coalition that brought major gains in the desegregation of elementary and junior high schools. Support from whites helped to accelerate the pace of desegregation.

Complete Desegregation Makes Planning Possible. White support for full desegregation was partly a by-product of the many, unresolved problems of partial desegregation. For years, needed school building was postponed, schools were overcrowded, dual facilities were not fully utilized, school boundaries were changed frequently, and hundreds of thousands of public tax dollars were poured into private schools. Therefore, many people in Charlottesville were relieved when the school district finally accepted major desegregation and began to move ahead with planning, school building, and solving of other problems that had accumulated during the long period when the district was neither segregated nor desegregated. Major desegregation ended a long period of uncertainty and chronic chaos and freed the district to plan ahead on a rational, systemwide basis, giving more time, money, and energy to confronting basic problems.

No Alternative to Public Education. Another factor influencing white acceptance of desegregation was the growing realization that there was, for most, no really viable alternative to public education. School closings in Charlottesville in 1958 under Virginia's massive resistance laws and the shortcomings of "private" academies financed with the help of public tuition grants under Virginia's Pupil Scholarship Program, helped to bring this lesson home. Between 1959 and 1969 Charlottesville spent hundreds of thousands of public tax dollars on tuition grants to whites who attended private schools to avoid desegregation. Yet the private schools never enrolled more than a small minority of the district's normal public school age population. Whites came to accept the fact that desegregated public education—if this was the only kind of public education available—offered the best alternative for most of the city's children.

Combining Desegregation with Major Reorganization. Charlottesville's first major desegregation move, which completely desegregated the junior high schools in one step, combined a major grade and school reorganization change with the desegregation of grades 7–9. The fact that the junior high school program was new, that new buildings were underway, and that the change to separate junior and senior high schools was considered desirable by the community, all contributed to a relatively easy transition. Elimination of the black elementary school that had previously taught grade 7 was another factor that helped make desegregation at the junior high school level successful. It appears that linking desegregation to a popular school and grade reorganization plan can greatly ease the transition.

Myth of "Natural" School Boundaries. The Charlottesville school board's use of elementary attendance zones throughout the period since desegregation explodes the myth that there is such a thing as "natural" boundaries for a school that accidentally result in segregation. Elementary attendance zones were first drawn to contain most whites in white schools and most blacks in the Jefferson School. Later, elementary zones were changed in order to desegregate some white schools, and, finally, full desegregation was achieved by means of new attendance areas that distributed black pupils among all schools. The district now draws attendance areas to avoid heavy concentrations of blacks in any particular elementary or junior high school. School attendance zones *coupled with a goal of racial balance* have become an effective tool of desegregation.

Acceptance of Principle of Racial Balance. Gradual acceptance of the principle of maintaining racial balance is the key to Charlottesville's recent success in desegregating all of the pupils and teachers in the regular schools. The district moved toward this principle slowly, making successive "hard" decisions to abandon the traditional use of black segregated facilities, rezone black elementary children throughout the city, operate some schools on a citywide basis, bus to reduce racial concentrations, and desegregate all-white as well as all-black schools. Although the board had not made a *formal* commitment to establish racial balance except in the case of proposed new high school facilities, the district was in fact controlling and "evening out" the distribution of blacks in all of its schools by 1969. Pressures from whites as well as blacks were responsible for the board's most recent steps in the direction of racial balance.

Need for Formal Policies on Racial Balance, Busing, and Nondiscrimination. Although the district's informal policy of maintaining racial balance was effective when this study was made, it was vague and undefined and did not appear in the district's new written code of *School Board Policies and Regulations* adopted in 1969. There was, in fact no statement regarding race, nondiscrimination, or busing in this code. What proportion of blacks in a school constitutes imbalance? Will the district permit all-white schools in the future? What racial concentrations will warrant busing or a redrawing of attendance zones? With new building, shifts in the racial composition of individual schools, and future annexations of suburban residential areas, Charlottesville will surely face these questions. A formal policy statement on racial balance, spelling out definite goals as to the desired racial proportions of individual schools and criteria for correcting imbalance, would help the district maintain the desegregation it has accomplished and should help the board avoid future community upheavals over resegregation.

Need to Plan New Facilities for Racial Balance. The board's present practice of locating or attempting to locate, new buildings in the midst of all-white neighborhoods or near predominantly black areas in itself raises the question of possible future resegregation. While the defeat of the 1969 bond referendum checked the board's action with respect to proposed high school facilities, the community does not have the opportunity to pass judgment on proposed school sites unless a bond issue is involved. The new Jackson-Via school, for example, was voted in closed executive session and financed without a bond issue through the city's capital improvement fund. New schools should be located to maximize racial balance and where possible, large new facilities, such as one citywide high school as opposed to two, should be considered to help prevent resegregation.

Black School Counterbalance to One-Way Desegregation.
Recent use of the formerly all-black Jefferson school as a city-wide Sixth Grade Center in connection with the district's major elementary desegregation plan has been an equalizing force in Charlottesville's desegregation efforts. In addition to the fact that all black and white children have attended Jefferson on an equal basis, use of a formerly black school as a desegregated facility has helped to balance out the one-way character of most of Charlottesville's desegregation. Whites have made the adjustment of coming to a formerly black institution; perhaps more important, a black school was considered adequate for the city's total population. Utilization of this formerly black institution on a desegregated basis not only salvaged the district's economic investment in the buildings, but also helped maintain pride in the black community and was a step in the direction of evening out travel hardships and adjustments involved in desegregation.

Black Students' "Adjustment" in Desegregated Schools.
One of the basic weaknesses in Charlottesville's overall desegregation has been the assumption on the part of many whites that desegregation is a one-way street that brings blacks into "their" schools; blacks are expected to "adjust" and accept conditions in these schools. The long period of token desegregation, where black adjustment to whites was pretty much the pattern, undoubtedly helped to reinforce this limited view of desegregation. While many whites do not want to admit it, black students in formerly white schools face racial slurs, some prejudiced teachers, white-oriented and white-biased curricula, and rejection by many students. Black students' strengths and interests are ignored and they have no channels for grievances. Black students should not in any case be expected to make all of the adjustments when attending formerly white schools. Most definitely, black students should not be expected to "adjust" to discriminatory and racist attitudes and practices.

Student Confrontations Raise Legitimate Problems. A recent element in Charlottesville's school desegregation that is difficult for many whites to accept is the open and aggressive way in which some black students are challenging racism and racial practices in the high schools. In early 1969, whites even at high policy levels were "running scared" and overreacting to student challenges and confrontations. Instead of addressing themselves to the legitimate issues raised by the black students, many whites became preoccupied with keeping the black students from getting out of control, even to the point of penalizing them severely for things they had not done. Others were harking back to an earlier period of desegregation when blacks were less demanding and "when everything was going along so well." Although disturbing to many, the Lane student confrontations brought some of the district's racial problems out into the open where they could be faced and dealt with by school authorities. Student demands and confrontations which raise legitimate problems and issues are a positive force in solving a school system's racial problems.

Black and Proud and for a New Kind of Integration. The new race consciousness and race pride among black students, their identification with black power symbols and their use of more militant tactics were also being misinterpreted by many whites and some older blacks, who criticized the students for being "separatist" and "going too far." Regarding the students' tactics, it should be noted that there was almost no change on racial issues in the schools during the period when black students were blending in, politely "taking" student and staff racism. Regarding their goals: even the most militant students complained that whites do not want blacks in their schools. In its totality, the black student movement seemed to have a dual thrust. In their formal demands, especially, black students were asking for more representation, more attention to their special needs, and fairer treatment *within* the integrated school. Informally, through the use of black power symbols, their new hair styles, and increased willingness to stand up and voice complaints, the black students were also saying that they *must be accepted on new terms,* as equals who bring something of their own to the integration process. While some black students would have preferred to remain in Burley, the all-black high school that was closed, and many black students were dissatisfied with *the kind of integration they experienced at Lane,* the majority of black pupils were not basically anti-integration or anti-white in 1969. Most seemed to be "black and proud," drawn to black power slogans and symbols as a new form of hope and protest, and seeking "acceptance in their blackness as whites are accepted in their whiteness."

Coping with Educational Problems of Desegregation. Although the academic weakness of black students in the early phases of desegregation is often stressed, Charlottesville's experiences with major desegregation suggest that a number of factors other than pupils' own educational backgrounds influence the academic progress of black children in newly desegregated schools. Among these are teachers' acceptance of the ability of black children to learn; willingness of teachers to modify or change teaching styles and approaches to motivating children; teachers' ability to work with children with different educational and social backgrounds; staff avoidance of racial stereotyping in judging and interacting with individual students; the ability of school leadership to reevaluate and reorganize the existing school program; the availability of special help for children in the form of remedial teachers, teaching aides, and educational materials suited to their needs; and, above all, the ability of staff to communicate to students that this is their school and that the staff is fair and concerned about them. The Venable Model School Program, particularly, indicates that positive staff attitudes, school leadership and organization, and a willingness to be sensitive to the needs of a changing enrollment are ingredients of a good learning situation for black children. These leadership, organizational, and attitudinal factors seem to be crucial to coping with the educational problems accompanying desegregation.

Ability Grouping and Resegregation. The grouping of children for instruction by ability or achievement levels is not a uniform practice throughout the Charlottesville schools, but ability grouping is used to some extent at the elementary, junior high, and high school levels. Ability grouping tends to result in a top ability level that is all white or nearly all white and a preponderance of blacks at the bottom ability level. To counteract the trend toward classroom segregation caused by ability grouping, at least some schools: (1) cut down on the number of ability levels, since fewer levels seem to cause less segregation; (2) combine adjacent ability levels, such as "average" and "below average" to get a better racial mix; (3) "borrow" individual children from adjacent levels in making classroom assignments so that the racial composition can be balanced; and (4) use teacher evaluations, the child's total record, and other criteria in addition to test scores for determining a child's "ability." The choice of using ability grouping in the first place, modifying it, using heterogeneous classrooms, or introducing a nongraded program, seems to be left largely to the individual principal. The district needs to reexamine the entire question of classroom grouping, including the use of test scores as a basis for determining a child's ability. Grouping practices that result in the segregation of black and white children in the classroom throughout most or all of the school day should be prohibited.

Need for Strong Measures Against In-School Racism. Evidence of in-school bias and racism, particularly among the teachers and staff of Lane High School, pointed to the need for strong leadership from the board and administration in bringing discrimination within the schools under control. The board's policy statement of November 1969, banning discrimination by teachers, students, and administrators, and affirming the intention of the board to work for maximum participation of all students and teachers in all school and professional activities, was an important first step toward resolving the problem of racism in Lane and other Charlottesville schools. Teachers, administrators, and students need to know that controlling individual prejudices is a matter of top priority, that complying with such a policy is important, and that they will be penalized if they persist in racist and discriminatory behavior. Follow-up on a policy statement in this area is of course necessary to demonstrate the seriousness of the matter and the fact that the board intends to live up to its pronouncements.

Realistic In-Service Orientation and Teacher Preparation. It is doubtful that any kind of voluntarily attended lecture-type in-service human relations orientation would help in schools such as Lane, where racial divisions are severe and a prejudiced entrenched faculty is a key factor in the problem. Certainly, in Lane or in any other school for that matter a seminar on how to lead Great Books discussions is completely useless in preparing teachers for desegregation. Placing staff who have been unable to handle racial problems in their own schools in charge of desegregation technical assistance programs also makes little sense.

Several different kinds of in-service situations should be of assistance, *provided they are coupled with strong administrative leadership in solving the schools' racial problems.*

(1) *All* teachers and staff need to explore and discuss the similarities and differences between white and black Americans, including the real problems faced by black students and staff in predominantly white institutions. Knowledgeable community leaders and students need to be brought into these discussions, and the goal should be determining what changes should be made so that both individual teachers and the school as an institution can better serve a biracial population. Full consideration

of demands posed by the black community, such as those put forth by the black students and the NAACP, should be items on the agenda.

(2) Specialized courses in black history and black experience literature are needed for Social Studies and English teachers, and counselors need special sessions to broaden their knowledge of colleges, scholarship opportunities, and job training possibilities of special interest to blacks. These courses should be required of all staff employed in these areas.

(3) Work sessions should be set up to revise teaching outlines to incorporate material by and about blacks where appropriate and to select supplementary classroom materials to be used with the new outlines. The current practice at Lane of buying many individual paperback books on blacks, for example, does not result in enough copies of any one book so that a teacher can assign a whole class a particular reading.

(4) Other work sessions on special problem areas, such as discipline procedures and codes, should be held in individual schools where the situations seem to warrant them. These should be problem-solving meetings, designed to implement or develop a positive policy. Again, the sessions should be compulsory.

It cannot be stressed too much that in-service training for desegregation without proper school administrative leadership and willingness to make concrete changes will probably be of little benefit.

More Black Representation at Decision-Making Levels. More blacks in top decision-making positions—on the school board, in responsible central administration positions, and in principals' jobs—are essential if Charlottesville is to fully resolve its school racial problems. More black representation on the school board is especially crucial, since the board acts as a court of appeals on school problems and issues, in addition to setting overall policy for the district. Placing more black staff in principals' jobs is important from the standpoint of fair treatment and understanding of black students' problems, maintaining fair discipline, and convincing students that the schools are not racist institutions. It is also important that black persons put in these positions be respected by the black community, sensitive to the students' needs and problems, and strong enough to give leadership on racial issues.

Hiring, Acceptance and Upgrading of Black Professionals. The plight of black teachers and professional staff

since major desegregation is legitimately of much concern, both
to the black adult community and to black students in Charlottesville. The gradual decline in the number of black teachers
employed, the loss of positions of prestige and responsibility,
and the district's failure to hire more than a few new black
professionals in the early stages of desegregation were particularly sore points in view of the high turnover of white professionals and the number of whites that are brought in from
outside the local system. The stability of black professionals in
the community is a decided asset to the district, apart from the
need for more black staff demanded by the racial situation.
More black professionals should be hired, placed in responsible
leadership positions, and accepted on a level where they feel
free to contribute ideas, take initiative, and be real participants
in shaping the direction of the schools.

**Coordination of Federal Enforcement of Desegregation
Needed.** Between 1967 and 1969, at least, Charlottesville
seemed to have slipped through the net of federal agencies
enforcing school desegregation, owing to lack of coordination
between the bureaucracies. Although Charlottesville's school suit
was dismissed in March 1967, as much as a year and a half
later the HEW Regional Office in Charlottesville and the Justice
Department refused to let the Regional HEW Office for Civil
Rights assume jurisdiction in a local school civil rights complaint
because the district "was under court order." Independent civil
rights organizations have protested such a "hands off" policy
toward school districts under court order since the early stages
of the Title VI enforcement program. Without adequate coordination and liaison, a district's immunity to HEW's compliance
program can apparently go on long past the actual dismissal
of a court suit. Coordination between the federal courts, the
Justice Department, and HEW is imperative, so that citizens'
rights will be protected at all times.

Need for Continued Leadership at Local Level. Although the
process was unnecessarily slow and required an inordinate
amount of citizen pressure, Charlottesville has done what many
other communities have failed to do—completely desegregated
its regular schools. Having accomplished this, the district must
now go on to the next set of tasks, what the NAACP has described
as "integrating a physically desegregated school system."[61] Ending racism on the part of teachers and staff, hiring and upgrading
black faculty, providing realistic in-service teacher training,

insuring more black representation at decision-making levels, modifying the white-oriented curricula—these are the pressing racial issues that now face the Charlottesville schools. Local leadership must mobilize to resolve these issues quickly, so that, as one civic leader put it, another generation—white and black —"will not be lost."

Epilogue

By the fall of 1971, two blacks were serving on the Charlottesville school board: the Reverend Henry Mitchell and a black woman, Mrs. Robert Tinsley, appointed after the Quaker Action Group protests in 1969 to secure more black representation on the school board. Mrs. Tinsley is the third black person to be named to the board since 1965. There were also two additional blacks in administrative positions in the schools formerly held by whites. A black principal was named to Walker Junior High School in the fall of 1971, and a black assistant principal was assigned to Lane Senior High School. With these two staff appointments, there were four black administrators in the Charlottesville schools in 1971.

Although black representation at the decision-making level was improved by the naming of a new board member and the principalships, the comparatively lower ratio of blacks to whites at all levels of employment in the schools was still a matter of major concern to the black community. Citizens for Progress, a black group including city and county residents, met with the school board and actively advocated the hiring of more black teachers and administrators in the schools in 1971.

The issue of racial balance had dropped into the background by 1971, but the gains made in the late 1960s were apparently intact. The fall 1970 HEW survey of school districts in compliance with Title VI of the Civil Rights Act showed that the percent of blacks in the elementary schools was between 17 and 22 percent in all schools except Venable, where the enrollment was 45 percent black. Two community leaders contacted in the fall of 1971 said that racial proportions in the elementary schools had stayed about the same since 1969, when new attendance zones were adopted, and that the percentage of blacks in individual elementary schools had ceased to be a community issue. Even in Venable, where the black enrollment was still possibly as high as 45 percent, the Venable Model School Program and other efforts, such as that of the Venable PTA to involve parents and pupils in a cooperative school grounds planting project, were effective in checking white panic over the high percentage of blacks in the school.

Busing for purposes of racial balance ended with the implementation of the new elementary attendance areas in 1969, but some children are now bused to elementary schools for other reasons. Children are bused to the new Jackson-Via School for safety reasons—for example, because of construction and lack of sidewalks. The Jackson-Via School opened officially in the fall of 1969, although the building was not completed. Pupils assigned to that school were housed in Clark and Johnson Elementary Schools the first year, and the school moved into the new building the next year. Jackson-Via was scheduled to open with a 19 percent black enrollment, and its black/white proportions were 17/83 in 1971.

The racial situation in Lane had improved by 1971, according to community leaders contacted, but black/white problems in that school were by no means solved. More black students were participating in Lane school activities, according to these spokesmen, and tensions within the school had leveled off. Although key leaders in the 1968 student protests had graduated, some of their goals were still being implemented. An elective black studies course, taught separately from the regular history classes, had been added to the curriculum, and a black assistant principal appointed. Mrs. Garrett, a black staff member formerly at Burley High School and formerly principal of the Sixth Grade Center at Jefferson, was on the staff at Lane in 1971 as a guidance counselor. Mrs. Garrett was succeeded at Jefferson by another black principal, who was moved from McGuffey to Jefferson. Two portable classroom structures were in use at Lane in 1971 to relieve overcrowding. The new high school, finally located in the northwestern part of the city, was scheduled to open in April 1974. A bond issue to finance the new high schoo¹ was approved by the voters in 1970.

Lane's racial problems surfaced again in early 1972 with another student walkout. According to the *Washington Post*, 50 white pupils walked out of Lane in mid-February 1972 to protest a black culture assembly. Lane's 300 black students then refused to attend classes as a counter-protest to the white walkout. Superintendent Rushton described the climate created by the two demonstrations as "highly charged and emotional" and closed all schools in the city to permit a "cooling-off period." Rushton said that he shut down all of Charlottesville's schools to prevent Lane students from infiltrating and causing disruptions at other schools. Students of both races and school officials were to meet before the schools reopened to seek ways to solve Lane's racial problems.[62]

In another important area, textbook reform, the Virginia State Board of Education voted unanimously in January 1972 to allow local school districts to select social studies and history texts from a list of alternative books, the list to be updated every two years by the board. The board's new position on social studies textbooks avoided mentioning by name the much criticized, ultra-conservative books on Virginia history previously required in elementary and high school social studies classes throughout the state. But the effect of the new policy, according to spokesmen interviewed after the board's decision was announced, was to end the official role of the prescribed Virginia history books in the public schools. Two of these textbooks, *Virginia: History, Government, Geography* and *Cavalier Commonwealth,* used in grades 7 and 11, respectively, were singled out for criticism in Charlottesville. Common complaints against the texts were that they were biased and distorted on racial questions and that they were inadequate from an historical point of view because of the glorification of Virginia's past and the highly selective material presented.

Dr. Harold W. Ramsey, chairman of the state board's Committee on Textbooks and Curriculum, stated after the board's action that the controversial Virginia histories, written to the specifications of a state history and government textbook commission in the 1950s, had become "obsolete" and people "objected to some of the phrases and the philosophy they expressed." He said future instructional materials would "try to relate Virginia history more to the history of the country as a whole."[63] Hilary H. Jones, Jr., the only black member of the state board of education, got assurances from Dr. Ramsey that the new history materials placed on the list for local adoption would emphasize a multiracial approach wherever possible.

Press reports indicated that contracts between the state board of education and the publishers of the required Virginia histories would be allowed to lapse without renewal on June 30, 1972. Beginning in the fall of 1972, history teachers in the state were to be advised of a variety of film strips, television presentations, and other materials that could be used in implementing a social studies curriculum.

NOTES

1. *Daily Progress* (Charlottesville, Virginia), Feb. 27, 1969, p. 1B.
2. *Daily Progress*, Mar. 5, 1969, p. 25.
3. *Daily Progress*, Sept. 21, 1969, p. 1B.
4. *Charlottesville-Albemarle Tribune*, Oct. 16, 1969, p. 2.
5. *Daily Progress*, Feb. 17, 1969, p. 11.
6. James W. Barksdale, *A Comparative Study of Contemporary White and Negro Standards in Health, Education and Welfare*, Phelps Stokes Fellowship Papers, No. 20 (Charlottesville, Virginia; University of Virginia), 1949, pp. 77—83.
7. *Charlottesville-Albemarle Tribune*, June 19, 1969, p. 1.
8. *Charlottesville, Virginia, Public Schools* (the Peabody report) (Nashville, Tennessee; Division of Surveys and Field Services, George Peabody College for Teachers), 1967, pp. 18, 32.
9. Barksdale, *op. cit.*, p. 53.
10. *Ibid.*, pp. 42—43.
11. *Ibid.*, p. 47.
12. *Southern School News* (Nashville, Tennessee), November 1955, p. 12.
13. Quoted in Dan Wakefield, "Charlottesville Battle: Symbol of the Divided South," *Nation*, 183:11, Sept. 15, 1956, p. 210.
14. *Ibid.*
15. Paul M. Gaston and Thomas T. Hammond, "Public School Desegregation: Charlottesville, Virginia, 1955—1962," a report presented to the Nashville Conference on "The South: The Ethical Demands of Integration," Dec. 28, 1962, pp. 2—3.
16. *Ibid.*, pp. 3—4.
17. *Ibid.*, pp. 1a—2a.
18. *Ibid.*, pp. 8a—9a.
19. *Ibid.*, pp. 5—6.
20. Benjamin Muse, *Virginia's Massive Resistance* (Bloomington, Indiana; Indiana University Press), 1961, p. 136.
21. Statement of Fendall R. Ellis, Superintendent of Schools, Charlottesville, Va., in U. S. Commission on Civil Rights, *Conference Before the U. S. Commission on Civil Rights, Second Annual Conference on the Problems of Schools in Transition from the Educator's Viewpoint*, March 21—22, 1960, Gattinburg, Tenn. (Washington, D.C.; U. S. Government Printing Office), 1960, p. 106.
22. Sarah Patton Boyle, *The Desegregated Heart: A Virginian's Stand in a Time of Transition* (New York; William Morrow and Company), 1962, p. 20.
23. *Ibid.*, p. 90.
24. *Doris Marie Allen vs. School Board of the City of Charlottesville, Virginia* (Civil Action No. 51 in the U. S. District Court for the Western District of Virginia, at Charlottesville), Opinion by the Court, Dec. 18, 1961, mimeographed, p. 4.
25. *Doris Dillard et al. vs. School Board of the City of Charlottesville,*

Virginia (U. S. Court of Appeals for the Fourth Circuit), Opinion of the Court, Sept. 17, 1962, mimeographed, pp. 3, 5—6, 14—18.

26. "Virginia," *in* U. S. Commission on Civil Rights, *Civil Rights U. S. A. Public Schools, Southern States, 1962* (Washington, D.C.; U. S. Government Printing Office), 1962, p. 171.

27. Gaston and Hammond, *op. cit.*, p. 18.

28. Letter from Mrs. Thelma J. Townsend, President, Charlottesville Branch NAACP, to Chester R. Babcock, Chairman, Charlottesville School Board, Dec. 1, 1964.

29. Letter from H. A. Haden, Chairman, Community Relations Committee, to Chester R. Babcock, Oct. 22, 1964.

30. Letter from Chester R. Babcock to Henry A. Haden, Chairman, Community Relations Committee, Oct. 25, 1964.

31. *Daily Progress*, May 21, 1965, p. 1.

32. Letter from Drewary Brown, President, Charlottesville NAACP, to School Board and Office of Superintendent of Schools, Sept. 8, 1965.

33. Letter from Chairman, Charlottesville School Board, to Drewary Brown, President, Charlottesville NAACP, Sept. 9, 1965.

34. *Daily Progress*, Apr. 16, 1968.

35. James E. Bash, *Effective Teaching in the Desegregated School*, (Bloomington, Indiana; Phi Delta Kappa), 1966.

36. Minutes of the regular meeting of the School Board, Charlottesville, Virginia, June 20, 1968, p. 20.

37. *Daily Progress*, Mar. 19, 1969, p. 1B.

38. *James A. Harris et al. vs. Charlottesville Development and Housing Authority and the School Board of the City of Charlottesville*, Civil Action No. 68—C—25—C in the U. S. District Court for the Western District of Virginia, Charlottesville Division, Answer, Nov. 4, 1968, p. 3.

39. *Ibid.*, Nov. 30, 1968, p. 3.

40. *Daily Progress*, Mar. 20, 1969, p. 13.

41. *Daily Progress*, Dec. 7, 1966, p. 1B.

42. Minutes, Board Conference of the School Board of the City of Charlottesville, May 17, 1968, p. 6.

43. Letter from Charlottesville parent to Edward W. Rushton, Superintendent, Charlottesville Public Schools, May 17, 1968.

44. *Daily Progress*, Nov. 7, 1968.

45. *Daily Progress*, Sept. 7, 1969, p. 4B.

46. *Daily Progress*, Feb. 2, 1969, p. 1B.

47. *Daily Progress*, Apr. 18, 1969.

48. *Daily Progress*, Aug. 5, 1969, p. 13.

49. *Daily Progress*, Sept. 3, 1969, p. 1B.

50. *Daily Progress*, Aug. 5, 1969, p. 13.

51. *Charlottesville-Albemarle Tribune*, Aug. 21, 1969, p. 1.

52. *Daily Progress*, Sept. 19, 1969, p. 1B.

53. *Ibid.*

54. *Washington Post*, Oct. 19, 1969, p. A3.

55. Frances Butler Simkins, Spottswood Hunnicutt Jones, and Sidman P. Poole, *Virginia: History, Government, Geography* (rev. ed.) (New York; Scribner's), 1964.

56. Quoted in the *Virginian-Pilot,* Oct. 27, 1965, p. 9–D.
57. *Ibid.*
58. William Edwin Hemphill, Marvin Wilson Schlegel, and Sadie Ethel Engelberg, *Cavalier Commonwealth: History and Government of Virginia* (2nd ed.) (St. Louis; Webster Division, McGraw-Hill Book Company), 1963, pp. 120–21.
59. *Ibid.,* pp. 395–97.
60. Landis R. Heller, Jr., and Norris W. Potter, *One Nation Indivisible* (Columbus, Ohio; Charles E. Merrill Books, Inc.), 1966, p. 315.
61. *Daily Progress,* Sept. 19, 1969, p. 1B.
62. *Washington Post,* Feb. 19, 1972, p. C2.
63. *Ibid.,* Jan. 29, 1972, p. B1.

PART 2

Providence, Rhode Island: White and Black Power and Citywide Dispersal of Blacks in the Public Schools

Foreword

Providence, Rhode Island's elementary schools were desegregated in the fall of 1967, as the culmination of several years of insistent and consistent community pressure. Many city and state educational, religious, civic, and humanitarian leaders and organizations supported desegregation, but a viable program, acceptable to both blacks and whites, was worked out only after a long series of false starts and controversy in both the black and white communities. The Providence Plan, the city's first elementary desegregation plan, took months to forge and, even so, was modified during the first school year to meet the demands of South Providence blacks for a more equitable process. The Providence Plan was augmented in the fall of 1970 by a Phase II plan, which eliminated resegregation in the elementary schools and established racial balance in the middle schools and junior high schools. Phase III, put into effect in September 1971, brought about a better distribution of blacks and whites in the senior high schools.

This Part describes the status of black education prior to desegregation, early unsuccessful efforts to desegregate Providence schools, the development of the Providence Plan for elementary desegregation, implementation of the Providence Plan, changes in the plan made early in 1968, and racial problems in the schools after the first phase of desegregation. While the Providence Plan was directly concerned with elementary desegregation only, the many auxiliary moves of older pupils that accompanied elementary desegregation had serious effects on racial situations in some of the middle schools and junior and senior high schools. The backlash of racial problems in other schools, the reorganization of the school board, and new policies of the school committee relevant to desegregation are also discussed. This Part mainly concentrates on the Providence Plan, Phase I of elementary desegregation, but Phase II and Phase III are summarized briefly in the last section.

1.

Community Background

Location. Providence, Rhode Island, is an old New England port city located on the Providence River at the head of the Narragansett Bay. It is about 25 miles from the Atlantic Ocean and is 44 miles southwest of Boston and 180 miles northeast of New York.

Early Settlement. Providence was settled in 1636 by Roger Williams, a religious dissenter banished from the colony of Massachusetts for his unorthodox beliefs. Williams did not intend to found a new colony, but brought other religious refugees with him and was soon joined by more dissenters. In 1638, Williams and the group of outcasts who gathered in Providence formed a town based on the principle of religious tolerance. They divided land they had secured from Narragansett Indian chieftains into plots for houses and farms and called themselves the Proprietors Company for Providence Plantations. Their settlement ran along the Providence riverfront in what is now the East Side of Providence. A board of governors controlled by a town meeting was established in 1640, and in 1644 Providence joined other nearby communities of religious dissenters in a common political association that became the basis for the colony and then the state of Rhode Island. Both the city of Providence and the state of Rhode Island became havens for New Englanders of British ancestry seeking religious freedom.

Economic Development. Providence became an important shipbuilding center and a major trading port after 1680. In spite of the strong religious principles on which Providence was founded, much of its early, thriving overseas commerce was based on the profitable "triangular trade" that then existed between New England, Africa, and the West Indies. Molasses and sugar from the West Indies were distilled into rum, carried to Africa, and traded for slaves, who were then taken to the West Indies and sold to plantation owners for more sugar and molasses. Newport, Rhode Island, only 30 miles away from Providence, was the capital of the American slave trade, with as many as 22 distilleries manufacturing rum for the African "market" at the height of its prosperity. While Providence's merchant-traders were not as outstanding in the "triangular trade" as Newport's, they "played a prominent role in the early slave trade."[1] Providence's merchant-shippers were also engaged in whaling and entered the world commercial market after the American Revolution, sending ships to the East, to India, and to China. Providence soon replaced Newport as the major port and center of commerce for Rhode Island and the surrounding region.

Although commerce and trade continued to flourish in Providence, industry became of prime importance in the late 1800s. Textiles were Providence's first important industry, and jewelry manufacture became a major enterprise after 1850. By 1880 the state of Rhode Island was first in the nation in jewelry manufacture, with almost all of its jewelry factories located in Providence. Other industries based on the manufacture of silverware, machine tools, metal goods, rubber products, and electronics equipment developed later, making Providence a highly industrialized town in the center of the nation's most industrialized state. Providence declined as a world port after the 1800s, but has remained an important commercial and trading center.

Ethnic Migrations. Through the 1700s, most of the newcomers who settled in Providence and Rhode Island were Yankees, native American-born New Englanders of British ancestry. The development of industry soon changed the Yankee character of the population, however, as wave after wave of immigrants of different ethnic backgrounds came to build and man the new factories. Irish immigrants began migrating to New England and Rhode Island in large numbers in the 1830s, their ranks swelling greatly after the famine of 1841. By 1850, 16 percent of all the residents of Rhode Island were foreign-born, primarily of Irish background (70 percent). The Irish first worked as ditchdiggers, bricklayers, and construction hands in the building of railroads and mills. But during the 1840s, as the need for factory workers increased, the Irish began to drift into the textile mills. The flow of Irish immigrants to Rhode Island reached a peak between 1850 and 1860, and continued on a smaller scale after this time. As Irish immigration tapered off, there was a large influx of French Canadians to Rhode Island. French Canadians began moving to Providence and the state of Rhode Island in large numbers after the Civil War, with this migration increasing to its highest level about 1890. The French Canadian immigrants were followed by a large number of Italians in the early 1900s, and there were also many Eastern European and Portuguese immigrants about this time. By 1910 one-third of Rhode

Island's population was foreign-born; seven out of every ten residents of the state were of foreign birth or parentage. Rhode Island had the largest proportion of foreign-born of any state in the union from 1860 to 1910. Since many of the immigrants came from Catholic countries or largely Catholic areas, by 1905 Rhode Island was a predominantly Catholic state. Rhode Island is the only state in the United States where Roman Catholics have ever made up the majority of the population. The Roman Catholic Church is still the largest denomination in both the state and the city of Providence.

As the largest city in Rhode Island and the center of much of the manufacturing activity that attracted immigrants, Providence's population became dominated by a combination of ethnic groups that outnumbered the original Yankee settlers. As late as 1960, 44 percent of Providence's population were of foreign birth or parentage, with the largest number of Providence's residents of foreign stock coming from Italy, Ireland, and Canada, in that order. Providence in 1960 also had a large number of people of foreign birth or parentage whose origin was Russian and Portuguese. Portuguese immigration to Providence has increased recently with changes in U. S. immigration laws.

Providence Today. Providence today is a highly compact, highly industrialized, densely populated city in the center of a metropolitan area that includes the bulk of the state's population. Manufacturing is still the chief economic activity in the city, although Providence is also a retail trade center for half the state of Rhode Island, the hub of the second largest market area in New England, the capital of the state, and an important port for coastal and some foreign shipping. As much as one-third (34 percent) of the total work force in Providence was employed in some kind of manufacturing in 1960, with the bulk of the factory workers found in plants producing textiles, jewelry, silverware, machine tools, electrical machinery, and rubber and plastic products. Since manufacturing and the movement of goods are among the city's main economic enterprises, Providence is a predominantly blue-collar town. According to the 1960 Census, about three out of every five men in Providence (57 percent) are employed in blue-collar jobs as skilled and unskilled factory workers, as laborers, and in service jobs. Even though Rhode Island state government offices are located in Providence and Providence is the seat of government for Providence County, only one out of every three employed men (34 percent) in the city are in professional, technical, managerial, clerical, or sales jobs.

Providence is the largest city in Rhode Island and also the chief city in the Providence-Pawtucket-Warwick Standard Metropolitan Statistical Area, which accounts for 83 percent of the state's population. Although Providence has been losing population steadily since 1940, the city is still over twice the size of Warwick, the next largest city in the state. Providence's 1970 population was 179,213, accounting for 19 percent of Rhode Island's population.

Residential areas in the city of Providence rise on hills on three sides of the central business district and tend to be settled by concentrations of one or more ethnic groups. The East Side, site of Roger Williams' first settlement and home of many of the early Yankee merchant-shippers and industrialists, is still the center of "entrenched wealth" in Providence and stands apart from the city in several respects. What is left of the once dominant Yankee community is found on the East Side and it is here that the one political ward in the city that consistently votes Republican is located. The East Side is also the center for college and university "liberals," as there are several prestigious colleges, universities, and private schools on College Hill on the East Side, including Brown University, Pembroke College, the Rhode Island School of Design, and Moses Brown, an old and well-known private school for boys. Historically, the East Side has also been the center of Providence's small black population, and Portuguese residents of the city are concentrated in the southernmost part of the East Side, in a community called Fox Point. Federal Hill, immediately to the west of Providence's downtown business district, was once an Irish enclave, but is now an Italian stronghold, declining in population and vitality, but still an important segment of the Italian community. Italians have settled in large numbers to the west of Federal Hill and also along the city's northern boundary. Many Irish and French Canadians are also concentrated to the north of the downtown business area. The upper part of South Providence is now heavily black, while lower South Providence is predominantly white with some largely Irish sections. (See Figure 1.)

The tendency for ethnic groups to concentrate by neighborhood or section, developing their own social life, organizations, and patterns of survival still persists. There are alliances, loyalties, and bonds that cut across ethnic lines, such as those of church and political party, but the bonds are strained and sometimes broken in times of stress, and there is not yet what could

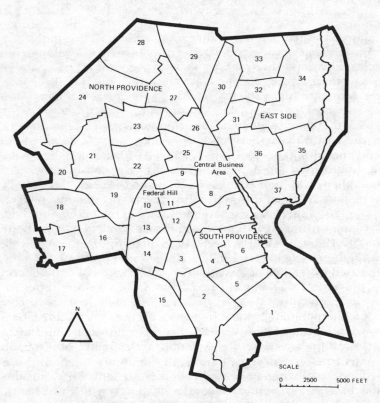

Figure 1. *Major areas of Providence, Rhode Island*

be called a cohesive white community. As a knowledgeable newspaper reporter commented recently during the third phase of Providence's school desegregation, Phase III revealed

. . . Providence as it is: a collection of ethnic groups eyeing each other warily, each with its prides and prejudices, cherishing their turfs and their traditions, feeling threatened at times by the thought of others stepping in, or of what will happen to them if they step elsewhere.[2]

Many upwardly mobile Yankees and ethnics have moved or are moving out of the city in large numbers to new developments and subdivisions surrounding Providence. Out-migration also has an ethnic flavor, with young better-off Italian families more likely to leave the city than their counterparts in the Irish population. The central fact about present-day Providence is, indeed, that the city has been losing population in large numbers for the past 30 years. Although Providence grew steadily and sometimes dramatically from 1790 to 1940, a major move to the suburbs that began after World War II and has continued since then has depleted a large proportion of the city's population. Between 1940 and 1970 there was a net loss of 74,291 people, 29 percent of the city's population. Providence's total population dropped from 253,504 in 1940 to 248,674 in 1950 and 207,498 in 1960. The greatest number of residents moved out of the city between 1950 and 1960, when the population decreased by 41,176 people. The movement out of Providence is a movement of whites. There were 79,032 fewer whites in the city population in 1970 than in 1950; 33 percent of the city's white population left Providence between 1950 and 1970. Providence's population decline is predicted to continue, with the total number of residents dropping to 165,000 by 1975.

As is true elsewhere in the country, whites who are leaving the city are moving to residential cities and townships on the suburban fringes. Suburban communities that ring Providence, such as North Providence, Warwick, Barrington, Johnson, and Smithfield, increased in size by as much as 41 percent between 1960 and 1970, while the total Standard Metropolitan Statistical Area (SMSA) in which Providence is located grew only 10 percent. This SMSA includes the central cities of Providence and Pawtucket, both old manufacturing cities, as well as their suburban fringes. The relatively small gain for the total Providence-Pawtucket SMSA in recent years, coupled with declining populations in Providence and Pawtucket, indicates that population change in the area is primarily a reshuffling of people, with many whites moving from the central cities to their suburbs and little new in-migration. With the depressed state of industry in Providence, Pawtucket, and other established manufacturing centers throughout the state, large numbers of newcomers are no longer attracted to this area. The relatively small net population gain experienced in the Providence-Pawtucket SMSA between recent Census periods in no way compares with the phenomenal growth in these industrial cities during the late 1800s and early 1900s. Between 1900 and 1910, for example, Providence alone increased by nearly 49,000 people.

Providence's politics, long dominated by the Democratic Party and the Irish, have been characterized as the "old style" urban machine politics "of wakes and push carts, conceived and born of power to the neglect of issues."[3] Ethnic identifications and loyalties play an important role in this kind of politics, with the Irish, who control the Democratic city committee, holding the top posts for themselves but nominating Italians, who represent a larger proportion of the city's population, for the less important offices. The Irish also share patronage with Italians and other ethnic groups in order to insure their support. It is only recently that blacks, whose numbers are comparatively small, have been able to gain any representation in these ethnic oriented politics. The first black city councilman was elected in 1969.

In addition to catering to ethnic interests of the voters, the "old style" politics in Providence gives the mayor a tremendous amount of power to influence the affairs of the city. This power, which was used to thwart and then to promote school desegregation, is part of the reality of political life in Providence. The support that Providence's mayor, Joseph A. Doorley, ultimately gave to school desegregation was said to be linked to his desire to stand shoulder to shoulder with the progressive big city Democratic mayors of the country and to his ties to the national Democratic administration.

Providence's Black Community.   While the white population has been leaving the city in large numbers since 1940, Providence's small black community is growing. Blacks in Providence numbered 15,875 in 1970 when the U. S. Census was taken—3,902 more than in 1960 and 7,194 more than in 1950.[4] Blacks made up 9 percent of the city's residents in 1970, compared with 3 percent in 1950 and 6 percent in 1960. The number of black people in Providence nearly doubled in the 20-year period between 1950 and 1970. According to a 1966 report of the Urban League of Rhode Island, "The Nonwhite in Providence," much of the growth in the state's black population is now the result of natural increase rather than migration. The bulk of Rhode Island's tiny black population lives in Providence, with nearly two out of every three black persons in the state residing in Providence in 1970.

Like the state of Rhode Island, the black population of Providence is quite small. It is also quite old, tracing its origins back to slavery days and the "triangular trade" discussed earlier. Slaves were first brought to Newport, Rhode Island in 1696 on a brig called the "Seaflower." As the "triangular trade" developed, Africans who were not sold when Rhode Island ships completed their stops at West Indian and southern slave markets were carried to home ports and sold within Rhode Island. Slavery flourished to the greatest extent in the southern part of Rhode Island, in Narragansett County and South Kingston, but also existed in other parts of the state. Slavery and slave trading in Rhode Island were abolished between 1774 and 1787 by a series of laws voted by the General Assembly.

While the city of Providence developed "an effective and viable antislavery tradition" in response to the slave trade, the 1,500 "free people of color" living in the city after slavery ended experienced hostility and discrimination from the general body of citizens.[5] Blacks lost their right to vote in 1822 and there were two anti-Negro riots in Providence in 1824 and 1831, with mobs razing segregated black settlements and taking the household possessions of blacks to sell at auction. The black community survived, however, developing many of its own separate associations and institutions.

Historically, Providence's black community was concentrated in the East Side, close to the old Yankee families and the wealthy merchant-shippers who profited by the slave trade. The black residential pattern changed drastically after 1950, however, as a result of broad-scale urban renewal projects that cut through heavily black areas on the East Side. Urban renewal displaced large numbers of both black and white families on the East Side in the 1950s and early 1960s and destroyed a great deal of housing formerly available to the black population. In 1950, 53 percent of the black people in the city of Providence lived on the East Side, with virtually all of this population concentrated in two census tracts, Census Tracts 31 and 37. (See Table 1.) Only 32 percent of the city's black residents were left in these East Side census tracts by 1960, and five years later only 26 percent. By 1965, the major locus of the black population had

Table 1—Changes in Black Population in East Side and South
Providence Census Tracts, 1950—1965

	1950		1960		1965	
Census Tract	No. of Blacks	% of Total	No. of Blacks	% of Total	No. of Blacks	% of Total
East Side						
31	2,930	38	2,645	56	2,215	63
32	12	—	156	4	915	22
37	1,459	20	1,043	18	706	15
TOTAL	4,401	22	3,844	26	3,836	31
South Providence						
4	407	5	850	13	1,508	26
5	298	4	926	13	1,994	36
6	231	4	515	14	1,120	37
7	289	2	1,204	15	1,917	35
TOTAL	1,225	3	3,495	14	6,539	33
Total City	8,681	3	11,973	6	14,809	8

Source: Urban League of Rhode Island, "The Non-White in Providence,"
Providence, Rhode Island, 1966; and U.S. Bureau of the Census, *U.S. Census of
Population: 1950*, Vol. III, Census Tract Statistics, Chapter 44 (Washington, D.C.:
Government Printing Office), 1952

shifted to South Providence, where 44 percent of the black people
of the city were concentrated in four census tracts, Census Tracts
4–7. Together the East Side and South Providence ghetto areas
now house at least seven out of every ten black people in
Providence. Blacks have also settled in smaller numbers just to
the west of the South Providence ghetto in Census Tracts 12
and 14 and in a pocket in North Providence in Census Tract
27.

Racial residential segregation in Providence has intensified
in the past 20 years, with the exodus of whites contributing
to the higher proportion of blacks now found in certain areas
of the city. Although over half of the black people of Providence
lived on the East Side in 1950, for example, the only census
tract there or in any part of the city with a population more
than one-fifth black was Census Tract 31, where 38 percent
of the residents were black. Between 1950 and 1965, the white
population of Census Tract 31 diminished by 3,522 people and

the black population, by 715 persons. As a result, in 1965 Census Tract 31 was 63 percent black. In South Providence, Census Tracts 4–7, the four census tracts where most black people now live, were 2, 4, and 5 percent black in 1950. By 1965 these census tracts were from 26 to 37 percent black. Although 5,314 blacks moved into these four South Providence census tracts between 1950 and 1965, 21,380 whites moved out. There were seven census tracts in the city of Providence with more than a 20-percent black population in 1965, in contrast to one census tract in 1950.

The total impact of urban renewal on the black community in Providence has been no less than massive. The 1960 Census found that only two out of five people in the black population five years of age or older were living in the same house in 1960 and in 1955. The Census also reported that 46 percent of the city's blacks had moved during this period within the county—which means the city, since the black population of Providence County is concentrated in the city. Urban renewal projects completed or proposed by the early 1960s were expected to eventually displace four out of every five black residents in Providence.

White Over Black in Providence. Commenting on the overall situation of blacks in the city of Providence in the early 1960s, Dr. Harold W. Pfautz of Brown University stated:

> ... Providence Negroes clearly continue to be economically depressed and the object of considerable discrimination and prejudice. In part this is due to the small size and proportion of the Negro population in comparison to the dominant white group, a fact which inevitably minimizes the former as a political threat. Another factor is the generally depressed economic situation of the city and state which, in the nature of the case, bears hardest on the minority members of the community.[6]

The 1960 Census documented major gaps between whites and blacks in the areas of job opportunities, income, and housing, and there were no signs that this situation was changing through the decade of the 1960s and into the 1970s. According to the 1960 Census, only about one out of ten black men were working in professional and managerial jobs in Providence in 1960, compared with about two out of every ten employed men in the general population. Blacks also worked less frequently in jobs in manufacturing plants, which pay the next highest wages to skilled and semi-skilled workmen. While about one-third (34

percent) of the total work force in Providence was employed
in manufacturing jobs in 1960, only 21 percent of all black workers were found in these jobs in 1960. Nearly half (45 percent)
of all women working in 1960 were in clerical, professional,
technical, and other white collar jobs, but 64 percent of the
black women in Providence worked in blue collar jobs, with the
largest number doing private household work. Two out of every
three black men also worked in blue collar jobs, with only 11
percent in skilled industrial jobs, compared with 19 percent in
the total work force. Such job discrepancies existed in spite of
the fact that the educational level of adult whites and blacks
in the city is about the same—both groups had attained between
nine and ten years of school in 1960. The median income for
black families in Providence was only $3,524 per year in 1959,
compared to $5,059 for white families. As many as two-fifths
of Providence's black families were at officially defined poverty
levels when the 1960 Census was taken, having annual incomes
of less than $3,000. Just a little over half (55 percent) of the
housing that blacks in Providence occupied in 1960 was sound;
about one-fourth was deteriorating and another one-fifth was
classified as dilapidated. Only about 2 percent of the houses
in which whites lived were dilapidated, however, and in the city
as a whole, 83 percent of the occupied housing was sound.

Since the 1960 Census, a 1966 Urban League of Rhode Island
report, "The Non-White in Providence," found that blacks in
the city are "poor," "employed mostly in the lowest paying positions and in positions requiring the least skills," and unemployed
at a rate "more than twice that of whites." The Urban League
also stated in this study that the housing in which blacks in
Providence live "is much poorer than that of whites."

A newspaper report describing a newly formed union of unemployed workers, which began recruiting members and demanding increased benefits for jobless workers in the early fall of
1971, pointed out that minority employment in inner-city areas
like South Providence's Model Cities area "probably reaches
depression levels."[7] The reporter felt that the activities of the
Unemployed Workers Union in inner-city areas, which included
demonstrations, were justified on the basis of the unemployment
rate alone. Investigation and hearings carried out by the Providence Branch of the National Association for the Advancement
of Colored People (NAACP) and the Rhode Island Advisory
Committee to the U.S. Commission on Civil Rights in 1970 and
1971 showed that almost no blacks—less than 1 percent—were
employed in skilled jobs in the construction industry, even where

these jobs were covered by federal, state, and municipal non-discrimination laws or executive orders.

Although the economic status of blacks in Providence in the early and mid-1960s was closer to that in major southern cities than in comparable northern communities, the city had not experienced massive civil rights demands and demonstrations. The drive for school desegregation, which became an overriding community issue in 1966 and 1967, was the first major move to expand opportunities for blacks that involved picketing, boycotts, and sit-ins on the part of the black community.

2.
Providence Public Schools

General Background. The Providence school district serves the city of Providence only, and for the last few years has enrolled between about 25,000 and 27,000 children, approximately two-thirds of the school age children in the city. The rest of Providence's public school age children, about 13,000 in number, are enrolled in private schools, mainly Roman Catholic parochial and diocesan schools. Providence is not only a predominantly Roman Catholic city, but on a statewide basis an unusually high proportion of the Catholic population—77 percent—attends Catholic schools. During the 1967–68 school year, when field work for this study was conducted, Providence public school children were taught in 51 different schools—39 elementary schools, 2 middle schools, 6 junior high schools, and 4 senior high schools. (See Figure 2.) The public schools are governed by the Providence school committee, a body of seven men and women now appointed by the mayor.

Enrollment Trends. Enrollment in the Providence schools has fluctuated over the past few years, growing from 25,908 in 1965–66 to roughly 27,000 in the 1969–70 school year, then dropping back to 25,116 in the fall of 1970. A 1965 study of enrollment trends carried out by the Providence City Plan Commission showed that the pupil population in the public schools peaked at a little over 28,000 during the late 1950s and early 1960s and that a downward trend began in 1964. This study

Figure 2. *Providence Public Schools, 1967*

projected a slight but steady decline in enrollment through 1980. The reasons for the current ups and downs in enrollment are not clear, but there is some hope that the public school population has at least temporarily stabilized.

While the trend in overall enrollment is one of general decline, the number and percentage of blacks in the Providence public schools is growing slowly. Although blacks make up only 9 percent of the total city population, black children now constitute about one-fifth of the Providence school population. In the fall of 1970, there were 5,002 black children in the Providence public schools out of a total enrollment of 25,116. Black enrollment was then 20 percent of the total. The number of black children in the Providence schools was 4,159 in the 1965–66 school year. Blacks made up 16 percent of the total school enrollment at that time. White enrollment on the other hand is falling off slowly as the city loses white population. Between 1965–66 and 1970–71 white enrollment dropped from 21,749 to 19,779.

Blacks are the only sizable racial or ethnic group in the school system officially considered a minority group. An October 1970 report from the Providence school department to the Department of Health, Education and Welfare showed that there were only 222 Spanish-surnamed pupils in the Providence public schools; 111 Orientals; and no American Indians. Dark-skinned Portuguese in the city who have immigrated from the Cape Verde Islands have presented an identity dilemma and have sometimes been white, sometimes black, in official records. While the school system is beginning to sponsor language programs for new Portuguese immigrants who do not speak English, the dark Cape Verdeans, with negroid as well as Portuguese ancestry, were not officially considered as members of a minority group by the school system when desegregation took place. Under new state guidelines on equal educational opportunities adopted in June 1970, children whose primary language is other than English are considered minority students.

Transition to Middle School Grade Organization Plan. The Providence public schools are now in the process of shifting from a grade organizational plan that more or less approximated a K–6–3–3 pattern to a "middle school" plan, with a K–4–4–4 grade breakdown. Because of partial changes to middle schools and inconsistencies in the number of grades in elementary schools under the old system, the present grade organization defies classification. Most of the changes to date have taken place in the junior high schools, where the school department is slowly converting the grade structure of existing junior high schools from a 7–9 to a 5–8 pattern. The shift to middle schools began on an experimental basis in January 1967 and by the 1970–71 school year, at least five former junior high schools were officially designated as middle schools. Three other schools at the junior high school level had partially converted to a middle school plan by 1970, having added the fifth, or fifth and sixth, grades to their curriculum. All senior high schools in the city now include four grades, although enrollment in the ninth grade in some schools is limited. Prior to 1967 there was only one four-year senior high school in the city, Classical High School, which operates on a citywide basis as a specialized academic school for college-bound Providence students.

Although the middle-school plan will eventually affect the grade structure of elementary schools in the city, as well as that of high schools and junior high schools, there had been no effort to begin implementing the middle school plan at the elementary level when this study was completed. Elementary schools in the city vary widely in size and grade structure, with some teaching grades K–6 or PK–6 and others enrolling pupils in grades K–2, K–3, K–4, or K–5. There was one elementary unit in the system in 1968–69 that offered a kindergarten program only and one that offered grades 1–2 only. A few elementary schools teach grades 2–5, 2–6 and 3–6. The general hodge-podge in grade organization at the elementary level stems from a long-standing tradition within the Providence school system of maintaining small, inefficient, even antiquated neighborhood schools so that, as one authority expressed it, "a relatively small number of pupils can walk a shorter distance to poor schools."[8] No target date for converting the elementary schools to a K–4 plan was set. Considering the strong tradition and the political support for neighborhood schools in the city and the long history of a proliferation of neighborhood schools, the change to the K-4 plan at the elementary level will require a tremendous amount of leadership and a tough political struggle.

"Decades of Indifference . . . and Powerful Opposition." Dr. Myron Lieberman, formerly a professor of education and director of education research and development at Rhode Island College, characterized the city schools of Providence in 1969 as suffering from "decades of indifference at best and powerful opposition at worst."[9] A long-time critic of the Providence public schools, Dr. Lieberman described the Providence school system in 1966 as the "worst in the North."[10] Most of the major problems Dr. Lieberman outlined in his 1969 critique of the school system were documented earlier in other studies of the school system and have been discussed widely in the press over the past few years.

The "antiquated physical plant," which Dr. Lieberman cites as the "most obvious deficiency of the Providence school system," was surveyed in 1967 by a team of registered architects on the faculty of the Rhode Island School of Design (RISD). Their study, part of an overall evaluation of the school system carried out cooperatively by several area colleges and universities, recommended the immediate closing of 18 elementary schools and one junior high school considered obsolete and completely unsuitable for continued use. Project COPE—"Cooperative Planning for Excellence"—as the total study was known, was an attempt on the part of then Superintendent Charles A. O'Connor to pinpoint the overriding problems of the Providence schools and lay a foundation for long-needed improvements. A key study in Project COPE, the RISD survey of the physical plant, showed that 30 of the 39 elementary schools then in use were at least 50 years old; one was 120 years old and only six of the 39 had been built since 1950. Inadequacies in elementary school facilities outlined by the RISD team included small and poorly ventilated classrooms; insufficient lighting; lack of facilities for health and guidance services, assemblies, and hot lunches; and an absence of equipment and facilities for modern teaching methods in science, art, language, music, drama, and physical education. The older schools tended to be small in size, Victorian in design, and located on tiny paved lots without adequate play space. Individual schools were described as "unattractive," "gloomy and intimidating," and "altogether forbidding." One school built in 1898 was still in service and still using the original furniture, which was bolted to the floor. Toilet facilities in several schools were described as "thoroughly unsanitary." Abandonment of at least two of these schools had been recommended in a series of surveys dating back to 1923.[11]

The RISD report found that junior and senior high schools, with the exception of Classical High School, were newer, better equipped, and more substantial in structure than the elementary schools. Most of these schools had been poorly maintained, however, and lacked new furnishings and equipment. Most needed up-to-date lighting, new public address and intercommunication systems, and facilities for individual student experimentation in science and the visual arts. Libraries in the junior high schools were below minimum Rhode Island standards. The RISD report recommended modernization of six existing junior high schools and two senior high schools. Plans for replacing the original 1897 Classical High School building were already underway when the study was made. Major renovation and expansion of another high school, Central High School, was also in progress at the time the RISD study took place.

The RISD study recommended renovation of eight junior high and high school plants and also proposed a long-range building program that included seven new K-4 schools and five additions to existing elementary schools. These new facilities, the study stated, would permit the closing of nine elementary schools in addition to the 18 mentioned earlier, plus one additional junior high school. All recommendations were based on the assumption that the school system would convert to a "middle school," or K–4–4–4 plan, as recommended in a companion COPE report on grade reorganization. The RISD team found that pupils in the 18 elementary schools recommended for immediate closing could be accommodated in existing facilities without any new construction if the district went ahead with a K–4–4–4 plan of grade organization that permitted fuller use of existing junior high schools.

Although the school committee largely ignored the RISD study and its recommendations, three elementary schools in the worst physical condition of any in the system were abandoned between 1967 and 1969. One was already scheduled to be replaced when the RISD report was written. The rest of the schools cited for immediate closing are still in use and many are still in need of major repairs and renovations. In June 1969 school officials stated that $10 million was needed to bring all buildings in use "up to par." They said that at least half this amount—a little over $5 million—was needed in the next fiscal year for repair work that was "dire." The initial 1969–70 proposed budget contained $1.8 million earmarked for immediate repair work.[12]

Another major, pressing problem in the Providence school system is weak administrative leadership. At the heart of the leadership problem, according to Dr. Lieberman and others, is a promotional policy that virtually insures appointment of administrators from within the system. Although there has been some reform in recent years to help remove principals' appointments, particularly, from political influence, the current promotional system is "designed more to provide jobs for the faithful than to encourage the employment of the most able."[13] The problem of weak administrative leadership and "inbreeding" among principals was detailed in another COPE report, a *Survey of Curriculum and Instruction in the Providence Public Schools,* carried out by the faculty of Rhode Island College. Although the Rhode Island College study was mainly concerned with course content and teaching methods in the various subject areas taught throughout the system, this report also evaluated the administration of Providence's elementary and secondary schools. The Rhode Island College team found a "pressing need for dynamic central leadership" for planning, developing a modern curriculum, and improving both administration and teaching in the elementary schools. Principals in the elementary schools, the report concluded, were not sufficiently strong, nor were work loads small enough to enable principals to properly supervise curriculum and instructional activities within their schools.[14] At the secondary level, one of the main findings was that "very little leadership in innovation is taking place." Sameness of background among principals at the secondary level seemed to account for the fact that the spark of new ideas and practices seems to be missing. At both the elementary and secondary level, the COPE report found that homogeneity of principals' backgrounds "is carried to an extreme," with virtually all principals gaining their teaching experience in the city of Providence, nearly all being educated in local colleges or in a limited number of nearby New England colleges, and almost all acquiring their administrative experience within the Providence public schools.

Other factors contributing to weak administrative leadership include frequent and prolonged vacancies in key central administrative positions and a high turnover of superintendents and acting superintendents in the past eight years. After having the same superintendent of schools for 27 years, from 1936 to 1963, Providence has had three superintendents and three acting superintendents in the past eight years. Charles A. O'Connor, superintendent at the time that pressure for school desegregation mounted, stayed through the initial year of elementary desegregation, but resigned suddenly and unexpectedly at the end of the first year of desegregation to take an administrative position with the U. S. Office of Education. There were two acting superintendents in the year following his resignation. A new permanent superintendent was appointed in the late summer of 1969, but he stayed in the post only a little over a year, to be replaced by another superintendent in March 1971.

The Rhode Island College COPE report cited above concentrated most of its attention on curriculum and teaching methods, assessing both the content of courses and the instructional practices in individual subjects at all grade levels throughout the system. Two overall conclusions reached by this study were that "there is little evidence that much change has been taking place in the Providence public schools" and that "even outstanding teachers are severely hampered by outmoded curricula, inadequate facilities, and a serious lack of materials necessary for teaching and learning." Consultants surveying the elementary curricula gave consistent reports that "curriculum guides are inadequate, outdated and often not being utilized." They found no new curriculum guides in the process of development at that time. Evaluation of curriculum and instruction in specific subject areas at the secondary level indicated that much teaching is traditional and confined to a textbook approach and that shortages of textbooks, supplementary reading materials, supplies, and laboratory equipment handicap teachers in a variety of courses. The social studies curriculum was described as "ethnocentric," top-heavy with American history, "without any clear-cut aims or goals," and "pre-1920" in orientation. By 1967 there had been virtually no overall reform in updating the social studies curriculum, despite the fact that the school system was in the third year of a federally financed project designed to prepare up-to-date teaching guides, develop new course materials, and train teachers in the social studies field. Some individual courses other than the social studies courses were described as "archaic" and "worse than useless."[15] There has since been progress in implementing a new social studies curriculum, which will be discussed later in the report.

School Funding and Fiscal Crises. In addition to the almost overwhelming problems of an antiquated physical plant, weak top administrative leadership, and outdated curricula, the Providence public schools also suffered over a period of many years from inadequate budgets, lack of fiscal coordination and control, and a funding structure that forced the schools to depend heavily on the mayor and the City Council for fiscal support.

Prior to a referendum vote held on August 20, 1968, the Providence schools were governed by an elected school committee that operated the schools with funds provided through a tax formula established by state law. The Strayer Act, which regulated both the election of the school board and financing of the public schools, provided for a nonpartisan school committee election and annual revenues based on a maximum of 1.1 percent of the city's total taxable valuations on real estate and tangible property. The intent of the Strayer Act was to remove the public schools from city politics by providing for independent funding. Beginning about 1957, however, monies available under the Strayer Act did not keep pace with actual expenses for the Providence city schools. From 1957 through the late 1960s, the school committee annually overspent Strayer Act funds, ending each year with a sizable deficit that grew progressively larger. To make up these deficits, the school committee went to the City Council periodically for supplementary finances. In the fall of 1967, for instance, it was expected that Strayer Act funds would meet only half the operating budget projected for the school year. The gap between state aid, federal aid, and Strayer Act revenues had to be obtained through special appropriations from the City Council. These special appropriations from the City Council defeated the purpose of the Strayer Act, which was to provide independent funding for the schools. In 1968, when changes in the Strayer Act were proposed and debated, the public schools of Providence were roughly $2.9 million in debt.

The actual expenses of the school department and the exact state of the running deficit were unknown at almost any given point in time because of the unbelievable state of fiscal records and the inadequate procedures for keeping track of public school expenditures. Peat, Marwick and Mitchell, an outside auditing firm brought in in 1968 to determine the exact amount of the deficit, found that they could not begin to calculate the total deficit until accounts dating back five to six years were audited. The final Peat, Marwick and Mitchell report to the school committee, dated February 12, 1969, cited "excessive duplication in processing financial transactions" between the school department and the city's finance department, "overlapping functions between the city and school maintenance departments," "inadequate procedures for processing school department purchase orders and vendor invoices," and "a serious lack of accounting records and proper procedures for maintaining control over school department expenditures." Some actual line item expenditures for the 1967–68 school year exceeded budgeted allocations by over $200,000. Actual expenses for "Transportation," for instance, exceeded the amount budgeted by $223,134. An interim report prepared on August 15, 1968, by Peat, Marwick and Mitchell stated:

> We are convinced that there is no single person within the school department at present who is attempting to exercise any degree of budgetary controls over the department's many operating units.[16]

In the face of a growing annual deficit, lack of control over school expenditures, and a new teachers' contract that raised the cost of teachers salaries by about $1.8 million for the 1967–68 school year, Mayor Joseph A. Doorley initiated a successful campaign in the state legislature in the spring of 1968 to amend the Strayer Act. Mayor Doorley sought changes in the Strayer Act that would permit complete reorganization of the school committee and a new method of financing the schools. Following enabling legislation at the state level, a referendum vote in Providence on August 20, 1968, approved a change to a school committee appointed by the mayor, with City Council confirmation. The proposal for an appointed school committee was tied to specific provisions for funding the schools through an annual operating budget appropriated by the City Council following approval by the city finance director and recommendation by the mayor. Under the new fiscal procedures, the school committee cannot spend in excess of funds appropriated and the City Council has the authority to allocate the distribution of funds within the school department, as well as to fix the total amount of the school budget. Details of the change in the organization and makeup of the school committee will be discussed later in the report.

There was still an air of mystery surrounding school finances when this study was made, but data from Peat, Marwick and Mitchell's final report and from other sources indicate that 61 percent of the school department's total operating expenditures for the 1968–69 school year, including federal programs, was derived from city revenues; 19 percent from state sources; and 14 percent from the federal government.[17] The school department received $3.7 million in federal aid in 1968–69 and $4.8 million in funds from state sources. Actual expenditures for the 1968–69 school year, exclusive of federal programs, totaled $21.9 million. With federally funded projects added, all 1968–69 school expenditures totaled $25.6 million. The mayor and the City Council have kept the school budget at about the same level since the reorganization of the school committee. The 1970–71 budget was a little over $26 million and the Providence schools received about $4.5 million in federal funds in the 1970–71 school year.

Factors Underlying the State of Providence Schools. Most of the blame for the sorry state of the Providence public schools in the mid-1960s has been put on the old school committee, a seven-man body elected on a nonpartisan ward basis. The old school committee, which was in office at the time that the desegregation of the elementary schools began, was notorious for its susceptibility to vocal neighborhood pressure, the ethnic-based interests of individual members, and a general lack of concern with public education in the city. A *Providence Journal* editorial of September 27, 1967, commented on the old school committee as follows:

> Supposed to be politically nonpartisan it has been the target of not-very-secret interference on occasion by political ward committees; supposed to run the schools, it has fumbled the task at a time when changes have been sweeping the world of education; intended to be representative of the people, it has been narrowly parochial in outlook.

Most of the faults of the school committee were personified in the chairman. The old school committee's last chairman, Raymond F. Fricker, a white man whose ward included the South Providence black ghetto, was absent from school committee meetings for nine consecutive months while the battle to desegregate the elementary schools was being waged. During his 15 years on the school committee, Chairman Fricker consistently opposed tenure for married women teachers, the closing of surplus schools, and annual promotions. Following the dissolution of the old school committee in 1968, Fricker was elected by the voters of South Providence to represent them in the General Assembly of Rhode Island. As of May 9, 1969, he had no recorded vote in the Assembly for his entire first term of office.

Use of school jobs and job prerogatives accompanying public school positions for purposes of patronage was a common complaint against the old school committee. When campaigning to change the selection and funding of the school committee in 1968, Mayor Doorley attacked the committee for excessive expenses for janitorial services. According to Mayor Doorley, the Providence school custodial force was about three times the average size for the nation and involved exorbitant amounts of overtime pay. Interviews for this study indicated that for many years both janitorial and principals' appointments were rooted in ethnic politics. A college faculty member who served as an informal consultant to a previous superintendent said that this superintendent told him that he spent more time one year trying to get a janitor of the "wrong ethnic group" appointed to a particular school than he spent working on the budget. A school administrator described the past system of appointing principals, which prevailed prior to a merit promotion plan adopted in the early 1960s, as a political, ethnic version of Russian roulette. He said that school committeemen were elected on an ethnic basis in the wards and when a principal's vacancy came up, the committeemen would go around the table, each taking his "turn" at filling open positions. When an Italian committeeman's turn came up, he would chose an Italian principal and when an Irish committeeman got his turn, he would pick an Irishman. There was not a Jewish principal in the system until about 1960. Blacks were pretty much out of these ethnic politics as they were not sufficiently strong in any political ward to elect or control a committeeman. There was not a black principal in the system prior to desegregation, and the school committee was all white at the time school desegregation became an issue. The roll call of members in the fall of 1966, as desegregation was being debated, suggests the ethnic makeup of the old school committee: Casey, DiMeo, Fricker, Gizzarelli, Kelly, Mulvey, and Robin.

The most frequently criticized abuse of the old school committee, however, was their failure to close obsolete schools. The overabundance of small, inefficient, and educationally unsound elementary schools discussed earlier is a direct result of committeemen yielding to short-sighted, neighborhood pressure to keep nearby schools open. The old school committee's legacy of decaying school plants will plague the Providence school system for many years to come.

Another background factor that cannot be ignored is the degree to which the mayor of Providence influences the schools. Dr. Lieberman maintains that the mayor "has more influence over school operations than any other individual" in Providence and that "decades of mismanagement of municipal affairs by Democratic mayors and city councils" is one of the reasons the Providence public schools "are in [a] deplorable condition." The mayor's role in school desegregation, which will be discussed fully in the body of the report, illustrates the degree to which that office influenced the conduct of the schools, even under the old "nonpartisan" school committee. With an appointed school committee, the mayor's role is somewhat more obvious, but still "blurred" by the existence of a school committee. Dr. Lieberman and others have suggested that the school committee be completely abolished and all responsibility for running the schools be placed directly in the hands of the mayor, so that he is "clearly accountable for school operations" and citizens will not get "lost in the shuffle between the mayor and the school committee."[18]

A final factor in the generally poor condition of Providence's public schools is the unusually large enrollment in private schools. There is fairly general agreement among community leaders and students of the public school problem that the number of children attending Roman Catholic schools contributes heavily to citizen apathy toward the public schools. Dr. Lieberman feels that "the fact that so many Jews have abandoned the public schools" is also a factor in the low level of community involvement in the Providence schools.[19] The high enrollment in Roman Catholic schools coupled with the fact that Providence's political leadership is concentrated among persons of traditional Catholic Irish and Italian backgrounds is critical, however.

While the lack of interest and support for public schools among large numbers of Catholics is an old problem, recent public financial aid to Catholic education, first under state and then under municipal auspices, raises a new question of Catholic schools draining off the already limited funds set aside for public schools. Catholic schools in Providence and throughout the state are currently in a state of crisis that has certain similarities to the Providence public school situation. Catholic schools are having difficulties meeting current expenses with available operating funds, and the Catholic school system is saddled with small and inefficient school plants located in areas where population shifts have reduced enrollments. A 1969 state law providing for subsidizing the salaries of secular teachers in nonpublic schools was ruled unconstitutional by the United States Supreme Court, only to be followed by local plans in Providence and throughout the state for the hiring of lay teachers of secular subjects in parochial schools. Serious students of the city's and state's education problems have suggested "some form of support for Catholic schools in exchange for Catholic support of measures to improve the public schools" as a possible solution to the many problems facing both systems.[20] What seems to be happening in Providence, where there is strong grass roots and political opposition to raising taxes, is that the already underfinanced existing public school budget will be tapped for stop-gap funds to check the decline of particular parochial schools. A taxpayer's suit challenging the constitutionality of Providence's new "semi-public" school aid program was filed in September 1971 just before the opening of school and before funds budgeted for aid to parochial schools were released.

3.
Black Education in Providence

Early State Anti-Segregation Law. The city of Providence established separate schools for blacks and whites in 1838, when the first public schools were voted. Officially segregated schools were abandoned after 1866, upon passage of a state law forbidding this practice. The General Assembly adopted this early antisegregation law in the field of education under pressure from black citizens led by an abolitonist named George Downing, whose children were refused admission to the Newport, Rhode Island schools. Downing, who operated businesses in both Providence and Newport, maintained that the establishment of segregated schools "wars against the principles of the state." After several unsuccessful attempts to get the General Assembly to end separate schools, the state legislature voted in 1866 that:

> In deciding upon the application for admission to any school in this state, maintained wholly or in part at the public expense, no distinction shall be made on account of the race or color of the applicant.[21]

Recent Segregation in Providence Schools. Although Providence has not maintained officially segregated schools in recent years, there were six elementary schools in the city with black populations of 50 percent or more in the early 1960s. A racial count of elementary schools conducted by the school department in November 1963 showed that two East Side schools, Doyle and Jenkins, were 90 percent or more black and that three South Providence schools, Beacon, Flynn, and Fogarty, were between 50 and 63 percent black. Hammond Elementary School, in the West End near the central downtown business area, was also over half black (52 percent) in 1963. At that time blacks made up 17 percent of the total elementary enrollment in the Providence public schools. Black enrollment in five of the city's 42 elementary schools was between 17 and 49 percent of their totals. Thirteen schools enrolled no blacks at all in 1963 or had a total black enrollment of less than 1 percent. In another 18 schools the black population was between 1 and 16 percent. (See Table 2.)

The concentration of black pupils in south and central Providence elementary schools in the early 1960s was not as extreme as on the East Side but was growing rapidly. In the two largest

Table 2—Providence Elementary Schools with High Black Enrollments
1963—1967

| | Black Enrollment | | | | | |
| | November 1963 | | March 1965 | | April 1967 | |
School	No.	%	No.	%	No.	%
Beacon	129	54	138	73	77	67
Doyle	254	98	189	94	160	97
Flynn	545	63	570	69	686	82
Fogarty	377	50	411	56	575	66
Hammond	69	52	87	61	69	57
Jenkins	161	90	243	93	142	95
Temple	176	37	212	47	169	58
Vineyard	158	39	158	41	115	37
TOTAL	2,679	17	2,954	19	2,437	21

Source: Providence Evening Bulletin, June 29, 1966, p. 39, and March 25, 1968; Department of Public Schools, "Integration Plan, Citywide, 1967," Providence, Rhode Island.

South Providence schools, Flynn and Fogarty, black enrollment and the percentage of black pupils increased markedly between 1963 and 1967. In Flynn, which had the largest black enrollment of any school in Providence in the early 1960s, the number of black pupils grew from 545 in 1963 to 686 in April 1967. In percentages, black enrollment increased from 63 to 82 in this four-year period. Fogarty, with the second largest black enrollment in the city, had 377 black pupils in November 1963 and 575 in April 1967. Fogarty's black enrollment increased from 50 to 66 percent between the two racial counts. The percentage of black children in Beacon, Hammond, Temple, and Vineyard schools also grew during the early and mid-1960s. Temple, for example, was 37 percent black in 1963 and 58 percent black in 1967.

Although black students were concentrated in several junior high schools above their proportion in the total population, there were no majority black junior high schools in the mid-1960s. Black students were enrolled in the largest numbers in Roger Williams Junior High School in South Providence, where they made up 41 percent of the population in June 1966. Although black students constituted only 16 percent of the junior high enrollment on a citywide basis at this time, they made up 24 percent of the student body in Nathan Bishop Junior High School on the East Side and 22 percent of the enrollment at Gilbert Stuart Junior High School, which also serves South Providence neighborhoods.

Black students were unevenly distributed at the high school level in the mid-1960s, but did not make up more than 17 percent of the student body of any single senior high school. In June 1966, the largest number of black high school students were enrolled in Hope High School on the East Side, where they made up 15 percent of the student population, and in Central High School in downtown Providence, where they constituted 17 percent of the total enrollment. By contrast, the other two senior high schools in the city, Classical and Mt. Pleasant, enrolled only a handful of black students at this time. Eleven black students were attending the citywide Classical High School in 1966 and 15 were enrolled in Mt. Pleasant, which serves the western part of the city. Blacks made up 1 percent of the total enrollment of both Classical and Mt. Pleasant in 1966. Differences in the racial population of the senior high schools were and are augmented by social class distinctions. Classical and Central High Schools, less than a block apart, with entirely separate facilities, also have completely different student populations, "socially, culturally and educationally," as well as racially.[22] Both schools serve a citywide enrollment, but Classical's student body is made up of elite, college-bound pupils, while Central, with a vocational emphasis, attracts lower-income, less socially prominent white and black students. Classical High School also recruits white students from the surrounding suburban areas on a tuition basis. Community leaders criticized the school department for building entirely new separate facilities for these two schools in the late 1960s, and for maintaining a rigid, outmoded curriculum at Classical that contributed to its failure to attract black students.

The high dropout rate among black students at the secondary level and the small number of college-bound black youth is a matter of concern to community leaders and to some extent explains the comparatively lower concentrations of blacks in the senior high schools, compared to the elementary and junior high schools. In June 1966, there were 2,954 black children enrolled in all elementary schools, 790 in all junior high schools, and only 415 in the four senior high schools. Only 76 black students graduated from all Providence high schools in 1965, and there were more black African than black Rhode Island students enrolled at the University of Rhode Island in the early 1960s. Black enrollment in the junior and senior high school grades is now higher, but this is partly a function of the change to the middle schools, which has added the upper elementary pupils to the old junior high schools and the upper junior high school grades to the senior high schools. There were only 119 black twelfth graders enrolled in the Providence public schools in February 1969.

Reasons for School Segregation. The trend toward a greater concentration of blacks in a few East Side and South Providence elementary and junior high schools in the mid-1960s was related to several factors. Neighborhoods surrounding some of the schools were losing white population and gaining black residents, but the "permit" system in practice in the mid-1960s also allowed whites who did not want to attend racially mixed or predominantly black schools to transfer to other attendance areas. Under the "permit" policy, any parent, theoretically, could transfer a child to any public school in the city as long as there was space in the school. With underenrollment in many elementary schools, there was room for a good many transfers between schools. Whites often moved their children to another school when the enrollment of blacks grew to substantial proportions. With whites leaving, the percentage of blacks increased even where the numbers did not grow sharply. Beacon School, for example, added only nine black children between 1963 and 1965, but the percentage of blacks in the school grew from 54 to 73 percent. Berkshire Elementary, a small school north of the downtown business section, lost five black children between racial counts in 1963 and 1965, but the percentage of blacks in the school rose from 27 to 31 percent. In 1966, George J. O'Brien, assistant superintendent for elementary schools stated:

> Once the trend [to nonwhite enrollment] begins, then it's a continuing trend. . . . Once it starts to move, it accelerates. The pattern seems to be the same—the nonwhites move in, the whites move out.[23]

Some school department officials apparently encouraged this trend prior to the build-up of community pressure to desegregate the schools. An East Side mother active in several civic organizations concerned with school problems said that some years ago, when the Benefit Elementary School became predominantly black, school department officials approached white parents stating: "I assume you want a permit for Howland." John Howland was at that time an overwhelmingly white school on the East Side. The Benefit Street School is no longer in existence.

Black children could "permit out" also, but did not leave predominantly black schools in sufficient numbers to accomplish massive desegregation. A special study of the Doyle and Jenkins attendance areas conducted by Dr. Sarah T. Curwood in 1963 showed that nearly twice as many black as white public school children in these two East Side school zones were attending schools in other neighborhoods on permits. Children in the Doyle-Jenkins area out on permits usually attended Summit and Howland, two predominantly white elementary schools adjacent to their home zone. Dr. Curwood interviewed a sample of mothers and found that 54 percent of the black and white mothers of children then attending Doyle and Jenkins did not want to keep their children in these schools, but could not send them elsewhere. Lack of transportation and school department refusals to give them permits to other schools were the two reasons these mothers gave most frequently for keeping their children in Doyle and Jenkins. A child "permitting out" had to furnish his own transportation.

Black parents have also complained that the principal of Summit, a predominantly white K–6 school north of Doyle and Jenkins, practiced discrimination in the granting of permits prior to school desegregation. Black children from Doyle and Jenkins did transfer to Summit on permits, but their parents sometimes had to go to the central administration to arrange the transfer after being refused by the principal. One black parent who obtained a permit through the central office was then asked by the principal if she would not be more "comfortable" if she took her child to the predominantly black Jenkins School. When this mother had previously placed her older children in Summit on permits the principal told her she was doing her a "favor" to admit them. The mother asked the principal what she meant by "doing her a favor" and the principal replied: "This belongs to me. This is my school." Black parents with children enrolled in Summit on permits in the mid-1960s said that the principal frequently threatened to send the children back to Jenkins if they were late to school or misbehaved. There was an unwritten school department policy that children who attended schools out of their zone could be sent back to their own attendance area if they became disciplinary problems.

School attendance boundaries were also a factor contributing to school segregation, particularly on the East Side. An older black woman who had been involved in community/school issues over a long period of time said that the school department "gerrymandered" attendance lines over a period of years to "confine" Negroes in certain schools. The *Providence Sunday Journal* shared this view. An editorial of July 3, 1966 stated:

> Not only housing patterns, but school department policy is responsible for racial imbalance in Providence schools. The Doyle Avenue and Jenkins Street school district lines, for example, insure segregated schools. A totally free transfer system reinforces this situation.

In addition to some elementary attendance boundaries that were deliberately racially drawn, elementary zones were generally rigidly fixed, with no changes being made unless a new school was added. There was a great deal of resistance to the idea of changing them for any purpose. In the early stages of the desegregation debate in 1966, school committee chairman Raymond L. Fricker stated that attendance lines for neighborhood schools in Providence "have existed for 100 years with only minor revisions" and he would "resist any attempt to change these lines."[24] A school department spokesman stated about the same time that attendance area lines had been moved or changed when new schools were built, but there were no specific references in board records to changes in attendance lines for at least 50 years.

School planning and enlargement was a final factor contributing to segregation in the Providence schools. The Master Plan for Public Schools drafted by the City Plan Commission in 1965 placed high priority on immediate construction of additions to both Flynn and Fogarty schools in South Providence, and the Providence school department built "relocatable" classrooms at these two schools in 1966 with federal money obtained under Title I of the Elementary and Secondary Education Act. These schools were 69 and 56 percent black when the Master Plan was drafted. The Master Plan also proposed a new PK-3 elementary facility for upper South Providence which would enroll approximately 400 pupils and "relieve the pressure on Flynn." This school was to be built in the Beacon attendance area that was 73 percent black when the Commission's plan was adopted in 1966.

Segregated East Side Schools. The Thomas A. Doyle and Jenkins Street elementary schools on the East Side were not only the most extremely segregated elementary schools in Providence, but were also the most criticized by parents and community groups. Doyle and Jenkins served a mixed area known as Lippitt Hill that had once been predominantly Irish, with a sizable representation of Polish, Jewish, French, and black families. With urban redevelopment and a movement out by Irish families, the black population became predominant. The 1963 Curwood study found that blacks were in a majority in the public school population in the Doyle-Jenkins area but that the zone contained a sizable group of white children attending private schools, primarily Roman Catholic parochial schools. Over one-third of the total East Side school age population was enrolled in parochial and other private schools in about 1966. The Curwood study identified 579 black and white public school children in the Doyle and Jenkins attendance areas in August 1963. Blacks made up 86 percent of this total group. About three-fourths (73 percent) of these children were attending the Doyle and Jenkins schools, with the rest enrolled in Summit and John Howland. A total of 97 blacks and 59 whites were "permitting out" to the Summit and Howland schools. The Curwood study concluded that ending the permit system in the Lippitt Hill area would not change the racial balance of the two schools appreciably.

Dr. Curwood's interviews with mothers of public school children in the two attendance areas revealed "a generalized, if not a specific, dissatisfaction with the education that their children are receiving in public schools, especially Thomas A. Doyle and Jenkins Street." This was true of black parents, particularly. Only 42 percent of the black parents with children attending the Doyle-Jenkins schools rated the teachers as good or excellent; 47 percent believed the curriculum there was adequate; and 81 percent of the black parents felt that their children could learn more, if more were offered. The two schools, Dr. Curwood said, "are presently considered low-status schools with an undesirable student body." Of the black mothers from this zone sending their children to Summit and John Howland schools on permits, 54 percent gave "good education" as their reason for transferring their children out of the Doyle-Jenkins attendance area. Another 23 percent of these mothers said that they were using the permits to avoid the "social situation" in their own attendance area. "Dirty children" and "socially unaware teachers" were among the social conditions these mothers wished to bypass.[25]

Dr. Curwood found that mothers in the Doyle-Jenkins attendance area were aware of the racial imbalance in the schools and that 67 percent of all the black mothers thought that education in a segregated school was a little worse or much worse than education in an integrated school. Black mothers with children attending the Summit and Howland schools, particularly, believed education in a segregated school to be inferior to education in an integrated school (84 percent). The majority of the mothers with children in the Doyle and Jenkins schools "see themselves as a captured population . . . and want out," Dr. Curwood said. She felt that the permit system had contributed to dissatisfaction and to school racial problems in the area, since it "fostered the idea that what is 'out' is better than what is 'in,' " "added friction to the relationship between administrator and parent and between parents of different racial groups," and "tended to cream off the leadership potential from the Thomas A. Doyle and Jenkins Street schools." Dr. Curwood also reported "an implied disapproval of present public school education" among whites in the area attending private schools other than parochial schools. This would have to be overcome before these parents would send their children to public schools.[26]

Both the Doyle and Jenkins schools were older structures, Doyle being one of the worst schools in the city, as far as the physical plant was concerned. Community leaders who were active in the desegregation struggle on the East Side described Doyle as "awful" and "terrible." A white man involved in school/racial questions said he "can't believe the white community would have stood for it." The Rhode Island School of Design COPE report described the Thomas A. Doyle building as follows:

> The school is in a state of complete disrepair. Its unfinished wooden floors, bolted down furniture and incredibly dim incandescent lights have apparently remained unchanged throughout their 71 years of use. It has a third floor auditorium and the building as a whole is lacking in adequate fire protection.

The Jenkins Street School was in an older building also, and lacked special facilities such as an auditorium, library, cafeteria, and space for physical education. It had been recently updated with new lighting, toilet facilities, and flooring, however, and was considered "structurally sound and in good repair" by the Rhode Island School of Design architects who examined it.[27]

Other complaints against Doyle and Jenkins focused on the failure of the school department to provide any special programs or facilities for the schools and on the lack of interest on the part of the school leadership in parents and parent participation. The schools were "pauperized," one community leader stated, and had nothing in the way of a good program, teaching facilities, and equipment. The Curwood study found that some mothers felt they "definitely are not wanted at the schools." There was no Parent-Teacher Association at Doyle in the early 1960s and there was less participation in school activities by parents sending their children to these schools than by Doyle-Jenkins parents whose children were in Summit and Howland. According to Dr. Curwood:

> The Negro mothers whose children attend schools outside of their home districts are conscious of the participation of the white mothers in the school and accept for themselves the established pattern of participation.[28]

Central and South Providence Segregated Schools. The four predominantly black schools in central and South Providence presented striking contrasts, as far as the facilities and the physical conditions of the buildings are concerned. Flynn and Fogarty, the schools that enrolled the largest number of black students in South Providence, offered grades PK–6, and both were housed in new buildings. Flynn was constructed in 1958 and Fogarty in 1962. Both schools were large, on adequate plots of ground and adjacent to public playgrounds. Both had special facilities such as an auditorium, a kitchen, a gymnasium, and a health suite. Flynn's auditorium and gymnasium were separate, while Fogarty had a combined auditorium-cafeteria-gymnasium. The Rhode Island School of Design's COPE study found both schools in good condition in 1967, but indicated there were certain deficiencies as regards the use or availability of special facilities. Flynn and Fogarty both had over-capacity enrollments at the time the COPE study was carried out and, owing to lack of space, shower rooms in the Flynn school were used for remedial reading classes. There was "too intensive use" of the multi-purpose room in Fogarty, according to the RISD COPE report.[29] Flynn had no library and no equipment for a science program.

Beacon and Hammond Elementary Schools were small, old primary schools teaching grades PK–3. Neither had an auditorium, a gymnasium, or any health facilities, and Hammond did not even have an office for the principal. Hammond, the oldest school in use in the system, was built in 1848. It was estimated that 40,000 children had passed through Hammond in its century-plus history. Situated on a paved lot about one-third of an acre in size, Hammond had only six classrooms and no library. The fire escapes were "in questionable condition." The girls had to walk past the boiler room to get to their rest room and both the boys' and girls' rest rooms were old, "poorly ventilated and thoroughly unsanitary." The molding was coming loose from the walls. The RISD COPE report and several previous studies had recommended that this school be "closed immediately and torn down."[30] On the fringes of the downtown business and commercial area, Hammond was losing enrollment from year to year. The percentage of blacks in the school fluctuated as whites moved out. The school lost black as well as white students between 1965 and 1967. (See Table 2.)

Beacon, built in 1891, was located in the upper part of South Providence in a "depressed residential neighborhood slated for urban renewal." This school was also on an extremely small paved lot with "minimal opportunity for outdoor play." Although facilities such as an auditorium and gymnasium were lacking, the interior had been redone to provide adequate lighting and heat. The toilet facilities were sanitary, and the building was equipped with sprinklers and fire doors. The school also had a small reading room. While improvements made the interior reasonably satisfactory, the RISD survey team considered the school "an obsolete educational plant in terms of contemporary curriculum and grade organization." They recommended that the school be closed as soon as possible.[31]

Mrs. Ann D. Hill, a black social case worker appointed to the school committee in 1969, stated that in the period prior to desegregation South Providence, including the schools, "had become progressively worse from the relocation of East Side Negroes moving to South Providence." According to Mrs. Hill, the schools in South Providence had the "least qualified teachers, the least equipment, and the least concerned parents." Sensitive community leaders were well aware that South Providence was rapidly becoming a major ghetto area.

In 1965, the Rhode Island State Advisory Committee to the U. S. Commission on Civil Rights undertook a comparative study of three Providence schools with different racial compositions. The Advisory Committee wanted to determine the relative quality of education in a predominantly black school, compared to a predominantly white school and an "evenly mixed" school. Two South Providence schools, Flynn and Temple, were selected along with an all-white school, the Nelson School in North Providence, later renamed Robert F. Kennedy. Flynn was 69 percent black at this time and Temple, which was experiencing a rise in black enrollment, was 47 percent black. Nelson had no black students.

The Advisory Committee's investigation of the training and preparation of staff, the pupil-teacher ratio, expenditures, physi-

cal facilities, and special programs in the three schools showed
that "the school department is making a special effort to deal
with the predominantly nonwhite school."[32] Their report, which
reflected the changes that had come about with the advent of
recent compensatory programs, noted that teachers in Flynn
tended to have more training, the pupil-teacher ratio was lower,
and there were more special programs and services than in the
white school studied. Flynn had a newer building and better
physical facilities. Flynn and Temple received more money per
pupil for textbooks and supplies than all-white Nelson in 1965.
Nelson's faculty was more experienced and the school had less
faculty turnover than Temple or Flynn, however. (See Table
3.)

In spite of the better physical facilities, lower pupil-teacher
ratios, and increased special programs, the Advisory Committee
found that pupils in Flynn scored lower than pupils in the other
two schools on achievement and IQ tests given in grades 4 and
6. (See Table 4.) There was, in fact, a direct correlation between
the racial composition of the school and IQ and achievement
test scores. Pupils at Nelson, the all-white school, scored highest
on all tests except fourth-grade arithmetic. Temple students,
approximately half white and half black, scored second highest
on nearly all tests and highest in arithmetic. Flynn's predominantly black pupils scored below both Nelson and Temple children on all tests. In addition, there was a direct correlation
between the number of behavior referrals in the schools and
the preponderance of black pupils and between PTA activity
and the racial makeup of the schools. Nelson, the all-white school,
had an active, well-organized PTA with about 350 members.
Temple, the racially mixed school, had recently organized a PTA
under the leadership of a new principal. Flynn had no PTA,
although school authorities said there had been an effort to
start a PTA in the past.

Besides documenting the fact that children in segregated
schools were not achieving at the same level as those in well-mixed
or all-white schools, the Advisory Committee raised a second
concern about the way in which school department staff were
reacting to the educational and other problems of black children.
The Advisory Committee noted an "overeagerness" on the part
of school officials to attribute the educational problems of black
children to their family and cultural backgrounds, absolving the
schools of all responsibility. They were, as the Advisory Committee put it:

Table 3—A Comparison of Three Providence Elementary Schools with
Different Racial Compositions, May 1965

	All-White School (Nelson)	Racially Mixed School (Temple)	Segregated School (Edmund W. Flynn)
Age of Building	42	55	7
Auditorium Capacity	0	0	415
Number of Gymnasiums	0	0	2
Health Suite	No	No	Yes
Dental Clinic	No	Yes	Yes
Cafeteria	No	No	Yes
Pupil Enrollment	562	447	823
School Enrollment Capacity	470	544	788
Percent Black	0	47	69
Faculty (Excluding Principal)	17	18	28
Student Interns	1	1	3
Faculty with Advanced Degrees	6	3	8
Pupil-Teacher Ratio	33.0	24.8	29.4
Average Years of Teaching Experience	26.8	19.0	10.8
Personnel Turnover (1963-65)	1	8	7
Instructional Costs per Pupil	$224.60	$290.70	$218.60
Textbook Expenditures per Pupil	$ 2.78	$ 12.70	$ 3.01
Supplies Expenditures per Pupil	$ 5.15	$ 9.04	$ 7.08
Textbooks Delineating Integrated Situations	No	Yes	Yes
Field Trips	10	12	77
Special Programs*	4	2	8
Behavior Referrals (1961-64)	0	22	34
PTA	Yes	Yes	No

* Includes such extracurricular activities as Christmas plays, tasting parties,
science fairs, art shows, Red Cross service, etc.

Source: Rhode Island State Advisory Committee to the U.S. Commission on
Civil Rights.

Table 4—Test Scores in Three Providence Elementary Schools with Different Racial Compositions, 1965

	All-White School (Nelson)		Racially Mixed School (Temple)		Segregated School (Edmund W. Flynn)	
	Expectancy	Actual Score	Expectancy	Actual Score	Expectancy	Actual Score
Mean IQ						
Grade 4	105.9		94.9		85.9	
Grade 6	111.2		99.4		93.5	
State Test Scores, April 1965						
Grade 4	63–68	65.8	51–57	59.6	45–53	48.6
Language	68–75	78.4	57–64	68.8	49–62	48.9
Arithmetic	48–53	47.8	42–47	48.3	38–43	40.1
Work Study	19–20	20.7	17–18	18.9	14–16	16.3
Grade 6						
Reading	93–97	96.8	81–82	88.2	73–77	77.8
Language	101–105	99.8	88–92	93.3	76–85	84.7
Arithmetic	76–86	84.1	67–74	77.8	61–68	74.5
Work Study	30–31	31.7	25–26	28.9	22–24	25.3

Source: Rhode Island State Advisory Committee to the U.S. Commission on Civil Rights.

a little *too* ready to believe that the social-cultural environment in which the schools must operate is beyond their responsibility or control or concern.

The Advisory Committee was not able to obtain all the information it wanted in this area, but stated:

There is reason to believe that serious problems exist in handling children from "culturally deprived" homes, and this means a high proportion of the nonwhite pupils in the schools.

The report indicated concern that black children with behavior problems were too quickly assigned to ungraded classes for slow learners and that "too few teachers have the training requisite for teaching the disadvantaged." The Committee was almost certain that there were too few personnel and facilities for remedial work, especially in reading, and there were too few resources for training remedial teachers.[33] The school department's efforts to provide compensatory education programs and services in Providence's predominantly black schools were still relatively new, beginning around 1963, when community pressure to desegregate the East Side Schools accelerated.

4.
First Attempts at Desegregation:
False Starts

The Doyle-Jenkins Replacement. With growing dissatisfaction on the East Side over the Doyle and Jenkins schools, the school committee voted in 1960 to build a new K–6 school to replace the two structures. A $1.75 million bond issue was voted on November 7, 1962 to finance a new school in this area to be called the Lippitt Hill School. The Lippitt Hill School was to be ready for use by the fall of 1965.

Once the decision to build a new school was firm, East Side residents began exerting pressure on the school committee to influence the kind of school that would be built and the racial makeup of the school. According to an East Side mother active in several civic organizations concerned with schools, the school department's idea was first just to "build another school." Parents who wanted to use the new school, however, "did not want their children in a predominantly black school." A new organization called HOPE—Helping Our Public Education—was formed "to be sure the replacement would be integrated and not [have] a traditional structure and educational program." A biracial group, HOPE included whites as well as blacks who saw the possibility for a new departure in public education on the East Side. HOPE's membership extended beyond the Doyle-Jenkins attendance area to nearby white residential areas that could be included in the new Lippitt Hill School if it served a broader population than Doyle-Jenkins. The East Side Neighborhood Council, an established, predominantly black community group with a strong political orientation, also became involved in the community struggle to shape planning for the new Lippitt Hill School. Although the weight of East Side black leadership was pro-integration, there was some fear in the black community that whites would take over the new school.

Parents and community groups on the East Side were determined that the new school would be a modern educational facility and that teaching in the school would be up-to-date in method and philosophy. The school department's original, traditional design for the building was abandoned as a result of community protest. Building of the school was in fact delayed two years as community groups blocked plans they considered unsatisfactory. The school department eventually yielded to community pressure and Lippitt Hill was designated an experimental school. The Lippitt Hill curriculum was to be nongraded and the school plant was planned to accommodate team teaching and the use of other contemporary educational methods and equipment. The Lippitt Hill building was ultimately designed on a cluster plan, with "learning centers" grouped around common service and storage areas. Four times the size of normal classrooms, the "learning centers" are subdivided by partitions that can be moved to provide a large combined area. The kindergarten area, cafeteria, gymnasium, and administrative offices are in separate wings connected to the "learning centers" by hallways. The Lippitt Hill School is actually a grouping of six such semi-detached buildings, spaced out over a three-and-one-half acre campus, with separate play yards for different age groups.

Desegregation Proposal for Lippitt Hill. The school department responded to initial pressure from East Side community
groups to desegregate the proposed Lippitt Hill School by com-
missioning a study of the Doyle-Jenkins area. This study, completed August 31, 1963, was carried out by Dr. Sarah T. Curwood, a professor of sociology at Rhode Island College. Dr.
Curwood's report, quoted earlier, concluded that the school
department's existing plans to build the Lippitt Hill School "in
an area where Negroes are already the racial majority" would
not result in desegregation. She suggested several alternatives
for establishing racial balance in the Lippitt Hill School, but
recommended setting up a new attendance area which would
bring in a maximum number of white pupils and take out a
maximum number of black students. Specifically, she proposed:
(1) moving the northern boundary line of the Doyle zone about
six blocks south, assigning this area to the Summit Avenue
School, which many of the black and white children in this section were already attending; (2) extending the eastern boundary
of Doyle-Jenkins to take in predominantly white blocks then assigned to the Summit and Howland schools; and (3) extending
the southern Doyle-Jenkins boundary to take in a small section
of the Fox Point attendance zone, also predominantly white.
Along with these boundary changes, Dr. Curwood stressed ending the permit system as "crucial to the maintenance of an integrated Lippitt Hill school." Abandoning the permit system
would be necessary to hold former Summit and Howland white
students in Lippitt Hill, Dr. Curwood pointed out. Dr. Curwood's plan would place more black students in Summit but
would not change the predominantly white character of Howland. Attendance area lines would have to be reviewed periodically because of population shifts, Dr. Curwood stated, and revised to prevent resegregation. "Gerrymandered districts" carry
the "taint" of "tools of discrimination," she said, but, "their use
in the future may well be in support of racial integration." Before anything can be done, Dr. Curwood concluded:

two major decisions must be made by the Providence School Department and publicized widely. First, a firm, clear policy statement about
the department's commitment to the maintenance and establishment
of integrated schools in the Providence public school system must
be made. Second, a definition, in terms of the needs of the Providence
school system of "racially balanced" or "racially imbalanced" must
be formulated.[34]

The Curwood report contained a second set of recommendations for an effective interim program involving Doyle and Jenkins schools and both present and future parents whose children would be attending the Lippitt Hill School. At that time Doyle and Jenkins had separate principals and both taught all elementary grades. Dr. Curwood suggested that the two schools be unified, and that Thomas J. McDonald, the principal designated for the new Lippitt Hill School, become principal of both schools. She proposed raising the overall educational standards of these two schools prior to the opening of Lippitt Hill, with special attention being given to the children at grades 4 and below, who would be "educated according to the new Lippitt Hill curriculum." She stressed that every effort should be made to "widen the horizon of these children" and also said that "teachers in these schools may need some additional education in human relations in order to make this program effective." As far as parents were concerned, she suggested activating a PTA, securing assistance from voluntary groups in the area concerned about public education, a "maximum use of 'grass roots' techniques and active involvement of those persons most directly affected by the program," and consideration of the potential of the Lippitt Hill School as a community center for the neighborhood. Her final recommendation for this interim period was that a preschool education program be established in the area to help prepare the children for later schooling.[35]

Dr. Curwood's proposals reflected major concerns of East Side parents who were organizing actively around the Lippitt Hill school issue. In addition to the demand for integration, parents in the Doyle-Jenkins zones threatened a school boycott at the end of the summer of 1963 if remedial programs were not put into effect in the two schools immediately. A rally of about 300 persons was held to show support for community demands, and the National Association for the Advancement of Colored People (NAACP) sent in a field representative who threatened to file a suit if the school department did not initiate a desegregation plan for the entire city.

New Educational Thrust in Doyle-Jenkins. Doyle-Jenkins parents persisted in their demands to upgrade the old schools and by the fall of 1964 secured substantial changes in the organization and character of the two schools. "People began to realize," a white East Side parent stated, "that putting black and white together would be a more severe problem than just black and white."

Thomas J. McDonald, the principal designated for the new Lippitt Hill School, was appointed principal of Doyle and Jenkins in September 1964. He reorganized the schools on a paired basis, with both schools offering kindergarten, Jenkins teaching grades 1–3, and Doyle, grades 4–5. The two schools were only two blocks apart. With the assistance of federal funds, a remedial reading teacher was added, pupils were evaluated by a full-time psychologist, the school was given $6,000 extra for supplies and a nursery school program was added in both schools. The school department reduced the pupil-teacher ratio to 25. Doyle and Jenkins also began using the Detroit and Bank Street Readers, becoming the first schools in the Providence school system to introduce multi-ethnic textbooks. McDonald attempted to set up a nongraded program as well, but found he did not have the full range of students necessary.

In addition to the new educational programs and the reorganization of Doyle and Jenkins, McDonald encouraged parent participation in the two schools. When he first went to Doyle and Jenkins, McDonald said that parents came to the schools only when their children were suspended. A PTA was organized for the first time in 20 years and toward the latter half of the three years he served as principal, McDonald promoted what he calls a "motivational, inspirational program" aimed at both the parents and the children. McDonald found that "regardless of how bright they were, the kids felt inferior in a competitive situation." To help counteract this, the two schools held a series of special assemblies, which were featured in the press. McDonald tried to get the teachers to "build up the children" and the schools sponsored large-scale parents' nights where awards and trophies were given to children "for every situation we could think of." There was also an arts festival, with many people invited and displays in the downtown stores. These kinds of activities, with accompanying publicity and a public relations approach had never been done before. In 1969, McDonald said that the parents and children from the area still talk about the awards. About 250 parents turned out for the awards night, the biggest community turnout in the history of the two schools. Discipline improved and daily attendance went up to 95 percent, one of the highest rates in the city. Parent support for the schools became high.

Official changes within the Doyle-Jenkins schools were paralleled by, and were undoubtedly inspired by, community activity centering on the two schools. Even before the school department appointed a new principal and made compensatory funds and services available, parents on the East Side organized a volunteer tutorial program designed to help bridge the academic gap between black and white children who would be integrated in the new school. The Lippitt Hill Tutorial began in the Doyle School in 1963 and initially utilized Brown University and Pembroke College students, who worked with the children after school hours. The program, which included Jenkins pupils, utilized 70 to 80 student tutors. The number of tutors grew to 175 by the time the schools were desegregated. During the first year of the tutorial, the East Side Neighborhood Council paid the cost of keeping the schools open after hours for tutoring purposes. The Lippitt Hill Tutorial set up a library of some 3,000 books in each of the two schools, manning the libraries with adult volunteers throughout the school day. As the tutorial program evolved, adult volunteers began supplementing the regular school program, giving classroom lectures in their fields of specialty and individual help to students outside of class under the direction of the classroom teacher. About 30 women were involved in these in-school daytime activities. The Lippitt Hill Tutorial also sponsored creative dramatic performances at the schools and arranged other enrichment activities, such as visits to the airport, theater performances, "dine outs," and a talk on government by the mayor. The Lippitt Hill Tutorial became so well established and well integrated into the Doyle-Jenkins schools that school-community lines began to blur. Several persons interviewed for this study said that it became difficult to tell where the volunteer program stopped and the official school program began.

The Lippitt Hill Tutorial was initially a predominantly white group, involving wives of Brown University professors and other professionals on the East Side, as well as university area college students. Only a few blacks and a few adult men worked with the tutorial at first. About a dozen black mothers, however, were involved in Doyle-Jenkins after-school activities through a Community School program sponsored jointly by the school department and the local poverty program. According to McDonald, a total of 150 to 200 children stayed for the after-school programs each night in each school. Between the two programs, nearly the whole school population was involved in after-school activities. One black mother said that as the community activity built up, "everyone else wanted to get in on the show."

As a result of combined efforts in Doyle and Jenkins, the children made impressive progress in their test scores during the period from 1963 to 1967. According to principal McDonald, the Doyle-Jenkins children were reading one and one-half to two years below grade level in 1963 and were functioning a year below grade level in math. By 1967, they were up to grade level in both these subjects and were within average achievement ranges for all other subjects for which they were tested. An editorial in one of the local papers described the last four years of the Doyle-Jenkins schools as their "finest years" and paid tribute to those who had worked in the "crusade" to

> enrich instruction for the preponderantly Negro children from poor homes who were to mix with children of the East Side well-to-do when the new Lippitt school opened.

From the perspective of two years after desegregation, however, two of the key people in upgrading the calibre of education at Doyle and Jenkins questioned the basic approach of concentrating on the black children while ignoring the whites who were to be integrated with them. McDonald said in an interview, in 1969, for instance, that "any efforts should have gone to the whites." He found that "black children didn't seem to have adjustment problems" with desegregation and said he would now prepare whites instead of blacks if he had time to carry out a program preparing students for desegregation. One of the white women who organized the Lippitt Hill Tutorial and who was a prominent figure in it prior to desegregation stated:

> The tutorial was in preparation for integration. The fact that we spent so much time on the black kids seems queer to me now. It seems sort of insulting. I am not sure what we accomplished. . . . Maybe teachers feel the kids are better prepared. . . . Maybe being in a special project has given a better tone [to desegregation].

She said that in the tutorial they tried to "build an aura for the black child in a special program" and that working with the children as if they were very special helped the parents. As far as the white parents were concerned, she said the tutorial "developed status around the [black] child which is what white parents understand." Another mother who had worked in the tutorial project felt that one of the "side benefits" was the exposure of whites to the Doyle-Jenkins school community ahead of time, so that they got to understand the backgrounds of the black children and were prepared for desegregation. She found that the whites who had worked in the tutorial were more realistic and had a better idea of what to expect when the schools were finally desegregated. A minister, active in school desegregation on the East Side, said that the tutorial project developed "a sense of neighborhood and parent involvement" that is probably not present in "a half dozen schools in the country." He also noted that the people involved in the tutorial "provided the muscle for the East Side in school desegregation."

New Pressures for Desegregation. Following Dr. Curwood's study, the school committee agreed to a plan for racial balance in the Lippitt Hill School, without establishing an overall policy on desegregation or adopting a definition of segregation and racial imbalance for the entire school district. The new attendance boundaries set for Lippitt Hill did not achieve as good a racial mix in Lippitt Hill and Summit as those recommended by Dr. Curwood, but did bring more whites into the Lippitt Hill zone. After agreement on this plan, school segregation on this plan was dormant as a public issue until the spring of 1966, when Superintendent O'Connor stated that the Lippitt Hill desegregation plan was outdated and that the new school would be 75 percent black unless the plan were changed. He said that the school would not be racially balanced when it opened in the fall of 1967 unless new district lines were drawn and the permit system was ended. O'Connor did not make any immediate recommendations for revising the Lippitt Hill Plan to the school committee, and community pressure began to mount once more.

With no action from the superintendent or the school committee, early in June 1966, Thomas J. McDonald, principal designate of the new Lippitt Hill School, said publicly that he would give serious reconsideration to his appointment as principal of Lippitt Hill if the school were not truly integrated. He defined "truly integrated" as a 60/40 white/black ratio. McDonald had publicly backed an end to the permit system several years before when the Lippitt Hill desegregation issue was first debated. Another pressure on the superintendent, not publicized at the time, came from the Rhode Island State Advisory Committee to the U.S. Commission on Civil Rights. The Reverend Raymond E. Gibson, chairman of this group, said that following their study of the problems associated with race in the schools, he met with the superintendent about the segregation problem. Then early in the summer of 1966, he told the superintendent he would call in the U.S. Commission on Civil Rights for an open hearing if he did not do something about school segregation by the end of the summer.

With community pressure building up once more, a school committee member from the East Side, Sherwin J. Kapstein, introduced two resolutions on de facto segregation at the committee's June 27 meeting. One resolution directed the school department to "proceed forthwith" on planning "that will eliminate de facto segregation where it exists in the Providence schools." Specific schools were not named and the resolution did not define racial imbalance or set a timetable for the elimination of segregation. The second measure Kapstein introduced dealt with the Lippitt Hill School, proposing that it "shall be, to the best of our ability, racially balanced." The Lippitt Hill resolution called for a plan for new district lines and enrollment policies to be prepared by the Superintendent and submitted to the school committee "no later than September 30, 1966."[36] This proposal was amended at Superintendent O'Connor's request to provide that a plan for Lippitt Hill be ready by October 31. The school committee passed both resolutions but, as the *Providence Evening Bulletin* pointed out editorially, "the general tenor of the proceedings contained no new promise of vigor."[37]

More important and dramatic than the introduction of the two desegregation resolutions was the emergence that night of a new coalition of civil rights organizations and leaders called the Negro Leadership Conference. This group, led by James D. McDaniel, president of the Providence Branch of the NAACP, picketed the school committee and pledged to end segregation in the Providence public schools by September 1 using "any means necessary." The press reported about 25 pickets at the board meeting and identified the demonstration as one of the first such civil rights protests in the city. McDaniel, who acted as a spokesman for the Congress of Racial Equality (CORE), the East Side Neighborhood Council, and a group of civil rights leaders known as the "Fearless Fifty," told the school committee:

> We are determined that come September 1966, our children will not receive continued inferior education, even if it means keeping our children out of the segregated schools entirely.

McDaniel singled out Superintendent O'Connor for pointed criticism, stating that he had failed to show "real initiative" in tackling the problem. McDaniel was not impressed with the Kapstein resolutions and said his group expected a desegregation plan for the entire city by August 1. He said the plan should include all schools in the city that were 50 percent or more black. McDaniel did not specifically commit the coalition group to a boycott, but the threat of a boycott was present.

For a month following the June 27 school committee meeting, the Negro Leadership Conference, the press, and school committeeman Kapstein continued to exert pressure on the school committee and the superintendent to resolve the segregation problem. The *Providence Evening Bulletin* stressed the importance of ending the "foot dragging by the Providence School Committee and its administration," stating that "by continuing a policy of delay and evasion, the Providence School Committee and its administration will only invite further unnecessary discord."[38] The *Providence Sunday Journal* was critical of Superintendent O'Connor for not demonstrating "a sense of urgency in breaking up de facto segregation of Negroes."[39] Both papers pointed to the bad example of the mishandling of school segregation problems in nearby Boston.

McDaniel announced July 5 that the Negro Leadership Conference would "take steps to see that state, federal, and city funds are cut off" because of segregation in the schools. "We feel that many times when the question of money arises, that much activity is generated," he added. The state commissioner of education replied that segregation in Providence involves "no violation of any federal or state laws" and there was no basis for any action from the State Board of Education cutting off funds to Providence.[40] At the next meeting of the State Board of Education, on July 6, one board member, Robert Finkelstein of Woonsocket, urged the board to formally offer its services to Providence school officials in solving the segregation issue. The board rejected his suggestion.

On July 8, McDaniel sent an official complaint against segregation in the Providence public schools to David Seeley, Director of the Equal Educational Opportunities Program (EEOP) of the U. S. Department of Health, Education and Welfare. EEOP was then responsible for enforcement of Title VI of the 1964 Civil Rights Act in public schools throughout the country. The complaint was based on (1) the "nonwhite makeup" of the six Providence elementary schools which were predominantly black; (2) 1965 achievement test scores of pupils in the fourth grade which showed that students at Flynn, Beacon, and Temple were one to two years behind in reading skills; (3) school department plans to use over half of $190,181 in federal monies budgeted for an educational program to construct temporary additions to segregated schools in South Providence; and (4) evidence that school boundaries had been gerrymandered to maintain segregated schools—for example, in the Doyle and Jenkins zones. McDaniel closed the complaint with the statement: "We have put up with this debasing situation long enough." Seeley wrote McDaniel July 21, requesting more information on the points raised in the complaint and, on August 12, informed Superintendent O'Connor of the complaint and asked him to furnish data related to the charges made by McDaniel. On October 11, another staff member of the HEW assured McDaniel the complaint was being reviewed. There were subsequent letters and telephone calls in later months, but the Providence file in the Equal Educational Opportunities Program indicates that no meaningful follow-up action was ever taken on this complaint.

Policy and Principles of Desegregation Established. In mid-June 1966, just before the demand for desegregation was reactivated in the black community, Superintendent O'Connor attended a national school administration conference on "The Community and Integrated Quality Education," sponsored by the National Urban League and Teachers College, Columbia University. Here he heard U. S. Commissioner of Education Harold Howe challenge local school officials and board members to "form a third front for racial equality in the United States." With community demands for an end to segregation escalating, Dr. O'Connor began to respond to this challenge. His first step was to meet with several advisors on desegregation, including Dr. Harold Pfautz, a sociologist at Brown University; James N. Williams, then executive director of the Urban League of Rhode Island; William P. Robinson, Jr., then state commissioner of education; and Myrl G. Herman, director of laboratory experience at Rhode Island College.

On July 28, Dr. O'Connor held a press conference to release a "Position Paper of the Superintendent on the Integration of the Providence Public Schools." The position paper contained two sections, a statement of philosophy on de facto desegregation and a plan for implementation of desegregation in the Providence schools. The superintendent said that the school committee had unanimously approved the statement of philosophy the day before in a closed session, but that he alone was responsible for the plan of implementation.

The statement of philosophy included several broad generalizations linking "quality education" to "integrated education" and asserting the Providence School Committee's dedication to "immediate . . . forthright action to bring as many children as possible into integrated schools as rapidly as possible." It said that a new and bold plan for integration was needed to bring about "quality education as we have defined it—integrated education," and that the support and cooperation of the entire community would be required to attain this goal. The strongest aspect of this statement was an assertion that "there is no such thing as 'quality education' in our time and place unless it is integrated education." This July 28, 1966, statement of philosophy was the only overall policy position on school segregation adopted by the Providence school committee throughout the elementary desegregation controversy. No school committee member was present when the statement was issued.

The superintendent's plan for accomplishing desegregation, not endorsed by the school committee, included implementing a plan for South Providence by October 1 and developing a plan for the East Side by December 1. The timing of the East Side plan, the superintendent said, would understandably be governed by completion of the new Lippitt Hill School. As to the mechanics of how it would be done, the superintendent stated that all schools in South Providence and on the East Side would be considered "as a single functioning unit." Traditional concepts of school districts and the permit system would have to be revised, O'Connor warned, "and many, both white and black," would have to experience "the inconvenience of busing" and "having our expectations as to where our children will go to school changed." He promised, however, "that no child will be moved in or out of any school until I have addressed myself personally to the parents in the school. . . ." This pledge and subsequent promises of the superintendent to hold public hearings on any plan before presenting it to the school committee caused a certain amount of resentment and bitterness in later stages of the desegregation struggle. The superintendent did not live up to either of these promises although he did attempt to hold school-by-school meetings with parents throughout the city.

On the crucial issue of federal funds, Dr. O'Connor said in his July 28 position paper that he had been in contact with the U. S. Office of Education about the need for more money "if we are serious about making an impact on the problem we face." He also announced receipt of a grant-in-aid under Title III of the Elementary and Secondary Education Act to be used to develop "the specifics of our program of action." This grant was used instead to fund the COPE study quoted earlier, which completely ignored racial factors in the school system. On July 29, Superintendent O'Connor sent a copy of his position paper to U.S. Commissioner of Education Harold Howe, explaining:

> since some question has been raised as to our eligibility for funds
> from the federal government under the poverty programs because

of the racial issue, this statement may serve as a clarification of our position.

The July 28 statement was followed by negotiations between the Negro Leadership Conference and the superintendent. These meetings resulted in agreement on six principles to be followed in desegregating the schools. The two parties agreed September 1, 1966 that: (1) both white and black children would be bused, if busing were necessary; (2) a hot lunch program would be continued for children moved into schools without cafeterias; (3) specially trained teachers would be used in staffing the newly desegregated schools; (4) qualified black school personnel would be upgraded; (5) a public information program on the necessity of desegregating the schools would be carried out; and (6) educational materials would be reevaluated, insuring accurate portrayal of the American Negro. The superintendent and administration shortly overlooked several of these important principles in the actual implementation of desegregation. But as a result of the agreement, black leaders waited to see what specific plans for desegregation the superintendent would develop.

"O'Connor Plan" for South Providence Desegregation.   On September 30 Dr. O'Connor announced his desegregation plan for South Providence. The plan involved the reassignment of about 1,000 black and white children in eight elementary schools and one junior high school in South Providence and the immediate vicinity. Specifically, O'Connor proposed new district lines for the four predominantly black elementary schools in South Providence—Beacon, Flynn, Fogarty, and Temple—and for three predominantly white schools in neighborhoods bordering the South Providence ghetto—Broad, Sackett, and Lexington schools. Hammond, a predominantly black school in the West End, was also to be desegregated as part of the South Providence plan. O'Connor estimated that about 500 youngsters in these schools in grades 1–5 would be moved by the new district lines, but that only about 200 of the children would have to be bused.

The second half of the "O'Connor Plan" called for converting Roger Williams Junior High School in South Providence to a "middle school." O'Connor proposed transferring all ninth grade Roger Williams students to various senior high schools in the city and moving all sixth graders in the elementary schools affected by the desegregation plan to Roger Williams. About 206 ninth graders and 365 sixth graders would be affected by

this portion of the O'Connor Plan. O'Connor maintained that
the middle-school shifts were necessary to provide space in the
elementary schools for a reduced pupil-teacher ratio, another
aspect of the desegregation plan. O'Connor had been discussing
the possibility of a middle-school plan for Providence for two
years when this proposal was linked to the desegregation plan.
The middle-school idea had not caught on by itself, so he now
tied it to the desegregation plan. Together, the middle-school
pupil shifts and the new elementary district lines were to reduce
the black population in the eight elementary schools in South
Providence to 45 percent and in Roger Williams to 37 percent.
The middle-school moves were to be made after the mid-year
high school graduation, and the elementary moves on January
30.

Educational improvements that were to accompany desegregation included: (1) reduction of the pupil-teacher ratio from "over
30" to 25 to 1; (2) an area supervisor for all elementary schools
affected by the plan; (3) a hot lunch program in all schools;
(4) libraries in all schools; and (5) specialized departmental programs at the sixth-grade level offering greater opportunities in
art, music, physical education, industrial arts, and home
economics. While his first concern was to make a "significant
impact on the pattern of de facto school segregation," O'Connor
said he would "see that in every school the cost of inconvenience
and change will be balanced by a clear increase in the quality
of education offered to the students."[41]

The plan made no mention of the permit system, which was
apparently to remain unchanged. Although O'Connor had initially said he would be responsible for implementing the desegregation plan as superintendent, he now indicated he would
present his plan to the school committee in October. Details
of cost were not worked out, but O'Connor estimated the cost
of busing for the second term of the school year at $12,000.

In announcing his plan, O'Connor also explained why he was
moving away from the so-called neighborhood school. He had
suggested in his July 28 statement that the segregation problem
would have to be solved on an area-wide basis on the East Side
and in South Providence, rather than school by school. O'Connor
now stressed "thinking in terms of larger area units than are
encompassed by the traditional concept of the neighborhood
school," noting "there is a good deal of expert testimony to
the fact that the concept of the neighborhood school has lost
its relevance as an educational concept in modern urban life."
He quoted Dr. Dan Dodson, the Director of the Center for

Human Relations and Community Studies of New York University, who has said that the neighborhood school no longer serves its original purpose of bringing together diverse elements in an area to share a common experience. While O'Connor did not explicitly recommend abandonment of the neighborhood school, he said he had concluded that the junior high school is "the most sensible and productive administrative unit." He therefore based his desegregation plan on a broader attendance area.[42]

Defeat of the O'Connor Plan. School committeemen, politicians, political candidates, and white "grass roots" resistance killed the O'Connor Plan within six weeks after it was announced. Although it was never officially presented to the school committee, the school board voted November 15 to table the O'Connor Plan. There was some debate as to the parliamentary correctness of tabling an item that had never been introduced. O'Connor had announced he would present his program to the school committee at several different meetings in October and November, but never did put the plan before the committee because all the school committee meetings between September 26 and November 15 were canceled. Both the superintendent and the school committee blamed each other in the press for the cancellation of the meetings. Meanwhile, Chairman Fricker and three other members of the school committee publicly opposed the plan almost as soon as it was released to the newspapers. In addition to their press statements, these four members of the school committee spoke against the plan at community meetings and political rallies. Committeeman Kapstein, who had sponsored the summer resolutions on ending school segregation, resigned from the school board in September, at about the time the plan was being introduced. He did not make a statement concerning the proposal, and Committeeman William T. O'Halloran also never took a public position on the O'Connor Plan. Only one school committee member, Gordon F. Mulvey, whose district was not affected by the O'Connor Plan, was publicly sympathetic with the plan. Mulvey said that the "concerns are valid" and the "recommendations are basic to the accomplishment of the objectives."[43]

Mayor Doorley quickly stated his opposition to the O'Connor Plan, opening the door for other political resistance. Mayor Doorley was running for reelection in November, and his opposition and the political debacle that followed were critical in the defeat of the O'Connor Plan. The mayor had been silent throughout

the summer on the question of school desegregation, but stated
several days after the release of the O'Connor Plan that he would
support it only if elementary pupils were transferred with the
consent of their parents and busing was voluntary. Both mandatory transfers and larger school attendance areas were at the
heart of the O'Connor Plan, making the mayor's condition of
voluntary transfers and busing tantamount to opposition. Mayor
Doorley favored the second half of the O'Connor Plan, the proposal to move ninth-grade students at Roger Williams Junior
High School to the senior high schools. This measure was not
controversial at all, as it was seen by many as a solution to discipline problems at the junior high school level. The mayor proposed a voluntary "experimental" racial balance plan that would
allow sixth graders in South Providence elementary schools to
attend Roger Williams under a special program involving smaller classes and supplementary, volunteer teachers recruited from
the colleges and from professionals in the community.

Other political figures opposing the O'Connor Plan included
at least several city councilmen, three state senators and representatives, a former lieutenant governor of the state, and a number
of candidates for the city council, the school committee, the
state senate, and other offices. Unfortunately, the O'Connor
Plan was issued just as politicians were warming up for the
November elections. After the mayor's opposition, the plan
quickly became a political football, especially in the white
neighborhoods of South Providence directly affected by the
proposal.

A mother of public school children in the Washington Park
area said, for instance, that at a meeting of the Washington
Park Citizens Association "one by one the candidates got up
and promised to keep the area lily white." Washington Park
is a heavily Irish, neat, trim, white "middle American"
neighborhood where skilled workingmen, tradesmen, salesmen,
and small businessmen make their homes. Just south of the ghetto
there was much fear in this area of school desegregation and
of blacks moving in. Politicians and members of the school committee were all "heroes of the day," this mother said, telling
people in the area, "No, you won't be bused. No, it won't happen."
"They thought it was what voters wanted to hear, and it was,"
she commented. She herself was running for the state senate
on the Republican ticket and took the position that the plan
was good, although it contained flaws. She asked people to "wait
and listen to what Mr. O'Connor has to say." She "took a bad
beating this time" in the election and was called a "nigger lover."

The Broad Street Elementary School in the Washington Park area was one of the three predominantly white schools to be desegregated with black South Providence children.

Political opposition at the neighborhood level was also strong in Elmwood, another white section bordering the South Providence ghetto. The press reported a meeting of the Elmwood Civic League where nine political officeholders or political candidates spoke against the O'Connor Plan. This meeting was held at the Sackett Street School, another of the white schools to be desegregated by the O'Connor Plan. School committee chairman Fricker, whose school district included Elmwood, spoke in opposition to the O'Connor Plan at this meeting, as did a former state lieutenant governor who was a candidate for the position of U. S. Attorney. Following an evening of speakers against the South Providence desegregation plan, the Elmwood Civic League voted to oppose it. One woman who spoke against the political and "panic-stricken" character of the meeting had difficulty being heard because of loud interruptions.

White grass roots political oppositon also entered into the school committee elections. With the system of staggered terms, three of the strongest opponents of the O'Connor Plan—Chairman Fricker, Vice Chairman Edward L. Casey, and Kathryn R. Kelly—were not up for reelection. There were four seats being contested, however, with candidates in all four wards taking positions for or against the O'Connor Plan. Armando DiMeo, an incumbent seeking reelection in the predominantly Italian Federal Hill section, strongly opposed changing attendance area lines to accomplish desegregation. Federal Hill was not affected by the O'Connor Plan, but there was great opposition in the area and DiMeo won the largest number of votes of any candidate in the school committee election. All school committee candidates in the Mt. Pleasant-Elmhurst area, a mixed Irish and Italian section, came out solidly against the O'Connor Plan, objecting to busing and to desegregation plans that were not voluntary. Like Federal Hill, these neighborhoods were not directly involved in the South Providence desegregation plan, but contained many people upset by it. A PTA leader said that people in these areas were afraid their children would eventually be bused to South Providence or were simply afraid of busing per se. On the East Side, the contest for the school committee seat was waged primarily on the question of the O'Connor Plan. William L. Robin, who favored the South Providence plan, won the seat vacated by Kapstein. Incumbent Mulvey, who also supported the South Providence plan, was reelected. His ward includes the North

End and a section of the East Side.

Other political opposition came from the Republican candidate for mayor, who said busing would drive families out of Providence.

The main emphasis of the opposition was on the mandatory, or involuntary, nature of the proposed reassignments, on busing, on the change in district lines, on "rowdyism" and discipline problems in Roger Williams Junior High School, on expenditures for busing when there was not enough money for "necessities," and on the "unfairness" of sending black children to only three schools rather than having the entire city "share the burden."

Support for the O'Connor Plan came from many Providence and statewide educational, religious, civic, and humanitarian organizations without a strong base of community political power. Local college presidents, Catholic, Protestant, and Jewish religious leaders, the Negro Leadership Conference, the Providence Human Relations Commission, the East Side Neighborhood Council, the State Commission Against Discrimination, the League of Women Voters, the Rhode Island Conference of Social Work, the Urban League of Rhode Island, the American Civil Liberties Union, and similar groups endorsed the plan wholly or in principle or offered to help implement the plan. The two daily papers backed the O'Connor Plan as well as the combined Sunday edition of the two newspapers, the *Providence Sunday Journal.* Then State Commissioner of Education William P. Robinson, Jr. gave strong personal support to the desegregation proposal and called upon the "absent voices that should be heard from" to speak out.[44] The State Board of Education endorsed the July 28 policy statement adopted by the school committee and urged implementation, but did not endorse the O'Connor Plan per se.

The PTA was split on the issue, with the executive committee of the Providence PTA Council giving unanimous support to the plan, but with several school units opposing part or all of the plan. PTA leaders in some areas held educational meetings, bringing in black PTA leadership or black PTA members to discuss the issue. The Broad Street PTA, for example, invited a black PTA president to participate in a meeting involving small group discussions on the desegregation plan. These discussions apparently tempered the reactions of the membership, as the executive board of this unit opposed only that part of the O'Connor Plan that would transfer sixth graders in South Providence to Roger Williams Junior High School. They based their objection on the "educational and disciplinary" problems in the school. The Broad Street group also said that "the very premise that we have to accept the plan in order to acquire quality education for any child is indeed shocking."[45] The Regent Avenue PTA held a joint meeting on the school segregation problem with two East Side PTA's, those of Summit and Doyle-Jenkins. Governor Chafee, the only political figure of any stature to support the O'Connor Plan, spoke at this meeting.

On October 24, Mayor Doorley asked the school committee to postpone action on the O'Connor Plan until he could appoint a "working conference" to draft a plan on desegregation acceptable to the community. The mayor's action was taken at the request of 12 prominent citizens including a Catholic and an Episcopalian bishop, the presidents of Brown University and Providence College, a former state governor, and a Superior Court judge. These community leaders were afraid the O'Connor Plan would be "shot down in haste" if the school committee voted on it in the heat of the election campaign. The school committee did not meet again until after the election, when it voted to table the O'Connor Plan. This vote was the final blow to the O'Connor Plan, as there were not enough committeemen favorable to the plan to take it off the table for future action. The school committee thus "abdicated its obligation to try to solve de facto segregation in the South Providence schools,"[46] handing leadership on this issue over to the mayor of the city.

5.
Development of the Providence Plan for Elementary Desegregation

The Mayor's Working Conference on Desegregation. The original proposal for a "working conference" on desegregation put to Mayor Doorley during the election campaign suggested that the group include members of the school committee, the superintendent, the state commissioner of education, the president of Rhode Island College, a few specialists in educational organization and administration, and one or more representatives of the black community. In announcing the conference, Mayor Doorley said he would go along with the proposed list but would also add parents of both black and white children to be involved in desegregation of the South Providence schools. Doorley promised to appoint the conference immediately after the election and said that the conference should be able to find a solution to the South Providence problem "within a few weeks."[47] He said he would make the conference a broad-based citizens group that could come up with an acceptable plan without "cramming it down the people's throats."[48]

After a little prodding from the press, Doorley appointed a 27-man committee early in December 1966. The group included many recognized community leaders holding a wide range of opinions on school desegregation. In addition to the school committee, Superintendent O'Connor, the state commissioner of education, and the presidents of Brown University and Providence College, Doorley appointed a labor leader, the superintendent of Catholic schools for the city, the chairman of the Rhode Island State Advisory Committee to the U. S. Commission on Civil Rights, and representatives of the PTA, the Urban League of Rhode Island, the Providence Human Relations Commission, the Elmwood neighborhood, and other areas affected by the O'Connor Plan. Though the conference contained black members, there was later criticism that the "grass roots" South Providence black parents were not put on the committee. A black woman who chaired the NAACP's Education Committee and who was president of the Flynn PTA complained that "the NAACP people weren't called in." Another black woman active in civil rights and civic organizations interviewed for this study said South Providence mothers were not invited to participate in the planning, that only "the people they thought were civilized were invited to help plan." The mayor let it be known that he wished to serve as chairman of the conference and was elected to head the group.

Reaching a consensus on a plan that could be accepted by City Hall, the school committee, the superintendent, the whites on the fringes of South Providence, and pro-desegregation forces was a more difficult task than the mayor had anticipated. The conference met weekly from early in December until the middle of April. One member said that a "fantastic amount of education" went on in the committee. There was, he said, much "give and take," with some "real brawls," although "the meetings never got out of hand" and "no one became so alienated he left." School committee members were active in the conference, although Chairman Fricker stopped attending meetings after December, giving ill health as his reason for not participating. The conference "played its cards close to the chest" and had little public visibility in the first three months of its existence. Members of the conference did not want to give out newspaper releases until a firm position on a plan had been reached. They "did not want public sentiment to harden" over proposals under debate. The conference had so little public identity that it never even acquired a name that was used consistently. The press called it "the mayor's integration study committee," "the mayor's advisory panel on integration," "the Providence desegregation conference," and "the mayor's desegregation conference."

As far as the school committee was concerned, there was virtually no change in the newly elected committee's position on desegregation and the O'Connor Plan. The four members of the school committee who actively and publicly opposed the O'Connor Plan were still in control of the committee, with Fricker remaining as chairman. A newly elected member of the school committee, a teacher named Attilio L. Gizzarelli, also president-elect of the Rhode Island Education Association, attempted to unseat Fricker as chairman after the election. Fricker was reelected by a 5-2 vote, however. Gizzarelli had opposed the O'Connor Plan during the election campaign and was elected from the Mt. Pleasant-Elmhurst section, which strongly opposed desegregation. The "new" school committee contained only two members who would possibly support the O'Connor Plan and were considered sympathetic to desegregation.

"Middle School" Proposals Adopted. Soon after its formation, the mayor's working conference on desegregation recommended to the school committee that all ninth graders from Roger Williams Junior High School be transferred to senior high schools in the city. This move, which was part of the O'Connor South Providence desegregation plan, was voted by the school committee January 10, 1967, to be effective January 30. Approval of this segment of the O'Connor Plan was no real issue, as the mayor had endorsed this phase of the plan at the time it was suggested, indicating it would help resolve discipline problems at the junior high school level. Although Chairman Fricker thought the move should be voluntary, he said he was sure the ninth graders "will want to go, so there is no problem there."[49] This transfer was supposed to be a desegregation effort, but all Roger Williams ninth graders were assigned to Central and Hope High Schools, the two senior high schools with the heaviest concentrations of blacks. No black students were sent to Mt. Pleasant High School, for example, which had a 1 percent black population.

At the end of February 1967, while the mayor's conference was still studying an overall desegregation plan for South Providence, the school committee adopted a modified version of another phase of the O'Connor Plan, a proposal for transferring select sixth graders from all South Providence elementary schools to Roger Williams Junior High School. Superintendent O'Connor had earlier recommended mandatory transfer of these students to make room for a reorganization of the elementary grades, but he now recast his plan along the lines the mayor had suggested in the fall. He proposed establishing a sixth-grade special program for the "gifted child" in Roger Williams that would be open to certain students on a voluntary basis. Students were to be chosen on the basis of IQ, reading ability, and teachers' marks. The school committee had appointed a new principal and vice principal for Roger Williams in the fall, along with a new coordinating elementary principal for South Providence, the first such coordinating principal in the city. Groundwork for the sixth-grade plan had already been laid so that the program could begin the first week in March. Roughly half of the sixth-grade students in three predominantly white and three predominantly black South Providence schools—174 pupils altogether—could enroll in Roger Williams on March 6 if their parents chose. Transfer of those pupils would reduce the size of sixth-grade classes in the elementary schools and would enable sixth graders in Roger Williams to take specialized departmental work. Bringing in sixth-grade students from the same junior high school attendance area was to have little impact on the racial balance at Roger Williams, but did have the advantage of moving these children out of segregated schools prior to the adoption of an overall elementary desegregation plan. Roger Williams was 41 percent black at the time the proposal was made. Superintendent O'Connor estimated that there would be a 60/40 white-black ratio among sixth graders placed in Roger Williams with this program.

Although the sixth-grade transfers were voluntary, the superintendent was greeted with shouts and hostility on March 2 when he met with parents from all South Providence schools to explain the proposed moves. The day before this meeting, the mayor's working conference on desegregation had endorsed what was essentially the original O'Connor Plan for the desegregation of South Providence schools. The 500 predominantly white parents who attended the meeting on the sixth-grade program insisted on questioning the superintendent on the newly adopted South Providence plan. The meeting got out of order and the audience had to be brought under control by the principal of Roger Williams. Angry parents called for O'Connor's resignation, yelling, "Why here?" "Why here?" "Don't stick us with it," and, "Citywide, citywide. We accept it citywide."[50]

The Roger Williams sixth-grade program was implemented on schedule the next week in spite of parental dissatisfaction with the overall desegregation plan.

Citywide Desegregation Proposals.   Parents who yelled at the superintendent on March 2 represented a growing sentiment among whites that any plan that was mandatory would have to include the whole city. Pro-desegregation members of the mayor's working conference, such as the Reverend Raymond Gibson, chairman of the Rhode Island State Advisory Committee to the U.S. Commission on Civil Rights, and James N. Williams of the Urban League had insisted from the beginning that the desegregation plan had to be mandatory. On February 21 Reverend Gibson proposed that the Providence desegregation plan be aimed at all-white as well as at predominantly black schools, stating:

> A reasonable goal is that no public school in the city of Providence would be all-white, or no school would have more than 35 to 40 percent Negroes.

Reverend Gibson said that neighborhood resistance should not be considered and that he personally would "not be a party to any decision that exempts a neighborhood because we already know there will be strong neighborhood opposition."[51] Gibson's proposal was followed by another citywide plan suggested by school committee vice chairman Edward L. Casey. Casey proposed closing or converting to special use the four South Providence schools enrolling most of the black pupils—Flynn, Fogarty, Temple, and Beacon. He said that children attending these four schools should be redistributed throughout the city or possibly sent to suburban schools, limiting the black enrollment in any school to a maximum of 22 percent, 5 percent above the current enrollment of blacks in the total school system. The mayor's comments on the Casey Plan indicated the drift toward a citywide solution to the desegregation of South Providence schools. "Any successful plan," the mayor stated, "will require citywide participation. It's a community-wide problem, not a South Providence problem."[52]

The Casey proposal followed endorsement by the mayor's working conference of what was in effect the O'Connor Plan.

The conference had approved the O'Connor Plan on March 1 in the mayor's absence, but on March 15 they withdrew their backing. In the interim period, residents of Washington Park and Elmwood had banded together to form a Citizens Committee on Citywide Integration and had threatened a court suit. Elmwood and Washington Park residents said that they were being singled out to solve the problem of school segregation, which ought to be a responsibility for the whole city. In addition to withdrawing support from the O'Connor Plan, the mayor's conference said on March 15 that it would prepare a citywide plan that would limit black enrollment in any school to a maximum of 30 percent or "preferably a smaller percentage."[53]

At this point pro-desegregation groups were becoming increasingly impatient with the mayor's study committee. The NAACP accused the study group of deliberate delay and the League of Women Voters expressed concern that the "proliferation of integration proposals may be used to further delay the accomplishment of integration."[54] State Commissioner of Education William P. Robinson threatened to ask for a state racial balance law if city officials did not produce "a satisfactory solution" in "the next few weeks."[55] With no consensus emerging from the larger working conference, on March 31 the mayor appointed a subcommittee of seven men who were to develop a citywide plan for eliminating segregation. The mayor promised a workable solution that would be implemented by September 1967. The subcommittee included the state commissioner of education, Superintendent O'Connor, Reverend Gibson, the Reverend Herbert O. Edwards, Jr., then executive director of the Providence Human Relations Commission, James N. Williams, then executive director of the Urban League of Rhode Island, and the Reverend Arthur T. Geoghegan, superintendent of diocesan Catholic schools.

On April 12 the subcommittee presented a citywide desegregation plan to the mayor's conference that was approved and officially presented to the school committee the following night. The "Providence Plan," as the desegregation proposal was called, was supported by Mayor Doorley and endorsed by the five school committee members present at the April 12 meeting of the working conference. A sixth school committee member, Edward Casey, was unable to attend the April 12 meeting but gave the plan his public support. Only school committee chairman Fricker failed to support the desegregation proposal publicly. Fricker was absent from the working conference when the Providence Plan was approved, and from the school committee meeting the following evening when the plan was adopted unanimously. Fricker never publicly disavowed the plan, however. Both press reports and interviews for this study indicate that key backers of the Providence Plan had difficulty convincing Mayor Doorley that a voluntary desegregation plan would not work. He was finally persuaded to support the mandatory plan and did so without qualification.

Provisions of the Providence Plan.   Although the Providence Plan had certain features that applied throughout the city, it actually consisted of two plans: one for the East Side and one for the rest of the city. The East Side had not only experienced its own unique community struggle for desegregation, but is also a distinct geographic unit, separated from the main city of Providence by the Providence River, the Moshassuck River and a series of large industrial parks and cemeteries. Throughout the entire discussion of a "citywide" plan members of the mayor's working conference and school officials more or less agreed that the East Side would be considered separately from the rest of the city. This partitioning off of the East Side for desegregation purposes was probably a mistake as it sharpened existing cleavages between the East Side and the main body of Providence. The advantage of the separate plan for the East Side was that organized black and white leadership there were prepared to accept desegregation arrangements that the conference was afraid to impose on the rest of the city.

The overall Providence Plan set a goal of a maximum of 30 percent black children in any school and called for mandatory reassignment of children for desegregation purposes, busing of children assigned more than a mile from their new schools, and certain "quality education" features to be implemented as soon as feasible. As a gesture of compromise with Mayor Doorley, the plan included a provision for consideration of "hardship cases" after the first semester of desegregation. The total plan covered grades 1–6, leaving kindergarten and pre-kindergarten children in neighborhood schools. Twenty-seven of the city's 39 elementary schools were to be affected in some way by the plan. An estimated 2,400 children were to be transferred, about 1,300 black and 1,100 white.

Desegregation on the East Side was to be accomplished through a modified "Princeton Plan" involving three of the four East Side elementary schools—Summit Avenue, John Howland, and the new Lippitt Hill School, which was to be ready by the fall. All the children in these school attendance areas were to be assigned to Lippitt Hill for grades 1–3, and grades 4–6 were to be split between Summit and Howland, with each of these two schools gaining children from the old Doyle-Jenkins attendance zones. Kindergarten would be offered in all three schools, with parents having the option of enrolling their children in any one of the three. The Doyle building was to be abandoned for teaching purposes and the Jenkins School was to be converted to use for special education classes. The East Side plan called for two-way, or "cross," busing, with white children being brought into Lippitt Hill for primary work and black children being bused out to Summit and Howland for the upper elementary grades. A total of 1,071 children on the East Side were to be reassigned under the plan. The overwhelming majority (72 percent) of the children to be moved on the East Side were white.

Educational changes to be implemented along with desegregation on the East Side included an immediate reduction of class size to 25 and implementation of a nongraded curriculum at Lippitt Hill in the fall of 1967 and in other East Side schools as soon as possible. Thomas J. McDonald, principal designate of Lippitt Hill, was recommended as a new coordinating principal for all East Side schools, including Fox Point, which was omitted from the desegregation aspects of the plan. According to community leaders who participated in the mayor's conference, the Fox Point Elementary School was dropped from the desegregation plan because of the complicated nature of the community ethnic/racial situation and the degree of resistance within the area to mixing with other East Side schools. A heavily Portuguese area, Fox Point already had a 24 percent black population.

The "citywide" segment of the Providence Plan proposed that South Providence elementary schools be desegregated by a series of actions that included: (1) conversion of the Flynn and Temple schools to special citywide education centers for handicapped children and slow learners; (2) the transfer of black children from four segregated schools—Beacon, Flynn, Fogarty, and Temple—to "satellite schools" in all parts of Providence other than the East Side, primarily by means of busing; (3) reassignment of white children from Flynn and Temple, the two South Providence segregated schools slated for conversion, to Beacon and Fogarty in South Providence; (4) a change in the Broad Street school attendance boundary to permanently assign part of the Fogarty zone to Broad; and (5) enrollment of about 40 Fogarty children in the Henry Barnard School at Rhode Island College, with tuition and busing furnished by the Providence Department of Public Schools. In addition, a small number of black students were to be moved out of three schools in North Providence, the West End, and Elmwood. These three schools —Berkshire, Hammond, and Vineyard—had high and growing black enrollments—Hammond was already 69 percent black. Pupils from these schools were to be placed in adjacent elementary schools.

The "citywide" section of the Providence Plan was to affect 23 of the city's elementary schools—5 predominantly black and 16 predominantly white. It projected the transfer of a total of 1,351 pupils—1,022 black and 329 white. Over three-fourths (76 percent) of the children to be transferred under this part of the plan were black. The majority of the black children were to be bused out of their neighborhoods to "satellite schools," although a small number of black students reassigned from Berkshire, Hammond, and Vineyard were to walk to nearby schools. No white children in South Providence were to be bused, since all were to be transferred to the two predominantly black schools in the area kept open as desegregated schools.

As for the educational features of the citywide plan, a coordinating principal for South Providence had already been appointed and had helped in the preparation of the Providence Plan. Class size was to be reduced as much as possible, but the superintendent said that he could not bring average class size down to 25 immediately because of the scattering of the children to so many schools. Similarly, there was no commitment to introduce a nongraded curriculum or the other special educational services promised on the East Side. The superintendent said that he would spread existing Title I Elementary and Secondary Education Act services as far as possible among the receiving schools and would seek additional Title I funds to "build quality education into the city at large."[56]

Eleven elementary schools in north, south, and west Providence were left out of the citywide desegregation plan. While the thrust of the plan was to spread black children as extensively as possible throughout the city, the proposal avoided sending South Providence pupils to schools with unusually small enrollments. Schools that already had a black population of 10 percent or more were also generally overlooked as possible receiving schools. Two of the Elmwood schools originally involved in the O'Connor Plan—Sackett and Lexington—were left out of the Providence Plan, for example. Sackett had a 29 percent black population in 1967 and Lexington had an 18 percent black enrollment. The Broad Street Elementary School in Washington Park, which had a 3 percent black population in 1967, was to be one of the receiving schools for the black South Providence children, however. Several people interviewed for this study noted that there were simply not enough black children to desegregate all the schools.

The key selling feature of the Providence Plan from the standpoint of gaining both acceptance by whites and political support was that it spread the "burden" of desegregation throughout the city, diluting political opposition from any one segment of the population. The *Evening Bulletin* noted April 14 that the

> initial plan, prepared by Mr. O'Connor and based on educational reasoning, fell short on political grounds . . . because it concentrated its effect on a limited area.

Similarly, the *Providence Journal* of April 16 spoke of "the political reality of white power" and pointed out that

> under the new plan, the burden is not on the white parents of Washington Park and Elmwood alone. It is on the parents of white youngsters in schools scattered around the city. . . .

The fact that white children from outside the South Providence area were not to be reassigned or bused to formely black schools also eased acceptance of the Providence Plan by many whites. But, as the *Bulletin* pointed out on April 14, the wide dispersal of blacks, which "reinforced" the political attractiveness and white acceptance of the plan, at the same time "undercut" the educational features built into the O'Connor Plan.[57] In short, educational benefits that were possible when only a few schools were involved in desegregation were traded for a South Providence plan that was more politically acceptable.

Early Resistance to the Providence Plan. The East Side portion of the Providence Plan was discussed with community groups and released to the press about March 15. Organizations such as HOPE and the League of Women Voters were already pressing the superintendent and the mayor for a definite program so that desegregation could be implemented with the opening of the new Lippitt Hill School in September. With preliminary announcement of a plan for their section of the city, pro-desegregation groups on the East Side quickly mobilized to support the tentative proposal. A three-fourths page advertisement urging the adoption of the East Side plan was placed in the *Providence Journal* on April 10. The advertisement was signed by 287 East Side citizens, including Sherwin J. Kapstein, former East Side school committee member; the executive director of the Providence Human Relations Commission; the wife of the president of Brown University; and two black school teachers. The Howland PTA voted approval of the East Side plan "in principle" before it was adopted by the school committee. Both HOPE and the League of Women Voters circulated information about the proposed East Side plan, asking members to voice support to the mayor, their school committeemen, and their city councilmen. Both organizations circulated petitions and solicited names for the April 10 newspaper advertisement. On the night the school committee adopted the Providence Plan, representatives of HOPE and the League of Women Voters urged its adoption. The president of the League of Women Voters, an East Side resident, presented the school committee with 550 signatures to a petition backing the East Side desegregation plan.

Support for the East Side desegregation plan was not unanimous, however. On April 4, a group of East Side residents announced at a meeting of the Summit Avenue PTA that they would file a court suit to prevent implementation. Their attorney, Phillip S. Rosen, said that the busing plan was unconstitutional since it applied to only one segment of the city. Mr. Rosen spoke against the proposed plan at the school committee meeting April 13, advocating a statewide or metropolitan plan as an alternative to the Providence Plan. The promised suit was not filed. On May 22, however, a group of East Side parents, organized as the Providence Committee for Fair Integration, appeared before the school committee to ask for a voluntary desegregation plan based on new district lines for Lippitt Hill and free student transfers between all East Side school attendance areas. Backers of the Providence Plan, including Reverend Edwards of the Human Relations Commission and representatives of HOPE and the PTA, urged the school committee to go ahead with the adopted plan.

According to East Side community leaders, most opposition to the Providence Plan in their area came from the Summit Avenue School neighborhood. A white East Side League of Women Voters' officer said that people in the Summit School area were saying, "Fricker kept his neighborhood intact and others were moved." A citywide PTA leader reported that the principal of the Summit School, some of its teachers, and a school committee member who had voted for the Providence Plan were involved in the effort to secure a voluntary East Side integration plan. According to a black East Side mother, "Black parents as well as whites at Summit Avenue objected to the influx of kids from Doyle and Jenkins." The Summit School had a 21 percent black population immediately prior to desegregation because of widespread use of the permit system. Many felt the school was already sufficiently desegregated.

The East Side opposition "fizzled out," but there were protests from other quarters. Toward the end of May, a joint meeting of PTA's from eight all-white and predominantly white receiving schools in the Mt. Pleasant area had to be adjourned because of shouting, yelling, and repeated outbursts from the audience. This meeting was one of a series that Dr. O'Connor held throughout the city on the Providence Plan. It included a panel made up of three school committeemen and three community leaders from the mayor's working conference on desegregation. A white citywide PTA leader who attended the meeting described audience reaction as "unbelievable." She said she was present at many meetings on the Providence Plan, but that "this was the worst." The areas involved were heavily Irish and Italian and most hostile to desegregation. The PTA leader quoted above said that the people there did not want any children bused in or bused out, but "wanted things to remain as they were." Mrs. Kenneth W. Stanley, President of the Regent Avenue School PTA, presided over the meeting and laid down a ground rule that all questions must be submitted to the chair in writing. Some of the outbursts stemmed from the fact that Mrs. Stanley bypassed some of the "sensitive" questions handed in, such as "Would you want your daughter to marry. . . ?" People who had submitted these kinds of questions wanted to know why their questions were not asked. Of Italian background and a resident of the area in which the meeting was held, Mrs. Stanley was an active participant in organized efforts to back the Providence Plan. She said that she had not "witnessed or been a part of a large meeting on desegregation that didn't border on violence or an outburst." "Frustrations," Mrs. Stanley found, "became rampant" in large meetings. She personally felt small meetings were more effective. There were nearly 600 people at the meeting described above, which was held in the George J. West Junior High School.

More serious opposition to the Providence Plan began to surface in the black South Providence community shortly after the desegregation plan was adopted. South Providence residents led by Freeman Soares, chairman of a group called the "Fearless Fifty," protested on April 15 that the typical people of the area were not represented on the "handpicked" subcommittee that drafted the final desegregation plan. They also objected to the fact that South Providence would lose two neighborhood schools through desegregation. Conversion of the new Flynn School was a main point of objection, since Flynn had many facilities lacking in the white receiving schools that the children would attend. At rallies in late April and early May, South Providence residents denounced the Providence Plan and the loss of the schools to their community. A school boycott was threatened. The CORE newsletter of May 19 opposed the Providence Plan editorially because it placed the burden of South Providence's desegregation on the black community. On May 22, a spokesman for South Providence residents condemned the Providence Plan at a school committee meeting, demanding the resignation of their official representative on the committee, Chairman Fricker. Fricker, who had been absent from school committee sessions since December, said he was recovering from an operation and an illness and had been told by his doctors to stay away from meetings.

Although there were no further rallies or demonstrations, opposition to the Providence Plan by South Providence residents persisted through the summer. A round-up on school desegregation published in the *Providence Journal* on July 16, 1967 noted "parents in the Flynn area want their own school in their own neighborhood" and

> also bitterly resent the fact that their children are being bused out of the neighborhood in order to partake of the benefits of rubbing elbows with middle class whites, whereas no whites are being bused in to rub elbows with them.

Freeman Soares was quoted as saying that removal of the Flynn school was just one more instance of white oppression, designed to divide blacks. He also said that closing the Flynn School would take away "community pride." The article reported that Mrs. Anita M. Baker, another of the more vocal critics of the Providence Plan, had stated, "After the meeting at George West, I wouldn't care if they never integrated."[58]

The mayor, the school committee and the superintendent stood firm in the face of early resistance to the Providence Plan and, on the whole, the balance of organized community sentiment seemed favorable. The "elite" organizations, as one community leader put it, supported implementation of the plan. The press endorsed it and the State Board of Education went on record as "pledging its support and assistance in implementing and financing to the best of its ability this or a similar plan."[59] Most organizations that had endorsed the O'Connor Plan earlier did not pass new, formal resolutions backing the Providence

Plan, but considered themselves already behind it. The Human Relations Commission met with the superintendent to see how their members could help "put the plan across," and the Providence branch of the NAACP brought in a speaker late in the summer to assist in mobilizing support for desegregation. As for the East Side push for a voluntary plan, the mayor noted he had "proposed a voluntary program when the issue first came up" and "there was unanimous agreement from the governor on down that a voluntary plan would not work." A voluntary plan was now out of the question. He said objections to the Providence Plan were expected, but it had received solid support from a number of persons and organizations, would remove de facto segregation, and should be put into effect.[60]

Final Planning and Preparations.   Detailed planning to implement the Providence Plan was largely in the hands of the two new coordinating principals appointed as part of the superintendent's overall strategy for desegregation: Miss Mary K. Joyce in South Providence and Thomas J. McDonald on the East Side. Miss Joyce, who was appointed to her new position in November 1966, had gained most of her experience as a teacher and principal in the key sending and receiving schools associated with the desegregation of South Providence—Flynn, Beacon, and Temple in South Providence and Kenyon in Federal Hill. Miss Joyce had spent about half of her time on desegregation throughout the 1966–67 school year, working closely with Dr. O'Connor on the development of the proposed Providence Plan. McDonald was appointed coordinating principal for the East Side near the end of the school year and was replaced as principal of Lippitt Hill by Miss Mary C. O'Brien, a Doyle teacher. Miss O'Brien finished out the school year as acting principal of Doyle-Jenkins. Several persons interviewed for this study pointed out that there was a noticeable lack of participation in preparation and planning for desegregation at the "middle levels" of administration. There was also no involvement in the details of planning and preparation on the part of the school committee, since its members took the position that implementation of the Providence Plan was the superintendent's responsibility.

Since Superintendent O'Connor had stressed the upgrading of education in the Providence schools as an adjunct to desegregation, securing additional funds and organizing supplementary and compensatory educational services in the receiving schools were important aspects of the preparation. To assist in this effort, the Rhode Island Department of Education gave the Providence school department two planning grants in the spring of 1967 totaling about $5,000. The planning grants were funded under Title I of the Elementary and Secondary Education Act and provided for part-time staff and consultants to work out the coordination of existing Title I services in the desegregated schools, as well as plans for a broader compensatory program to accompany desegregation.

In addition to the reduction of class size to 25 on the East Side and 30 in the rest of the city, the educational component of the Providence Plan provided for the addition of 11 new elementary guidance teachers, 8 reading specialists, and 72 teacher aides to be placed in receiving schools throughout the city. The services of this special staff were divided among the receiving schools, with all schools getting one or more teacher aides, but some schools sharing guidance counselors and reading teachers on a part-time basis. Reading teachers were available to the receiving schools on a much broader basis than guidance teachers, since there were already 19 reading specialists at the elementary and junior high levels in the Providence school system under the district's Title I program. With desegregation, most of the Title I elementary reading teachers in formerly segregated schools followed the children to the receiving schools. A few reading teachers were still assigned to elementary schools not directly affected by desegregation, however. Reading teachers were thus a new resource to many of the receiving schools, and guidance teachers were new to nearly all schools. Guidance teachers were not generally available in Providence's elementary schools prior to desegregation. The use of teacher aides, primarily women from the sending areas, was also new to the Providence school system. The 72 teacher aides placed in the Providence Plan receiving schools were hired under a New Careers project sponsored by the local poverty program. The aide program trained women to work as classroom, library, and audiovisual assistants and to help with school attendance activities, including neighborhood liaison work with parents where attendance problems existed. Some aides also rode the buses to school with the children.

Besides adding new educational personnel, the Providence Plan furnished libraries and new textbooks for many of the receiving schools. The citywide Providence School Clinic was expanded with Title I funds, giving children eligible for its services increased access to psychological testing and referral for followup help. This clinic was originally set up primarily for children in the South Providence and Doyle-Jenkins areas.

In addition to the supporting educational services outlined above, hot lunch programs were introduced in 18 of the elementary schools involved in the Providence Plan. Five of the receiving schools with cafeterias already had hot lunch programs, and in the 18 schools without cafeterias that had never had lunch programs, prepared "zip lunches" were delivered to the schools in insulated, individual containers. Lunch was available to all children in these 23 schools, with children from the Providence Plan sending areas automatically eligible for a reduced price of 25 cents per meal (the regular price of school lunches was 40 cents). Only three of the schools involved in the Providence Plan—Berkshire, Hammond, and Willow—did not participate in the hot lunch program. Two schools, including Lippitt Hill, added free breakfast programs after desegregation got underway.

In other changes instituted with the Providence Plan, about 50 elementary teachers in the regular schools were transferred because of school closings, school conversions, and the shifting of children. Teacher reassignments were made within the framework of established union procedures, with all displaced teachers having the right to transfer and bid for open positions on the basis of seniority. In South Providence, teachers from the schools converted to special education centers were given the opportunity to move with the children. On the East Side, Superintendent O'Connor and coordinating principal McDonald talked personally with each teacher, giving information about plans for desegregation and a general idea of what to expect with the changes to be brought about by desegregation. Teachers had the option of transferring to schools not as greatly affected by desegregation if they did not think they could fit into the new situation. About five teachers in Howland, Summit, and Doyle-Jenkins requested moves to other schools after these talks. Because the school was new and experimental, the Lippitt Hill faculty was essentially a volunteer staff made up primarily of teachers transferred from Doyle, Jenkins, Summit, and Howland, plus other teachers who moved to Lippitt Hill from Flynn and other schools in the city.

Final pupil assignments were completed near the end of the summer. East Side upper elementary children were divided between Summit and Howland on the basis of geographic zones, but the assignment of black South Providence children to "satellite" schools was made on the basis of several factors, including available classroom space at different grade levels. There was an attempt to keep families intact, but this goal was not always achieved. Coordinating principal Joyce said that families were split up because of space considerations and lack of knowledge of family ties where children had different surnames or were already enrolled in separate South Providence schools. There was also an attempt to "balance" classrooms racially within the receiving schools, keeping the classroom, as well as the school population as a whole, at a maximum of 30 percent black. Assignment of only one or two black children to a classroom was also avoided where possible, to prevent social isolation.

The Providence Plan as adopted in April provided for the transfer of all children in grades one through six to the elementary "satellite" schools scattered throughout the city. By late summer, however, the school committee agreed to go ahead with a partial "middle school" plan and transfer some sixth graders to the junior high schools. Following this decision, all sixth graders in South Providence were assigned to Roger Williams Junior High School, as originally proposed in the O'Connor Plan. There were other shifts at the sixth-grade level in some Providence Plan receiving schools to make room for the bused children. Some sixth graders in Regent, for example, were transferred to Nathaniel Greene Junior High School. Superintendent O'Connor also announced at the end of August that all students in ungraded special education classes and other types of special education classes at Roger Williams would be transferred out, partly to make room for the incoming sixth graders. These pupils were moved to Samuel W. Bridgham and Esek Hopkins Junior High Schools. A total of a little over 600 elementary children in ungraded and other special education classes for the handicapped, the mentally retarded, and the emotionally disturbed were moved throughout the city, with most of these children being transferred to the new centers established at Temple and Flynn. Other special education classes were distributed between regular elementary and junior high schools.

On the East Side, parents were notified of their children's new school assignment in June. In South Providence and in the rest of the city notices were not sent out until a little over a week before school opened. There were two reasons for the delay in sending out assignments in South Providence: the greater mobility of South Providence families and the fact that last-minute notices allowed less time for opposition to crystalize. Resentment over one-way busing and school closings was building up in South Providence as September approached, and the superintendent wanted to stave off protest that might develop over school assignments. Just prior to the opening of school, all parents throughout the city whose children were reassigned because of desegregation were sent details about bus schedules, bus stops, and the hot lunch program. Bus passes and identification stickers for children to wear on the first day of school were also mailed, plus a fact sheet with the office telephone numbers of the two coordinating principals in charge of desegregation. On the East Side, coordinating principal McDonald and Miss O'Brien, the new principal of Lippitt Hill, placed an advertisement in the newspapers stating they would hold office hours in the Jenkins School for two weeks before school started. There was a good deal of parent response to this opportunity to contact coordinating principals in both parts of the city.

Other preparations for the first stage of desegregation included an all-day orientation meeting for principals and teacher aides held the day before school opened. The two coordinating principals went over the final details of the desegregation plan, including the number of black children each school would receive. Superintendent O'Connor made a plea for cooperation and several leaders from the black community spoke, among them Reverend Edwards of the Providence Human Relations Commission, James Williams of the Urban League, and a representative of the NAACP.

Cost of Providence Plan. State and federal funds were obtained to finance the bulk of the Providence desegregation plan, with most of the cost of busing and the hot lunch program paid for by two special grants from the state Department of Education. The state Department of Education also financed a program of voluntary in-service training for 30 teachers at Rhode Island College in the summer of 1967. The budget for direct costs of the Providence Plan totaled $670,222, with $324,610 earmarked for compensatory personnel; $161,612 for transportation, and $184,000 for the hot lunch program. The compensatory personnel budget covered the cost of 11 guidance teachers, reading teachers, coordinators, and 32 of the 72 teacher aides to be added to receiving schools, but did not include classroom teachers added to reduce class size. The transportation budget provided $65,000 for busing handicapped and special education children to the Flynn and Temple schools, as well as $89,550 to bus children to receiving schools and $7,000 to move necessary furniture and equipment. The actual cost of busing children was much higher than anticipated and over twice this amount, $217,673, was budgeted for the second year of desegregation. The state Department of Education voted

$184,000 to Providence to meet the cost of the hot lunch program and another $268,000 for transportation, desegregation coordinators, and other special supporting personnel for the Providence Plan. These funds constituted the largest part of a special appropriation of $500,000 that the state legislature had earmarked to assist localities in the resolution of de facto school segregation problems. In addition to costs that were directly budgeted to the Providence Plan, a number of special personnel and services from other federal and state programs were also diverted to the receiving schools. The teacher aide program, for example, was developed on a broader basis than originally anticipated in the Providence Plan budget, and was ultimately funded through the Economic Opportunities Act in conjunction with a citywide New Careers aide-training program. The cost for training New Careers aides in the Providence Plan schools, most of which does not show up in the Providence Plan budget, was set at $229,204. Estimates of the total cost of implementing the Providence Plan, including all supporting and auxiliary programs and services, are as high as $2 million.

6.
Implementation and Revision of Providence Plan

Providence Plan Transfers. The Providence Plan was fully implemented on September 6, 1967, in spite of demonstrations demanding the reopening of Flynn as a neighborhood school and an agreement from the school committee that Flynn would be converted back to a regular elementary school in October 1967.

Final school department desegregation plans called for the transfer of a total of 2,655 children. The number of children moved was higher than projected in the spring because of the assignment of all sixth graders in the Roger Williams feeder area to Roger Williams Junior High School. The Providence Plan as adopted in April had assumed the continuation of the more limited voluntary enrollment of South Providence sixth graders in Roger Williams that had begun the previous March. On a citywide basis, more children in South Providence were moved than in any other part of the community. Roughly three out of every five children (56 percent) who were transferred to accomplish desegregation lived in South Providence; about two out of five lived on the East Side; and only 4 percent lived elsewhere in the city. The overwhelming majority (72 percent) of the children reassigned in South Providence and in the three high black enrollment schools in North Providence and the West End were black, while on the East Side the exact opposite was true. Nearly three-fourths (72 percent) of the children shifted on the East Side were white. On a citywide basis, 54 percent of the pupils transferred were black and 46 percent were white.

The busing of children to accomplish desegregation was the most dramatic and publicized aspect of the Providence Plan. The number and racial identity of the sixth grade children bused to Roger Williams Junior High School are not available, but in grades one through five 59 percent of about 1600 children reassigned because of desegregation were bused. Blacks bore the brunt of busing both in South Providence and in the city at large. A total of about 850 black children were bused out of South Providence to white "satellite" schools scattered throughout the city, but no white children at all were bused in connection with the South Providence desegregation plan. Nearly three-fourths (74 percent) of the children bused on the East Side were white but the total number of children bused in that area—750 approximately—was too small to counterbalance the large numbers of black children bused out of South Providence. On a citywide basis, seven out of every ten elementary children bused were black.

While the busing captured public attention, 41 percent of the children assigned to new elementary schools were close enough to school to walk. The 231 white South Providence children shifted from Flynn and Temple to Beacon and Fogarty walked, as did about 194 black students transferred from Berkshire to Camden, Vineyard to Gilbert Stuart, Hammond to Kenyon and Willow, and Fogarty to Broad. On the East Side, about half of the children moved were within walking distance of their new schools. Most of the 340 sixth graders assigned to Roger Williams also walked.

In addition to transfers that were directly related to the desegregation of elementary classrooms, at least 755 other children were shifted in related moves that took place simultaneously with desegregation. About 611 special education students were moved to the new centers established at Flynn and Temple schools and to special classrooms in regular elementary and junior high schools. Most of these children were bused. At least 144 upper elementary children in the white "satellite" schools were transferred to junior high schools in a further extension of "middle school" conversions that also made room for black children coming in as a result of desegregation.

The overall assignment pattern developed for South Providence was to send as many black children as possible to nearby white schools bordering the South Providence ghetto, busing the rest in groups to schools at greater distances, mainly in the northern and western sections of the city. In the first group of assignments to schools adjacent to predominantly black areas, most black children from Beacon were assigned to Kenyon; black children from Hammond were split between Kenyon and Willow; 93 black children from Fogarty were rezoned in the Broad Street attendance area; and black Vineyard pupils were placed in adjoining Gilbert Stuart. Black children from Temple, the smaller of the two South Providence schools converted to special use, were bused to only three schools—Laurel Hill, Ralph and Windmill. Black Fogarty pupils were spread a little more widely, being bused to six schools—five public schools (Academy, Laurel Hill, Regent, Reservoir, and Webster) and Henry Barnard on the Rhode Island College campus. Flynn was by far the largest school affected by desegregation and Flynn children were the most widely distributed of all, being bused to nine receiving schools in the northern and western parts of Providence. Flynn children were assigned to Academy, Branch, Kenyon, Laurel Hill, Mt. Pleasant, Nelson (Robert F. Kennedy), Ralph, Veazie, and Windmill in groups ranging from 10 to 113 pupils. The Kenyon school in Federal Hill received the most South Providence children, being assigned 190 black pupils; Windmill, at the extreme northern tip of the city received the second highest number of black students, 126; and Veazie, also in the northern part of the city near Windmill, got 102 black transfers. Academy, Camden, and Mt. Pleasant got the lowest number of black children, with Academy and Camden each receiving 10 and Mt. Pleasant, 20. (See Figure 3.)

On the East Side, the modified Princeton Plan was carried out as anticipated, placing 88 black pupils in grades 4–6 in Howland and 100 black children in these upper elementary grades in Summit. As a primary school for the equivalent of three attendance areas, Lippitt Hill had the highest enrollment of the three schools and the largest number of black students of any of the East Side schools after desegregation. Lippitt Hill enrolled 233 black students in grades 1–3 and was 38 percent black. Sum-

Figure 3. *Transfer of black elementary pupils under Providence Plan for School Deseg-regation, September 1967*

KEY

KINDERGARTEN   ◇
ELEMENTARY SCHOOLS   △
JUNIOR HIGH SCHOOLS   □
HIGH SCHOOLS   ○

RECEIVED BLACK STUDENTS   +
BLACK STUDENTS TRANSFERRED OUT   −
SCHOOL CLOSED OR CONVERTED TO OTHER USE   ×
CHILDREN WALKED TO RECEIVING SCHOOL   ▲
CHILDREN BUSED TO RECEIVING SCHOOL   ▲

mit was also 38 percent black after desegregation, while Howland became 30 percent black.

Although a racial count of pupils was not made with the opening of school and the exact distribution of students in individual schools was not known, the immediate impact of the Providence Plan was to (1) reduce the black population in nine schools that were already considered segregated or had high and growing black enrollments, (2) eliminate all concentrations of black students as high as 50 percent of the total student population, (3) enroll black students in five Providence schools that had previously been all-white; (4) increase the number of black students in 13 predominantly white elementary schools; and (5) reduce the number of all-white schools in the system from six to two.

Early Period of Desegregation. Desegregation commenced with a great deal of concern on the part of many black and white parents, but with no major incidents. While school department officials and community leaders who had helped plan desegregation were worried about the bus schedules and timing, individual parents tended to be anxious about the situation the children would meet on the buses and in the schools. There was a great deal of anxiety among black parents, especially, as to what might happen to the children in school, what would be done if a child got sick, and what would happen if he missed the bus. A white mother sympathetic to desegregation said that she would never forget the faces of black mothers shown on TV, with tears in their eyes and tears running down their cheeks as they put their children on the buses. Miss Joyce, South Providence coordinating principal, confirmed the fact that black parents were "fearful of the busing" and "afraid to part with their youngsters." She said that in many cases the fears of parents were communicated to the children. There were no provisions for late buses, but the coordinating principals attempted to cover this situation. In South Providence, if a parent could not take a late child or send him in a cab, the child was to go to the nearest school, where Miss Joyce would pick him up. On the East Side, parent volunteers were lined up to help transport children in case of emergencies. In spite of parental anxiety over the busing, several persons interviewed said there was no question that the children liked the buses. A white parent in the John Howland area said that with the busing some parents actually felt better about their children's safety then they did before, because of traffic problems on the way to school.

On the opening day of school, through the first week, and into the second week of classes, mothers in some parts of town, particularly white mothers, gathered in the school yards in numbers. There was no yelling or jeering, but something of a "circus atmosphere," as one school official described it. There were several hundred women on the grounds outside the Lippitt Hill School for the first few days after school opened and similar gatherings took place at other East Side schools and at some schools in northern and western Providence, such as at Nelson (Robert F. Kennedy), Regent, and other schools in the Mt. Pleasant area. A citywide PTA leader said that there were "mothers at school many days after school opened, more than would be otherwise."

The situations that black children encountered initially varied a great deal from school to school. At John Howland on the East Side, one of the schools where faculty resistance to desegregation was greatest, the first days of desegregation were described by one teacher as "terrible." She said that the principal told the children at an assembly the first day, "This used to be the best school in the city and we expect it to stay that way." A white East Side boy in Howland told his mother that the kids from Lippitt Hill came in and stood together in a group the first day and the teachers did nothing to welcome them or direct them. This boy's mother said that it was a "shock" for the black kids to "go into the Howland situation" after being at Doyle and Jenkins, "where teachers had begun to work with them, were more sympathetic and did not 'label' [children]." The principal of Regent said that there were no real incidents, but that there were some name-calling and some comments. Some of the black children were upset and refused to go into the classroom. There was also a situation where a white child refused to sit in a chair after a black child had sat in it. The principal indicated that children were reflecting home situations where parents were upset or making derogatory comments. At the Lippitt Hill School, however, the principal and many of the teachers were familiar to the children and the atmosphere was one of acceptance for the children and of making a success of desegregation. At the Webster Avenue School on the western edge of the city, a buddy system was set up among the youngsters and, according to Miss Joyce, many South Providence children were included in birthday parties and "treats." The Webster Avenue School PTA had voted in October to oppose the O'Connor Plan in the early stages of controversy over South Providence desegregation.

There was fairly general agreement that most of the initial adjustment problems were adult problems—those of parents, teachers, and principals. School staff and community leaders noted that during the first year of desegregation white parents complaining about fights between children would always mention it if a black child was involved and "it was always a major problem." When there were instances of white children being pushed or threatened by black children, the parents were "more upset than the children." According to an East Side white mother, the white parents "looked for" problems, such as children being shoved. Mr. McDonald, the East Side coordinating principal, reported that there were many rumors in the early days of desegregation of black children assaulting white children physically and of white children "abusing black children," often by name-calling. He immediately investigated all cases reported to him. He said that in instances of supposed physical assault, the typical pattern was that "a threat becomes a happening" in the parent's mind. He said that he did not have one substantiated case of physical assault among the many complaints made to him, although there were some cases of black children threatening whites and of following a white child home. McDonald and others mentioned the fact that many white parents and teachers on the East Side were preoccupied with the "vulgar language" used by black children, particularly black boys. "Foul language" was a prime complaint in the first two to three months of desegregation.

A great deal of effort had been expended on the East Side to secure desegregation and prepare black children academically, but it was here that the greatest number of problems surfaced. Desegregation on the East Side, as many people pointed out, brought together "extremes" more so than in other parts of the city—extremes in terms of income, education, cultural advantages, and opportunity. Complaints of whites in the early stages of desegregation were greatest in the John Howland area where the East Side contrasts were greatest. Coordinating principal McDonald said that the complaints of white parents in the Howland area during the first few months of desegregation "verged on hysteria." Parents told him black children were threatening white children with knives in the corridor, throwing food recklessly around in the cafeteria, ripping the clothes off white children, and beating up white children in the classrooms in the presence of teachers. They also objected to the black children's manners, their clothes, their "vulgarity," and their "dirty noses." He said that during the first three months of desegregation about 50 percent of his time was spent investigating specific parental complaints about children's behavior. The number of complaints then dropped sharply. McDonald associated the volume and nature of complaints in the Howland area to the vast differences in the socioeconomic status of the Howland and Doyle-Jenkins children and to the lack of exposure in the Howland area to children from low-income families. He felt that the children's blackness intensified the other contrasts. Howland is in one of the highest income areas of the city and the school had the highest academic standing of any elementary school in the city prior to desegregation.

Other early complaints on the East Side and in the Howland area, particularly, came from property owners who said that the black children walking home from school ran through their yards and destroyed plants and property. McDonald was able to verify only one property complaint, where a black boy pulled down a clothes line. The people complaining about children destroying property insisted that it be compulsory for black children to ride the buses. McDonald took the position that riding the bus was optional and permitted children to walk to school with their parent's permission. Children traveled relatively short distances on the bus on the East Side and both McDonald and Miss O'Brien, the principal of Lippitt Hill, maintained that the buses were a convenience, to be utilized as best suited the individual or school situation. Lippitt Hill had the most flexible attitude toward use of the buses of any school in the city, the general idea being to regard the buses as a resource and get as much out of them as possible. The Lippitt Hill buses picked up children living closer to school than the official walking limit, and late buses leaving Lippitt Hill at the close of the after-school community school program detoured to take home regular school children who had missed the bus at the close of the school day. Parents who needed to come to school for conferences or any other reason were free to ride the buses along with the children and children could get bus passes to ride home with friends for after-school visits. In the fall of 1968, the second year of desegregation, approximately the same number of black children as in the first year were walking to and from school in good weather, but there were no complaints from property owners in the Summit and Howland areas.

Teachers' adjustments were a major problem throughout the city, especially in schools that had not previously enrolled any black or low-income children. Black leaders complained that some teachers were "at a complete loss" to understand the black

children and their problems. A principal of an all-white school
that received 66 bused South Providence students stated:

> A great many teachers were presented with a type of child they
> had never encountered. It was quite overwhelming. They were not
> used to a child different from those in their own residential area
> . . . Some teachers are used to a conforming, middle class child.
> It was a new experience to have a child rebel, answer back or refuse
> to obey an order. The language of the street was quite shocking
> to some teachers, especially the older teachers.

She also said that there was more fighting in her school than
there was prior to desegregation and that there were more children wandering around the building, as the white children had
"copied" this from the black children. This was upsetting to
some of the teachers who felt that too much of their time was
taken up with settling fights and checking up on children away
from the classroom. Children arriving at school "angry" constituted another new problem the teachers faced. Teachers in
one school found that some of the bused children were angry
and upset when they got to school and did not settle down for
15 to 20 minutes. The principal thought that crowding and fights
on the bus upset some of the children, in addition to problems
at home. The teachers in her school also had difficulty with
learning to work with the aides, who were a new element in
the school and who held different views from those of the
teachers as to their role and responsibilities.

Staff in other schools and community leaders noted a tendency
in some schools to "pretend nothing has changed" and continue
to "run the school on straight middle class values." Teachers
apparently overreacted to the children's language in many
schools and an East Side community leader said the "rigidity
of the teachers was so great the kids exploded at the end of
the day." A teacher on the East Side felt that in-school pressures
and frustrations contributed to after-school problems, with black
kids taking out their hostilities on white children and on property
in the "receiving" neighborhoods when school let out. Discipline
problems increased where teachers were inconsistent and uneven
in their handling of children, "afraid of being accused of discrimination if they try to cope with the kids," and "afraid to talk
about race relations." For example, black children who were
not discipline problems in Doyle and Jenkins became discipline
problems in Howland and to some degree at Summit Avenue.
White children in these and other schools complained that the
black kids were getting away with things they could not do.

A mother in Washington Park noted that "teachers always have favorites," pointing out that "Negro children will not be their favorites if they have the least bit of prejudice."

In some schools, the problems of teacher adjustment gradually lessened as the teachers became accustomed to the new children and the new situation. A school department administrator noted the changed view of the bused children held by teachers in South Providence receiving schools after the early phases of desegregation. Teachers said that the children were "wild" when they first came, but "now they have quieted down." She suggested that the difference "may be in the eyes of the beholder," that the teachers had expected certain behavior of the children in the initial stage of desegregation and got what they expected. She noted that teachers "realized they were involved" and "were trying to cope, many in mistaken ways, but they were trying."

Principals, on the other hand, were frequently mentioned as one of the main sources of problems in desegregation. The tradition of principal autonomy was strong in the Providence school system, so much so that several community leaders likened the Providence principals to ship captains of old who were a law unto themselves at sea. Desegregation not only brought in black children, but caused a number of other changes such as the all-day "single sessions," the lunch program, specialized personnel, aides, the addition of libraries, and, in some schools, new curricula and textbooks. Desegregation was "a traumatic thing" for some of the principals and the changes that took place were sometimes "too much for the principals to cope with." A school department administrator who worked closely with desegregation attributed most of the problems in the first year of desegregation to "failure" at the principal's level. Prior to desegregation, principals did not take a position on the Providence Plan through their official association, were reluctant to accept the fact that desegregation would actually take place, and were slow to furnish information and make necessary arrangements to implement the Providence Plan. Even after desegregation began, "some felt it would fail and go away." Top administration began to take a "harder line" after the first few months, emphasizing, "Integration is here to stay" and "This is part of your job."

In addition to the problems that centered around adult adjustment to desegregation, there were several scheduling and organizational problems that became apparent in the early stages of desegregation. At some schools only bused children participated in the hot lunch program, making an obvious distinction between the sending and receiving pupils. After complaints from community leaders, all children were required to eat lunch at school, bringing bag lunches if they did not wish to buy the "zip lunches" or cafeteria food. Some of the pickup stops for the South Providence buses were also unsatisfactory and were changed after a few weeks. Other busing problems—the lack of late morning and afternoon buses and children having to wait a long time at bus stops in cold weather—were never really resolved.

Community Campaign to Reopen Flynn. At the end of the summer of 1967, shortly before school opened and the Providence Plan was implemented, dissatisfaction over desegregation plans for South Providence developed into a full-blown community issue. As discussed earlier, the closing of neighborhood schools and the one-way character of the busing were sources of resentment and targets of criticism from the time the plan was announced. Following the release of children's school assignments on August 29, some South Providence parents found that their children would be attending as many as three different receiving schools. Few details concerning the implementation of the Providence Plan had been made public and parents were concerned about other aspects of the desegregation plan. On August 31 a group of South Providence residents made up primarily of mothers of children to be bused out of the area went to the school administration offices to discuss: (1) children in the same family being sent to different schools; (2) plans for the teacher aide program; (3) plans for changing teacher attitudes in the receiving schools; (4) the need for improvement in teaching techniques and methods; and (5) the school department's long-range plan for the Edmund W. Flynn School, including future use of Flynn in the after-school community school program and as a community organizing center for the anti-poverty program.

The future of Flynn's after-school community school program, sponsored jointly by the school department and the anti-poverty program, was of much concern to area residents. The Flynn community school was headed by Jarvis D. Jones, the only black person heading any school program throughout the city and one of two black persons employed in a supervisory capacity by the Providence Department of Public Schools in 1966. The other black person employed as a supervisor also worked with the community school program. There were no black principals or vice principals or any other black administrators in any of the regular Providence schools in 1967, and there were none

on the staff of the central administration. The common bond
of interest in Flynn shared by area residents and the anti-poverty
program was clear from the first protests over Flynn's closing.
Several of the most vocal critics of the South Providence desegregation plan were staff members of Progress for Providence
and other anti-poverty agencies, and anti-poverty centers such
as the youth "Drop-In-Center" in South Providence were frequently used as meeting places for the Flynn protest group.

Following unsatisfactory meetings with the superintendent and
members of the subcommittee of the mayor's working conference
on desegregation, about 60 South Providence residents staged
a 36-hour sit-in/sleep-in August 31 at the school committee meeting room. They demanded: (1) that Flynn be kept open as a
regular, quality, integrated elementary school; (2) that all the
children in any given family attend the same school; (3) that
a black principal or vice principal be appointed to Flynn; and
(4) that a meeting be arranged with the school committee to
resolve their demands. A position paper issued by the demonstrating group on September 2 pointed out that the protesters
were not opposed to the integration of public schools and did
not object to their children being bused out of South Providence.
Indeed, they would welcome busing "if all children are going
to be given the same treatment in regard to transportation"
and "all parents are given the same options in regard to their
children." They protested the "double standard" in South Providence's desegregation plan, which involved busing out black children only, splitting up black families, and placing a center for
special education in their neighborhood, which they said no white
neighborhood would accept.[61]

The demand for the reopening of Flynn as a desegregated
elementary school was not settled until October 4, after a school
boycott and a great deal of divided opinion as to the wisdom
of "tampering with" the Providence Plan as it was initially
adopted. School committee members met with South Providence
residents as a result of the sit-in and on September 4 agreed
at an "unofficial" meeting to retain Flynn as an elementary school
and appoint a black principal or assistant principal in "some
Providence school." The school committee also made a commitment to consult South Providence residents with respect to future
plans for Flynn. South Providence protesters in turn agreed
to go along with the Providence Plan transfers until the next
regular school committee meeting, when terms of the agreement
were to be officially adopted in a formal resolution. The 150
South Providence residents who attended the September 4 meet-

ing also pointed out Chairman Fricker's absence from this and all school committee meetings for the past eight months and demanded his resignation.

Shortly after the school committee's September 4 Flynn agreement, Mayor Doorley took a strong stand against "nibbling at the Providence Plan" and urged the school committee not to make any changes.[62] Under pressure from the mayor, the state commissioner of education, the press, at least two city councilmen, and the Rhode Island Chapter of the Council for Exceptional Children, the school committee voted unanimously September 11 to go ahead with the Providence Plan, backing down on its agreement of September 4. The school committee's direct repudiation of its commitment to South Providence residents, plus an incident that took place at the September 11 meeting, greatly increased support for the Flynn campaign, particularly in the black community. On September 11, in the midst of "outraged shouts" of "white racists" following the school committee's vote, a South Providence leader called for "the cops to come out from behind the curtains."[63] Two members of the audience then jumped on the stage of the auditorium where the meeting was being held and pulled back the curtains, revealing six plainclothesmen. About 420 persons, mainly black, were present at this meeting and were greatly angered by the hiding policemen, as well as by the insulting way in which the school committee had broken its word. The base of community support for reopening Flynn broadened after the September 11 meeting to include the black Ministers Alliance of Greater Providence, the Reverend Herbert O. Edwards, director of the Providence Human Relations Commission, and the chairman of the NAACP Education Committee. The NAACP as an organization continued to back the Providence Plan. Other support for the Flynn campaign came from a former director of the city's anti-poverty program, Progress for Providence; the Cooperating Clergymen of South Providence, a group of Catholic and Protestant ministers; the Social Action Department of the Rhode Island Council of Churches; and several individual white ministers including the Reverend Albert Q. Perry of the Church of the Mediator, the Reverend McKinnon White, pastor of the Washington Park Methodist Church, and the Reverend Henry J. Shelton, a South Providence Catholic priest.

Anticipating the school committee's repudiation of its agreement after the mayor's statement, South Providence leaders initiated a school boycott on September 11. The boycott led to the development of four Freedom Schools, which were in

operation by September 18. According to the press, approximately 175 families, primarily from South Providence, participated in the school boycott. The boycott had little or no effect
on the East Side, which was not involved in the controversy.
Up to 120 children were enrolled in the Freedom Schools, set
up at the anti-poverty Drop-In-Center in South Providence, the
Washington Park Methodist Church, the Church of the
Mediator, and the Episcopal Church House. The Urban League
of Rhode Island helped recruit teachers, and a professor at
Brown University was named principal of the Freedom Schools.
A *Journal-Bulletin* opinion survey showed that a large portion
of the South Providence blacks were upset about the Flynn
situation, even if they had not reached the point where they
would boycott the schools.

South Providence residents agreed to call off their boycott
on October 4, after the school committee issued a public apology
for "the implied affront to the dignity of the South Providence
people"[64] and made a firm agreement to establish a "quality,
integrated" elementary school at Flynn that would enroll whites
from all over the city on a voluntary basis. Other terms of the
agreement, which had the mayor's sanction, were: (1) the racial
population of Flynn would be 70 percent white, reflecting the
goal for all schools set by the Providence Plan; (2) children attending Freedom Schools would be given priority in making up the
150 black children to be enrolled at Flynn; (3) white children
living in the Flynn area would also have priority in enrollment;
(4) South Providence parents would choose professional
educators, as well as community representatives, to help plan
a model school program; and (5) Flynn would open as a regular
elementary school on January 29, regardless of the racial composition of the enrollment.

Another condition of the agreement reached between Flynn
protesters and the school department was that a black principal
or vice principal would be appointed in one of the secondary
schools. Jarvis Jones was then the only black person in the school
system on the principal's promotional list. The school department
would not appoint him principal of Flynn as community groups
requested, as he was certified to be a principal at the secondary,
rather than the elementary, level. He was named vice principal
at Roger Williams shortly after the Flynn agreement was
finalized, stayed there only a short time, and was reassigned
to Gilbert Stuart Junior High School for the remainder of the
year. Jones was appointed vice principal of Hope High School
at the beginning of the 1968–69 school year.

Development of Flynn Model School. After agreeing to establish a quality, integrated school at Flynn, South Providence protesters, school department officials, and a wide range of citizens and educators spent the next few months planning a "model school" and recruiting students to attend. A 30-member steering committee for the Flynn Model School was formed, including South Providence parents, educators from area colleges selected by the South Providence protest group, school department officials, and representatives of the teacher's union, the state Department of Education, and the city anti-poverty agency. The committee formulated a "rationale" for Flynn that set as goals class sizes limited to 25; recruitment of teachers on a voluntary basis; transfer "without prejudice" of teachers not suited to the school at the end of the first year; hiring of full-time specialists in music, art, physical education, and reading; hiring of other part-time and full-time special personnel, such as a counselor, social worker, nurse, librarian, and speech and hearing therapist; utilization of auxiliary community and college personnel on the Flynn staff; hiring of a school-community liaison staff member; in-service human relations training for the entire staff; and after-school educational, recreational, and cultural programs for children and adults in the neighborhood.

Other plans for the Flynn Model School included a nongraded curriculum in reading and mathematics at the primary level and departmentalized instruction in grades 4 and 5. Students were to be assigned to individual classrooms at a ratio of 70 percent white and 30 percent black. A cross-cultural approach to subject matter was to be used, emphasizing the contributions of blacks to the American heritage. Team teaching, audiovisual aids, field trips, and supplementary professional and community resources were to be used, rather than traditional teaching methods. The steering committee also decided to bypass the traditional school administrative pattern and planned for a Staff and Educational Coordinator (SEC) instead of a principal, and an administrative assistant to the SEC rather than a vice principal. A community liaison officer was to be the third person on the administrative team leading the staff at Flynn.

Immediately following formulation of plans for Flynn, an intensive campaign to recruit students was carried out by the school department and interested citizens. A committee of clergymen and civic leaders was appointed to help recruit white pupils and the superintendent sent letters to 3,825 parents inviting them to place their children in Flynn. Letters went to all families with children formerly enrolled in Flynn, plus selected white parents throughout the city. The superintendent held four large area meetings in December in different parts of the community to describe the advantages of the Flynn program, and the coordinating principals and the assistant superintendent of elementary education also spoke to parents' groups. The Flynn program was discussed on radio and television and there was editorial support from the press. The newspapers emphasized positive developments in reporting on the planning for Flynn and gave a running total of gains in white enrollment. Toward the end of this campaign, Flynn held an open house on January 21 that was attended by more than 700 parents and resulted in the registration of 43 white pupils.

School department officials appealed to whites on the basis of the quality academic offerings planned for Flynn, but also tried to create an impression of "selectivity" and "prestige" associated with attending the school. Dr. O'Connor spoke of a "selective" admissions policy, based on IQ and achievement scores, although there was an obvious difficulty with finding enough whites. Early in the effort to recruit students, Dr. Myron Lieberman of Rhode Island College, an advisor to South Providence parents, suggested publicly that Mayor Doorley and Governor Chafee place their children in Flynn. He said that "one thousand others would want to go too," if these public figures led the way.[65] Mayor Doorley enrolled one son in Flynn as the January 29 deadline approached, but Governor Chafee did not place any of his children there. He did, however, urge other whites to support Flynn. In addition to the mayor, other "prestige" parents enrolling children in Flynn included William L. Robin, a school committeeman from the East Side; State Senator Julius C. Michaelson; Mrs. Kenneth W. Stanley, then president of the Regent Avenue PTA and later president of the Providence Council of PTAs; and several faculty members from Brown University. A community leader active in desegregation efforts said that white liberals all over Providence were under a great deal of pressure to "put their children where their mouth is." There were also problems in filling out the quota of black children. A black leader in the Flynn campaign said that they had a great deal of difficulty recruiting the last 37 black children. Enrollment in Flynn meant a mid-year transfer into an unknown situation.

Flynn opened on January 30 with 265 white and 150 black students. The quota of 350 whites set for the school was not reached until February 28, one month after the model school was in operation. According to the press, Flynn students were

drawn from as many as 33 of the city's elementary public schools,
as well as from private schools. A newspaper report of January
19 indicated that registration at that date included 34 former
Flynn students transferred to Veazie under the desegregation
plan and 58 children placed in Kenyon with the Providence
Plan. A total of 21 pupils, primarily white, had enrolled in Flynn
from the Joslin School and a total 21 children were signed up
from all East Side schools. There was also "a concentration"
of white transfers from the Sackett and Lexington Street Schools,
which had been so controversial during the debate over the
O'Connor Plan. Thirty-three children who formerly attended
private schools were among the 350 whites ultimately enrolled.

Final plans for Flynn included the purchase of new mathematics books for children at all grade levels; the establishment of
a mathematics laboratory with approximately $1,000 worth of
new equipment; the hiring of two full-time physical education
teachers, one for boys and one for girls; the purchase of about
$1,500 worth of new gymnasium equipment; the equipping of
classrooms throughout the school for the use of projectors and
other audiovisual equipment; the purchase of about $13,000
worth of audiovisual equipment; the implementation of cross-
cultural social studies material developed by the federally
financed Social Studies Curriculum Project of the Providence
Public Schools; the initiation of an art program planned by the
Rhode Island School of Design, to be carried out with the help
of four RISD students; a week's in-service training for Flynn
staff prior to the opening of school; an in-service course on
urban education for all teachers and specialists, conducted by
Brown University staff in the winter of 1968; and organization
of the Flynn Model School Parents Association, an independent
group without the teacher-administrator component of the PTA
structure. Shortly after Flynn's reopening, the staff consisted
of 20 classroom teachers, 13 specialists, 14 teacher aides, and
18 student teachers from local colleges. All of the staff volun-
teered to teach at Flynn, with some teachers returning who left
Flynn under the Providence Plan.

Flynn's budget for the educational program for the second
semester of the 1967–68 school year totaled about $252,000 with
$239,000 of this amount needed from new sources beyond fund-
ing available for the school year. The $252,000 to be spent on
the educational program did not include the cost of busing white
children into the school, or federal funds from existing projects
channeled back into Flynn. A grant of $44,000 under Title IV
of the Civil Rights Act provided for a citywide desegregation

specialist who also served as Staff and Educational Coordinator for Flynn. The Title IV project covered the cost of in-service training for Flynn teachers and of additional in-service courses on a citywide basis. When initial appeals to private foundations were unsuccessful, Mayor Doorley was called upon to fulfill his promise to South Providence parents to help finance the project. The cost of the Flynn Model School apparently contributed to the large deficit in school department expenditures for the 1967–68 school year.

Repercussions of Flynn Model School Decision.   The decision to reopen Flynn as an elementary school meant that other provisions had to be made for the handicapped children moved to Flynn with desegregation. Parents of handicapped children and professional organizations and associations working with the handicapped considered the consolidated center established at Flynn to be a real gain and did not want to lose this special facility. While at least one organization working with the handicapped opposed the return of Flynn as an elementary school, most parents of the handicapped organized to secure a satisfactory alternative. Shortly after the decision to develop the Flynn Model School, a group of parents of the handicapped demanded a definite commitment from the school committee to continue a consolidated program at a site they considered adequate. When the school committee failed to act, the parent group began a sit-in at the school department on October 9. On October 11, the school committee voted to build a new $1 million center for the handicapped, meanwhile providing a suitable interim facility where special services would be concentrated. Parents rejected the first 11 sites suggested for the interim facility, but at the end of November they accepted a school committee offer to place a temporary center for the handicapped at Nathaniel Greene Junior High School in North Providence. The school committee delayed voting on the informal agreement, however, and before an official decision was made, Greene parents whose children would be displaced by this plan began protesting.

Controversy over the proposed placement of handicapped children in Greene continued until January 10, with school committee members and the superintendent vacillating greatly under the pressure of different parents groups. Parents of the handicapped picketed School Committee Chairman Fricker's drug store, circulated anti-Fricker petitions, and staged a second sit-in to back their demand for location of a center at Greene. Parents of sixth-grade and ninth-grade pupils who would be displaced by the center organized to keep their children in Greene. The sixth-grade students had been moved from Regent and Joslin in the fall with the "middle school" moves accompanying desegregation and their parents objected to the children being transferred again. Parents of ninth-grade students did not want their children assigned to senior high schools. In spite of their different goals, the sit-in begun by parents of handicapped children on January 4 was soon joined by mothers of sixth-grade Greene pupils, who demanded that their children be kept at Greene. The joint sit-in of the two parents groups continued until the school committee's final decision on January 10 to house the handicapped youngsters in Greene. This decision caused about 165 Greene ninth graders to be transferred to senior high schools and also resulted in all sixth graders in Greene being transferred back to Regent and Joslin Elementary Schools or to George J. West Junior High School. In some cases, at least, the schools to which sixth graders were assigned did not have adequate space for them. Regent, for example, was full to capacity due to desegregation and had to set up makeshift classes in the auditorium and use the basement to accommodate all of its pupils.

When the school committee voted in January to set up the temporary center for the handicapped at Greene, Superintendent O'Connor also promised Greene parents he would definitely establish a middle school at Greene the next fall. This meant that the interim center for the handicapped would have to be moved, but parents of the handicapped were promised another suitable facility by fall that could be used until the new center was completed. The school committee voted to convert Greene to a middle school beginning in September 1968, without making satisfactory plans for a new facility for the handicapped children, however. Parents of the handicapped were thus sitting in at the school department offices again by May 13, 1968, and took the position that their children would not leave Greene until an acceptable substitute was found. They rejected a proposal from the superintendent to place the interim center for handicapped children at John Howland and were joined in a 16-day sit-in by parents representing five East Side schools. The proposal to place the interim center at John Howland was part of a total reorganization "package" planned for the East Side, which included (1) converting John Howland to a center for the handicapped; (2) establishing a middle school at Nathan Bishop Junior High School for grades 6–8; and (3) assigning all children in grades 4–5 in the Lippitt Hill, Summit, and Howland attendance areas to the Summit Avenue School. East Siders opposed the total reorganization plan, with the result that the school committee voted May 29 to move the facility for the handicapped to Kenyon instead of Howland, and to postpone implementation of a middle school plan for the East Side pending development of a "true" middle school program by an outside consultant. The decision to place the temporary center for the handicapped at Kenyon displaced five special education classes already there. As one mother summed up the situation, "It always seems one bunch gets pushed around for another bunch."

The solidarity of all parents against the school committee was the most revealing aspect of the running controversy over relocation of the handicapped children from Flynn. While their demands were sometimes at odds, all parents involved—the South Providence parents who wanted Flynn returned as an elementary school, the parents of the handicapped, the Greene and the East Side parents—agreed to remain allies and not oppose each other. Some blacks joined the sit-ins demanding facilities for the handicapped, and parents of sixth-grade children at Greene sat in with the parents of the handicapped whose goals conflicted with their own. The degree of parental involvement, activity, and unity was completely new for the Providence schools, with the participation of whites in demonstrations over Greene and the East Side schools directly inspired by the successful campaign launched by black parents in South Providence.

Another repercussion of the decision to establish Flynn as a model school was the demand of parents in North Providence that all schools in the city be given the same educational improvements adopted for Flynn. In late January and early February 1968, a group of North Providence PTA units, including Windmill, Berkshire, Branch, and Veazie Elementary Schools, plus Esek Hopkins Junior High School, asked Mayor Doorley, Governor Chafee, Superintendent O'Connor, and four members of the General Assembly from Providence to make available "sufficient additional monies to finance the extension of quality education now being offered at Flynn." They specifically requested that a $3 million state aid fund earmarked for "culturally handicapped" children be used to raise the quality of education in the city in general. A spokesman for the combined North Providence PTA's wrote Mayor Doorley that the quality education anticipated under the Providence Plan had not been achieved. She reminded Superintendent O'Connor that hundreds of South Providence children were bused into North Providence schools. "It is these children we are concerned about as well as our own," she stated.[66] As a result of the combined PTA

protests, North Providence schools were placed under the supervision of the coordinating principal for the East Side and additional remedial reading, physical education, art, and music
teachers were added to the staffs of these schools. Nongraded
classes were also to be introduced in the primary grades.

Initial Impact of the Modified Providence Plan. In February
1968, following the reopening of Flynn as a regular elementary
school, the Providence school department released racial data
on all elementary schools in the city, making possible an evaluation of the initial impact of the modified Providence Plan. An
analysis of school department statistics carried out by Dr. Harold
W. Pfautz of Brown University indicates that the Providence
Plan was completely successful in removing black children from
majority black schools, but only moderately successful in fulfilling
two other primary goals set by the plan: (1) to reduce the black
population in grades 1–6 in all elementary schools to a maximum
of 30 percent and (2) to desegregate individual classrooms so
that each classroom in the Providence Plan schools approximated
a 30 percent black enrollment.

Nearly two-thirds (62 percent) of Providence's black school
children in grades 1–6 were enrolled in majority black schools
prior to school desegregation, according to Dr. Pfautz—that is,
in schools that were 50 percent or more black. During the first
year of desegregation, no black children in grades 1–6 were
found in majority black schools, although 12 percent were attending schools with an enrollment of 40 to 49 percent black, and
47 percent were enrolled in schools that were between 30 and
49 percent black. While majority black schools were eliminated,
only 53 percent of the black elementary children in grades 1–6
were in schools that met the Providence Plan's goal of desegregation—a maximum of 30 percent black. (See Table 5.) As
for classrooms, Dr. Pfautz's data show that 47 percent of the
black and white children in grades 1–6 in the Providence elementary schools were in segregated classrooms in 1966, prior to
desegregation. Dr. Pfautz defines "segregated" classrooms as
those that contain more black than white students, or are all
white. His 1968 followup study of classrooms indicated that
under the Providence Plan only 12 percent of all children in
grades 1–6 were taught in segregated classrooms. (See Table
6.) Only 55 percent of the Providence elementary children were
assigned to classrooms in 1968 that met the specific goal set
by the Providence Plan, however—a range of from four to nine
black students per classroom.

Table 5—Black Students Attending Elementary Schools, Grades 1—6,
Providence, Rhode Island, by Percentage of Blacks in School, Before
and After Desegregation.

School Percent Black	Before Desegregation, 1967		After Desegregation, 1968		After Desegregation, 1969	
	No.	%	No.	%	No.	%
50 percent or more	1,567	62	0	0	507	15
40—49	0	0	305	12	101	3
30—39	170	7	919	35	1,218	36
20—29	508	20	905	35	972	28
10—19	157	6	445	17	506	15
1— 9	125	5	30	1	120	3
TOTAL	2,527	100	2,604	100	3,424	100

Source: Data supplied by Providence Department of Public Schools; analyzed by
H. W. Pfautz, Brown University, Department of Sociology and Anthropology.

In addition to the impact of the Providence Plan on the racial
distribution of elementary students, East Side enrollment data
suggest that the opening of the new Lippitt Hill School and
educational reforms accompanying the Providence Plan brought
a number of black and white children back to the public school
system. Between 1964 and 1966, the total enrollment in Howland, Summit, Doyle, and Jenkins dropped from 1,671 to 1,127
pupils—a loss of 544 children. With desegregation, the combined enrollment in these attendance areas rose to 1,499 in the
fall of 1967, a gain of 372 pupils. White enrollment in these
schools was up 268 students in 1967 and black enrollment was
up 104 pupils.

All in all, the 1967—68 school year was, as school committeeman
Mulvey put it, the most unusual year in the history of the Providence school department.

Table 6—Desegregation Status of Classrooms in Elementary Schools, Providence, Rhode Island, by Grade Levels, Before and After School Desegregation

Classroom Desegregation Status

Grade Level	Before Desegregation, 1966 N = 444			After Desegregation, 1968 N = 431			After Desegregation, 1969 N = 478		
	Desegregated (%)	Segregated* (%)	Total (%)	Desegregated (%)	Segregated* (%)	Total (%)	Desegregated (%)	Segregated* (%)	Total (%)
1	47	53	100	86	14	100	79	21	100
2	49	51	100	92	8	100	84	16	100
3	50	50	100	93	7	100	95	5	100
4	60	40	100	94	6	100	93	7	100
5	57	43	100	92	8	100	97	3	100
6	56	44	100	65	35	100	95	5	100
AVERAGE	53	47	100	88	12	100	90	10	100

*More black than white students per classroom or no black students per classroom.

Source: Data Supplied by the Providence Department of Public Schools; collected by Mrs. Carol Fuller, Urban League of Rhode Island, and analyzed by H. W. Pfautz, Brown University, Department of Sociology and Anthropology.

7.
Problems and Protests in the Aftermath of Elementary Desegregation

THE Flynn School controversy marked a changeover from old to new forms of citizen involvement in the Providence public schools. Where prior to the Flynn protest the public had been largely apathetic and interested community leaders had limited their actions to petitions and statements, after the Flynn issue more and more people became involved in public school issues, and stalwarts in traditionally moderate groups such as the PTA and the League of Women Voters began picketing, sitting-in, and sleeping-in in response to a variety of problems. This heightened public participation continued in the aftermath of desegregation, focusing on racial tensions and problems in the nearly integrated schools, on the quality of education and administrative leadership, on reorganization of the school committee, on further extensions of the middle school plan, and on racial unrest at the junior and senior high school levels.

Racism in the Public Schools, Spring 1968. Racism in the public schools first became a public issue in March 1968, when parent dissatisfaction over several aspects of desegregation on the East Side came to a head. Dating back to October 1967, one month after desegregation, concerned East Side parents had held a series of conferences with individual school principals and the coordinating principal regarding teachers' and principals' attitudes toward desegregation, the failure of the school department to hire specialists promised with desegregation, and the slowness with which nongraded curricula were being introduced in schools other than Lippitt Hill. Their complaints centered on the Summit and Howland schools, where educational reforms were lagging and where both black and white parents agreed that a number of teachers were prejudiced. A biracial committee of representatives of East Side PTAs met with Superintendent O'Connor on March 4 and again on March 18 to voice these complaints. On March 13, a separate group of black parents conferred with Dr. O'Connor to raise the same issues, particularly the need for action on racial problems in Summit and Howland schools. The League of Women Voters of Providence, whose membership is concentrated on the East Side, wrote Superintendent O'Connor on March 15 pointing out that some teachers regard "the Negro child as a lesser

member of the group." The League also asked the superintendent to make a persistent and determined effort to implement
the promised curriculum changes and to hire the supportive
personnel who were supposed to accompany desegregation.[67]

Growing discontent among East Side parents became a public
issue about the middle of March 1968, after appeals to the
superintendent failed to achieve satisfactory results. Black East
Side parents who had organized as the Concerned East Side
Negro Parents Committee held a meeting at the Lippitt Hill
School on March 19 to gain broader support for seven demands
they had presented to the superintendent. Many of a predominantly white group of parents attending the meeting endorsed
the following demands: (1) replacement of the principals at Howland and Summit Schools; (2) sensitivity sessions for principals,
teachers, and parents; (3) a course in minority history in all East
Side schools; (4) appointment of a resource person for black history and minority problems to work with East Side schools; (5)
better information on curriculum, requirements, and programs
in the schools; (6) a committee of black parents to interview
guidance counselors to be assigned to the schools; and (7) renaming of the Summit Avenue School to honor the Reverend Alexander Crummell, a black minister who had preached in Providence
in the 1800s. Because of the interest of white parents, the Concerned East Side Negro Parents Committee was renamed the
Committee to Eliminate Racism in the Public Schools. The Committee soon received formal support from other community
organizations, such as CORE, the Rhode Island Chapter of the
American Civil Liberties Union, HOPE, the Afro-American Society of Brown University, and the Camp Neighborhood Advisory
Committee.

Although some whites were reluctant to call for the firing
of the principals of Summit and Howland, black parents felt
that removal of the principals was essential. As Mrs. John Rollins,
chairman of the Committee to Eliminate Racism in the Public
Schools, explained their feelings:

It is the principal who sets the tone of any school and it is the
prevailing tone in these schools rather than the actions of specific
teachers that concerns us.[68]

Charges and demands made by the Committee to Eliminate
Racism were reinforced by an individual campaign carried out
by Mrs. Marion Marrow, a black East Side mother with five
children in Howland. Mrs. Marrow withdrew her youngsters
from Howland in February 1968 in an attempt to get them

transferred to other schools where the faculty and principal were more sensitive to the needs of black children. A school-community liaison worker, Mrs. Marrow demanded that four of her children be placed in Fogarty in South Providence. She wanted the fifth child, who was assigned to a special education class at Howland, placed in a more sympathetic school that offered special education. Mrs. Marrow began her efforts to transfer her children from Howland following an incident on February 16 where the principal accused one of her girls of stealing 55 cents. The accusation took place in front of other children, with the principal taking the money away from the child and keeping it until she had reached Mrs. Marrow by telephone and verified that the 55 cents belonged to the child. There was no basis for the accusation, according to Mrs. Marrow, except that some money was missing and her child happened to have 55 cents. Mrs. Marrow said that in other incidents in the school, one of her girls was called "a big fat horse" by a teacher and another child was reprimanded by a teacher for not knowing a Negro spiritual. Mrs. Marrow maintained that teachers in Howland had told black children, "You're acting like a bunch of savages," "It wasn't like this before you got here," and "All you colored kids do is pick on kids smaller than you."[69] In addition to her complaints of specific incidents of racial discrimination and derogatory racial remarks, Mrs. Marrow stated that the school system was failing to motivate and help low-income children.

Superintendent O'Connor refused Mrs. Marrow's requests to transfer her children to Fogarty on the grounds that the school district was trying to maintain a 70/30 racial ratio in Fogarty and reduce class size there. He also said he could not justify busing black children into a school where other black children were being bused out. Although no action was taken on Mrs. Marrow's transfer requests, East Side Coordinating Principal McDonald stated publicly that the stealing accusation was not handled in the way he would have liked and that Mrs. Marrow's children were doing well academically at Howland. He said further that he had met with Mrs. Marrow several times to try to resolve the problem and had asked for her help as a parent and a leader in fighting prejudice in the school.

For several weeks after the East Side parents first publicized their demands, the superintendent, the school hierarchy, and community groups lined up for and against the parents' charges. Superintendent O'Connor immediately stated to the press that the committee was acting as a "kangaroo court" in demanding the removal of the principals without a fair hearing. He said further that the manner in which the committee was proceeding was "un-American." The Providence School Principals Association, the Administrative Staff Association of the Providence Public Schools, and the Rhode Island Education Association all backed the principals, criticizing the committee for their accusations. Two of these organizations, the principals' and administrative staff associations, expressed confidence in the principals.

A citywide meeting of the Committee to Eliminate Racism in the Public Schools March 27 attracted about 500 persons who voted to endorse six of the committee's original demands. The meeting did not vote on the demand for the removal of the Howland and Summit principals, but instead called for an open public hearing on the charges of racism on the part of the principals. The Committee to Eliminate Racism had already requested such a hearing. The March 27 meeting also adopted a general resolution decrying the problem of racial discrimination in the city schools and asking immediate action by Superintendent O'Connor. In another area of concern, the assembly called for the establishment of a citywide planning committee to help create a model school system for the city of Providence. Members of the South Providence Parents Association, who had spearheaded the drive to return Flynn as a regular elementary school, attended the March 19 meeting and pledged their full support. The Providence Teachers Union endorsed the model school proposal, but delayed judgment on charges against the principals until after a hearing.

Although Superintendent O'Connor agreed to a public hearing on the charges of racism, to be held under the auspices of the Human Relations Commission, he later backed down on this commitment and scheduled a closed hearing before the superintendent on April 4 and 5. The April 4 hearing dealt specifically with the charges of racism leveled against the principals of Summit and Howland, but neither principal was present. In the absence of the two principals, a total of 13 black and white parents testified to their own and their children's experiences with the Summit and Howland principals and teachers. Parents took the position that the two principals condoned and sanctioned the racist conduct of teachers in the schools, as well as personally engaging in racist behavior themselves.

Parents' testimony in the two-day hearing indicated that:

(1) at least one of the principals, Miss Mary A. Powers of John Howland School, made negative statements about deseg-

regation, black children, and black aides at a PTA meeting;

(2) at least some black children were being individually harassed by the two principals by such tactics as being kept out of class in the office, being barred from riding the bus, and being reported unfairly to the truant office for lateness;

(3) black children were being penalized and punished by teachers when they were actually the victims of the misbehavior of other children, with one of the principals backing up the teacher in at least two cases where a black child had been injured by white children;

(4) black children were under a great deal of pressure in the schools because of differential treatment, with one mother testifying that her child's grades had gone down because of the pressure;

(5) at least some teachers referred to "those children," "children who ride on the bus," and "the new children" in a disparaging tone of voice and ridiculed both black and white children from Doyle-Jenkins in the classroom;

(6) one teacher in Howland had forbidden a black child to write down the name of a black person when "famous people" were being listed as part of a classroom exercise;

(7) at least one teacher in Howland was telling white parents that the black children were making "trouble" for their children;

(8) both black and white children were becoming more aware of racial differences because of the behavior of the teachers and principals and the general atmosphere in the schools;

(9) some parents felt that the racial climate in the schools had worsened since desegregation had brought in larger numbers of black children; and

(10) a long history of unsuccessful conferences with the two principals over their children's problems—some dating back prior to desegregation—had convinced black parents they could not receive fair treatment because of their race.

Following the April hearing, Superintendent O'Connor upheld the two principals with the backing of the school committee. He had said at the opening of the hearing that he would transfer the principals without loss of tenure or prejudice if overt acts of discrimination on their part were proved. After examining the hearing transcript and conducting further personal investigations, the superintendent concluded that the principals had not acted in a discriminatory way in recent months or directly and knowingly upheld teachers in discriminatory conduct. The superintendent discounted what he called "subjective interpretation of remarks" by parents who testified and he also

disregarded all incidents brought out in the hearing that pre-
dated the desegregation plan of September 1967. Although the
complaining parents had been promised a new hearing before
the school committee if they were dissatisfied with the superintendent's ruling, an appeal hearing was denied. Six members of
the school committee voted to back the superintendent's judgment and deny a further hearing after reading the first hearing
transcript. This decision, made at a closed session, prompted
the Committee to Eliminate Racism in the Public Schools to picket
City Hall and sit-in at the school department offices. There was
no formal action on the Summit and Howland principals after
these demonstrations, but during the summer of 1968 both principals were given the opportunity to transfer to schools with
fewer black students and less involvement in the desegregation
program. Miss Mary A. Powers, John Howland's principal, transferred to the Asa Messer and Willow Street Schools, and Miss
Florence I. McGwinn, Summit's principal, moved to the Joslin
and Sisson Street Schools. Neither Messer, Joslin, nor Sisson
were affected by the Providence Plan, and Willow Street enrolled
only a handful of black students after the Flynn Model School
opened.

Although the campaign to end racism in the public schools
did not result in a clearcut victory as far as the principals were
concerned, the committee's efforts did produce a series of actions
in the spring of 1968 designed to improve the racial and educational situation on the East Side. Even before the parents' public
campaign was well underway, East Side Coordinating Principal
McDonald scheduled the first parent-teacher conferences ever
to be held in the Providence school system, bringing parents
and teachers together in brief, person-to-person discussions of
the children's progress and problems. Parent participation in
the conferences was high in each of the three East Side schools
involved in desegregation. In mid-March, McDonald also
instituted night open houses in the East Side schools, where
parents and teachers could talk informally. Although all parents
were involved in the open houses and conferences, the primary
purpose was to bring about a confrontation between white
teachers and black parents. Beginning April 22, 1968, a series
of small, mandatory, in-school sensitivity sessions were held for
teachers at the Summit Avenue and Howland Schools. Eight
or nine teachers at a time were brought together on a weekly
basis for informal discussions conducted with the assistance of
a psychiatrist and psychiatric social worker from the Providence
School Clinic. Parent volunteers took over classes so that teachers

could attend these sessions. In addition to the teacher sensitivity sessions, the Reverend Herbert O. Edwards, formerly director of the Human Relations Commission, taught a special course in black history to pupils and teachers in grades 4–6 in Summit and Howland for about ten weeks, until the end of the school year. Other changes affecting the East Side included the renaming of the Lippitt Hill School for Dr. Martin Luther King, Jr., and an agreement to accelerate the nongraded reading and mathematics curriculum in John Howland, Summit, and Fox Point. New multi-ethnic textbooks already in use at the Martin Luther King School were to be introduced in these schools along with the nongraded reading and mathematics programs.

On a citywide basis, the school department agreed to immediately distribute a book called *How Immigrants Contributed to Our Culture* to all fifth-grade and junior high school social studies classes in the city. School officials also announced in April that the revised social studies curriculum prepared by the Providence Social Studies Curriculum Project would be implemented on a broader basis in elementary and junior high school grades during the 1968–69 school year. The new curriculum, which is based on an interdisciplinary and cross-cultural approach to social studies, was to be fully implemented in all city elementary schools in grades K and 1 and 4–6, with an experimental pilot program to be introduced in grades 2 and 3 in six schools. Junior high schools and middle schools were to fully incorporate the new curriculum in grades 7 and 8, with an experimental pilot program planned for grade 9. High schools were to be involved in the curriculum project on an experimental basis only. A pilot class in black history was introduced in Central High School in the second semester of the 1968–69 school year, for instance. The director of the Providence Social Studies Curriculum Project said that black and minority group history was being integrated into the new curriculum materials.

Following the East Side campaign, teachers and administrators throughout the city were encouraged to attend two voluntary in-service training courses sponsored under Title IV of the Civil Rights Act: (1) a weekly series of lectures on teaching "disadvantaged" children for teachers and administrators given by Brown University staff at the Flynn Model School; and (2) an elementary administrator's in-service workshop on urban education conducted weekly by a staff member of Rhode Island College. A total of 125 teachers and administrators participated in the course at Flynn and 22 elementary principals attended the administrator's workshop. Fees and stipends for attending these in-service training courses were available under the district's Title IV grant program.

Collapse of Public Confidence in Providence School Committee. By the end of the 1967–68 school year, parents' and citizens' groups actively concerned with school issues and problems had completely lost confidence in the Providence School Committee. Public criticism of the school committee's chairman, Raymond F. Fricker, was pronounced throughout the entire period when desegregation was debated, but was especially pointed during the crisis over the Flynn school. Community leaders actively involved in the Flynn issue frequently called attention to the chairman's prolonged absence from school committee meetings, with some demanding his resignation. Requests for Fricker's resignation extended beyond the South Providence protestors to the executive director of the Providence Human Relations Commission and to groups such as the Ministers' Alliance of Greater Providence. The degree to which the mayor controlled the school committee became common knowledge during the desegregation effort and contributed to a general loss of respect for school committee members. At the height of the Flynn controversy, Dal Nichols, a spokesman for South Providence residents, invited parents to attend the next school committee meeting, "if you people want to see a good puppet show." Nichols predicted the school committee would reverse its original agreement with the South Providence parents following the mayor's opposition to the Flynn agreement and urged South Providence activists to "come to the meeting and we'll see how good the mayor can pull the strings."[70] Nichols publicly stated his distrust of the school committee after the committee reversed its commitment to convert Flynn back to an elementary school.

By the spring of 1968 the number of parents and community groups that had lost faith in the school committee had grown considerably. In March and April, when a number of important issues were before the committee, five consecutive meetings were canceled, some with only a few hours' notice. Several groups attempting to speak before the school committee in March and April were denied a place on the agenda and the school committee continued its long-standing practice of making decisions on hotly debated issues in closed executive session. On April 25, 1968, following the school committee's vote in a closed session to deny a new hearing to the Committee to Eliminate Racism in the Public Schools, the executive board of the city's PTA's

issued a sharply worded statement to Mayor Doorley, criticizing
the school committee on a number of counts. The PTA protested
"secret sessions held in place of regularly scheduled meetings,"
"cancelling scheduled meetings without notice," the school committee's "blatant disregard of the public interest," and its recent
refusal to place items on the agenda properly requested by PTA
units and individual parents. The PTA board also condemned
the school committee's failure to keep complete minutes of meetings and to prepare an itemized annual budget by March 1,
in accordance with state law. The PTA asked the mayor for
a redrawing of election districts for school committee members
to provide "more equal representation" and stated that members
who are "repeatedly absent from meetings should be penalized."
The group also asked for a nationwide search to replace Superintendent O'Connor, who had recently announced his resignation.[71]

The day that the citywide PTA executive board formulated
its protest of the school committee, a broad coalition of parent
groups, including some individual PTA units, organized to seek
new solutions to the impasse individual organizations had
reached in their efforts to solve particular school problems. This
coalition, known as the Providence Committee for Better Schools,
was made up of representatives of the Committee to Eliminate
Racism in the Public Schools, five East Side PTA units, the Providence Parents and Teachers for Special Education, the South
Providence Parents Association, the Vineyard Street PTA, parents from Nathanael Greene Junior High School, and a Central
High School student. The group was chaired by the Reverend
Albert Q. Perry, pastor of the Church of the Mediator. In addition to the special concerns of these groups discussed earlier,
such as racism, extension of the middle school program, and
facilities for the handicapped, the Vineyard Street PTA
demanded immediate repair of their 83-year-old building. The
Vineyard Street School was scheduled for replacement but still
in use in a dilapidated condition. Possible approaches discussed
by the new coalition included impeaching or suing individual
school committee members for failure to perform their duties,
asking the governor to take over the school system, and complete
reorganization of the Providence school system, including abolishing the school committee and making the superintendent
directly responsible to the mayor. Although goals of some of
the different parents' groups were in direct conflict, they were
"up to [their] necks with frustration"[72] and convinced that some
kind of new, unified approach was necessary.

The Providence Committee for Better Schools asked the state Board of Education to intervene in the local school system in May 1968. At a special meeting with Richard Staples, chairman of the state Board of Education, on May 22, spokesmen for the various concerns represented in the coalition spent three hours detailing their complaints—the "filthy and unsafe" conditions in the Vineyard Street School, the unplanned shuffling of children from school to school in middle school and special education programs, the school committee's failure to hold the promised hearing on racism, and the complete abdication of the school committee's responsibility to hold public meetings. Reverend Perry, chairman of the coalition, said that he had never seen "such a loss of confidence in the integrity of an educational system, the word of public officials, or the institutions of democracy." Professor William G. McLoughlin of Brown University, vice chairman of the Martin Luther King, Jr., PTA, described the state of affairs in the Providence schools as a "crisis" and urged the state board to "come to the assistance of the frustrated, concerned, and despairing parents of the city," sparing Providence's children "another year of chaos."[73] Mr. Staples was presented a copy of the complete transcript of the April 4th and 5th hearing on the Howland and Summit principals. Although Mr. Staples indicated he was sympathetic with the parents' grievances, he raised the question of the state board's legal authority to intervene in such problems in a local school system. No followup action was taken on the issues raised at this meeting except for a hearing on the condition of the physical plant at Vineyard.

Reorganization of Providence School Committee. While parents' groups were unable to secure any direct or immediate help from the state Board of Education, their disenchantment with the school committee paved the way for Mayor Doorley to completely reorganize this body.

In May 1965, Mayor Doorley had appointed a nine-man advisory committee, headed by Representative Bernard Gladstone of Providence, to study the need for possible revision of the Strayer Act, the state law governing the election of the school committee and the financing of the Providence public schools. The Gladstone report, completed in September 1967, recommended an appointed school committee, selected by the mayor with the consent of the City Council. The Gladstone report also concluded that the schools should be funded under a budget appropriated by the City Council. Both these changes would require state legislation amending the Strayer Act. Little attention was given the Gladstone report when it was first completed, but in the spring of 1968 the mayor began a determined effort to replace the elected school committee with an appointed committee and change the basis of the school committee's funding. A *Providence Bulletin* reporter traced this concentrated effort on Mayor Doorley's part to a school committee decision in late April 1968 to raise teachers' salaries a total of $1.8 million in the coming fiscal year. With the school committee already greatly overspending its revenues, Doorley called the new teachers' contract "a grossly irresponsible fiscal act."[74] Although Doorley was critical of the school committee over its fiscal mismanagement long before this time and was said to be irritated with the school committee over its "vacillation in dealing with Negroes over school integration,"[75] he accelerated his efforts to reorganize the school committee after their agreement to raise teachers' salaries.

Against the backdrop of widespread public dissatisfaction with the school committee in the late spring of 1968, city solicitors worked with state legislators to draft legislation permitting a referendum in Providence to change the method of selecting the school committee and financing the schools. A bill providing for a referendum on two alternative proposals for school reorganization was introduced in the General Assembly on June 4 and passed both the Assembly and the Senate in a week's time, without a public hearing. The two choices to be given Providence voters in a referendum ballot were (1) an appointed school committee subject to confirmation by the City Council and (2) an elected school committee with the power to set its own taxes and no fixed limit as to the amount of taxes the school committee could raise. Although a number of organizations and individuals active on the Providence school scene asked the governor to veto the bill, he let it become a law without his signature, stating the two alternatives offered were better than the present situation in Providence. Those opposing the bill included many individuals and organizations who were dissatisfied with the existing school committee, but who opposed both "reforms" offered by the referendum bill. On August 20, 1968, a small turnout of Providence voters chose a school committee appointed by the mayor with the confirmation of the City Council. Public knowledge of the school committee's sizable fiscal deficit contributed to support for a change.

Within a few weeks after the referendum vote, Mayor Doorley appointed to the new school committee nine men and women who, for the most part, were unknown and had not been involved in recent public school issues. The new chairman, Charles A. Kilvert, had opposed Mayor Doorley in the elections of 1958 and 1964, and was about the only new committeeman with a public identity. The mayor's appointments included two black women, Mrs. Ann D. Hill, supervisor of the John Hope Settlement House's tutoring and preschool educational programs, and Mrs. Edna Frazier, a South Providence mother who had been active in the PTA and had served on the mayor's advisory committee recommending the appointed school committee. Mayor Doorley was immediately criticized for failing to appoint a black man to the school committee. In January 1969, following Mrs. Frazier's death, he named Wilson S. Williams, Jr., a black union liaison officer with the Concentrated Employment Program, to replace Mrs. Frazier.

During the 1968–69 school year, Mrs. Hill quickly became one of the most active and articulate members of the new school committee, and one of the few members of the committee to acquire a public identity. She frequently represented the school committee at parents' and citizens' meetings and became actively involved in attempts to settle racial and other school controversies that developed during her term of office. Mrs. Hill resigned in August 1969 when she was appointed director of the John Hope Settlement House. She was replaced by another black woman, Mrs. Robert L. Fowler, a licensed practical nurse.

Mayor Doorley indicated at the time of Mrs. Hill's resignation that he felt that two black school committeemen are appropriate in view of the size of the black school population. He had not, however, appointed blacks from the major ghetto areas. Mrs. Hill, Mr. Williams and Mrs. Fowler all resided in the West End section of Providence.

New School Committee Policies. One of the early decisions of the new school committee was to almost completely eliminate the school district's permit policy at the elementary and junior high school levels. The status of the permit system was unclear during the first year of school desegregation, as the Providence Plan avoided outlawing the permit system, but banned the reassignment of children transferred by the plan until after the first semester of desegregation. On November 2, 1968, the new school committee voted to permit transfers between schools in grades 1–9 for a limited number of reasons only: racial integration, medical problems, and "pupil adjustment." All new permits except those made by school officials in disciplinary cases were to require the approval of the superintendent in the future.

The virtual end of the permit system was defended on the basis of "unequal distribution of children in certain schools," specifically, overcrowding in particular buildings. The superintendent said that children already enrolled outside their attendance areas on permits could continue in these schools, but no new permits were to be granted except for the limited reasons stated. The implications of this decision for maintaining desegregated schools were clear. The *Providence Journal* hailed the restricted permit policy as "good news" and noted that "racial dislikes, fixations about prestige or 'better' schools, desires for greater convenience and other motives of self-interest" were giving way to "the interest of quality education for all." The *Journal* pointed out that maintaining racially desegregated classes becomes "a nightmare" when large numbers of parents are free to move their children at will.[76]

Changes in the permit policy did not stimulate wide protest from whites, but there was an undercurrent of resentment that surfaced in the spring of 1969, when the school committee voted to change the feeder status of Regent and Kennedy (formerly Nelson Street) Schools so that all children in these elementary attendance areas were assigned to Nathanael Greene Middle School. The school committee voted at the same time to send sixth graders in Regent to the Nathanael Greene Middle School. Prior to these decisions, some of the Regent and Robert F. Kennedy children attended Nathanael Greene and some attended George J. West Junior High School. Changes in the feeder status of these schools, particularly, touched off appeals to the school committee, parents' protest meetings, and pressure from city councilmen on the school committee.

A desire to keep their children in an almost all-white junior high school, resentment of desegregation, and a feeling that they were unfairly trapped by the new permit policy were all part of the parents' highly emotional reaction to changes in the feeder status of Regent and Kennedy. At the time the school committee voted the new feeder policy, Greene's black population was 20 percent, while George J. West's was only 1 percent. Regent, West, and Kennedy were all popular "receiving schools" for whites "permitting out" of their own attendance areas prior to desegregation, and all three schools had a reputation for being hostile to blacks. At a neighborhood protest meeting in April 1969 Regent parents stated they did not object to Greene because of the black population, but felt children should attend schools in their own neighborhoods. Parents at the meeting did not speak out against desegregation directly, but it was clear that they objected to South Providence children being bused into their schools, especially if neighborhood children were to be pushed out. City councilmen from the ward who were present at the meeting fed and inflamed the parents' anti-desegregation feelings, voicing their own objections to "involuntary busing" and pointing out that people in the neighborhood should have priority to attend schools in their home area. Councilmen Anthony Sciarretta and Raymond Cola, who represented the ward in which Regent is located, suggested that the Council could refuse to approve the school department budget or refuse to confirm appointments to the school committee if parents did not get satisfaction from the school committee on the issue. A PTA leader in the Regent area said that rumors were circulating to the effect that children in Greene were beaten up and "shaken down" by "that element" in Greene, meaning blacks. She said that people in the neighborhood were threatening to sell their houses and "not be particular who they sold to" if the feeder area changes were carried out. The fact that Regent sixth graders were sent to Nathanael Greene at the beginning of the 1967–68 school year and returned to Regent in mid-year was also a factor in parents' reluctance to go along with the new decision affecting sixth graders.

Kennedy parents were a little more open than the Regent parents in voicing their objections to Greene. Kennedy parents stated at a meeting with acting school superintendent Louis I. Kramer at the end of April 1969 that the area around Greene was poor, that Greene offered a poorer education than West, and that their children could be "contaminated" at Greene. Kramer, who became acting superintendent in the middle of the 1968–69 school year, answered that the remarks about children being "contaminated" reflected "a very dangerous philosophy, a racist philosophy."[77] City Councilman Louis A. Mascia, who represented the Kennedy area, called the city's integration program "a glorified permit system" and labeled the school committee's refusal to let Kennedy parents send their children to the school of their choice "discrimination in reverse." "These people want to be heard," he said, referring to his constituents in Kennedy. "They want your attention as much as Roger Williams or Hope."[78] Councilman Mascia's reference to Roger Williams and Hope alluded to public and school committee focus on these two schools, following demands of black students and a racial outburst at Hope in May 1969. The school committee went ahead with feeder changes at both Regent and Kennedy in the 1969–70 school year, in spite of parent dissatisfaction and pressure from city councilmen to reverse the decision.

Reactions to Racial Transfers, 1968–69. While desegregation moves were accompanied by marked racial tensions and problems in the East Side elementary schools during the first year of the Providence Plan, there were repercussions the second year at the junior high school level. During the first half of the 1968–69 school year, there were two flareups in junior high schools stemming from combined middle-school and desegregation moves and from the transfer of ungraded classes out of South Providence as part of the overall desegregation plan.

With the opening of school in September 1968, about 27 South Providence fifth and sixth graders were bused to Oliver Hazard Perry Junior High School in West Providence. Perry is located in a predominantly white area and had only four black students in a total population of 575 pupils in February 1968. Perry began a transition to a middle school in the fall of 1968, adding the fifth and sixth grades and increasing its enrollment by 300 students. With the 27 bused students from South Providence there were 37 blacks in the school in November 1968, making up 4 percent of the total school population.

Perry experienced a brief racial outburst when school opened in the fall of 1968, with more than one-third of the white students staying out of school for a day following unfounded rumors that there was rioting in the school. Some parents in the Perry area said they had heard reports on local radio stations that youths with knives were roaming through the corridors. Others apparently got reports of violence from their own children and other parents. School department officials contacted radio stations in the area, but spokesmen for the stations denied broadcasting inflamatory reports on the school. Press coverage of the Perry situation indicated that a schoolyard fight between a white ninth-grader and a black sixth-grader was probably the basis for at least some of the rumors. Eight white youths not enrolled in Perry were arrested in the schoolyard the day many parents withdrew their children from school. The boys failed to follow police instructions to move out of the schoolyard. Press interviews with some mothers gathered at the school revealed they were critical of the busing and felt the South Providence youngsters should attend school in their own neighborhood. Some white students and teachers had insulted the new black students, according to subsequent press reports. Elmer V. Devolve, a former Perry principal who acted as school superintendent at the beginning of the 1968–69 school year, appealed to students over the Perry public address system, asking them to assure their families there was no trouble and request that they stay away from the school. Superintendent Devolve and other school department officials conferred with black South Providence leaders and agreed to hold a meeting with community and PTA leaders to see what could be done to ease any tension accompanying the busing.

Black fifth and sixth grade South Providence pupils were bused to Perry in 1968 to help maintain racial balance in Roger Williams Middle School. Roger Williams was 41 percent black prior to desegregation and began the 1967–68 school year with the addition of sixth graders from all South Providence schools, a move that was supposed to result in a 37 percent black sixth grade population and a school population approximating a 60/40 white/black ratio. When a racial count was made in all Providence schools in February 1968, Roger Williams' enrollment was 48 percent black. Community leaders said that Roger Williams was about 50 percent black by the end of the 1967–68 school year. A white mother in the Roger Williams attendance area said that whites in her neighborhood were "frantic to get out" after the decision to start a middle school at Roger Williams, applying for permits to George West Junior High School in Mount Pleasant and trying to get into private schools—"anyplace but Roger Williams." She said that the school had a reputation for poor discipline and a high turnover before the middle school program was initiated and that there was much resistance among whites to the idea of placing sixth graders in the school. She herself had a daughter moved to Roger Williams with the middle school plan and was quite satisfied with the new principal and the program introduced in the school. Whites continued to leave the school, however. In February 1969 Roger Williams' enrollment was down 143 pupils from February 1968. With the busing of black students to Perry and a change in Roger Williams' attendance lines, the school was 40 percent black in February 1969.

The most serious racial situation at the junior high school level erupted at Esek Hopkins Junior High School in North Providence in February 1969. Racial problems at Esek Hopkins were slow to come to a head, but were a direct outgrowth of the way in which groups of children were shifted around the Providence schools in auxiliary moves accompanying desegregation.

As part of the "domino game" that accompanied the Providence Plan, four predominantly black ungraded classes with a total of about 60 students were bused from Roger Williams to Esek Hopkins Junior High School in September 1967. The ungraded class in Providence schools is an old, established program that enrolls "slow learners" with IQs of from 75 to 90 who are also two or more years educationally retarded. The program is disproportionately black on a citywide basis and is greatly resented by black parents and leaders who feel that the children are further handicapped by additional isolation. Although Esek Hopkins had a small black resident enrollment prior to the busing of South Providence pupils, the area Hopkins serves is predominantly white and heavily Italian, with Italians dominating the school life. The school is old, is in need of renovation, and was overcrowded prior to the busing of black students. In June 1966, Esek Hopkins enrolled 27 black students out of a total of 447 pupils. The climate in Esek Hopkins prior to busing is illustrated by the experience of a black mother who enrolled a child in Hopkins in 1965. The family had just moved into the community and met much harassment and hostility from the neighborhood. When this mother took her son to school, "a man wanted to know if he was a behavior problem. They knew he was a transfer student and that he was a Negro, so they assume he must be a discipline case."[79] With the bused students, Hopkins had a 15 percent black population during the 1967–68 and 1968–69 school years.

Ungraded students from Roger Williams were completely segregated when first transferred to Esek Hopkins and racial problems soon developed. The Roger Williams classes were not only moved intact and taught separately from the ungraded classes already established at Hopkins, but the children also ate lunch separately from the other students, and, according to a knowledgeable community leader, were "without even a book." These classes were 95 percent black. A teacher in Esek Hopkins said there were fights and name-calling by kids "on both sides" beginning with the busing and that racially derogatory terms were written on the walls in the lavatory. This teacher also said that, on the whole, staff at Hopkins did not have a good response to the situation because "they figure the kids can't learn anyhow." There were at least two outbursts of fighting with racial overtones during the 1967–68 school year. In one of these fights in April 1968 a black pupil was knocked unconscious by a rock. School officials said white youth involved in the April incident were not pupils at Esek Hopkins.

In January 1969, after black community leaders protested the segregation of South Providence pupils in ungraded classes, students in these classes were assigned to the regular classrooms. The mixing of the two groups of students took place without any preparation of students or teachers, although some of the ungraded students were overage and had a history as discipline problems. Racial problems in the school built up quickly following the integration of ungraded and regular students, with white students initiating a school boycott on February 3, 1969. White pupils in Hopkins claimed that black students got "preferential treatment" in disciplinary cases and that black students threatened and intimidated whites. The 100 white pupils participating in the boycott agreed to go back to classes after three days of protesting, but the school was closed when racial fighting broke out in the corridors.

A special meeting to hear student grievances, a faculty statement, an investigation by a special committee of the Human Relations Commission and a community meeting attended by about 100 parents indicated that the handling of discipline was a key problem in the school, although problems surrounding discipline were not entirely racial. While white students resented the fact that black students could not be kept after school because of busing, faculty spokesmen indicated that all students were violating school rules because of weak discipline on the principal's part. The president of the Providence Teachers Union, a teacher at Hopkins, stated that the worst troublemakers were not the bused students, but pupils transferred out of other attendance areas because they were discipline problems in other schools. Some white students interviewed by the press were openly hostile to the bused black students and resented these students being placed in class with them. Reporters found the black students "acutely aware of the resentment that numbers of whites felt at their presence in the school."[80] Similarly, black mothers of Hopkins pupils did not feel welcome to participate in adult school activities, such as the PTA. Mrs. Kenneth W. Stanley, President of the Providence Council of PTAs, stated that the resentment of blacks in Hopkins could be at least partly attributed to the preponderance of Italians in the area, since Italians have felt "on the bottom of the ethnic ladder and tend to view any upward movement by Negroes as a direct threat."[81] Mrs. Ann D. Hill, one of the new black school committee members, told Hopkins parents that they themselves had an obligation to make integration work. She stated:

Parents in this neighborhood had better search their hearts. You sit there and say, "I'm not prejudiced." Big deal. That means nothing. That means you are prejudiced. If you weren't you wouldn't have to say it.[82]

After a series of meetings with parents, teachers, and students, in which the new school committee chairman, Charles A. Kilvert, participated, a number of steps were taken to ease school tensions and resolve major sources of complaint. The vice principal of Hopkins was placed in charge of discipline, with the understanding there was to be a general "tightening up" and no "preferential treatment." A late bus to South Providence was provided so that black students could participate in after-school activities and be detained for punishment. A few "hard core" problem students were transferred to other schools, a "merry-go-round" practice throughout the district that has been criticized by community leaders for some time. In addition to these measures, aides were stationed near and in the lavatories to prevent possible incidents and a special committee was appointed to hear and evaluate student complaints. The Hopkins student council was reorganized to include black student representation, previously lacking, and the one black faculty member in the school was asked to be a staff co-sponsor to the council. School counselors were asked to develop a program of group guidance classes on human relations, and students were banned from wearing black jackets to class—an "in" practice among white resident students that was resented by black students. A special reading program was set up in the school and two resource teachers were assigned to work with the students who were transferred from ungraded to regular classes. Some students were also promoted to higher grades and were to receive special help through an after-school program financed by Title I funds. A voluntary breakfast program was initiated and school department officials promised to try to improve the physical condition of the building. Esek Hopkins was in need of complete renovation when the COPE study of school physical plants was conducted in 1967 and was one of the schools the RISD faculty recommended for abandonment.

Black Students' Demands and Racial Tensions: Spring 1969. Racial problems of a very different nature emerged in the late spring of 1969, following a series of demands by black students for changes in the secondary schools, including curriculum changes and the removal of "racist" teachers and administrators.

The organized effort of black students first came to public

attention early in May, when about 150 black Hope High School students staged a walkout. Hope High School students left their school on May 9, after the principal, Max H. Flaxman, refused to discuss a list of grievances prepared by the students. Students met the next day in the Hope auditorium with acting school superintendent Kramer and other school officials, who agreed to (1) a "crash" course in black history and literature to be taught through the end of the current school year; (2) a change in summer school requirements to waive grade requirements for summer school eligibility; and (3) a waiver of summer school examinations for students earning a grade of "C" or better. The first meeting between Hope black students and school officials did not successfully resolve all student complaints, however, particularly as regards the demand for action against "racist" teachers.

When negotiations between black students, acting superintendent Kramer, and Hope's principal resumed, the two sides reached an impasse over the question of school department action against "racist" teachers. Kramer agreed to investigate documented charges of racism against teachers, but in accord with school department procedures, which include written statements supporting a claim and parents being present when pupils make charges against teachers. Black students did not want their parents involved and asked that immediate charges be brought against the teachers they had named. Black students' full demands, which the superintendent said were "escalated" in the second meeting, included elimination of tuition for summer school, getting rid of racist teachers, giving black students an opportunity to determine what is read in black history and literature classes, and removing locks and chains from the doors to the auditorium and other rooms.

The black students' May demands and demonstration emerged at the end of a year characterized by growing racial tensions at Hope. Community leaders had been concerned about Hope for some time and the school was described by the school committee chairman in April 1969 as "close to eruption." A Providence high school teacher said early in April that something could be done at Hope, but problems were being handled badly and black students were very discouraged. The recent growth of the black enrollment at Hope was in part an outgrowth of the auxiliary moves accompanying elementary desegregation. Although located on the East Side, Hope began receiving ninth graders from Roger Williams in January 1967, when the school committee decided to initiate a middle school at Roger Williams.

Later, ninth graders from Gilbert Stuart Junior High School, adjoining Roger Williams, were also bused to Hope. Hope's black population grew from 233 in 1966 to 336 in February 1969. Teachers said that many of the bused students from other parts of the city, particularly those from Gilbert Stuart, did not want to attend the school. Hope's black population made up 22 percent of the total student body of 1,544 by the middle of the 1968–69 school year.

Hope black students went on a "rampage" through the school following the impasse in negotiations on May 13—smashing windows, lightbulbs, and furniture, assaulting some teachers and white students, and doing extensive damage to sets and props in the auditorium where the negotiations were held. Fire extinguishers were emptied and flags were ripped and burned. Total property damage was estimated at $10,000. The violence and destruction on the part of black students was apparently triggered by a rumor that two white girls had told the principal that they had been attacked by blacks. Black students involved in the negotiations believed that they would be accused of these assaults. The Hope rampage was the first outburst of this nature by black students in Rhode Island and greatly shocked many whites. Faculty refused to teach at Hope for four days, returning only after several stipulated conditions were met. Faculty conditions included: (1) police protection in the school for students and faculty, which faculty maintained was necessary; (2) public disclosure of the racism charges, or withdrawal of these charges; and (3) use of the school's normal disciplinary procedures, which included suspension, to deal with black students involved in the outburst. The faculty also aired their grievances concerning the school's many educational deficiencies and called for implementation of recommendations from a 1959–61 evaluation of Hope by the New England Association of Secondary Schools and Colleges. A group of white students questioned by the school committee after the Hope disturbance described the school as "stifling," criticized some teachers as "incompetent," and told the school committee that outdated curriculum and materials were breeding dissatisfaction.[83] Both students and a representative of the teachers' union pointed out the faculty's fear of returning to the school. The school was finally opened when school officials stated that the black students' complaints against teachers were "vague statements, not charges," and would not receive followup action.[84] The Human Relations Commission agreed to investigate the students' charges and school officials assured black students they would act on documented evidence of racism through established procedures. Although classes resumed at Hope after four days, there was a great deal of divided sentiment over police in the school, disciplinary and police action against black students involved in property damage and physical assault, school department followup on charges of racist teachers, and the possible role of "outside agitators" in the Hope situation.

Demands similar to those of the Hope High School black students were made in two junior high schools of the city about the time Hope students first presented their grievances. Black students in both Nathanael Greene and Nathan Bishop Junior High Schools presented a list of complaints to their principals around May 8 or 9 and May 13. After the Hope outburst, a group of black students at Roger Williams Middle School also drew up a list of grievances that they attempted to negotiate with the principal. Black student demands at Nathanael Greene concentrated on black studies, while the Nathan Bishop students asked for more black teachers, a black studies program, and improvements in the physical condition of the building. Roger Williams pupils went further than the other junior high school students in their demands, calling for the removal of the principal, the assistant principal, and three white teachers. Black student leaders in Roger Williams said the principal and assistant principal were "incapable or unwilling to understand the problems facing black students."[85] Roger Williams black students also demanded improvement of the physical condition of the building, a black guidance counselor, and elimination of the requirement that students go through the principal to get an appointment with the guidance counselor. Students at this school telephoned at random by reporters stated that the three teachers in question included one who refused to help slow students improve their grades, one who mistreated black students in class, and one who gave preferential treatment to her almost entirely white class. Both Roger Williams and Nathan Bishop black students staged walkouts and Roger Williams was closed for one day by the faculty. Police were stationed in Roger Williams and Central High School after the Hope disturbance.

Black students' demands in the spring of 1969 placed a great deal of pressure on the school committee to move more rapidly in the areas of black history and literature, further in-service training for teachers, and the addition of more black staff. While the Hope situation inspired a great many whites to call for tighter discipline and punishment of students involved in assault and property destruction, there were other voices insisting that adults respond positively to the students' demands, particularly the demands for black studies and for action against racism on the part of staff. The Camp Street Neighborhood Interim Board, an East Side anti-poverty advisory organization, and a new group known as Concerned Parents and Citizens asked for amnesty for the students, removal of police from Hope, removal of all locks and chains on lavatory and other doors, at Hope, and immediate action on documented cases of racism. The League of Women Voters, the Urban League of Rhode Island, Rhode Island Educators for the Development of Human Resources, Woman Power of Rhode Island, and a group of 23 East Side Protestant and Jewish clergymen stressed the need for coming to grips with basic racial and educational problems at Hope. The state Commissioner of Education, William P. Robinson, immediately backed the students' demand for black history and literature courses and met with Hope and Roger Williams faculty to help resolve their reluctance to return to the schools. Robinson and staff members of the state Department of Education worked closely with the Hope situation releasing additional state and federal funds for some of the remedial action taken by the school department following the Hope crisis. The Providence PTA Council met with parents and students from the Roger Williams Middle School and agreed to press complaints regarding the condition of the building with school officials. Parents, civil rights leaders, and anti-poverty leaders worked with Nathanael Greene Middle School students to develop plans for an Afro-American Club, a black literature section in the school library, and a combination exhibit and entertainment for students and parents at Greene sponsored by the Afro-American Club on May 29. Parents and community leaders were called in by Nathanael Greene's principal to help students implement their black studies demands immediately after the demands were presented. Greene's principal credited the students with taking positive steps and acknowledged the help of black community leaders in developing a program. As a result of many pressures and efforts, a number of steps were taken at the end of the 1968–69 school year and through the summer to improve racial and educational conditions at Hope and other secondary schools:

(1) a black history course, carrying one-fifth of a credit was set up at Hope on an elective basis for the remainder of the 1968–69 school year; approximately 220 students enrolled in the course, which was taught on a volunteer basis by Charles H. Durant, executive director of the Human Relations Commission and a certified history teacher;

(2) elective black history courses were initiated in Classical, Hope, and Mount Pleasant High Schools for the 1969–70 school year and the number of sections of black history taught at Central High School was expanded (Central had the only black history course at the high school level in the 1968–69 school year);

(3) black history courses at the junior high and middle school levels were established at Esek Hopkins, Nathan Bishop, Nathanael Greene, and Roger Williams beginning in the fall of 1969;

(4) additional books by and about blacks were purchased for high schools, junior high schools, and middle schools before the end of the 1968–69 school year with state funds made available to Providence;

(5) a statewide conference on black history for school superintendents, curriculum directors, senior high school principals, and social studies department heads was held at the University of Rhode Island on June 7, 1969, by the state Department of Education;

(6) a conference on intergroup relations for Providence school administrators in secondary schools and staff of the central administrative office was sponsored by the state Department of Education on June 16 and 17;

(7) the faculty council at Hope was reactivitated following the disturbance and special faculty workshops financed by the state Board of Education were held in the summer of 1969 to make plans for curriculum changes at both Hope and Central High Schools;

(8) an interracial parents' council was organized at Hope;

(9) home room periods were eliminated at Hope, beginning in the fall of 1969 and the school also got a new student government constitution with reforms such as student representation on faculty committees, student government recognition of other student groups, and a provision that a minimum of 37 percent of the student council representatives would be black during the first year the new constitution was in force;

(10) painting and other repairs were promised at Hope, and portions of Roger Williams and Gilbert Stuart were also to be painted with the help of state and federal funds for disadvantaged children;

(11) a local black community leader accompanied by a representative of the state Department of Education was sent to black colleges in the South to recruit and hire black teachers for the Providence schools;

(12) twelve Providence social studies teachers were enrolled

in black history summer school courses at the University of Rhode
Island through funds made available by the state Department
of Education;

(13) voluntary, non-credit seminars on "Black Awareness and
Its Implications for the Education of Black Students" were con-
ducted for Providence and Providence area teachers at the Urban
Education Center in the city in August and September, 1969;

(14) a ten-week in-service training program in intergroup relations was planned for elementary teachers in the fall and winter
of 1969 and 1970, with the help of funds from the state Department of Education;

(15) human relations seminars for teachers and selected parents and students were to be held at Hope during the 1969-70
school year;

(16) five new black teachers were added to Hope's staff at
the beginning of the 1969-70 school year; and

(17) a total of 18 black teachers were added throughout the
Providence school system in the fall of 1969, bringing the total
number of black teachers in the Providence schools to 66, or
approximately 5 percent of the total.

In spite of student emphasis on staff racism and community
backing for investigation of charges of racism, the school department took no action in this area. An examination of complaints
in four key high schools, junior high schools, and middle schools
carried out by the Human Relations Commission in the summer
of 1969 did not find "sufficient evidence of individual acts of
racism to warrant disciplinary action against school employees."
The report concluded, however, that the "typical" school setting
"allows adequate opportunity for racist attitudes to exist and
to go unnoticed for lengthy periods of time." The Commission
noted that tenured teachers, particularly, operate almost completely free of any official observation, that discipline may be
administered at the whim of the disciplinarian, and courses of
study, such as black history, may be implemented contrary to
guidelines. The Commission examined a total of 50 reports of
incidents or conditions in these schools that it could not verify
or recommend for followup action for reasons such as witnesses'
fear of reprisals, unsolved problems as to school department
policy and teachers' contracts, and legal problems that arose
in the Commission's attempts to investigate evidence of bias.
The Commission established a core of nine "solid" cases of racism
but recommended broad-based programs to reorient staff rather
than charges against individual teachers.[86] At the height of the
Hope crisis, a Human Relations Commission field investigator

had antagonized the superintendent and many teachers by a statement that the teachers were largely responsible for the problems in the Providence system.

As the 1969 Hope crisis drew to a close, the school department's obvious reluctance to deal aggressively with teachers' and administrators' racial bias and with staff conduct offensive to blacks remained one of the key racial problems in the Providence schools. Webb Mangum, a black South Providence leader, had criticized the school department during the Esek Hopkins racial strife for failing to prepare school officials, teachers, and parents. Mangum predicted there would be continued "chaos, disruption, dissension, and even violence at other schools" until "there is a definite, specific program for teachers."[87] Community leaders interviewed in the spring of 1969, prior to the Hope outburst and other black student demonstrations, pointed out the continued failure of the school department to require intergroup relations training for principals and the reluctance to make teachers take sensitivity and intergroup relations training except under extreme circumstances. Although there were a number of opportunities for Providence school staff to participate in courses and workshops in urban education, race relations, black history and intergroup relations held by various institutions in the area, teachers and administrators who were most in need of the courses did not volunteer. In cases such as Summit and Howland schools, where biased principals transferred out under community pressure, parents were not satisfied with the replacements and felt there was a need for more direction and positive leadership from top administrative sources. The need for action on the issue of staff racism was stressed by Dr. Myron Lieberman, chairman of the Hope High Parents Advisory Council, in June 1969. There was, according to Dr. Lieberman, a need to win back the confidence of the black community and clear the air of racism. He urged the hiring of a special outside examiner to investigate charges of racism in Hope High School. The examiner should be black, Dr. Lieberman stated, and should be provided with a budget and full freedom to carry out an impartial investigation. He also recommended that the examiner be a person of outstanding calibre such as Bayard Rustin, civil rights leader and executive director of the A. Philip Randolph Institute. Dr. Lieberman proposed taking "a good look at the record" as to what has happened in the classroom and in extracurricular activities for the past five years and letting "the chips fall where they may."[88]

Status of Desegregation: Spring 1969. Racial counts of black
and white students in the Providence public schools in the spring
of 1969 indicated that desegregation was retrogressing at the
elementary level and that the number and percentage of black
students was growing in a few high schools and junior high
schools in the city, while other schools remained overwhelmingly
white.

Racial enrollment figures in May 1969 showed, for example,
that three regular elementary schools in racial fringe areas had
resegregated since implementation of the Providence Plan. Hammond and Almy Schools in the West End were 55 percent black
at the end of the 1968–69 school year, and Berkshire Elementary
School in North Providence was also 55 percent black. Black
enrollment in Hammond and Almy went up in the 1968–69
school year after nearby Beacon was converted to a special education center. The growing proportion of blacks in Berkshire was
partly due to a decline in the number of white pupils. Both
Hammond and Berkshire were "sending" schools under the
Providence Plan. Hammond was scheduled to be closed at the
end of the 1968–69 school year, with all Hammond pupils reassigned to Kenyon for the 1969–70 school term. In addition to
the three predominantly black regular elementary schools in
the Providence system in May 1969, there were also three special
education centers serving the elementary population that were
predominantly black: Beacon, in upper South Providence, was
79 percent black; Jenkins, in the East Side ghetto area, was 64
percent black; and Temple, in South Providence, was 63 percent
black. Other elementary schools with high black enrollments
in May 1969 included: Fogarty (39 percent); Flynn (38 percent);
Vineyard (37 percent); Howland (37 percent); Sackett (34 percent); Martin Luther King (33 percent); and Summit (31
percent).

The percentage of blacks in Fogarty, Flynn, Howland, and
Sackett increased in the second year of desegregation, while
the proportion in Summit and King dropped slightly. Although
some black pupils were transferred out of Vineyard with desegregation, the proportion of blacks in the school was about the
same after desegregation as before; the percentage of blacks
varied by only 1 percent between 1967 and 1969. There were
still elementary schools in Providence with only a few black students in 1969, but there were no all-white elementary schools
in the system at the end of the 1968–69 school year.

In addition to the resegregation of three regular elementary
schools, an analysis of racial enrollment carried out by Dr. Harold

Pfautz of Brown University in April 1969 showed that as many
as 15 percent of all black pupils in grades 1–6 were in majority
black schools in 1969—that is, schools with a 50 percent or more
black population. Dr. Pfautz' study found that an additional
39 percent of the elementary pupils in these grades were attending schools that were over 30 percent black, the maximum limit
set by the Providence Plan. A little less than half (46 percent)
of Providence's school children were in schools that met the
Providence Plan goal of less than 30 percent black, compared
with 53 percent the previous year. In a separate analysis of classroom racial patterns, Dr. Pfautz discovered that 21 percent
of all first graders in the Providence schools and 16 percent
of all second graders were attending segregated classrooms in
1969—that is, classrooms that were all-white or had more black
than white students. (See Tables 5 and 6.) Dr. Pfautz' figures
also showed that the greatest elementary classroom segregation
in the school system existed at the kindergarten and pre-
kindergarten levels, where 51 percent of the city's school children
were in all-white or predominantly black classrooms. (See Table
7.) Preschool and kindergarten children were left in
neighborhood schools under the Providence Plan, except on
the East Side, where parents could place their children in preschool programs in King, Summit, or Howland.

Table 7—Desegregation Status of Classrooms in Providence Public
Schools, February 1969

Type of School	No. of Class-rooms	*Classroom Desegregation Status*		
		Desegregated (%)	Segregated* (%)	Total (%)
Pre-kindergarten and Kindergarten	92	49	51	100
Elementary	478	90	10	100
Junior High School	187	68	32	100
Special and Other†	153	69	31	100
TOTAL	910	76 ††	24 ††	100 ††

* More black than white students or no black students per classroom.
† "Ungraded," "educable," and various types of handicapped.   ††Averages.
Source: Data supplied by the Providence Department of Public Schools, collected
by Mrs. Carol Fuller, Urban League of Rhode Island, and analyzed by H. W. Pfautz,
Brown University, Department of Sociology and Anthropology.

At the secondary level, 91 percent of black high school students in Providence attended Central or Hope High Schools in February 1969. Central High School was 33 percent black in 1969 and enrolled 47 percent of the city's black senior high school students; Hope was 22 percent black and enrolled 44 percent of the total black high school population. Classical and Mount Pleasant High Schools, in contrast, enrolled only a small number of black students, who made up 2 percent of their school population. Classical had a total of 24 black students in February 1969 and Mount Pleasant enrolled 49. While the total number of black students at Classical and Mount Pleasant had remained extremely low up to this time, black enrollment in Central more than doubled between 1966 and 1969, increasing from 156 to 363 in three years' time. The middle school plan, which transferred South Providence ninth graders to Central, contributed greatly to the rapid growth in Central's black student body. The growth in Hope's black population has already been discussed.

At the junior high school and middle school level, the largest number and proportion of black students in February 1969 were concentrated in Roger Williams, Gilbert Stuart, and Nathan Bishop. Roger Williams was 40 percent black; Stuart, 33 percent black; and Bishop, 27 percent black. Recent growth in Gilbert Stuart's black population was the result of a change in attendance lines between Gilbert Stuart and Roger Williams that became effective at the beginning of the 1968–69 school year. While a few black students were bused from Roger Williams to Esek Hopkins and Oliver H. Perry in 1967 and 1968 in attempts to maintain racial balance at Roger Williams, Gilbert Stuart absorbed more of Roger Williams' black students than either one of these schools. With the new attendance boundaries, Gilbert Stuart's black population increased from 193 to 316 between February and November, 1968, and the percentage of blacks grew from 26 to 35 percent. George J. West, in contrast, had only 10 black students in 1969 and was overcrowded with whites from other junior high schools attending West on permits. The number of black students in Nathan Bishop Junior High School on the East Side grew between 1966 and 1969, but the proportion of black students did not increase greatly. Bishop was 27 percent black in 1969. An analysis of the status of classroom desegregation at the junior high school level in April 1969 showed that about 32 percent of all junior high school pupils were in segregated classrooms. (See Table 7.)

Parents, students, and community leaders were particularly concerned about racial and social class divisions between Classical and Central High Schools in the spring of 1969. Prior to the Hope outburst community leaders saw Central as a potential spot for racial problems at the secondary level. As noted earlier, Classical and Central coexist side by side with completely different student bodies and course offerings and completely different statuses in the community. There were 24 black students in Classical in 1969, in contrast to 363 in Central. A black Classical student encouraging black junior high school pupils to attend Classical in the spring of 1969 said that the low number of black students in the school was "an outrage" and gave whites "a little sense of superiority." According to this young man, many white Classical students don't realize there are "blacks smart enough to go to Classical."[89] A Classical teacher told members of the school committee on April 10, 1969 there was reason to believe the school's rigid academic program "is a subterfuge to maintain segregation." He called the school department's failure to include Classical in the desegregation program "irresponsible and illegal" and said that two Classical teachers who attempted to work with the student movement to recruit black students were "reproved by the administration." Dr. Lieberman publicly criticized the school committee's decision to maintain Classical and Central as separate institutions in the new Classical-Central complex and a black South Providence leader interviewed for this study pointed out that Classical was getting a new building in the new joint educational complex, while Central was getting "nothing." Plans for the new educational complex including the two schools provided for replacing the old Classical building, but renovating Central.

Possible Reorganization of Rhode Island School Districts.

Although Providence's black school population is still a minority population and many whites are still left in the city to integrate with blacks, school desegregation could be affected on a long-term basis by possible reorganization and consolidation of the state's school districts, now under consideration by the relatively new Rhode Island Board of Regents. The Rhode Island Board of Regents was created by the state legislature in 1969 as a single governing body for all public elementary, secondary, and higher education in the state. The new Board of Regents is an outgrowth of recommendations made by a Special Commission to Study the Entire Field of Education and is charged with the responsibility for preparing a consolidation plan for the state's school districts. The Special Commission to Study the

Entire Field of Education, chaired by General Assembly Representative Joseph A. Thibeault, was appointed by the state legislature in the mid-1960's to formulate comprehensive plans for reorganization of the state's education system. The controversial report issued by the commission on June 1, 1968 included a proposal to reorganize the state's elementary and secondary schools into four districts for the entire state. The report specified that each district should be "heterogeneous in nature," containing urban, suburban, and rural areas in proportions "similar to the proportion existing in the state as a whole." Since Providence "has a disproportionate share of the state's disadvantaged and handicapped children" and "the trend is toward its gaining more such pupils in the future and becoming increasingly imbalanced," the Thibeault report concluded that the proper education of children in Providence demands "a different mixture of pupils for the school district." The report recommended extending Providence's present district beyond the city limits to encompass a total school population of about 40,000.[90] While the bill creating the new Board of Regents did not give it the power to regionalize and consolidate school districts as proposed by the Thibeault study, the legislature instructed the board to prepare a plan for consolidation to be presented to the General Assembly by January 31, 1971. It seems highly unlikely that the state's school districts will be consolidated to the extent recommended by the Thibeault report, but it is possible that Providence could gain some suburban fringe areas in a consolidation move. A metropolitan area school district extending beyond the city limits would not only bring more whites into the Providence school system but would close the escape hatches to white suburbia and help stabilize the white population in the inner city. Reorganization on a metropolitan basis could greatly alter the character of the Providence school system.

8.
Providence School Desegregation: Recent Developments

CURRENT research updating the findings on school desegregation in Providence, presented in the November 1971 issue of *The Urban Review*, indicates that the Providence schools have undertaken two additional phases of desegregation since 1969 when the original data were collected.

Phase II of the Providence Plan, 1970. Phase II of Providence's school desegregation plan took effect in the fall of 1970 and was designed to accomplish two objectives: (1) to eliminate the resegregation in elementary schools that had occurred since the first desegregation plan was implemented in 1967, and (2) to extend the Providence Plan to the middle school-junior high school level.

In the elementary grades, there were minor revisions of the attendance lines of six predominantly white schools. Five schools are located in North Providence and in the Mt. Pleasant area, white sections that received bused black pupils from South Providence in Phase I of the Providence Plan. The new attendance lines shifted 145 resident pupils among these schools, redistributing the white population to make room for an increased number of bused black students to be brought into the area. Three of the schools were new to the Providence Plan—that is, they did not receive bused black students prior to 1970. In another change in attendance lines, ten black pupils were moved from Lexington, an elementary school on the edge of the South Providence ghetto, to Sackett, a nearby school that enrolled fewer black students. The only pupils bused with these changes in the elementary zone lines were 18 whites reassigned in the Mt. Pleasant area. Although "forced busing" became a major issue in Mt. Pleasant, these 18 pupils were already eligible for busing prior to Phase II because of the distance from their homes to their previous school. In addition to revising school attendance boundaries, Phase II stepped up the busing of blacks out of segregated neighborhoods that had begun with Phase I of the desegregation plan. A total of 85 more black elementary students were bused out of South Providence with Phase II. The original plan proposed busing 65 East Side black pupils to three North Providence and Mt. Pleasant schools, but this segment of the Phase II plan was dropped. Altogether, 240 elementary children—145 white and 95 black—were reassigned with Phase II of the Providence Plan. No whites were added to the numbers of black elementary pupils already participating in long-distance busing.

At the middle school-junior high school level, Phase II involved the busing of 100 black students from schools serving the South Providence ghetto areas to overwhelmingly white Mt. Pleasant and West Providence schools. Limited busing from South Providence middle and junior high schools had begun in 1967 simultaneously with Phase I of desegregation. Phase II added to the numbers of black pupils being moved out of high black enrollment schools at the middle school level and brought about a better balance of black pupils in George J. West, which had been 97 percent white prior to Phase II. A proposal to bus 30 East Side middle school pupils across town to the western part of the city was abandoned.

An important part of Phase II was a new racial balance formula for the Providence schools that stipulated that the racial composition of any school could not deviate by more than 10 percent from the overall black-white ratio of all schools at the same grade level. Under the new formula, based on racial balance guidelines adopted in June 1970 by the State Board of Education, elementary schools in Providence that were under 12 or over 32 percent black were considered segregated. Similarly, middle schools that were less than 10 percent or more than 30 percent black were defined as segregated. Before Phase II was implemented, a racial count in the district indicated that 11 out of 30 regular elementary schools were segregated when the new policy was applied; five out of eight middle schools were also found to be segregated. After Phase II, eight of the regular elementary schools failed to meet the new racial balance formula. These schools had black populations of from 9 to 11 percent. No regular elementary school had a concentration of blacks higher than 30 percent, although the three special education centers in the district enrolling elementary pupils had black enrollments ranging from 33 to 49 percent. At the middle school/junior high school level, all schools met the new racial balance standards in the fall of 1970, after implementation of Phase II.

Federal Pressures for More Desegregation. During the first phase of Providence's elementary desegregation, Providence received a grant under Title IV of the Civil Rights Act, which was to be used for teacher in-service training and the activities of an advisory specialist who was to promote desegregation and work with problems incident to desegregation. Flynn's Staff and Education Coordinator served in a dual role as a desegregation specialist and an educational leader at Flynn from the beginning of Phase I through the fall of 1969. He was mainly occupied by the demands of Flynn, and both community leaders and federal Title IV officials were dissatisfied with the combining of these two major responsibilities. Beginning in the winter of 1969, federal Title IV officials began negotiating with Providence's superintendent to appoint a full-time desegregation specialist who would work throughout the entire system and see that more desegregation was accomplished. The Washington Title IV monitor for Providence's grant was concerned about the situation in Hope and insisted that the Title IV program had to begin developing ways and means to desegregate the high schools. He also stipulated that the program should be used to correct problems and maintain gains made in the desegregation of the elementary schools. After federal Title IV officials took the position that Providence's grant could not continue unless it was used to further desegregation, the 1970–71 Title IV program was specifically designed to plan Phase II of the Providence Plan and to complete desegregation of the high schools by September 1, 1971. Dr. Richard C. Briggs, who became superintendent in the fall of 1969, testified in court in September 1970 that he had worked out an agreement with federal officials when he first became superintendent to carry out full integration at all grade levels in two years' time.

Phase III of the Providence Plan, 1971. Phase III of the Providence Plan began in September 1971, focusing on the senior high schools. Under the new racial balance guidelines, Providence high school enrollments were to range from 8 to 28 percent black. With reference to this criterion, all four senior high schools were segregated in the 1970–71 school year. Mt. Pleasant and Classical High Schools had overwhelmingly white student bodies, with black enrollments making up only 3 and 6 percent of their populations, respectively. Hope and Central were 32 and 42 percent black by November 1970, partly because black South Providence ninth graders were assigned to these two schools with the conversion to middle schools beginning in 1967. Phase III set up a racially oriented feeder system from some of the middle schools and junior high schools to the three regular senior high schools, with some white eighth and ninth grade students

who would have previously attended Mt. Pleasant being assigned
to Hope and Central, and some eighth and ninth grade black
pupils who would have gone to Hope and Central attending
Mt. Pleasant. Classical, a special citywide college preparatory
school with an open enrollment, modified its admission standards
somewhat to make it possible for more blacks to qualify. No
busing was involved in Phase III, but many of the reassigned
students were eligible for special rates on the city buses. A major
thrust of Phase III was to help even out the burden of crosstown
travel, which blacks had borne exclusively in Phases I and II.
Phase III assigned more whites than blacks to schools at long
distances. Phase III was designed to just meet the new racial
balance guidelines, and press reports after school opened in
September indicated that three of the senior high schools were
still out of balance, in spite of the pupil exchanges. Mt. Pleasant
and Classical were only 7 percent black in September 1971, falling
short by 1 percent; Central had a 31 percent black enrollment,
exceeding the prescribed limit by 2 percent. A total of 715 high
school students, 603 white and 112 black, were transferred by
Phase III.

Recent Opposition to Desegregation.

Opposition to deseg-
regation plans has continued in both the white and black communities, with politicians getting into the act once more, making
political capital out of "forced busing."

With the opening of school in 1970, white parents of elementary children from the Mt. Pleasant-Manton area filed suit in
the Superior Court against the extension of the desegregation
plan, asking for an injunction to restrain school officials from
transferring their children out of "neighborhood schools." These
parents were represented in court by a city councilman from
their area and by two elected members of the Rhode Island
General Assembly. Parents from the Mt. Pleasant-Manton area
also held protest meetings, leafleted, sat-in in the schools, placed
their children in their old schools, and appealed to both the
State Department of Education and the governor. The parents
claimed they did not mind black pupils being bused to their
schools, but wanted their own children to remain in
"neighborhood schools." Although these parents made public
protests against "forced busing," very few of the children were
to be bused, no more than the number already eligible for busing
prior to the revised desegregation plan. A major concern that
emerged during the campaign was the effect the change in

elementary schools would have on the middle schools and high schools these children would later attend. Many parents objected to the fact that the children's new elementary assignments would eventually put them in middle schools and high schools with greater concentrations of blacks and low-income children, assuming current feeder patterns and other conditions remained constant.

East Side black parents also opposed Phase II of the Providence Plan, sitting-in and speaking out publicly against assignment of their children to schools at further distances from home. A spokesman for East Side blacks said that they did not mind doing their fair share, but considered the September 1970 busing plan unfair because it placed the burden on blacks. Black parents in South Providence also protested Phase II, demanding a 50/50 racial breakdown at the Flynn Model School. An estimated two-fifths of the white and black pupils reassigned with Phase II were initially withheld from schools all over the city in protest against the desegregation plan.

The court ruled against the Mt. Pleasant-Manton parents, and school department officials and school board members held firm on the majority of the transfers included in Phase II. Plans to bus East Side black pupils across town were canceled, however, and school officials permitted the enrollment of 25 additional black children in the Flynn Model School with the understanding that the 32/68 racial ratio would be met by admitting more white children. The judge hearing the Mt. Pleasant-Manton parents' suit ordered the school department to present a plan for the correction of racial imbalance in the middle schools and senior high schools no later than May 1, 1971, so that parents would have ample notice and an opportunity to be heard in advance of the implementation of the plan.

Plans for Phase III, which was concerned mainly with the senior high schools, were the subject of controversy for months prior to the opening of school in September 1971. White parents again filed suit to block implementation of the plan, the suit originating with the parents of a girl who would have attended Mt. Pleasant Senior High School but, under Phase III, had been assigned to Hope. Several Senators and Assemblymen from Providence introduced a series of bills in the state legislature in the spring of 1971 designed to thwart the city's desegregation plan. Provisions of these bills included a requirement that local desegregation plans be approved by the General Assembly and the state Board of Regents before they could be implemented. Another bill would have prohibited the state Board of Regents from implementing policy statements on desegregation or any program at any school level that would result in forced busing. None of these bills passed. Rhode Island CORE introduced an alternative plan for community controlled schools that would set up a dual set of school districts along racial and ethnic lines, permitting children to attend the school of their choice. When school opened in September 1971, Flynn parents sat-in again, demanding a 50/50 racial ratio that would permit more children from the area to attend school in the neighborhood. White attempts to block Phase III failed, but more black children were enrolled in Flynn, with the provision that the 32/68 ratio would be maintained.

School opened smoothly in September 1971, but early in October, Central High School was closed for nearly a week after a day of racial disturbances. Newspaper accounts quoted conflicting opinions concerning the impact of high school desegregation on racial conditions in Central, but there was fairly general agreement that white students who came to school armed with bricks and sticks initiated the violence. Black students and community leaders complained that the police used dogs and weapons against black students in dispersing them, while armed white students were allowed to congregate outside the school and were not subjected to the same heavy-handed force of police weapons. Parents, students, teachers, community leaders, area settlement house staff, clergymen, central administration staff, and the state Commissioner of Education were involved in emergency meetings to discuss the background issues and work out plans for reopening the schools.

Other Race and Education Issues.   Five black administrators were on the staff of the Providence schools in the fall of 1971. These included: a deputy school superintendent, a middle school principal, two senior high school assistant principals, and a special assistant to the superintendent for equal educational opportunities. The hiring of blacks in principal's and other administrative positions was an important issue when the first phase of school desegregation began. There were none in the regular schools or on the central administration staff of the school department until 1967, when a black assistant principal was appointed.

Community pressure to employ more black teachers continued, with one of the goals of Phase II being to place at least one black teacher in schools that were newly desegregated in the 1970–71 school year. This goal was not fully met, but by fall 1970 there were 78 full-time black professionals in the system who were distributed fairly well among all school levels. All senior high schools, junior high schools, and middle schools had at least one black teacher at the beginning of the 1970–71 school year, and there were one to four black teachers in 12 of the elementary schools. Eighteen elementary schools still had no black teachers. Black professionals made up 6 percent of the total full-time professional staff in the Providence schools in the fall of 1970, with the greatest concentration of black staff being assigned to the secondary schools with the largest enrollments of black students. Central had the most black faculty members, a total of 13 black professional staff members out of 110.

Recent controversy surrounding staff leadership in the Flynn Model School has raised serious questions about the future of that school, a specially planned elementary magnet school in a black neighborhood that enrolls white pupils bused from all over the city on a voluntary basis. Flynn's first Staff and Education Coordinator, the equivalent of a principal, was asked to resign in 1970, and in 1971 his successor, a black man appointed on an acting basis, was also removed. A special quality education program and educational resources not available in most Providence elementary schools have been key factors in attracting Flynn's white students.

Overview. Developments in school desegregation in the Providence schools over the past two years indicate: (1) the continuing need to revise and update desegregation plans, particularly those that rely heavily on individual pupil assignments; (2) the inadvisability of approaching major desegregation over a period of several years and several phases, in the hope that the problems will become simpler as time goes on or that opposition will disappear; (3) the staying power of resistance to desegregation in certain sections of the white community, especially where politicians periodically fan the flames of opposition by seizing upon phony issues such as "forced busing"; (4) the problems of equity raised by a desegregation approach that places the major burden of desegregation on the black community; and (5) the overall positive effect of a racial balance policy that provides for a definite goal ratio of whites and blacks in the schools, for periodic racial counts, and for the revision of school assignments to meet changes in the racial distribution of school populations.

9.

Conclusions and Implications of Providence's Desegregation Experiences

School and City Officials Foster Segregated Schools. While school and city officials in northern cities such as Providence frequently disclaim any responsibility for segregated schools, these same officials have usually carried out definite policies and actions that have, over a period of years, fostered school segregation. In Providence, gerrymandered school districts, enlargement of majority black schools, a transfer policy that permitted whites to leave predominantly or heavily black schools, and a master plan that called for replacing segregated schools near the same sites were among the official actions of the school committee and City Plan Commission that created and maintained segregated schools. Increased housing segregation, another factor contributing to segregated schools in Providence, was at least partly a product of city urban renewal programs that displaced large numbers of black families without providing alternative housing on a nonsegregated basis within the economic means of these families. These policies and practices challenge the popular myth that northern school segregation is "accidental" and is not the result of official policy.

State and Federal Officials Share Responsibility for Segregated Schools. State and federal officials also contributed to the maintenance of segregated schools in Providence by allocating funds to enlarge predominantly black segregated schools. Federal Title I ESEA funds, channeled through the Rhode Island Department of Education, were used to add classrooms to segregated schools in South Providence. These classrooms were planned after passage of the 1964 Civil Rights Act over the protest of local community groups actively demanding school desegregation. While citizen complaints to the U.S. Department of Health, Education and Welfare (HEW) and the state Board of Education calling for a cutoff of funds did not receive favorable action, the complaints, coupled with public exposure of the continued use of federal monies to segregate, increased the pressure on Providence school officials.

Gains in Black Students' Academic Achievement Prior to Desegregation. The greatest gains in raising the academic achievement scores of black pupils prior to desegregation were made in East Side ghetto schools where there was an intensive, enthusiastic and organized community effort to prepare black students for desegregation. Community-sponsored tutorial and enrichment programs, combined with positive leadership and a new approach to education within the schools brought black students' achievement scores up to grade level in a period of several years' time. Although these gains took place within a framework of segregated schools, the whole East Side education thrust was linked to plans for desegregation. Desegregation provided the impetus, the interest, and the motivation for joint community-school efforts to upgrade the education of black children. The outstanding success of the East Side community-school compensatory programs suggests the tremendous potential for accelerating children's academic growth where parents, community leaders, and school officials are working actively together toward this common goal. It also indicates the vast resources of time, effort, and money whites will devote to preparation for desegregation when they see their own children's educational welfare at stake.

Importance of Title VI in the Desegregation of Schools. While federal Title I ESEA funds added classrooms to majority black schools in Providence in 1966, the belief that federal funds could be cut off or cut back because of continued segregation played a crucial role in the desegregation of Providence schools. School and city officials apparently looked beyond the rather sizable federal monies already coming into the system to the possibility of more funds for other projects, as a kind of reward for desegregation. The assumption that the federal government would "smile more favorably" on communities that went ahead with desegregation was noted by several community leaders as one of the most important factors influencing desegregation. The fact that HEW never took meaningful action to follow up on citizens' complaints under Title VI of the Civil Rights Act did not seem to diminish its influence. The belief that there would eventually be a day of reckoning, or reward, as far as federal money was concerned was enough to keep pressure on the local school system. Title VI thus played an important though indirect role in the desegregation of Providence's schools.

Importance of State Support in Local School Desegregation. The state Commissioner of Education's strong personal support for desegregation and for state funds channeled to Providence to help with desegregation were also important in developing and carrying out the Providence Plan. The state's role in the desegregation of Providence's elementary schools was largely one of support for and cooperation with local forces for change, however, as opposed to the setting of policies and standards that initiated desegregation at the local level. The state Board of Education's first general policy statement on desegregation was not adopted until August 8, 1968, after Providence had already carried out a desegregation plan. This statement, which endorses racial integration as a "positive good" and pledges the state's resources to assure racially integrated schools, fails to define de facto segregation or establish a deadline for an end to school segregation in the state of Rhode Island. To be most effective, a state policy on school desegregation should (1) include a definition or criteria for identifying segregation; (2) set a positive goal for racial balance; (3) establish target dates for meeting desegregation and racial balance standards; (4) set up an enforcement agency, or designate enforcement officers, who could also supply technical assistance to local districts undertaking desegregation; and (5) impose economic sanctions, in the form of cutoffs or cutbacks in funds, against local districts that fail to comply with desegregation.

Role of Black Leadership in Desegregation Struggle. Organization of an effective coalition of black leaders of civil rights and community groups, plus the willingness of this coalition to use tactics such as demonstrations and boycotts, marked the real turning point in the struggle to achieve desegregated schools in Providence. Picketing, boycotts, sit-ins, and sleep-ins were first used in Providence on the school desegregation issue, but were soon applied in efforts to solve other educational problems. The overall strategy of black leaders was to mount a variety of pressures on the superintendent, the board of education, and eventually, the mayor, seizing the initiative with new demands and direct action protests when progress slowed down or unsatisfactory decisions were made. Sympathetic white leaders supported or worked along with black leaders, supplementing this basic strategy. An important element in Providence's total community leadership on desegregation was that blacks were able to gain support from at least some whites for even their most militant positions and demonstrations. The working coalition of blacks and whites on desegregation quickly spilled over into other areas, so that the superintendent and school board were faced for the first time with a large group of activist parents determined to fight a range of educational issues as a united front.

Timing of Desegregation Plan. Delays and postponements in the formulation of desegregation plans for Providence in the spring and summer of 1966 caused the O'Connor Plan, the first major proposal for eliminating segregation in the city's schools, to be announced just prior to fall elections. The "timing" of the O'Connor Plan almost inevitably thrust it into the political arena, where politicians—including school committee members —quickly defeated it. Providence's experience with the timing of the O'Connor Plan suggests avoiding, if possible, presentation of a major desegregation proposal at a time when it can become an election issue.

Need to "Sell" Desegregation Plan. Another factor related to "timing," brought out by Providence's experience with the O'Connor Plan, is the inadvisability of releasing a desegregation plan to the public before any commitment or strategy to support the plan has developed. Since any plan will generate some opposition, an overall strategy for building support for a plan and for meeting possible criticisms should be developed in advance. A plan that a superintendent or board is not prepared to defend should not be proposed publicly.

"How Not to Desegregate Schools." School officials' initial responses to the demand for an end to segregated schools in Providence provide a model for "how *not* to desegregate schools." Actions—and inactions—by the superintendent and school committee that insured the defeat of the O'Connor Plan included: failure of the school committee to commit itself to any definite course of action for resolving segregation at the time a general policy statement on desegregation was adopted; failure of the board to assume any responsibility for a plan for eliminating segregation; failure of the board to support the plan developed by the superintendent; suspension of school board meetings at the time the O'Connor Plan was being hotly debated by the public; failure of the superintendent to present and defend his plan for desegregation to the school committee; vacillation by the superintendent in the face of opposition to his plan; and the school committee's complete abdication of its responsibility for resolving the problem of school segregation.

Factors Encouraging Opposition to Desegregation. The open opposition of school committee members, the mayor, and other public officials to the O'Connor Plan not only defeated that plan, but also encouraged widespread public opposition to subsequent desegregation plans. As individual school board members, the mayor, and the superintendent later worked positively to develop support for the Providence Plan, they were faced with protests, shouts, and organized opposition from citizens who assumed that a second plan could be defeated by a loud public outcry. Opposition to desegregation on the part of the citizenry is stimulated and encouraged by opposition from highly placed officials. Failure seems to breed more failure so that the defeat of one desegregation plan encourages opposition to the next proposal.

"How to Desegregate Schools." In contrast to the O'Connor Plan, the chances for success of the Providence Plan were greatly enhanced by strong and unified support from school and city officials. The school committee adopted and unanimously approved the Providence Plan; the superintendent, individual members of the school committee, and representatives of the mayor's working conference on desegregation interpreted and defended the plan at public meetings; the mayor gave strong and unqualified support; and city officials who disagreed with the plan refrained from attacking it publicly. Unified support and positive leadership on the part of school and city officials make it possible to implement a desegregation plan successfully even where desegregation is unpopular and there is widespread, vocal opposition.

Desegregation and Quality Education. Use of the desegregation plan as a "wedge" to force other gains in quality education brought many improvements to the Providence schools, but had a mixed effect on both white and black parents. While "quality education" gains, such as reduced class sizes, the addition of specialists, and changes in curricula, were welcomed by a large segment of the public school community, there were many whites who did not see why these gains should necessarily depend on school desegregation. Others were antagonized when improvements that were promised with desegregation were not forthcoming. There was also some resentment among blacks over the fact that white support for desegregation was in effect being purchased with a better educational program, which they felt rightfully belonged to all children. This was particularly true in the development of the Flynn Model School. With desegregation, an all-out effort was made to set up a superior program that would draw whites, whereas no such effort was made when Flynn was a predominantly black school. Use of quality education improvements as a tactic to appease whites involved in desegregation appears to have certain drawbacks as well as advantages and may backfire if the promised improvements are not delivered.

Middle School Plan and Desegregation. The introduction of a partial middle school plan simultaneously with desegregation was another attempt to upgrade Providence's school system that compounded parent resistance and hostility to the Providence Plan. The middle school program, already under discussion in Providence but rejected prior to desegregation, called for major changes in school organization that were almost as controversial and threatening to parents as school integration. Instead of building support and understanding for middle schools as an independent issue, the superintendent gradually added more partial middle school conversions to planning for desegregation, justifying the middle school transfers on the basis of space needed for desegregation. Parent unrest and anxiety over desegregation, already high, was increased by the uncertainty and controversy surrounding the middle school conversions. Providence's experience with combining these two school reorganization efforts suggests that a second, unpopular, major school reorganization effort should not be attached as a "rider" to a desegregation plan. Two major changes of the magnitude of school desegregation and middle schools should probably not be attempted at the same time, unless the need for fusion of the two programs is clear and both sets of changes are adopted as a unified program.

Pressures of Whites Establish Racial Balance. Providence's decision to adopt a citywide desegregation plan that emphasized the dispersal of blacks and that set a racial balance goal of a maximum of 30 percent blacks in any school was largely a product of the political pressures of whites who wanted to even out the "burden" of desegregation and reduce its impact in any one area. Many of the whites responsible for the grass roots opposition that led to citywide desegregation and racial balance were fundamentally opposed to desegregation. But they preferred a plan that would spread blacks all over the city to one that would bring many blacks into their areas, leaving predominantly

white schools in other parts of the city intact. It appears that
once the "fact" that there will be desegregation is established,
a districtwide plan with a racial balance or racial control formula
tends to neutralize and homogenize white opposition, making
desegregation more palatable and thus more politically feasible.

Establishing and Monitoring Racial Balance Goals. Setting
a definite goal for racial balance, at the classroom as well as
at the school level, is one of the unique aspects of the Providence
desegregation plan that has had very favorable results. The
classroom goal, not usually included in school desegregation
plans at that time, helped prevent resegregation of black children within the regular school program and insured their direct
contact with other children. Records of classroom assignments
by race, kept by both principals and the school department administrative office, allow both school officials and community
leaders to check periodically on implementation of this goal.
Similarly, periodic racial counts of total school enrollments provide the information needed to monitor changes in racial balance in individual schools. While goals for school and classroom
desegregation were not fully met in carrying out the Providence
Plan, the fact that the goals are clear and that continuing follow-
up information is available, makes it possible for both school
department officials and community groups to see that racial
imbalance is corrected.

Need for More Coordinated, Comprehensive Planning. One
of the major weaknesses of the Providence Plan is that many
of the auxiliary moves connected with elementary desegregation
were not planned or coordinated to avoid further racial concentrations of blacks. As a result, some of the pupil transfers made
to free classroom space for desegregation resulted in resegregation of special education students in their new schools and an
added buildup of black students in high schools that already
enrolled the bulk of the city's black pupils. At a minimum, all
transfers connected with the Providence Plan should have max-
imized the desegregation of blacks throughout the system.
Ideally, since schools at all levels were affected by the Providence
Plan, the district should have gone ahead with a comprehensive,
coordinated desegregation plan for the entire system. A total
desegregation plan, implemented at the time the Providence
Plan was put into effect, might have avoided some of the racial
problems that emerged later in schools receiving blacks as a
result of the auxiliary moves associated with desegregation. A

total desegregation plan also might have prevented another major community confrontation over desegregation at the high school level at a later date.

One Community, One Plan. A truly comprehensive and coordinated desegregation plan would also avoid special concessions and "easier" versus "harder" approaches in different parts of the city. While school location, capacity, and the racial distribution of pupils may suggest pairing schools in one part of the city, as compared with long-distance busing in another, there does not seem to be any justification for shielding whites in one part of the city from attending ghetto schools and from busing, while requiring these in another section. The allocation of compensatory education features, such as lower pupil/teacher ratios and the assignment of specialists, should also be based on objective criteria applied consistently, such as the number of children needing or qualified for assistance. Providence's experiences with basically different desegregation approaches in different parts of the city indicates that lack of a consistent, overall plan for a city tends to increase sectional divisions and rivalries and gives rise to charges of favoritism. Conversely, applying the same overall standards on a citywide basis should play down sectional divisions and homogenize complaints and criticisms.

Need for Two-Way, Mutual Exchange. One of the most obvious and objectionable sectional differences in the Providence Plan as originally designed was the use of a two-way, or "cross busing," approach on the East Side and a one-way busing approach in the rest of the city. The decision to bus whites on a voluntary basis to the Flynn school in South Providence helped correct this imbalance. But even with the Flynn busing, Providence blacks were bearing the major inconveniences of the Providence Plan. The largely one-way nature of the plan for South Providence schools continued to be a source of resentment on the part of black South Providence leaders, whereas blacks on the East Side accepted the more equal exchange features of desegregation for their part of the city. It is not only unfair to expect blacks to bear the major inconveniences and hardships of desegregation, it is also clear from Providence's experience that blacks will not continue to accept such plans, which reinforce the idea of white superiority and to some extent undermine the very goals of desegregation. On a long-term basis, a one-way desegregation plan takes on the character of another form of discrimination.

Busing Vis-à-vis Total Desegregation Plan.   The idea of busing children for desegregation purposes initially touched off fear and uneasiness in many quarters—among some parents and school officials who were favorable to desegregation and among whites who made busing a major focal point for resistance to desegregation. The emotional atmosphere surrounding busing tended to dissipate once desegregation got underway, with busing soon becoming a fairly routine way of getting to school. There were some recurring problems related to schedules, discipline on the buses, and the impact of busing on after-school discipline, but the major long-term problem associated with busing was the complaint of South Providence blacks that there was a "double standard" with regard to who was bused. Busing per se is not the real issue, but rather whose children will be bused where and what schools will be closed or reorganized as part of the total desegregation plan. When the broader desegregation issues associated with busing are resolved, busing is, after all, only a means of transportation.

Need for Black Representation in Decision-Making Bodies. The open rejection of the Providence Plan by South Providence blacks points up better than any theoretical argument could the need for including a wide range of black leadership on planning and decision-making bodies concerned with school racial issues. Blacks did serve on the citizens' committee that hammered out the Providence Plan, but blacks on that body did not reflect the mood and temper of the total ghetto community. Black representation should include militant and grass roots as well as "elite" black leaders. Appointment of blacks to the reorganized Providence School Committee after desegregation helped improve representation at that level, but there were no black principals or blacks in administrative positions in the school system at the time this study ended. Black participation at all levels of top decision-making is essential if the interests of the black community are to be represented in official planning.

Need for Firm Policy Against Racism.   One of the major weaknesses in the Providence school system that became highly visible with desegregation was the failure of many teachers and administrators to accept, understand, and work positively with black children. Many parents and community leaders were concerned, and rightfully so, that the hope of integrated education would be destroyed by a new kind of isolation—the isolation of the black child within the desegregated classroom. The fact that there was no formal, mandatory preparation of teachers and administrators for desegregation was a criticism frequently voiced by community leaders. While preparation or orientation to the needs and problems of black children would undoubtedly benefit staff, it is doubtful that preparation alone would solve the problems of racism in the schools. There was a pressing need for the school committee and top school department officials to assume leadership to end subtle as well as obvious ways of differentiating between white and black children and to make it clear that racist and discriminatory behavior on the part of school staff would not be tolerated.

School Teachers and Administrators vs. Children. Parents and community leaders attempting to cope with the problems of discrimination and racism in Providence's schools have made several observations that suggest other possible approaches to solving the problem of racism: (1) tenured teachers, particularly, operate almost completely free from any kind of official observation; (2) the career interests of tenured staff who engage in racist behavior have to be weighed against the interests of hundreds of children who are affected by the negative actions of these staff members; and (3) the racist attitudes and behavior of teachers that have brought on widespread community complaints do not exist to any degree in schools where principals have a positive attitude toward desegregation and black children. These observations suggest that the racial climate in desegregated schools could be improved by: (1) evaluation of staff with respect to possible racist behavior in the schools; (2) establishment of a grievance procedure in conjunction with the teachers union that would set up clearcut guidelines for handling charges of racism, including provisions for transfer, reassignment or dismissal of staff who persist in negative, discriminatory, and differential treatment of black children; and (3) more careful selection and orientation of principals assigned to racially mixed schools. Tenure and seniority in the school system should not insulate teachers and administrators from disciplinary action if they refuse to comply with board and administration policy related to racial equality in the schools.

Mandatory Orientation of Principals and Teachers. Within a framework of a clearcut policy and procedures for handling racist and discriminatory behavior on the part of staff, the preparation of teachers and principals for desegregation should be effective. Providence's early desegregation history suggests that orientation should be mandatory, should stress the serious implications of teachers' and principals' showing of racial bias in their treatment of children, and should provide teachers and administrators with an opportunity to work out concrete problems that they face on a daily basis. Providence administrators who had attended different intergroup relations training sessions since desegregation pointed out the value of small group discussion sessions with specialists and resource persons who gave them the opportunity to discuss their problems and concerns informally and learn more about available resources in the community. The need for in-service teacher training where a nongraded curriculum is being introduced was also emphasized, but should not be considered as a substitute for in-service education that would focus on developing positive intergroup relations within schools, including an understanding of the backgrounds, needs, and problems of black pupils.

Need for Followup Action on Providence Plan. The fact that several schools resegregated in the second year of the Providence Plan indicates the need for continued followup action to maintain desegregation, particularly where a plan is based primarily on individual pupil assignments. New pupils must continually be assigned with desegregation goals in mind and old assignments must be reviewed, if racial balance is to be maintained. Several community leaders expressed concern in 1969 that the desegregation gains they had worked so hard to obtain might "slip" with community attention focused on other, more current issues. The tendency for community pressure groups to shift their interests to the most pressing problems of the moment suggests the possibility of establishing a joint school-community review board that would periodically check the progress of a desegregation plan.

Overall Value of School Desegregation to Providence. Providence's school desegregation plan was effective in almost completely eliminating school and classroom segregation from the city's elementary schools. In addition, after nearly two years of desegregation, most community leaders, parents, and Providence school department staff interviewed for this study felt that there were decided advantages to desegregated schools. Offering the same educational opportunities to all children, preparing children to live in a pluralistic society, giving black children the advantages of better educational facilities, developing incentive and self-confidence among black pupils, correcting white arrogance, and making the classroom a part of the real world were among the chief benefits associated with desegregation. In addition to gains such as these, which were closely related to the education and development of children, several community leaders pointed to the marked impact of the total desegregation campaign on public interest in the schools. In a city where public schools have suffered over a period of years from the apathy of citizens, the desegregation struggle aroused wider interest in the schools and inspired parents to begin attending school committee meetings, organizing, and demonstrating on other vital school matters. More concerned citizens, an improved school committee, and the beginnings of educational reform in several key areas were all by-products of a general public awakening that began with the desegregation of schools in Providence.

NOTES

1. Harold W. Pfautz, "The Power Structure of the Negro Sub-Community: A Case Study and a Comparative View," *Phylon*, 23:2, Summer 1962, p. 157.
2. Charles M. Baskt, "The School Board Acts Daringly on Desegration," *Providence Sunday Journal*, Mar. 14, 1971, p. N-39.
3. Richard A. Gabriel, "The Political Machine Is Still Alive and Well in Rhode Island," in *The Rhode Islander, Providence Sunday Journal*, Mar. 21, 1971, p. 18.
4. "Black" is substituted for the official U.S. Census category "nonwhite." since 90 percent of all nonwhites in Providence are black (i.e., American Negroes).
5. Pfautz, *op. cit.*, p. 157.
6. *Ibid.*, p. 160.
7. *Providence Sunday Journal*, Sept. 26, 1971, p. G-5.
8. Myron Lieberman, "The City's Schools After Decades of Indifference," *Providence Sunday Journal*, Aug. 17, 1969, p. N-41.
9. *Ibid.*
10. *Providence Evening Bulletin*, Apr. 15, 1966, p. 1.

11. Rhode Island School of Design, *Survey and Recommendations: Physical Plant, Public Schools of the City of Providence*, Project COPE (Cooperative Planning for Excellence), (Providence, R.I.; Rhode Island School of Design), June 1967, passim.

12. *Providence Evening Bulletin*, June 24, 1969, p. 1.

13. *Providence Sunday Journal*, Aug. 17, 1969, p. N-41.

14. Sidney P. Rollins, *Survey of Curriculum and Instruction in the Providence Public Schools*, Project COPE (Cooperative Planning for Excellence), (Providence, R.I.; Rhode Island College), June 1967, pp. vii, 15, 37—38, 42.

15. *Ibid.*, pp. i, viii, 353—54.

16. *Providence Evening Bulletin*, Aug. 21, 1968.

17. These figures reflect actual expenditures, rather than budgeted figures or sums appropriated for the 1968—69 school year. When the Peat, Marwick and Mitchell report was prepared in the middle of the 1968—69 school year, only $10.9 million in city funds had actually been appropriated to the Providence School Department for the 1968—69 school year. At that time, the grand total of $20.9 million in city, state, federal, and other funds was available for the school year. In addition to appropriated funds, the Peat, Marwick and Mitchell report projected a total of $4.6 million in deficit spending for the 1968—69 school year. The cumulative deficit, including spending in excess of the budget prior to 1968—69, was later fixed at $6.8 million. Since the City Council voted $5.5 million in May 1969 toward the cumulative deficit, for purposes of calculating meaningful distributions, $4.6 million was added to the $10.9 million in city revenues shown in the Peat, Marwick and Mitchell report, bringing total school funds derived from city revenues for the 1968—69 school year to $15.5 million.

18. *Providence Sunday Journal*, Aug. 17, 1969, p. N-41.

19. *Ibid.*

20. *Ibid.*

21. Charles H. Durant, Soraya More, Arline R. Kiven, and Bradford F. Swan, "The Negro in Rhode Island from Slavery to Community," in "Our Black Heritage," *Providence Sunday Journal Magazine*, Oct. 12, 1969, p. 22.

22. Myron Lieberman, "The City's Schools After Decades of Indifference," *Providence Sunday Journal*, Aug. 17, 1969.

23. *Providence Evening Bulletin*, June 29, 1966, p. 39.

24. *Providence Journal*, Oct. 19, 1966, p. 26.

25. Sarah T. Curwood, "A Report on Lippitt Hill, Providence, R.I.," a report to William Gaige, President, Rhode Island College (Providence, R.I.), Aug. 31, 1963, pp. 1, 25, 34.

26. *Ibid.*, pp. 2, 8, 33.

27. Rhode Island School of Design, *Survey and Recommendations: Physical Plant, Public Schools of the City of Providence*, Project COPE (Cooperative Planning for Excellence), (Providence, R.I.; Rhode Island School of Design), June 1967, pp. 25, 46.

28. Curwood, *op. cit.*, p. 32.

29. Rhode Island School of Design, *op. cit.*, p. 21.
30. *Ibid.*, p. 24.
31. *Ibid.*, p. 16.
32. Rhode Island State Advisory Committee to the U. S. Commission on Civil Rights, "A Comparative Study of Three Elementary Schools in Providence" (Providence, R.I.), May 4, 1965, p. 2.
33. *Ibid.*, pp. 4–5.
34. Sarah T. Curwood, "A Report on Lippitt Hill, Providence, R.I.," a report to William Gaige, President, Rhode Island College (Providence, R.I.), Aug. 31, 1963, pp. 1, 4, 8–9.
35. *Ibid.*, pp. 10–10a.
36. *Providence Sunday Journal*, June 26, 1966.
37. *Ibid.*, June 29, 1966, p. 44.
38. *Ibid.*, Editorial, June 29, 1966, p. 44.
39. *Ibid.*, Editorial, July 3, 1966.
40. *Providence Evening Bulletin*, July 6, 1966, p. 1.
41. *Ibid.*, Sept. 30, 1966, p. 18.
42. *Ibid.*
43. *Ibid.*, Oct. 15, 1966, p. 1.
44. *Providence Journal*, Oct. 5, 1966, p. 8.
45. *Ibid.*
46. *Ibid.*, Editorial, Nov. 16, 1966.
47. *Providence Evening Bulletin*, Oct. 24, 1966.
48. *Providence Journal*, Nov. 23, 1966.
49. *Providence Evening Bulletin*, Oct. 7, 1966.
50. *Providence Journal*, Mar. 3, 1967.
51. *Ibid.*, Feb. 22, 1967, p. 1.
52. *Providence Evening Bulletin*, Mar. 6, 1967.
53. *Ibid.*, Mar. 16, 1967.
54. Letter from Mrs. Barrett Hazeltine, President of the League of Women Voters of Providence, to the Honorable Joseph A. Doorley, Mar. 9, 1967.
55. *Providence Journal*, Feb. 22, 1967, p. 1.
56. *Ibid.*, Apr. 14, 1967.
57. *Providence Evening Bulletin*, Apr. 14, 1967, p. 26.
58. *Providence Journal*, July 16, 1967, p. N-35.
59. Minutes of the meeting of the State Board of Education, Apr. 13, 1967.
60. *Providence Evening Bulletin*, May 26, 1967, p. 31.
61. *Providence Journal*, Sept. 3, 1967, p. 7.
62. *Providence Evening Bulletin*, Sept. 7, 1967.
63. *Providence Journal*, Sept. 12, 1967.
64. *Providence Evening Bulletin*, Sept. 22, 1967, p. 29.
65. *Providence Journal*, Oct. 8, 1967, p. H-1.
66. *Ibid.*, Feb. 7, 1968.
67. *Providence Journal*, Mar. 17, 1968.
68. *Ibid.*, Apr. 3, 1968.
69. *Providence Sunday Journal*, Mar. 17, 1968, p. 53.
70. *Providence Journal*, Sept. 11, 1967.
71. *Ibid.*, Apr. 26, 1968.

72. *Ibid.*
73. *Ibid.,* May 23, 1968.
74. *Providence Evening Bulletin,* Aug. 14, 1968.
75. *Ibid.,* Mar. 28, 1968, p. 1.
76. *Providence Journal,* Editorial, Nov. 7, 1968.
77. *Providence Evening Bulletin,* Apr. 24, 1969, p. 33.
78. *Ibid.,* May 23, 1969, p. 31.
79. *Providence Sunday Journal,* Feb. 16, 1969, p. N-12.
80. *Ibid.*
81. *Ibid.*
82. *Ibid.*
83. *Providence Journal,* May 17, 1969, p. 1.
84. *Providence Sunday Journal,* May 18, 1969, p. 1.
85. *Providence Evening Bulletin,* May 23, 1969, p. 1.
86. *Ibid.,* Aug. 20, 1969, p. 1.
87. *Providence Journal,* Feb. 4, 1969.
88. *Providence Evening Bulletin,* June 16, 1969, p. 29.
89. *Ibid.,* Mar. 26, 1969, p. 18.
90. Rhode Island Special Commission to Study the Entire Field of Educa-
    tion, *Education in Rhode Island: A Plan for the Future. Final Report to
    the General Assembly* (Providence, Rhode Island: The Commission),
    June 1968, pp. 75–77.

PART 3

Sacramento, California: Partial Desegregation in a Racially Imbalanced, Multiethnic School District

Foreword

BETWEEN 1963 and 1969, the Sacramento City Unified School
District was involved in three major school desegregation efforts
in its junior high schools and elementary schools. These undertakings resulted in desegregation involving a substantial number
of black and Mexican children and eliminated segregation in
the junior high schools as defined by the Board of Education.
The district had not completed desegregation of the elementary
schools when this report was written. Other, related racial problems also existed, including violations of the State Administrative Code regarding ethnic imbalance, too few minority representatives at decision-making levels, tensions between racial
groups, insufficient minority staff, and a need for curriculum
and textbook reform with respect to inclusion and accurate portrayal of minority groups.

This report concentrates on the district's three desegregation
programs in black and Mexican segregated elementary and
junior high schools and on racial problems in the district as
they affect black and Mexican children at these school levels.
It was not possible to give major attention to other racial and
ethnic groups present in the district's enrollment or to explore
racial problems at the high school level in any depth. This report
is limited to the Sacramento City Unified School District, which
includes most of the city of Sacramento and some territory outside the city limits.

1.
Community Background

SACRAMENTO is a growing, medium-sized city in the north central part of California, located at the confluence of the Sacramento and American Rivers. It is the capital city of California,
the largest city in Sacramento County, and the seat of govern-

ment for the county. Sacramento is 72 miles by air from San Francisco and is situated on a flat plain midway between two mountain ranges—the Coastal Range on the west and the Sierra Nevada on the east. It is in almost the exact center of the long north-south Great Central Valley of California. The city's fortuitous location, including its strategic access to main lines of transportation and the farm lands of the Valley, has played a decisive role in Sacramento's growth and development.

History. The Sacramento Valley was the first inland area in northern California permanently colonized by white settlers. John Sutter, a German-born Swiss citizen, established a settlement within the boundaries of the present city of Sacramento on the south banks of the American River in 1839. Sutter had immigrated from Europe, intending to become a citizen of the United States. California was then under Mexican rule, however, and Sutter applied for Mexican citizenship to facilitate his obtaining a land grant. Sutter received his Mexican citizenship and, shortly after, the land he sought from the Mexican governor. Although Sutter befriended and harbored Americans coming into the territory, his original settlement was a Mexican colony and remained under Mexican rule until the United States took California from Mexico in the late 1840s.

The fort Sutter built at his settlement quickly became a wayside station for immigrant trains coming westward from the United States. When gold was discovered to the northeast of Sutter's Fort in 1848, Sutter's son opened up a new settlement on the east banks of the Sacramento River which he named Sacramento. The new city was soon a staging ground for prospectors pouring into the area and rapidly became a boom town. Food production in the fertile valley, water transportation to the coast, and Sacramento's established position as a stopping point for the overland wagon trains were all important to the city's growth during this period.

After the Gold Rush subsided, the city settled down to a more mundane existence. Sacramento became the capital of California in 1854. In the 1850s and the 1860s the city of Sacramento and its citizens played important roles in the establishment of overland mail routes, the Pony Express, and western links in the transcontinental railroad. As time went by, both the state government and agricultural development in the rich farm lands around the city became increasingly important to the city's growth and prosperity.

Recent Growth and Expansion. The present city of Sacramento has grown south and east of the two original settlements established by Sutter and his son and has spread across the American River to the north. (See Figure 1.) Sacramento's 1970 population was 254,413. This figure represents a net growth of 62,746 people since the 1960 Census and an increase of 116,841 people since the 1950 Census.

The bulk of Sacramento's recent growth is the result of a number of annexations that began in 1946. There were, for instance, 27 annexations to the city on the south side of the American River between 1946 and 1955. Most of these additions were small tracts of land, and until 1959, the entire city was located south of the American River. A series of piecemeal annexations north of the American River began in 1959 and culminated in the merger of the cities of Sacramento and North Sacramento on January 1, 1965. The merger with North Sacramento increased the city's population by 20,110 and extended the city's total land area to 92.75 square miles. The merger also consolidated most of the heavily populated area immediately north of the American River within the city government of Sacramento. Between 1960 and 1965, roughly 52,000 people north of the American River were added to Sacramento's population through annexation and the North Sacramento merger. During the same period, there was another series of small annexations south of the American River. A total of 63,882 people were added to the city between 1960 and 1970 through annexation. Sacramento's land area jumped from 23.46 square miles in 1955, to 50.25 square miles in 1961, and to 92.75 square miles in 1965.

Reasons for Consolidation and Unification. The many recent annexations, which culminated in the North Sacramento merger, were for the most part byproducts of two separate sets of pressures for consolidation of government and municipal services.

Since 1955, a series of government-appointed study and planning commissions and independent citizens campaigns have promoted various solutions to the problems of overlapping, uncoordinated, and "fractionated" governments in the Sacramento suburbs. The basic problem is that Sacramento County outside the city of Sacramento has been urbanizing rapidly since the early 1930s. The county is, in fact, growing at a faster rate than the city of Sacramento itself. By 1960, the total population of Sacramento County was 502,778, with more people living in unincorporated areas in the county than in Sacramento or in the other small incorporated cities in the county. Sacramento County's 1970 population was 631,498. Municipal services—including schools—have traditionally been provided by small, independent tax districts set up as needed. In 1957, for example, there were 157 special tax districts exclusive of school districts in existence in Sacramento County to provide municipal services for the heavily populated unincorporated areas. There were 45 separate school districts in the county in 1956. The total number of special tax districts in the county had been reduced to 123 by 1970, but all major efforts to bring about a merger of city and county governments, large-scale consolidation of municipal services, or mass annexations of the Sacramento suburbs to the city had failed. An abortive effort to incorporate a big, new city northeast of Sacramento also failed. While all campaigns for mass consolidation have been unsuccessful, many of the areas closest to the city have gradually joined the city in the piecemeal annexations described above.

The other major factor influencing annexations to Sacramento were new policies from the State Department of Education and the state legislature that required a certain amount of unification of the schools. State policy in this area had a mixed effect on the annexation campaigns, contributing to annexation in some areas and hindering it in others. The impact of state policy and legislation on annexation and the reorganization of the Sacramento City Unified School District will be discussed in a later section.

Sacramento's Present Economy. A team of social scientists in their study, *Growth and Government in Sacramento,* published in 1965, concluded that the economy of both the city and the metropolitan area in the mid-1960s was "dominated by government activity, either directly or indirectly."[1] This team, headed by Christian L. Larsen, stated that the "steady and rather spectacular growth" of the Sacramento metropolitan area in recent years could be "attributed largely to the burgeoning state government and to the expansion of federal field offices."[2] In addition to the state capital and the headquarters for most state agencies, which are located in the city, there are two U. S. Air Force bases and a U. S. Army Signal Corps depot on the northeastern and eastern outskirts of Sacramento. There are also two major aircraft and missile plants in Sacramento's suburban fringes, Douglas and Aerojet. In the late 1960's, both these plants were mainly occupied with defense-related work supported by federal contracts.

In addition to the various government agencies and activities, food shipping and food processing have over a period of decades formed a stable and important part of Sacramento's economy. The Sacramento Valley is one of the largest truck farming areas in the country, and Sacramento is a major distributing point for the fresh fruits, vegetables, nuts, and rice that grow in abundance in the surrounding farm lands. In 1963 there were 34 plants with 20 or more employees in the city of Sacramento and in Sacramento County where agricultural products of the Sacramento Valley were canned, frozen, milled, shelled, processed, and refined. Also in Sacramento are railroad shops and a large soap and detergent plant. In 1963 the city opened up deep-water port facilities with direct access to the Pacific.

Government activities account for Sacramento's large, relatively well off, middle class population. According to the 1960 Census, the median income of families in the city in 1959 was $6,943, and 55 percent of the persons in the Sacramento labor force in 1960 were working in white collar occupations. A high proportion of the city's housing was sound in 1960, 83 percent having all plumbing facilities. The median educational level of all persons 25 years old and older was 12.1 years of school.

Early Multi-Ethnic Population. From the earliest days of Sutter's settlement, the Sacramento Valley has had a multi-ethnic population. Sutter sailed to California via Hawaii and brought with him ten Hawaiian workers to help with the founding of his original colony. Prior to the Gold Rush, Sutter hired Mexican as well as native Indian laborers to help clear land, dig irrigation ditches, plant crops, and build his fort. Although Sutter was personally partial to U. S. immigrants, Sutter's Fort was officially a Mexican colony until 1848, with Mexicans migrating into the vicinity from the south. The first black settler arrived in 1841. He was William Alexander Leidesdorff, a West Indian of mixed Dutch and Negro ancestry, who obtained a land grant of 35,000 acres on the American River near the present city of Folsom. Other blacks were among the early miners who came to Sacramento with the Gold Rush in the late 1840s.

Some Chinese also came into the Sacramento area during the Gold Rush, but the first major influx of Chinese took place during the Civil War when labor was short. At that time, 12,000 Chinese were brought into the area to help build the Central

Pacific Railroad. The 1868 City Directory for Sacramento listed
a 3 percent Chinese population, and a 6 percent "colored" population that apparently was black. There were enough blacks in
Sacramento by 1856 to warrant establishing a segregated public
school. The black population later declined in proportion to
Caucasians and Asians, however. Japanese began coming to
California in large numbers after the annexation of Hawaii in
1898 and many became farm workers and settled in the Sacramento Valley. Mexicans migrated to the southwest in great
numbers during the Revolution of 1910 and shortly after, and
still later, during World Wars I and II, when farm labor was
acutely short. Since World War II, black movement into the
area has again increased rapidly and the black population has
displaced other racial and ethnic groups as Sacramento's most
numerous minority.

Chinese, Japanese, and Mexicans who have settled in the Sacramento area have undergone a somewhat similar experience
in that each group was imported or welcomed as workers at
a time when it was needed, only to be resented, discriminated
against, and persecuted at a later date. During World War
II, for example, Japanese in Sacramento and the Sacramento
Valley were placed in concentration camps as "security risks,"
along with Japanese from the coastal areas. Some Japanese came
back to Sacramento after they were released, but Sacramento's
Japanese population was lower in 1950 than it had been before
the war. Although many Japanese, Chinese, and Mexicans originally settled in the Sacramento Valley as farm workers they have
now become urbanized. The bulk of both the Asian and Mexican
populations in Sacramento are also native-born Americans,
more typically the descendants of immigrants, rather than immigrants themselves. In 1960, for instance, only 14 percent of Sacramento's Spanish background population had been born in
Mexico and only about three out of every ten Mexicans in the
city had at least one parent born in Mexico. Although Mexicans
represent the largest group of foreign born in the city, the
families of 56 percent of Sacramento's Mexican people had lived
in this country for at least two generations when the 1960 Census was taken.

Sacramento's Present Minorities.   Today, the combined total
of all racial and ethnic minorities in Sacramento makes up a
little more than one-fourth of the city's population. According
to the 1970 Census, 11 percent of the people of Sacramento
are black; 3 percent are Chinese; 3 percent are Japanese; and

2 percent belong to other nonwhite racial groups. The 1970 Census count of the Mexican population was not available when this report was completed, but the 1960 Census showed that 8 percent of the total population was then Mexican.[3] The Mexican community is a little smaller and is growing more slowly than the black community.

Although still relatively small in comparison to the Caucasian population,[4] both the black and Mexican populations are growing and have displaced Asians as the city's largest racial and ethnic minorities. The black population, especially, has increased drastically in the last 25 years. Blacks made up only 1 percent of Sacramento's population in 1940. A great deal of the growth of the black population has come from recent annexations. While the suburban areas brought into the city in the last 20 years were largely populated by whites, recent annexations have included two predominantly black sections. Glen Elder, a predominantly black subdivision on the southeastern edge of the city, was annexed in 1956. (See Figure 1, Census Tracts 32 and 48.) Del Paso Heights, north of the American River, annexed to the city in the early 1960s, also has a large black population. (See Figure 1, Census Tracts 65–67.) Two other recent additions to the city have had concentrations of Mexican-Americans: a former part of the city of North Sacramento on the south side of the American River near the waterfront (see Figure 1, Census Tract 53); and Gardenland, immediately across the American River in the northwestern part of Sacramento (see Figure 1, Census Tract 70). Few Asians live in any of the newly annexed areas.

Growth of Ghettos and Barrios. Although a scattering of the different minorities live in most predominantly Caucasian areas, the majority of blacks, Mexicans, and Asians live concentrated in older inner city neighborhoods or in particular sections of the outlying parts of the city, such as Glen Elder, Del Paso Heights, and Gardenland. While the older minority areas of the inner city, such as the West End and Southside, tended to be multi-ethnic, with several racial and ethnic groups living in close proximity, the present trend is toward more concentration and separation of minorities into separate ghettos and barrios. Blacks, especially, are becoming more ghettoized.

In 1950, for example, the largest numbers of blacks, Mexicans, and Asians[5] were found in the old West End (Census Tracts 7 and 8) and in Southside (Census Tract 21). The West End, especially, served as the center of both the black and the

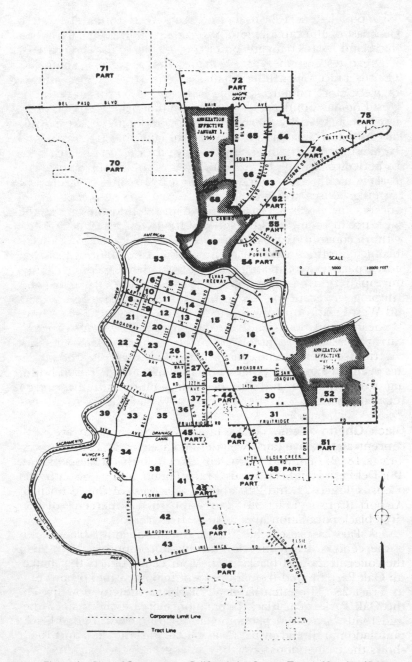

Figure 1. *City of Sacramento, California by Census Tracts, May 15, 1965*

Asian populations. Census Tract 8 in the West End, immediately southeast of the capitol along the Sacramento River, had more blacks and Asians than any other census tract in the city in 1950. The greatest number of Mexicans was found in Southside (Census Tract 21) in 1950. Asians, then the largest ethnic minority, were more numerous than blacks and Mexicans in both the West End and Southside. Sacramento's first urban renewal project, launched in the early 1950s, focused on the West End. Part of the original city of Sacramento laid out by Sutter's son, the West End along the river was once the largest "hiring hall" for agricultural workers west of Chicago, and thousands of farm workers of all races, colors, and creeds lived there. Hotels and rooming houses in the West End catered to single, male farm workers and it was here that Sacramento's skid row was found. With urban renewal, old residential housing in the West End, within economic reach of the down and out and the lowest income minorities, gave way to new state office buildings, banks, stores, parking lots, and high income apartment buildings. Many unemployed farm workers were forced into the "Weed Hotel," camping in vacant lots on the river bank. Destruction of the old West End, coupled with the increases in both the black and Mexican populations, led to the development of new ghetto and barrio areas. The economic plight of blacks and Mexicans has contributed to this trend, but continued housing discrimination has been a major cause. Blacks, particularly, are victims of housing discrimination and are becoming more and more segregated.

Black Ghetto Areas. Black families in Sacramento are now concentrated in five fairly well defined areas: Oak Park (Census Tracts 18, 27, 28, and 37); Glen Elder (Census Tracts 32 and 48); Del Paso Heights (Census Tracts 65, 66, and 67); Southside (Census Tracts 21 and 22); and an area west of the Municipal Airport (Census Tract 34). Three-fourths (76 percent) of the city's black population lives in these five areas.

Oak Park at present has the largest numbers of blacks and is the center of activities for the black community. In 1964, the concentration of blacks in the four census tracts that make up Oak Park ranged from 28 percent in Tract 18 to 60 percent in Tract 28. Three-tenths of all blacks in the city now live in the Oak Park area. Black population increases here since the mid-1950s have been phenomenal. A comparison of the black population in three census tracts in Oak Park in 1950 and 1964 shows the tremendous growth:

Black Population

U. S. Census Tracts	1950 Number	Percent of Total	1964 Number	Percent of Total
Tract 18	422	6	1,742	28
Tract 27	194	3	1,525	39
Tract 28	260	7	2,225	60

Many of the city's black institutions are located in Oak Park and most of the "happenings" in the black community take place here. Malcolm X Day was celebrated in McClatchy Park in Oak Park in May 1969, for example, and the School of Afro-American Thought, sponsored by the Ethnic Studies Department of Sacramento City College, was set up in Oak Park on the site of an abandoned city junior high school. With the rapid increase in the black population, Oak Park has taken on more and more of the characteristics of a typical ghetto area. City services in Oak Park have declined and the press has identified this section as "perhaps the city's most problem plagued neighborhood."[6] Black merchants accuse the city of conspiring to permit the decay of Oak Park, so that it can become an urban renewal area. Oak Park experienced a brief flare-up of racial violence in June of 1969, after police attempted to close off key streets and raided and fired into Black Panther headquarters, located on the "Main Street" of the Oak Park business district. One of the factors contributing to the buildup of tension was police suppression of an attempt by young blacks to change the name of McClatchy Park to "Brotherhood Park."

The second largest concentration of Sacramento blacks is in Del Paso Heights, a comparatively low income community north of the American River. This territory was added to the city on a piecemeal basis in the early 1960s through a series of annexations. Del Paso Heights contains some of the worst housing in Sacramento and the area was given first priority in the city's recent attempts to secure federal funds to increase the supply of low and moderate income housing. One census tract (65) in Del Paso Heights, the most populous in that section, is 62 percent black. Nearly one-fourth of Sacramento's black residents live in Del Paso Heights.

Glen Elder, a subdivision in the southeast corner of Sacramento, has the third largest concentration of blacks in the city. Most of the Glen Elder subdivision is located in Census Tract 48, which is now 77 percent black. Eleven percent of the city's black population lives in the two census tracts in which the Glen Elder subdivision is located. Although Glen Elder began as a new interracial development in 1954, the few whites who moved in were soon outnumbered. Whites stopped moving in altogether when houses proved to be poorly constructed and promised community services did not materialize. In addition to changing from a predominantly white to a predominantly black area between 1950 and 1960, the Glen Elder section has also undergone a transition from being predominantly middle class to a rather wide-ranging mix of middle class and lower class blacks, Mexicans, and Caucasians. The *Sacramento Bee* described Glen Elder and the adjacent Elder Creek area in 1971 as "impoverished, poorly planned neighborhoods [that] cry out for revitalization."[7]

The fourth area where blacks are concentrated over their proportion in the general population is Southside, a neighborhod made up of two census tracts (21 and 22) along the Sacramento River, south of the old West End and the downtown business area. Unlike the other major centers of black population, Southside is a well-mixed multi-racial area where blacks are outnumbered by Asians and Mexicans. The northern half of the Southside community, especially, has been affected by changes in the West End and is now losing much of its old residential population. The black population in Census Tract 21 increased between 1950 and 1955, for instance, but is now declining. The Caucasian and the Mexican populations in Census Tract 21 are also decreasing, while the number of Asians living there remains about the same. Altogether, 6 percent of Sacramento's black population lived in Southside in 1964.

The fifth area where blacks live is a small pocket west of the Municipal Airport in Census Tract 34. Over 1,000 blacks, constituting about 5 percent of the total black city population, lived in Census Tract 34 in 1964.

Mexican "Barrios." Sacramento's Mexican population is now centered in two areas—in Washington Heights, immediately north of the Sacramento downtown business section (Census Tracts 5, 6, and 53); and in Gardenland, an area across the American River, north of Washington (Census Tract 70, Part). Mexican-Americans in Sacramento are not as segregated as blacks, but many are concentrated in these two areas above their proportions in the general population. Dr. Clark Taylor, an anthropologist at Sacramento State College, who specializes in Mexican culture, considers Gardenland, but not Washington Heights, a genuine barrio.

Data from the 1960 Census indicates that a little over one-fourth of the Mexican people living in the present city of Sacramento are found in the three census tracts that comprise the Washington area. The population of the Washington area is 26 percent Mexican. Washington borders the downtown shopping area and Mexicans there are mixed primarily with a Caucasian or "Anglo" population. Although the adult population of Washington is predominantly Anglo, the Washington Elementary School had a majority of Mexican children before it was desegregated. Washington is now the center of activities for Mexicans in the Sacramento area. The neighborhood is served by two Mexican-staffed antipoverty agencies, the Washington Community Council, part of the Sacramento Area Economic Opportunity Council, and Concilio, a relatively new community center developed by a federation of Mexican civic organizations in the late 60s. A proposed Mexican commercial-cultural center, La Plaza de Las Flores, will be located in Washington as part of the city's downtown urban renewal plan. Plans for La Plaza de Las Flores include low cost rental housing, as well as shops and a community hall. The Washington community is a transitional area and has a high turnover of population, which is part of a broad process of assimilation of Mexican families into the mainstream of Sacramento's life. According to Dr. Clark Taylor, Mexican families first move to the Washington area from Yolo County to the west of Sacramento and then move on to "better" areas when they have acquired enough money and English to do so.

Because of the large numbers of Mexicans in the surrounding area and the pattern of migration from the rural areas into Washington and other downtown sections, the Washington comunity is actually a focal point for Mexicans in the entire Sacramento metropolitan area. Concilio, for instance, serves people from the outlying areas, and the city's antipoverty program, which has a neighborhood center in Washington, is organized on a metropolitan basis. Approximately 75,000 Mexicans live in the total Sacramento labor market area, which extends beyond Sacramento County.

Gardenland, the other center of Mexican population in the city, was 18 percent Mexican in 1960. Approximately one-tenth of the Mexican population of the present city of Sacramento lived in Gardenland in 1960.

Outside Washington and Gardenland, Mexican-Americans tend to live mixed with other minorities in the old West End, in Oak Park and Southside, and in areas adjacent to the Sacramento Municipal Airport. Some Mexicans also live in the southeastern part of the city (Census Tracts 30 and 31) where the population is predominantly Caucasian. Altogether, there were 11 census tracts outside of Washington and Gardenland, within the present city limits of Sacramento, where there were 400 or more Mexicans in 1960.

Asian Housing Patterns. While Sacramento's Asian population was most heavily concentrated in the old West End in 1950, with urban renewal and the razing of so many residences, Asians have shifted southward along the Sacramento River to neighborhoods such as Southside, Riverside, Land Park, and Sutterville Heights (Census Tracts 20–22, 33 & 34, and 39 & 40). There are also concentrations of Asians to the north and south of the old Municipal Airport, which is located within Sacramento's city limits in the southern part of the town (Census Tracts 35, 38, and 42). In 1964, 71 percent of Sacramento's Asian population lived in 14 census tracts in a corridor running south from the downtown business area, between the Sacramento River on the west and the Western Pacific Railroad on the east. Generally speaking, the concentration of Asians diminishes as you move south from the downtown area and away from the river. With one exception, all the census tracts in the city with Asian populations of 250 or more persons were located in this corridor in 1964. The largest number of Asians are now found in Census Tract 22 in Southside, which has a 23 percent Asian population. The largest percentage of Asians was also found in Southside in Census Tract 21, which is 36 percent Asian.

Asians, like Mexicans, are less segregated than blacks, but tend to live in defined areas. In the older neighborhoods nearer the downtown area, such as Southside, Asians are mixed with blacks and Mexicans and outnumber both these minorities. A breakdown of the racial and ethnic composition of Southside illustrates both the multi-ethnic character of this section and the kind of mix that was characteristic of Sacramento's downtown population before the trend toward more separation took over:

U. S. Census Tract	Caucasian Population, 1964	Black Population, 1964	Asian Population, 1964	Mexican Population, 1960
21	26%	21%	36%	17%
22	53%	10%	23%	14%

Asians in neighborhoods farther south live in predominantly Caucasian areas. For example, the area around and south of the old Municipal Airport (Census Tracts 35, 38, and 42) is predominantly Caucasian. The largest number of Asians in this area are found in Census Tract 35, where Asians make up 12 percent of the total population. Blacks constituted 6 percent of this census tract in 1964, and Mexicans made up 5 percent of the tract's total population.

Gaps Between Minorities and the Majority Population. As indicated earlier, Sacramento has a large, relatively well off white collar population. The racial and ethnic minorities of the city are less well off than Caucasians, however, and there are large numbers of blacks and Mexicans who do not fall within the comfortable middle class that is dominant. Comparison of key indices from the 1960 Census shows some of the gaps between the total city population and the major minority groups:

	Total City	Blacks & Asians	Mexicans
Median Years of School Completed (Persons 25 and Over)	12.1	11.5	8.8
Median Family Income	$6,943	$5,710	$5,582
Unemployed Males in Labor Force	6%	8%	12%
Sound Housing Units with All Plumbing Facilities	83%	72%	75%
Population per Household	2.8	3.5	—

Target poverty areas set up by the Sacramento Area Economic Opportunity Council (SAEOC) coincide with neighborhoods where there are large concentrations of minorities: Oak Park, Del Paso Heights, Gardenland, Southside, Washington, and Glen Elder. Data compiled by SAEOC from the 1960 Census and other sources indicate that median family income and median years of school completed by adults are lower in these areas than for the city and county as a whole. The percentages of unsound housing, unemployment, and children receiving Aid to Families of Dependent Children (AFDC) is higher than for the total city. In the Washington area, for instance, median family income in 1960 was $4,247; the median number of school years completed by adults was 9.1 years; and 15 percent of the labor force was unemployed. One-fourth of the children were receiving AFDC.

Substandard housing is also prevalent in heavily minority-inhabitated neighborhoods. The areas of Oak Park, Del Paso Heights, and Washington were singled out in July 1969 for a proposed urban renewal program that would provide low and moderate income housing under the federal Neighborhood Development Program. The city's projected housing plans for these areas followed a *Sacramento Bee* editorial that called for swift action to begin low cost housing projects

> for such blighted areas as are to be found in profusion in Del Paso Heights, Gardenland, the area north of the American River, Oak Park, Alkali-Washington, Southside, Glen Elder and Elder Creek.[8]

A *Bee* editorial on June 21, 1969, pointed out that the Oak Park neighborhood had "been allowed to deteriorate while the city failed repeatedly to apply for funds [for] decent low cost housing."[9] The housing program that was ultimately funded in 1970 focused on Del Paso Heights only, since the city could not get enough federal money to build or rehabilitate houses in all three areas. The city applied for more federal funds for low income housing in the Washington neighborhood in 1971, with a small amount to be used to develop a planning proposal for Oak Park.

The gap between the majority white middle class population and the masses of black and Mexican citizens is wide, and there are no adequate programs to bridge the differences. The $2.5 million in federal money that Sacramento requested in 1969 to begin the proposed Neighborhood Development Program in Del Paso Heights, Washington, and Oak Park stands in sharp contrast to the $65 million appropriation for a new state capitol building then under consideration by the California legislature. Plans for the new capitol building called for a toilet in every office, a conference room for every legislator, and a parking space for every legislator's car. The existence of such marked differences between Sacramento's "haves" and "have nots" caused a 1969 Sacramento League of Women Voters housing report to refer to the several "ghetto-slums" developing in Sacramento as "islands of need in a sea of plenty."[10] As elsewhere, young militants are becoming increasingly aware of these gaps and the failure of both private agencies and government to narrow them.

2.
Sacramento City
Unified School District

Formation and Additions. Sacramento's first schools date back to 1840, with the city's first public schools being established in 1853. The present Sacramento City Unified School District was formed in 1936. At that time separately organized elementary school, high school, and junior college districts in the city were brought together in one system. The new district boundaries corresponded closely to the city limits, and the Board of Education had an understanding with the city government that the district would extend its boundaries only in conjunction with identical extensions of the city limits. The school board for the district was then appointed by the city council and this policy was closely followed.

In the late 1950s the Sacramento City Unified School District's policy of keeping its boundaries identical with the city limits broke down under the cross pressures of annexation and school unification campaigns in areas immediately surrounding the city.

California has had a long history of many separate community districts for elementary schools, high schools, and junior colleges, independent of other governmental structures. Increasing state pressure on local districts to consolidate and enlarge culminated in a 1956 law requiring all elementary districts to affiliate with a high school or unified school district. At the time this law was passed, there were 45 separate school districts in Sacramento County.

Passage of the 1956 law stimulated both annexation and school district unification campaigns in the independent districts on the periphery of Sacramento. In July 1958 the city unified district enlarged its boundaries to include seven elementary districts south of the American River on the southern and eastern fringes of the city. These additions nearly doubled the district's land area and included large parcels of sparsely inhabited land suitable for subdivisions. Some of the districts that came into the city school system in 1958 failed in their annexation campaigns and are still outside the Sacramento city limits. A year after this large expansion of the district, the Elder Creek School District in Glen Elder was annexed to the city and joined the Sacramento City Unified School District.

North of the American River, schools became a central issue in the first major mass annexation campaign in 1958. School superintendents and trustees in the Hagginwood-Del Paso Heights area fought annexation vigorously, publicly, and successfully, and the Hagginwood-Del Paso Heights annexation proposal was defeated in January 1959. Although most of the area has subsequently been annexed to Sacramento's city government on a piecemeal basis, the schools have remained in other districts. All annexation and merger proposals affecting territory north of the American River have omitted the schools since the failure of the 1958–59 Hagginwood-Del Paso Heights annexation campaign. As a result, there are approximately 14,500 school age children living in the city of Sacramento who attend schools in five elementary and high school districts other than the city district. Most of these children are located north of the American River, but there are also a few children in a section north of the downtown Sacramento business district who attend school in other districts.

Present School District. In the 1968–69 school year, when field work for this study was carried out, the Sacramento City Unified School District operated 74 regular schools, 57 elementary schools, 12 junior high schools, and 5 high schools. Total enrollment in grades K–12 was 51,292 pupils. The physical boundaries of the district were essentially the same as in 1959, when the last major additions to the district took place. (See Figure 2.)

The district's total school population has fluctuated over the past few years, going down between 1966 and 1968, gaining between 1969 and 1970, and falling off again in 1971. Enrollment during this period has ranged from about 49,00 to 52,000 students. In the 14-year period prior to 1966, however, the number of pupils in the district more than doubled. The district enrolled 23,037 students in 1952, 40,892 in 1959, and 51,641 in 1966. Gains in enrollment in this period were primarily the result of the addition of new territory to the Sacramento City Unified District and of the rapid population growth in many of these outlying areas, where new subdivisions were being developed.

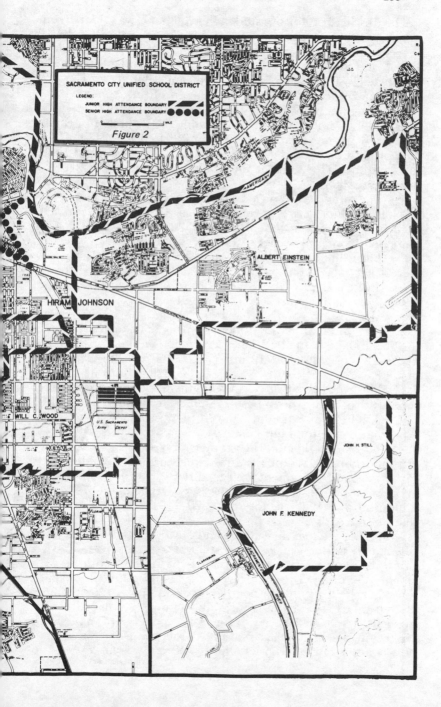

SACRAMENTO CITY UNIFIED SCHOOL DISTRICT

LEGEND:
JUNIOR HIGH ATTENDANCE BOUNDARY
SENIOR HIGH ATTENDANCE BOUNDARY

Figure 2

The district's 1968–69 student enrollment was 35 percent minority, with 14 percent of the enrollment being black; 12 percent, Mexican; 8 percent, Asian; and 1 percent, American Indian and other nonwhites. An annual racial and ethnic census conducted by the district between 1963 and 1968 showed several important trends in the racial population of the schools:

(1) Both the number and proportion of Caucasian students in the school system are gradually declining. The number of whites decreased from a peak of 34,455 in 1964 to 33,431 in 1968. The proportion of whites also dropped between 1963 and 1968, falling from 71 percent of the total enrollment in 1963 to 65 percent in 1968.

(2) The number and proportion of black students are increasing steadily. Black enrollment grew from 4,848 in 1963 to 7,040 in 1968. The proportion of blacks in the total school system increased from 10 percent to 14 percent in this period.

(3) The number and proportion of Mexican students are also increasing, but not as rapidly as with black students. The district's method of classifying Spanish-background students changed in 1966, suggesting a greater increase than has actually taken place.[11] Adjusting for the change in definition, there were an estimated 5,122 Mexican students enrolled in district schools in 1963 and 5,981 in 1968. The percentage of Mexican students in the school system grew from 10 percent in 1963 to 12 percent in 1968.

(4) The enrollment of Asian students has begun to decrease slightly, dropping from a peak of 4,358 pupils in 1966 to 4,146 in 1968. The proportion of Asian students remained the same, 8 percent of the total enrollment.

Though no single minority group is present in large numbers or proportions, as a combined group the various minorities make up a substantial segment of the district's enrollment. Racial enrollment figures reported to the U. S. Department of Health, Education and Welfare for the 1970–71 school year indicate that these trends are continuing.

In spite of the fact that a large and obviously growing number of minority students make up the student body, the district Board of Education was 100 percent Caucasian in 1969, with no representation of any of the different racial and ethnic minorities. Since November 1960, the board has consisted of seven members elected on a citywide basis in nonpartisan elections. Although Mexicans and blacks have run for seats on the board, none were elected in the 1960's. Early in 1967, following the resignation of a board member who left the city, there was an attempt to get a black candidate who had run in a previous election appointed to fill the unexpired term. The board decided, however, to appoint a white candidate who had been the highest runner-up in the same election.

Until 1963, Sacramento schools were organized on a neighborhood school basis at all levels, without any special efforts on the part of the school board to select sites, adjust boundaries, or in any way insure that school organization would transcend community patterns of housing segregation. The neighborhod school pattern, combined with the district's rapid expansion into predominantly Caucasian suburbs, created a kind of double segregation for minority students. Blacks, Mexicans, and Asians were not only heavily concentrated in certain inner city schools, but the majority were also attending the older schools, while the district built new schools in the suburbs that primarily served Caucasian children. This was particularly true at the elementary level. From 1954 to 1968, the district built a total of 20 new elementary schools. Nineteen of these schools are located outside Sacramento's 1950 city limits, and 19 are in predominantly Caucasian areas. One new elementary school, Camellia, is in the predominantly black Glen Elder subdivision. The sharp contrast in school buildings and in money spent in the outlying Caucasian areas as compared with the older minority neighborhods heightened minority dissatisfaction with the schools.

3.
Desegregation of Stanford Junior High School

Fire Destroys Stanford Junior High School. Sacramento's confrontation with school segregation began in August 1963, when Stanford Junior High School was set on fire by a mentally retarded, disgruntled minority student.[12]

Located at Tenth Avenue and Sacramento Boulevard in Oak Park, Stanford Junior High School was in the center of one of the heaviest concentrations of blacks in the school district (Census Tract 28). The school drew students from several predominantly black elementary feeder schools in the surrounding Oak Park community. While official figures on the racial and ethnic composition of Sacramento schools were not available at the time, it was known that Stanford and several of its feeder schools were predominantly·black. Stanford was 30 years old at the time of the fire and had served substantially the same geographic attendance area, the Oak Park community, since it opened February 20, 1933.

The Reverend Cyrus Keller, President of the National Association for the Advancement of Colored People (NAACP) in 1963, described the situation at Stanford as "negative." The school was overcrowded and, according to Reverend Keller, "the principal didn't care." Although district officials insisted at that time that there was no relationship between achievement and racially imbalanced schools, results of standardized achievement and ability tests indicated otherwise. Students at Stanford and Lincoln junior high schools, the two junior high schools with the highest minority enrollments in the city, did more poorly on tests given eighth graders than did pupils at other schools. For example, Stanford and Lincoln eighth graders had mean IQ scores of 94 and 95, respectively, compared to average scores of 100 to 109 in other schools. Both Stanford and Lincoln had the smallest proportion of students scoring in the "high group" on other tests and the largest percentage of pupils in the "low group."

Firemen were unable to control or stop the Stanford fire, and on August 17, 1963, the bulk of the school plant was destroyed. Only the cafeteria and five portable classrooms were left when the fire was quenched. The Stanford plant was insured on a replacement basis for $1,419,116 minus 5.3 percent for noninsurable property.

Temporary Plans for Stanford Students. Since school was scheduled to open September 10, emergency action was necessary. In a special board meeting held two days·after the fire, then Superintendent of Schools F. Melvyn Lawson presented three alternative plans for immediate housing of the Stanford students. Each of the plans provided for keeping the Stanford student body and faculty together in an intact unit. Dr. Lawson suggested (1) moving Stanford Junior High School to the American Legion School, a nearby elementary school, and relocating American Legion children in neighboring elementary schools that were experiencing declining populations; (2) using one of the other junior high schools to house both its own and the Stanford student body on a double-session basis; and (3) placing 35 portable classrooms on the rear of the Stanford site and resuming operation of the school as soon as possible in portables. Lawson personally recommended a combination of approaches (2) and (3). He proposed that the Stanford students be housed at predominantly white Peter Lassen Junior High School on a double-session basis until 35 portable classrooms could be assembled and equipped for use at the rear of the Stanford site.

One board member, Mrs. Alba Kuchman, proposed that all Stanford students be immediately dispersed to surrounding junior high schools, eliminating the need for double-sessions at Lassen and giving the Stanford youth the benefit of a full-time education during the period needed to replace the Stanford structure. Both Superintendent Lawson and Assistant Superintendent Donald E. Hall, Director of Planning and Research Services, opposed this approach, stressing the administrative and transportation problems it would create. Several parents from the Lassen attendance area backed the idea of immediate dispersal. One Lassen parent stated that Lassen was willing to take its "share" of the Stanford students, but that it was unfair for Lassen to bear the entire burden.

When the floor was opened to public discussion, Robert Tyler, Chairman of the Congress of Racial Equality (CORE) Education Committee, identified the "real issue" as "breaking up an intense pattern of segregation in Oak Park."[13] Mr. Tyler urged that Stanford Junior High School be dissolved and its students dispersed to surrounding junior high schools, with the board perhaps using the insurance money to build a new junior high school in another area. He considered arguments about transportation costs, possible conflicts between student bodies, and scheduling difficulties to be a "smoke screen" to hide the real issue—ethnic containment at Stanford arising from segregated housing in Oak Park.

At the end of the evening's discussion, the board voted 6–1 to: (1) initiate double sessions at Peter Lassen Junior High School, housing both Lassen and Stanford students there for a maximum period of one year; (2) move portable classrooms to the Stanford site and reestablish Stanford temporarily until long-range plans could be made; and (3) evaluate the long-range problem of rebuilding Stanford. Mrs. Kuchman cast the only dissenting vote.

NAACP Challenges Plan for Stanford Students. On August 21, Reverend Cyrus Keller, the father of a Stanford student, as well as NAACP Branch President, wrote the president of the Board of Education, Mrs. Jewel Blucher, informing her of a resolution passed by the NAACP Executive Board. The letter asked the school board to reconsider its emergency plan for the Stanford students, pointing out the "grave problem of ethnic imbalance at Stanford."[14] The letter also stated that the NAACP would not let propagation of the racial status quo go unchallenged. When the board refused to reconsider its temporary plans for Stanford, the NAACP announced publicly on September 16 that it would force dispersal of the Stanford students by means of a court-ordered injunction. Later in the month, Reverend Keller filed an injunction suit in the Sacramento County Superior Court on behalf of his son, Cyrus S. Keller, Jr. The Keller suit, filed under the auspices of the NAACP, charged that Stanford was a segregated school and sought an injunction to prevent the school board from (1) erecting portables and returning students to a temporary campus on the site of the Stanford school; (2) selecting the old Stanford site for construction of a permanent junior high school; and (3) failing to evolve and execute a nondiscriminatory plan for distribution of the Stanford student population later than January 7, 1964.

On October 8, Judge Irving Perluss issued an opinion finding the Stanford Junior High School to be a segregated school. The Perluss opinion also (1) permitted use of portable classrooms on the Stanford site on a temporary basis; (2) ruled that an injunction against selection of the old Stanford site for a new school was "premature"; and (3) directed the board and superintendent to evolve a plan "in accordance with law" for the correction of racial imbalance at Stanford Junior High School no later than September 1, 1964.

In outlining the legal basis for his decision, Judge Perluss quoted a 1963 decision of the Supreme Court of California, which held, in *Jackson vs. Pasadena City School District:*

> The right to an equal opportunity for education and the harmful consequences of segregation require that school boards take steps, insofar as reasonably feasible, to alleviate racial imbalance in schools *regardless of its cause.*[15] (Emphasis added.)

Judge Perluss also cited a further statement in the Pasadena decision calling attention to regulations of the State Board of Education that "encourage transfers to avoid and eliminate racial segregation."[16] In a footnote, Judge Perluss quoted fully from Sections 2010 and 2011, Title 5, California Administrative Code, which state clearly that it is the policy of the State Board of Education to avoid and eliminate segregation and that the ethnic composition of the neighborhood and student body must be considered in establishing school attendance areas.[17] The legal framework provided by the Pasadena decision and the California Administrative Code played an important part in Sacramento's subsequent deliberations over school segregation.

Mounting Community Pressure for Desegregation. In the seven weeks between the emergency board meeting that voted to return Stanford students to the old site in portables and the Perluss decision, community pressure to desegregate the Sacramento schools began to build up. State Senator Albert S. Rodda (D-Sacramento County) wrote an open letter urging the board to reconsider its decision regarding the immediate housing of the Stanford students. Senator Rodda's letter pointed to the legal implications of Title 5, Sections 2010 and 2011, of the state administrative code, obligating districts to consider the ethnic factor when planning school attendance boundaries. He quoted and pointed to the implications of the *Jackson vs. Pasadena* decision and urged the district to confer with Dr. Wilson Riles, then State Department of Education Consultant in Intergroup Relations. Community organizations, including the Sacramento Fair Housing Committee, the Oak Park Neighborhood Council, the Social Relations and Action Commission of the Sacramento Council of Churches, the American Civil Liberties Union, the Sacramento Council of Democratic Clubs, and the Sacramento Chapter of the National Association of Social Workers, sent representatives to school board meetings to call for dispersal of the Stanford students and abandonment of the Stanford Junior High School site. Some of the groups wanted immediate dispersal of Stanford students, while others were amenable to a reasonable interim period for planning. Nearly all went on record against reestablishing Stanford in portable classrooms. On September 16, the Sacramento Council of Democratic Clubs urged the Board to appoint a broadly representative Citizens' Advisory Committee to investigate the entire problem of racial imbalance in the Sacramento schools. On September 24, 11 community organizations, including NAACP, CORE, the American Civil Liberties Union, and the National Council of Jewish Women, formed a coalition called the Sacramento Council for Equal Education. This group was organized to press for the elimination of segregation in the city's schools.

When school opened on September 10, 1964, Stanford and Peter Lassen students were attending half-day sessions at Peter Lassen, with each group of students being taught separately by its own faculty. A newly formed group of Peter Lassen parents protested the board's apparent delay in making plans to end the double sessions.

Racial and Ethnic Census. Following the initial pressure for dispersal of the Stanford students and an exploratory conference with Dr. Wilson Riles of the State Department of Education, School Superintendent Lawson proposed a districtwide racial and ethnic census. The board authorized this census on September 3, making Sacramento one of the first, if not the first, city in California to conduct such a census on a voluntary basis. According to Superintendent Lawson, the survey, which was "a new idea" then, caused much discussion. The district has continued to conduct an annual racial and ethnic census each year since 1963, and the State Department of Education now carries out such a yearly census in all districts.

Results of the district's racial and ethnic census, completed September 25, 1963, substantiated charges of community groups that Sacramento did, indeed, have segregated schools.

At the junior high school level, Stanford was found to be 71 percent minority—50 percent black; 14 percent Mexican; 6 percent Asian; and 1 percent other nonwhites. (See Table 1.) The census also showed that a second junior high school, Lincoln, located near the downtown business area in the old West End, was overwhelmingly minority. Only 17 percent of the Lincoln students were Caucasian; 37 percent were Asian; 30 percent Mexican; 14 percent black; and 3 percent other nonwhites. The nine other junior high schools in the district ranged from 63 to 90 percent Caucasian.

The 1963 racial and ethnic census found the most extensive segregation at the elementary level, however, where neighborhood schools closely overlapped with segregated housing. The census identified 13 elementary schools out of a total of 54 where more than 50 percent of the students were from minority groups. Five elementary schools were more than 50 percent black—American Legion (67 percent) and Donner (54 percent) in Oak Park; Argonaut (61 percent), located just west of the Municipal Airport; and Elder Creek (52 percent) and Camellia (91 percent) in the Glen Elder section of southeast Sacramento.

One school, Riverside, near the east bank of the Sacramento River, was 51 percent Asian, and the Washington Elementary School in Washington Heights was 54 percent Mexican. (See Figure 3.)

In addition to these seven schools with concentrations of one minority exceeding half the student body, there were six schools where a combination of all minority enrollments exceeded 50 percent, but where no single minority predominated. The student enrollment at Lincoln Elementary School, for example, was 95 percent minority, with a fairly even division among Mexican (33 percent), black (31 percent), and Asian (28 percent) children. William Land, located not far from Lincoln in Southside, was 83 percent minority, with 43 percent of the student body made up of Asians; 20 percent, Mexicans; 17 percent, blacks; and 3 percent, other nonwhites. Other schools with multi-ethnic populations of more than 50 percent, but no single predominating minority, included Jedediah Smith (60 percent minority), Oak Ridge (63 percent minority), Ethel Philips (54 percent minority), and Newton Booth (54 percent minority).

The 1963 ethnic census also indicated that all the Sacramento high schools were at least two-thirds Caucasian. The largest clustering of minority groups at the high school level was found at Sacramento High School, where nearly one-third of the enrollment (32 percent) was made up of racial and ethnic minorities. Blacks at Sacramento High constituted the largest concentration of a single minority group at the high school level, making up 13 percent of the Sacramento High enrollment in 1963.

Stanford Desegregation Plan. Approximately one week after the Perluss ruling, the Board of Education adopted a far-reaching desegregation plan for Stanford Junior High School. The Stanford desegregation plan consisted of three main parts: (1) abandoning the Stanford site as a permanent location for a junior high school; (2) opening a new junior high school, the Albert Einstein Junior High School, in the eastern extremity of the district in the fall of 1964; and (3) redrawing attendance boundaries of six junior high schools in the central and eastern part of the city to redistribute the Stanford students and create a new student body for Albert Einstein.

The Einstein site had been acquired several years earlier, and with increased growth of the eastern edge of the city the board had expected to build a new junior high school on this site by the fall of 1966. By using the Stanford insurance money to

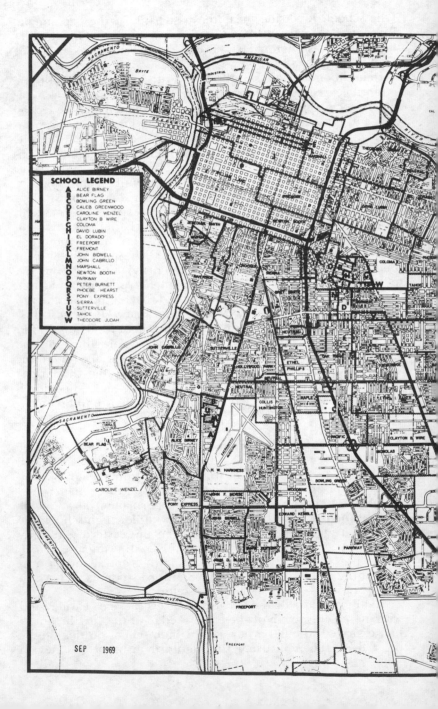

SCHOOL LEGEND

A	ALICE BIRNEY
B	BEAR FLAG
C	BOWLING GREEN
D	CALEB GREENWOOD
E	CAROLINE WENZEL
F	CLAYTON B WIRE
G	COLOMA
H	DAVID LUBIN
I	EL DORADO
J	FREEPORT
K	FREMONT
L	JOHN BIDWELL
M	JOHN CABRILLO
N	MARSHALL
O	NEWTON BOOTH
P	PARKWAY
Q	PETER BURNETT
R	PHOEBE HEARST
S	PONY EXPRESS
T	SIERRA
U	SUTTERVILLE
V	TAHOE
W	THEODORE JUDAH

SEP   1969

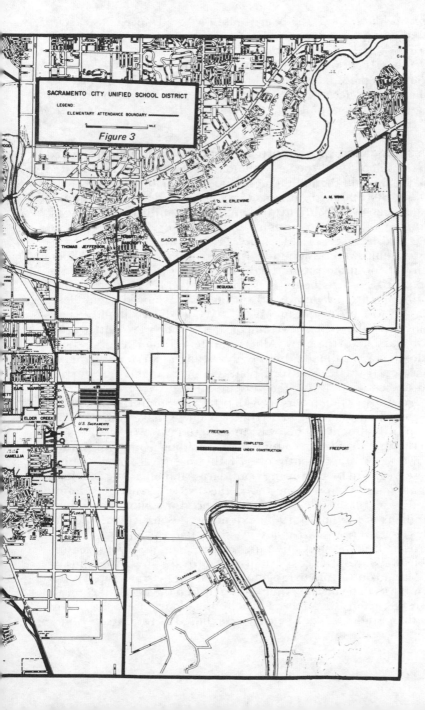

SACRAMENTO CITY UNIFIED SCHOOL DISTRICT

LEGEND:

ELEMENTARY ATTENDANCE BOUNDARY ───────

Figure 3

initiate the project, the board was able to advance construction of a junior high school in the area by two years.

The board's desegregation plan for Stanford was adopted on October 16, 1963, and put into effect in the fall of 1964. The court accepted the plan and there was no appeal. Stanford students completed the fall 1963 term in double sessions at Peter Lassen and were taught in portables at the Stanford site in the spring of 1964.

Desegregation of Stanford Students. When school opened in the fall of 1964, the new attendance boundaries caused three major shifts in the junior high school population.

The 808 Stanford students were distributed among the junior high schools in closest proximity to Stanford. The largest number of Stanford students went to Peter Lassen (344) and the next largest, to California (224). Approximately 138 Stanford pupils were assigned to Kit Carson, 81 to Joaquin Miller, and 11 to Sutter Junior High School. To make room for the Stanford students being reassigned to Peter Lassen, a total of 445 students, predominantly white, were moved from Peter Lassen to Kit Carson and Will C. Wood. In addition to these moves, 473 students, nearly all of these white, were shifted from Kit Carson to the new Albert Einstein Junior High School. Altogether, 726 junior high school students were permanently reassigned by the Stanford plan. Of the students transferred, 63 percent were white. (See Figure 4.)

No transportation was provided for the Stanford students or for the Caucasians moved from Lassen to make room for the Stanford students. This was and continues to be a sore spot in the Stanford desegregation plan. Avoiding a busing program, however, was apparently one of the incentives to accomplish desegregation by redrawing boundaries and engaging in a kind of "domino" plan. Furthermore, the district changed its definition of a "reasonable" walking distance for junior high school students in the fall of 1963, extending the limit from one and three-quarters to two miles. At that time the district did not provide free transportation for regular students beyond reasonable walking distances, but it did provide subsidized busing under a contractual arrangement with the Sacramento Transit Authority. The new two-mile limit reduced the need for contract bus service in the Albert Einstein attendance area, since most of these students had formerly been bused to Kit Carson Junior High School.

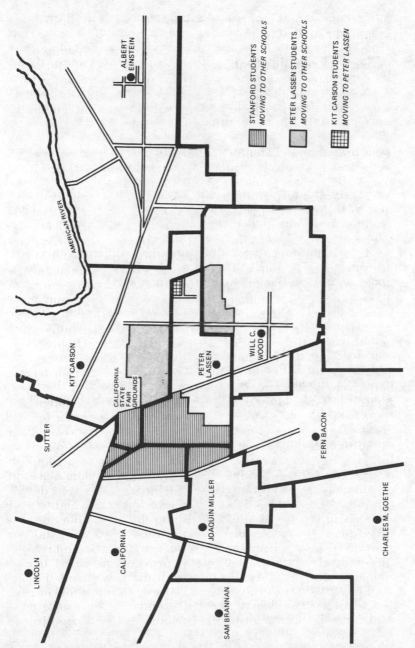

Figure 4. *Change in Junior High School Attendance Boundaries to Accomplish Stanford Desegregation, Fall 1964*

Immediate Impact of Stanford Desegregation Plan. The Stanford plan had the following impact on the racial and ethnic compositions of district junior high schools in the fall of 1964:

(1) No junior high school in the district had more than a 20 percent black enrollment.

(2) California, Joaquin Miller, Kit Carson, and Peter Lassen experienced increases in the proportion of minority students enrolled, with Peter Lassen and California, especially, gaining black students. The percentage of black students in California rose from 6 to 16 percent and the percentage of black students in Peter Lassen increased from 2 to 20 percent.

(3) The proportion of minority students in Will C. Wood decreased slightly, owing to the block of white students transferred from Peter Lassen to make room for Stanford students. Will C. Wood was 37 percent minority in 1963 and 35 percent minority in 1964.

(4) The number of Stanford minority students transferred to Sutter was so small that it had no effect on the minority-majority ratio in the school. Sutter remained 35 percent minority.

(5) Albert Einstein opened in the fall of 1964 with a 93 percent Caucasian enrollment. Although no blacks at all were anticipated, two enrolled. Asians made up 6 percent of Einstein's enrollment in 1964; Mexicans, 1 percent.

Four junior high schools in the district were completely unaffected by the Stanford plan. These schools included three predominantly white junior high schools—Charles M. Goethe, Fern Bacon, and Sam Brannon—that ranged from 71 to 90 percent Caucasian. Lincoln Junior High School, with an 83 percent minority enrollment, was also unaffected by the Stanford plan.

Follow-up Study of Stanford Students. In January 1967, the district released results of a follow-up study of Stanford students transferred to other junior high schools as part of the Stanford desegregation plan. The study covered the 1964–65 and 1965–66 school years and showed some gains over the two years, particularly for those students who transferred as seventh graders. The results were mixed, however, particularly with regard to scores on ability and achievement tests given before and after desegregation. District officials summarized the findings as "positive" but "not dramatic."[18]

The study showed, for instance, that the grade averages of the Stanford students who transferred as seventh graders improved over the two-year period, particularly during the first

year after their transfer and the first semester of the second
year. Grade averages dropped the second semester of the second year, but were still above the students' grade averages as
a group at Stanford. The increases in grade point averages after
the students left Stanford were statistically significant—that is,
the gains were large enough not to have happened by chance.
Grade averages of the eighth grade Stanford transfers were not
studied.

School attendance on the part of the seventh grade transfers
from Stanford to other schools was satisfactory during the first
two years of desegregation, but dropped slightly in the two-year
period, from 93 percent daily attendance at Stanford to 91 percent in desegregated schools. District officials considered the
slight drop a "plus," considering the added distances the former
Stanford students had to walk to their new schools. Attendance
records of the eighth grade transfer students following desegregation were not evaluated.

Seventh and eighth grade Stanford students' scores on
achievement and ability tests prior to and after desegregation
were also compared to those of resident pupils in the six junior
high schools affected by the desegregation. Students already
in these schools were matched with Stanford students on the
basis of age, sex, ethnic group, eighth grade ability tests, and
eighth grade reading achievement test scores. Because of
absences when tests were given, moves away from the district,
and other circumstances, only 121 of the 222 seventh graders
involved in the Stanford desegregation completed all the tests
and were represented in the report. Similarly, only 127 of the
221 eighth graders transferred from Stanford to other schools
participated in all the tests and were included in the two-year
evaluation.

As a group, both the seventh and eighth grade Stanford students who were tested scored below the national averages on
two standardized tests that they took both before and after
desegregation. The tests were designed to measure general
academic ability and achievement in specific subject areas, such
as reading, writing, and mathematics. Scores from both tests,
the School and College Ability Test (SCAT) and the Sequential
Test of Educational Progress (STEP), were broken down by
ethnic group. These breakdowns indicated that the small number of Asian students among the seventh and eighth grade
transfers scored higher than Stanford students in other racial
and ethnic groups on most tests both before and after desegregation. The Asian students tested above the national averages

in all areas while in Stanford and scored even higher after they transferred to other schools. Black and Mexican students, however, tested below the national averages while in Stanford and while in desegregated schools as well. Caucasian students from Stanford scored near the national averages both before and after desegregation. Caucasians scored a little better than average in some areas and a little lower than average in other areas while in Stanford and two years later in the other junior high schools. When the test scores of seventh grade Stanford transfer students were compared with those of resident students with similar backgrounds, the Stanford students' reading scores had improved more than the resident students' scores in the first two years of desegregation. Both groups made similar gains in tests of general academic ability, writing, and mathematics. The Stanford students who transferred as eighth graders, however, made approximately the same gains as their matched peers in tests of general academic ability, writing, and mathematics, but did not make as much improvement in reading as the resident students with similar backgrounds.

Ethnic Status of Junior High Schools, 1968.   No changes were made in the attendance boundaries of junior high schools affected by the Stanford desegregation plan between 1964 and the 1968–69 school year, when field work for this study was done. Only one new junior high school, John H. Still, was built in this period. The John H. Still Junior High School, located in the southernmost part of the school district, opened in 1966 with a 20 percent minority enrollment—10 percent black, 7 percent Mexican, 2 percent Asian, and 1 percent other nonwhites. (See Figure 2.) Still is in a predominantly white area that has a small but growing black population. By the 1968–69 school year, Still was 16 percent black and 26 percent minority.

The fall 1968 district census indicated that no junior high school in the district had an enrollment made up predominantly of blacks, Mexicans, or any single minority group. (See Table 1.) The highest concentration of any one minority at the junior high school level was found at Lincoln Junior High School, where Mexicans made up 40 percent of the total student population. The highest concentration of blacks was at Peter Lassen, where black students made up 26 percent of the total enrollment. Asians were enrolled in greatest numbers at Sam Brannon, where they constituted 22 percent of the student population.

The Stanford desegregation plan was aimed at dispersing black students and was successful in this respect in the first few

Table 1—Racial and Ethnic Distribution of Pupils in Sacramento Junior High Schools, 1963 and 1968

School	Fall 1963 Racial and Ethnic Composition						Fall 1968 Racial and Ethnic Composition					
	Total Enroll-ment	Cau-casian %	Black %	Mexi-can* %	Asian %	Other Non-White %	Total Enroll-ment	Cau-casian %	Black %	Mexi-can %	Asian %	Other Non-White %
Albert Einstein†							890	88	5	4	2	1
California	866	66	6	6	22	—	914	49	25	12	13	1
Charles M. Goethe	1,339	86	3	6	4	1	1,289	68	15	7	7	2
Fern Bacon	1,342	90	1	6	2	1	1,296	83	5	9	2	1
Joaquin Miller	985	71	4	7	18	—	955	53	11	14	21	1
John H. Still†							673	74	16	6	3	1
Kit Carson	1,246	89	1	3	4	3	942	77	13	7	2	1
Lincoln	560	17	14	30	37	2	385	17	19	40	21	3
Peter Lassen	1,480	90	2	5	2	1	1,086	54	26	15	4	1
Sam Brannon	874	72	9	1	17	1	1,132	65	9	3	22	1
Stanford‡	773	29	50	14	6	1						
Sutter	974	65	3	16	14	2	689	56	5	26	11	2
Will C. Wood	707	63	21	13	2	1	943	57	23	16	2	2
TOTAL	11,146	73**	8	8	10	1	11,194	65**	14	11	9	1

*Not adjusted for changes in definition of Spanish background population.   **Averages.

†Built after 1963.

‡Not in existence in 1968.

Source: Sacramento City Unified School District, *Preliminary Report on the Ethnic Composition of the Pupil Population of the Sacramento City Unified School District*, Research Report No. 3, Series 1963-64 (Sept. 25, 1963), p. 7; and *The Ethnic Composition of the Pupil Population of the Sacramento City Unified School District, Fall, 1968*, Research Report No. 8, Series 1968-69 (Nov. 20, 1968), p. 15.

years following desegregation. In 1963, 42 percent of the black junior high school students were enrolled in Stanford, which was 50 percent black. Of all black students in the district, 51 percent were then enrolled in predominantly minority junior high schools. In 1968, no junior high school was over one-fourth black and only one-fifth of the black students were enrolled in predominantly minority junior high schools.

While black segregation was eliminated and single minorities did not dominate any junior high school in 1968, two schools, California and Lincoln, had predominantly minority student populations. Lincoln was 83 percent minority and California was 51 percent minority. Four other junior high schools had student populations between 43 and 47 percent minority: Joaquin Miller, Peter Lassen, Sutter, and Will C. Wood.

Racial Problems in the Junior High Schools.   District officials considered the desegregation of junior high schools a closed matter in 1969, although they were aware of current problems. Some of these problems stemmed from the district's initial approach to desegregation. Others were related to the district's slowness in responding to the growing race and ethnic consciousness among black and Mexican students and the general trend of minorities to be more open and direct in expressing dissatisfaction and hostility.

The distance Oak Park students walk to school is a continuing problem and one that seemingly will not be solved. District officials have stood firm on the position that no busing will be provided, although parents, principals, and PTAs have asked for busing. The two schools receiving the most Oak Park students, Peter Lassen and California, have attendance areas that extend as far as 2.7 and 3 miles from the schools. The majority of the Oak Park children cannot afford the commercial, feeder buses run by the transit system, and their families do not have cars. There is, therefore, more tardiness among minority children and less participation in after-school activities. Many of the minority pupils do not have raincoats and sufficiently heavy clothing for the rainy winter season, which further compounds the problem. The principals of California and Lassen were concerned in 1969, but saw little they could do, having tried unsuccessfully to get the district to bus the children. The California principal said he is lenient with lateness. The Peter Lassen principal allowed the girls to wear slacks to school in the winter, which was generally taboo at that time, and some teachers tried to help by taking home a car load of students after school and picking children up for special events.

There is also a great deal of hostility toward Oak Park students in the Caucasian neighborhoods through which the California and Lassen students pass going to and from school. Police cars follow the students home on a routine basis, apparently because of complaints from whites in the neighborhoods. Neither principal felt this was justified and the students resented the police patrol. The principal of California had set up meetings with representatives of Curtis Park, the white area involved, Oak Park, and the central administration. The student Intergroup Relations Club at California also invited the Sacramento police to the school to talk about the situation and explain the students' point of view. The police patrols continued, however, and central administration officials said they could not stop it. Police cars were frequently parked in sight of the schools. The principal of Peter Lassen felt that the hostile stares and remarks of Caucasians in these neighborhoods created a situation where the kids "put on a show" because it was expected. This hostility dates back to the early days of desegregation and, like the transportation problem, remains one of the "givens" in the junior high school situation.

Peter Lassen, especially, has undergone many changes since desegregation and has had to overcome many difficult problems. Lassen got the most Oak Park students with desegregation and shifted from a 90 percent Caucasian school to nearly half minority in a five-year period. There has also been a change in the white population of the area, which was more professional when the school opened in 1954 but is now predominantly working class. By the spring of 1969, Lassen had had three principals in the last three years, five vice-principals in the last six years, and a high faculty turnover. Lassen still had a nucleus of teachers who were on the staff when the school opened and some of these had not accepted the new population and changes that had come about. Courses like Latin had been dropped and extracurricular activities were nonexistent for several years, except for sports. There were divisions in the faculty between the younger, more liberal teachers and the older, more conservative teachers, who regretted the changes in Lassen. White parents did not work with the school as they did before desegregation.

The 1968-69 Lassen principal felt that much damage was done in the "preparation" of pupils, parents, and teachers for desegregation. He said that Oak Park parents still threw it up to him that the Stanford students were told they were "guests"

tend to mingle with the Caucasians, in contrast to the other minority groups. He sees "little difference between the Orientals and Caucasians," and "doesn't know" the difference if he "doesn't pay attention."

New Programs for Minority Students. Lassen, California, and Will C. Wood have the largest proportions of blacks in their student body and all three schools are to some degree beginning to initiate some programs of special interest or help to black and Mexican students. During the 1968-69 school year, Lassen had both a black history and a Mexican-American history course, taught as electives, and a special class for Mexican background students who needed help with their English. Both Lassen and Will C. Wood had Afro-American Clubs and chapters of the Mexican-American Youth Association (MAYA). The minority history courses at Lassen were begun without major confrontations, following walkouts and formal demands by high school students for ethnic history,courses and other changes in the spring of 1968. Lassen's principal said that he added these courses and clubs because

> I felt that many things the kids are doing is for a sense of identity and that we as educators could help out and help children reap the benefits inherent within.

The ethnic history courses and the special English class for Mexican students at Lassen were begun without special funds. Although the ethnic history courses and clubs are open to all in both schools they are almost completely made up of the particular minority groups. The principal of Lassen planned to add weight lifting to physical education classes the next year and also wanted to add boxing because of the interest of boys with a Mexican background. Mexican students had requested these sports for several years.

At California, however, the principal felt it would be better to "keep all the students in one group." There are no special clubs or courses for individual minorities and the principal channeled activities recognizing special traditions and interests through an Intergroup Relations Club, set up at the beginning of the 1968-69 school year. Activities of the Intergroup Relations Club have included a Mexican cultural program and assemblies on blacks and on African culture and tradition. The principal initiated this club because of the poor participation of black and Mexican students in student activities. The club meets at lunch time, as after-school activities present problems for the minority students who have to walk home. Both black and Mexican students have responded favorably to programs on their own group.

There were no compensatory or supportive educational services for desegregated schools instituted with the initial transfer of Stanford students, but both Peter Lassen and Will C. Wood were later identified as compensatory education schools. During the 1968-69 school year, both schools had reading resource teachers who they were to lose in the 1969-70 school year because of Title I budget cuts. California had already lost its reading teachers because of reductions in the budget, but the principal expected to be able to partially restore this program during the 1969-70 school year, owing to a new district policy giving extra teachers to secondary schools with over 40 percent minority enrollments. The special reading teachers were in the schools to assist all children from low income areas but served a high proportion of blacks and Mexicans. Will C. Wood had a State-funded program for average and above average intelligence students who were behind in reading and/or mathematics. This program also enrolled a high proportion of black and Mexican pupils.

Other measures the principals of these schools took to assist black and Mexican students with their academic problems included encouraging students to study in the neighborhood study centers sponsored by the poverty program, working with teachers to increase their expectations of minority children and improve their teaching methods, placing pictures of black students on the honor roll in the local black newspaper, sending out home visitors to discuss academic and attendance problems with parents, and encouraging students to stay after school for help when they have problems. Some teachers tutored students on an individual basis. In the fall of 1968, the Oak Park Community Council sponsored a parents workshop in which Lassen teachers participated on how to help children with school work. Lassen was dropping ability grouping in subjects such as mathematics and English beginning with the 1969-70 school year, and California had already dropped all ability grouping. The principals believe this is in the interest of minority students, who are heavily concentrated in the lowest groupings, where students are classified by achievement scores. These changes followed demands of minority high school students that the track system in the senior high schools be eliminated.

In spite of clustering at the lower levels where there has been ability grouping, there is a wide range of academic ability among minority students in the three schools. Some black and Mexican students are found in all academic subjects and at all achievement levels. Two college preparatory classes visited at Will C. Wood had the following racial and ethnic breakdowns:

	Students				
Class	Total	Caucasian	Black	Mexican	Asian
Eighth Grade English	31	24	3	2	2
Algebra	29	13	10	4	2

A teacher at Lassen said that their school had a "solid core of achieving black students, many right out of the ghetto." She said that the black students, especially, were doing better even though it is "so rough for them." In her observation, the black students went through a period of "being loud" and "condemning others," but then settled down to "more constructive things." She said that the black students were "becoming so mobilized, many will make it regardless of who stands in the way." California's principal noted that "many Negro students don't have the background in education to take algebra and foreign languages, but many do." He has found the parents interested in their children's getting an education and commented that "even the militant organizations are talking about staying in school."

Lincoln Closing Furthers Racial Imbalance.
On April 20, 1969, after a long period of study and debate, the board voted to close Lincoln as a regular school, including both the junior high school and elementary departments. Although discontinuation of Lincoln's primary grades had been considered earlier as part of a proposed elementary desegregation plan, the 1969 decision to close Lincoln was promoted by the central administration on financial grounds. Lincoln's enrollment had been declining for a number of years and projections for the 1969–70 school year indicated that the junior high school department would enroll only 384 students, while the elementary grades would enroll 134. Operational costs were high, and the age and structural condition of the building also figured in the administration's recommendations. Like many other older, inner-city schools, Lincoln was in need of major rehabilitation to bring the physical plant in line with state legal requirements for earthquake safety. This aspect of the district's present deliberations on the question of closing most of the older, inner-

city schools will be discussed later in the report.

Shortly after the board's decision to close Lincoln, presumably to save money, the district's then superintendent, Paul Salmon, proposed an increase in the tax rate to finance a new "continuation" school for the district. A "continuation school" is a special school for youngsters under the compulsory school age limit who have been suspended from the regular junior high and high schools for periods of more than ten days. Special programs for these students are mandated by state law, but can be provided in the regular schools, as the district was then doing at the junior high school level. The board refused to support a proposed tax increase for a new continuation school, but ultimately sanctioned the establishment of a continuation school for junior and senior high school pupils in the Lincoln building, on a smaller scale than originally proposed by the superintendent. Superintendent Salmon assured board members that the $89,000 saving promised with the closing of Lincoln would not be washed out by the new continuation school, which would receive special state aid.

Though the closing of Lincoln did not become a major issue in the minority communities, it added fuel to a growing resentment over the district's treatment of minorities and a trend toward elimination of schools in inner-city neighborhoods. The separate continuation schools are particularly resented and criticized by members of minority groups whose children make up a disproportionate segment of the enrollments. School officials also argued for the conversion of Lincoln to a continuation school because of the need to isolate and rehabilitate "rowdies." This remark greatly incensed several Mexican leaders, including a mother whose son had had a very unfortunate experience in a similar school.

The Lincoln conversion was not tied in with a desegregation plan and had the immediate effect of feeding more minority students into adjacent junior high school attendance areas, which were already heavily minority. As a result of the influx of Lincoln students, both Sutter and California became predominantly minority schools in 1970. After Lincoln was closed as a regular school, the racial and ethnic distribution of students in these two schools was as follows:

Fall 1970 Enrollment

School	Total	Caucasian	Black	Mexican	Asian	Other Nonwhite
California	983	44%	25%	15%	16%	less than 1%
Sutter	775	49%	6%	27%	18%	less than 1%

The administration anticipated this buildup of minorities, but made no proposals for a general realignment of junior high school attendance boundaries or for sending the Lincoln students to other schools with lower minority concentrations. No transportation was provided for the former Lincoln pupils, although some who were transferred to Sutter had to travel over three miles to their new school.

The continuation school set up at Lincoln was predominantly minority at the junior high school level when it opened, with a 37 percent black, 19 percent Mexican, and 2 percent Indian population. The high school section was 49 percent minority in 1970, with more Mexican (28 percent) than black (18 percent) pupils or other nonwhites (2 percent).

4.
District Desegregation Policy Adopted

Citizens Advisory Committee Proposals. On November 26, 1963, a little over a month after adopting a plan for the desegregation of Stanford, the Board of Education formed a Citizens Advisory Committee on Equal Educational Opportunity. The Advisory Committee, a response to mounting pressure to desegregate *all* the Sacramento schools, was set up to (1) study and evaluate evidence of racial tension arising from ethnic imbalance in the district's schools, especially at the elementary level; (2) recommend ways and. means to reduce or eliminate existing tensions; and (3) investigate and recommend means by which equal educational opportunities could be offered to all pupils in the district. Specifically, the board asked the Citizens Advisory Committee to recommend a definition of segregation and to examine the applicability of the neighborhood school concept at all school levels.

The committee of 15 men and women selected to carry out this undertaking was a "blue ribbon" group including professionals, businessmen, and a minister. There were ten Caucasians, two blacks, one Mexican, one Chinese, and one Japanese. According to one member of the committee, the group held a range of conservative, moderate, and liberal opinions on politics and racial issues. But the committee was not "representative" in terms of today's requirements, this same member pointed out. There were no poverty or grass roots level leaders or parents represented.

The Advisory Committee began its work in February 1964. For the next 15 months, committee members interviewed and consulted with parents, teachers, counselors, principals, and central administration staff. The committee held public hearings and requested special studies which the district central administration staff conducted. The committee examined and evaluated different approaches to desegregation and compensatory education in other parts of the state and throughout the country. The Chairman of the Advisory Committee felt that the committee heard "everyone who wanted to be heard" and that it was more representative of the district than the school board, which had no minority members at that time.

On May 22, 1965, the Citizens Advisory Committee issued a unanimous report that brought the major issues of Sacramento's school problems into sharp focus. The report identified and dealt with segregation as the main barrier to equal educational opportunity in the district and recommended sweeping changes in the organization of Sacramento schools.

By way of defining segregation the committee proposed that a school be considered segregated whenever (1) the total ethnic minority composition exceeds 40 percent of the enrollment or (2) a single minority group exceeds 25 percent of all students, then roughly twice the proportion of the largest minority in the district population. Applying this definition, the committee found that two of the 11 junior high schools were ethnically imbalanced during the 1964–65 school year. Lincoln was still 83 percent minority, and the committee also considered the new junior high school, Albert Einstein, ethnically imbalanced because of its 93 percent Caucasian enrollment. None of the high schools were segregated according to the committee's definition, but 23 of the 53 regular elementary schools had a single minority of 25 percent or more, or a total ethnic population of 40 percent or more. The report pointed to "most extreme" segregation in the seven elementary schools where single minorities made up over half of the school enrollment and also called attention to seven additional schools where a combination of several minorities exceeded 50 percent of the school population. By 1964, Bret Harte Elementary School also had a minority population of more than 50 percent. The committee noted there were six elementary schools with no black children at all enrolled.

The Citizens Advisory Committee report made a number of recommendations to the district Board of Education. Specifically, it asked the district to:

(1) recognize and deal with segregation as the "primary obstacle to equal educational opportunity";

(2) take positive steps to develop student populations in each school that approximate the ethnic composition of the district;

(3) establish an administrative position to coordinate and supervise all activities affecting equal educational opportunity;

(4) by active recruitment, increase the percentage of administrators, principals, teachers, and noncertificated personnel from ethnic minority groups;

(5) select administrative personnel with special consideration for successful experience in schools with minority enrollments;

(6) require in-service training for all personnel working with ethnic minority pupils;

(7) expand counseling services and increase counselors' competences in assisting pupils and parents of ethnic minority groups;

(8) revise the current suspension policy and practices and administer suspensions in such a way as to insure that parents and children of minority groups understand the policy, to "thus avoid feelings of discrimination";

(9) make every effort to insure that parents feel welcome and comfortable with teachers and principals and that an atmosphere of mutual respect and trust prevails between parents and school personnel;

(10) institute a program of compensatory education in all schools that recognizes and compensates for deficiencies in children who are educationally handicapped; and

(11) join in the efforts of federal, state, county, and local agency efforts to reverse the trend toward segregated housing patterns.

The committee's most far-reaching recommendation, and the one that provoked the most public controversy, was a proposal to eliminate ethnic imbalance in elementary schools by abolishing existing attendance areas and grouping schools together in "clusters." The clusters, which would contain at least three elementary schools, would combine heavily minority schools with nearby Caucasian schools, creating new attendance zones that would be balanced as to racial and ethnic groups. Within each cluster, the individual school would be balanced by such techniques as curtailing the growth of some schools, abandonment of schools, open enrollment, mandatory reassignment of students, development of a single central school, and interzone attendance agreements. An advisory committee of school staff, parents, and citizens-at-large in each area would develop specific plans for desegregating their particular cluster. The committee felt the plan could be implemented by September 1, 1966. To illustrate the feasibility of the cluster proposal, the committee grouped most of the elementary schools of the district into eight clusters that had minority student enrollments ranging from 27 to 49 percent. (See Figure 5.)

Reaction to Citizens Advisory Committee Report. Meeting with the Citizens Advisory Committee on May 27, school board members questioned and expressed doubts about several key recommendations of the committee's report, including the proposed definition of segregation and the feasibility of taking children out of neighborhood schools. At a meeting between the board and top administrative school staff on June 21, the staff went on record as agreeing with the bulk of the report, but recommended that the neighborhood school concept be maintained. Both these meetings were open to the public and were covered by the news media. Then Superintendent Lawson appealed for citizen reaction. A public hearing had already been set for June 30.

Public reaction to the report had begun early in June, in the form of a few letters to school board members and the superintendent. Beginning June 22, the day after staff defended the neighborhood school concept, letters, petitions, statements, and telegrams began to flood into the superintendent's office. The heavy influx of letters and petitions continued through the June 30 public hearing. Between June 10 and the early part of July, school board members, the superintendent, and other top school administrators received a total of 4,506 letters, petition signatures, telegrams, and other written communications reacting to the Citizens Advisory Committee report. The issue had crystalized publicly as "forced busing" versus the "neighborhood school," and those writing and petitioning the superintendent's office and the board overwhelmingly rejected busing and rallied to the neighborhood school. (See Table 2.)

At least ten different petitions and form letters hostile to busing or expressing support for the neighborhod school were circulated between June 22 and June 30. Though differently worded, petitions and form letters concentrated on several main

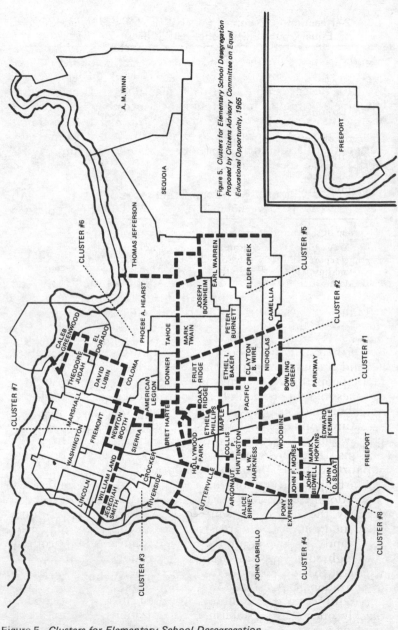

Figure 5. *Clusters for Elementary School Desegregation Proposed by Citizens Advisory Committee on Equal Educational Opportunity, 1965*

Table 2—Reaction to Report of the Citizens Advisory Committee on
Equal Opportunity, June—July 1965

Type of Communication	Total	In Favor of Report	Anti-Busing, Pro Neighbor-hood School	Ambiguous or Could Not Be Classified
Signatures on Petitions	3,764	26	3,549	189*
Form Letters	505	0	505	0
Individual Letters and Communications	237	7	227	3
TOTAL	4,506	33	4,281	192

*This group of signatures referred to an attached statement that was missing.

Source: Xerox file of communications to Sacramento City Unified School District
concerning report of Citizens Advisory Committee on Equal Educational Opportunity, June-July, 1965, loaned to the study by Board of Education member
Adolph Moskovitz.

themes: (1) opposition to any plan which would bus children
out of their neighborhood; (2) the cost of transporting children
beyond traditional neighborhood boundaries; (3) the fact that
many people bought homes in particular areas because of the
closeness of schools; and (4) their preference for the traditional
neighborhood school. Three petitions, accounting for 3,073
signatures, opposed the busing of children out of the neighborhood without the express consent of parents. Altogether, 4,054
persons signed petitions and form letters opposed to busing or
supporting the neighborhood school.

The bulk of the petitions and form letters came from residents
of predominantly white residential areas of the district, particularly the southwest, south central, and eastern suburbs.
Elementary attendance areas such as Caleb Greenwood, Parkway, and Thomas Jefferson were canvassed thoroughly.
Although some parents circulating petitions identified their
school at the top of petitions, most of the petitions carried no
organizational identification. Petitions and form letters were
apparently circulated by ad hoc groups of citizens who mobilized
quickly outside the established organizations. A note accompanying a batch of petitions from the Parkway attendance area
suggests something of the flavor of the petition campaign:

On two days notice we canvassed our Parkway area, door to door and obtained 436 signatures. With more time we could have reached every home in the Parkway area. Of those polled 99 percent were against transfers of students from neighborhood schools.

Only one petition, signed by 26 residents of the Caleb Greenwood attendance area, voiced support for the recommendations of the Citizens Advisory Committee. This statement endorsed the goals of equal education and called upon the school board to "develop the means and the method of implementation of the citizens' recommendations." The petition also said that signers were aware of anti-busing petitions circulating in their area and knew of the "unpublicized" meeting at the Caleb Greenwood Elementary School "for the purpose of organizing and indoctrinating the community against busing without regard to educational values to be gained from all of the seven recommendations of the committee." This statement closed with an expression of confidence in the school board.[19]

The 237 individually worded letters, statements, and telegrams sent in reaction to the Citizens Advisory Committee report were also overwhelmingly anti-busing or pro-neighborhood school. Only seven letters and statements supported the recommendations of the Citizens Advisory Committee or were favorable to busing children out of the neighborhood to resolve the school segregation problem. The most correspondence came from the same areas where petitions and form letters originated. There was in fact a degree of overlap between the two forms of protest—some people wrote a personal letter in addition to signing a petition. Common themes running through the letters were similar to the major points of the petitions, but many also said they would not object to black children being bused into their areas. A special study group of the David Lubin PTA opposed busing without parental consent, but also recognized the existence of racial imbalance in the schools and recommended "cluster committees" to study ways and means of promoting balance with "a minimum of disruption of the neighborhood school concept."[20]

At the public hearing on the Citizens Advisory Committee report at McClatchy Senior High School on June 30, 15 persons testified in support of the report, including part or all of the controversial cluster plan. Those in favor of implementing the report included a spokesman for the California Democratic Council and a representative of the Sacramento Citizens Council. Eighteen persons spoke against abandonment of the neighborhood schools, against busing, and against the cluster plan. Those against implementation of the report included a spokesman for the "Parkway homeowners" and a representative of the Sacramento Mothers Club, a group organized to "preserve the freedom of our children to attend their neighborhood school." Fourteen additional persons testified, but their statements were too ambiguous to classify as either for or against the report.

Emotions had built up to a peak by the time the June 30 hearing took place. A minority member of the Citizens Advisory Committee said he could not believe the "public uproar" over the report. Whites, he said, accused the committee of "trying to mongrelize our people." Although some protest came from the older, inner-city neighborhoods with minority populations, the wellsprings of opposition were the heavily segregated, newer white residential areas. In 1966, when actual desegregation of the elementary schools began, a newspaper reporter for the *Union*, Sacramento's more conservative morning paper stated:

> Nowhere was the Sacramento elementary school desegregation fought more actively than in trim, three- and four-bedroom River Park.[21]

He described River Park, a section of East Sacramento where Caleb Greenwood Elementary School is located, as a "natural enclave" and noted fear of busing among parents. When the desegregation plan was set and assigned more bused black-students to Caleb Greenwood than any other school, a teacher living in that area commented:

> Since the majority of people in this neighborhood are not willing to allow open housing in River Park, I think we're reaping the harvest.[22]

While some of the school attendance areas that generated much opposition to the Advisory Committee report had sizable Asian populations, the most protest came from attendance areas with no blacks at all or only a few blacks enrolled in their elementary schools. The Caleb Greenwood and Parkway elementary attendance areas had no black students when possible desegregation plans were first debated, and Thomas Jefferson had 8 black students out of an enrollment of 557 pupils.

The anti-busing hysteria was clearly a panic reaction of white homeowners who had by choice settled themselves away from the pressing problems of blacks and the inner city. One of the

ironies of the whole outburst was that many of those who wrote
letters and signed petitions opposing the busing of their children
away from "the neighborhood school" were living in new subdivisions where there were, in fact, no "neighborhood" schools
in operation. Their letters frequently mentioned that new
schools were under construction near them or were projected
for their neighborhood in the future. Their children were being
bused or transported by car to schools out of the neighborhood,
pending completion or building of schools in the area. Some
discussed their current or recent busing experience—to other
white schools—as arguments in favor of maintaining "neighborhood" schools. It was also ironical that some of the greatest
protest came from eastern and south-central suburban areas
outside the city limits that the committee had deliberately ex-
cluded from the suggested cluster proposal.

Adoption of Desegregation Policy.   No further action on the
Citizens Advisory Committee report was taken during the
summer of 1965. The Citizens Advisory Committee dissolved
with completion of the report and ceased to function as a group,
although some individual members continued to push for
implementation of the report and desegregation of the schools.

In the fall of 1965, with three school board seats up for election, some board members and administrative staff were concerned that busing might become a major issue in the election
and that "unenlightened" people might be voted to the board
in the aftermath of the furor over the Citizens Committee
report. Partly to help keep the desegregation issue "in perspective" for the election, the board issued a major policy statement
on equal educational opportunity on October 4, 1965. This
statement spelled out a definition of school segregation and
equal educational opportunity, instructed the superintendent
to prepare a plan for eliminating the adverse effects of segregation, and endorsed many of the less controversial recommendations of the Citizens Advisory Committee. This was the district's
first major policy statement on school segregation and it has
not been revised since 1965.

The 1965 policy statement defined segregation as

> the condition in a given school population where the concentration
> of *any one* ethnic minority is such that this group actually loses
> its identity as a minority group and thereby becomes the majority
> group in that situation. (Emphasis added.)

This definition ignored the school dominated by a combination of several racial minority groups and identified segregation as "*one* of the primary obstacles to the attainment of equal educational opportunity." (Emphasis added.) The board noted that "the adverse effects of de facto school segregation are compounded when accompanied by other factors, such as cultural and economic deprivation" and that equal educational opportunity

> recognizes that pupils of like ability are not able equally to benefit from the same educational programs due to such factors as differences in cultural background, economic deprivation, bilingualism, etc. So that pupils with these limitations may compete on an equal basis with other pupils of like ability, there must be equalizing opportunities.

The board then stated "its responsibility to provide an educational program for all pupils of the district which will allow them to achieve their potential as adult members of our democratic society." ". . . of particular concern," the board continued, "is the need to alleviate, or eliminate, if possible, the adverse effects of de facto school segregation."

The policy statement made no commitment to eliminate segregation, but instructed the superintendent to bring to the board on or before May 1, 1966, "the most practical and feasible plan for alleviation and, if possible, the elimination of the *adverse effects* of de facto segregation." (Emphasis added.) The board did not rule out the cluster plan, but stated that it did not believe the cluster plan "is the only method or even the most desirable method of fulfilling the Board's responsibility. . . ." Similarly, the board did not rule out busing but said that it

> wants to emphasize that it does not consider the mandatory reassignment of young children to schools relatively distant from their homes, requiring the transportation of large numbers of pupils, as a necessary or desirable method of fulfilling the board's responsibility in regard to de facto segregation.

Referring a second time to the "advantages of the neighborhood school concept," the superintendent was asked to "consider all reasonably feasible methods for dealing effectively with this problem."

The board accepted—in some cases in modified form—a number of recommendations of the Citizens Advisory Committee in the areas of compensatory education, personnel practices, counseling services, pupil discipline and communications. Specifically, the board adopted the Citizens Committee recommendations for:

(1) an administrator directly responsible to the superintendent to coordinate and supervise all activities affecting equal educational opportunity;

(2) continuation and expansion of the compensatory education program, consistent with the "ability to finance such programs";

(3) efforts to increase the percentage of ethnic minority personnel employed as teachers, administrators, specialists, and classified personnel;

(4) expansion of the in-service training program so that "all district personnel may develop skills and attitudes necessary to work effectively with those from minority groups";

(5) expansion of counseling services, including the extension of counselors to the elementary schools, and training of counselors in intergroup relations through in-service training;

(6) efforts to improve communication with parents so that there can be "an improved parental understanding of suspension as a disciplinary measure."

The statement also said that the board and staff "shall join the efforts of federal, state, county and local agencies, both public and private, to alleviate the perpetuation of segregated housing patterns." When called upon to oppose Proposition 14, a state constitutional amendment hostile to fair housing, the board declined to do so.[23]

Increased State Pressure for Desegregation.   In addition to the new local district policy, there was also increased pressure for desegregation in the fall of 1965 from the California legislature and the State Board of Education.

Late in 1965 the state legislature passed the McAteer Act, which enabled the State Board of Education to accept federal Elementary and Secondary Education Act funds. Section 6451 of the McAteer Act included a nondiscrimination provision that prohibited the perpetuation or promotion of racial or ethnic segregation of pupils in the California public schools. In interpreting this nondiscrimination provision to local school districts, the Office of Compensatory Education of the State Department of Education said that districts could be found in violation of the McAteer Act and declared ineligible for federal compensatory funds unless they took affirmative action to reduce high concentrations of ethnic minorities in their schools. The Office of Compensatory Education further recommended that districts avoid constructing new school plants in areas with high concentrations of ethnic minorities and refrain from adding permanent or portable classrooms in schools serving high percentages of minorities.

5.
Project Aspiration: Elementary Desegregation Begins

Formulation of Project Aspiration. In February 1966, Dr. Erwin Jackson, a black man with a Ph.D. in guidance and psychology from Oklahoma University, was hired to fill the new administrative post in intergroup education authorized by the October 1965 board statement. Dr. Jackson, formerly coordinator of compensatory education for the Santa Barbara County school system, was appointed as an Assistant to the Superintendent for Intergroup Relations. His responsibilities included helping to formulate plans for resolving Sacramento's segregation problems, interpreting the plans to the community, and acting as a troubleshooter for problems arising in the process of desegregating schools.

Late in March 1966 then-Superintendent Lawson presented four alternative plans for desegregation in black elementary schools. Each of these plans concentrated on the five schools in the district that were over 50 percent black: American Legion, Argonaut, Camellia, Donner, and Elder Creek. (See Figure 3.) Each of the four proposals represented an attempt to reconcile a possible solution of the segregation problem with the requirements of the McAteer Act and other immediate needs of the district.

In projecting enrollments for the 1966–67 school year, staff had found that the four schools that were segregated under the board's new policy would need additional classroom space for the coming year. These four schools were eligible for compensatory funds, but under the new guidelines for the McAteer Act, adding classroom space might jeopardize the district's total compensatory program. The district had initiated a compensatory program in 1963–64 with local funds, and expanded this program during the 1965–66 school year with the addition of federal Title I and Economic Opportunity Act monies. The compensatory program was then receiving nearly $1 million in federal funds. The district also planned to finance desegregation primarily with Title I funds.

The 1965 California legislature also amended the Education Code requiring that local districts establish full-time continuation high school programs for children under the compulsory school age suspended from regular schools. Since failure to comply with this new requirement carried a possible penalty of 10 percent of all district apportionments from the state school fund being withheld, it seemed imperative that the district establish a full-time continuation high school. The board had already voted to establish an adult education facility and had recently instructed the superintendent to bring in a plan that would recommend conversion of an elementary school for this purpose.

These considerations were taken into account in the proposed desegregation plans, and the staff also considered the negative reaction of whites to the Citizens Advisory Committee report. "One way" plans, only, were proposed, providing for the closing and/or readjustment of attendance areas of predominantly black schools and the busing of children out of black areas only. Segregated Mexican and Asian schools were left out of all proposals. Dr. Lawson described the proposals as "modest but realistic attempts" to begin coping with the district's segregation problem.[24] He promised long-range, more comprehensive plans at a later date. He and other district officials have since said a broader, two-way approach to desegregation was "not politically feasible."

Prior to a public hearing on alternative plans, Superintendent Lawson endorsed the plan that called for:

(1) converting the American Legion Elementary School in Oak Park to a combined adult education center and full-time continuation high school in the fall of 1966, with all the American Legion students being permanently reassigned to at least a half dozen schools in the vicinity where classroom space was available;

(2) reassigning kindergarten children from the Argonaut School, west of the Municipal Airport, to largely white schools in the vicinity in the fall of 1966, with the remaining elementary children to be transferred to other attendance areas in September 1967, when the Argonaut School would be phased out as a regular elementary school;

(3) reducing the size of the attendance areas of Camellia, Donner, and Elder Creek elementary schools so that children remaining in these schools could be served by available permanent classroom facilities; and

(4) reassigning portions of the Camellia, Donner, and Elder Creek attendance areas to other elementary schools with available classroom space.

Public Hearing on Proposed Plans. On April 11, approximately 500 persons gathered in Sacramento High School for a public hearing on the alternative desegregation plans. Thirty-six speakers testified, with more favoring than opposing some form of desegregation. Opposition was expected, since prior to the hearing several groups had been criticizing the proposals and mobilizing negative sentiment. The Sacramento Mothers Association, for example, was distributing leaflets warning "parents" and "taxpayers" that busing would separate them from their children in the event of an atomic attack. In the black community, Oak Park parents were circulating a petition protesting the proposed closing of American Legion. Other blacks objected to the one-way character of all alternative plans for desegregation. In addition to black opposition, a small group called the Justice Forum took the position that the white child is really the "culturally deprived child" of today and suggested that whites be bused into predominantly black schools.

Unlike the earlier hearing on the Citizens Advisory Committee report, opposition to desegregation at the April 11 hearing came from both blacks and whites and was not as sharply drawn along ethnic, economic, neighborhood, or school attendance lines. Several black parents from Oak Park spoke out against children being taken out of the neighborhood, the closing of American Legion School, being left out of planning for desegregation, the one-way approach built into all alternative plans, and the impliction that "our children ought to be like the white children." The Reverend W. P. Cooke, pastor of the Shiloh Baptist Church in Oak Park, predicted that the Oak Park community "will become an asphalt jungle without schools." Mrs. Margaret Norberg, representing the Sacramento Mothers Association, opposed compulsory busing, "biased interpretations" of laws pertaining to integration, and selection of defenseless minority children as "guinea pigs." Others pleaded that the board not give in to a "federal fund scare."[25]

Support for the proposed plans came from some of the affected parents in Oak Park, Argonaut, and River Park and

from the Sacramento City Teachers Association, the Oak Park
Neighborhood Council, the Congress of Racial Equality, several
ministers, and the Sacramento Committee for Improved Education. At least two members of the Citizens Advisory Committee,
the Reverend Robert Ferguson and James C. Dodd, testified
in support of immediate action on a desegregation plan. Mr.
Dodd was one of two black members of the Advisory Committee.
James Williams, a black parent elected to represent Argonaut
parents on a new Community Educational Advisory Committee
on compensatory education and school segregation, said that
he thought children "have a better chance of success outside
the ghettoized community."[26]

On April 25, the board voted 6 to 1 to adopt the desegregation
plan Dr. Lawson recommended. Before the vote, Dr. Lawson
urged the board to "take a positive attitude" and "get away from
a closed-eye attitude which has prevailed on this issue for 300
years." He emphasized that the plan was a first step and represented a "short range" solution for a problem bound to persist
for a long time.[27]

Robert Tyler of CORE, Sam Porter, President of the Oak
Park Neighborhood Council, and representatives of the Argonaut neighborhood applauded Lawson's stand and expressed
support for integrated schools as the "best hope for an orderly
society." Several white parents and a spokesman for the Sacramento Mothers Association said the board should have
adopted an "open enrollment" or a "freedom of choice" plan,
as the one dissenting board member had urged.[28]

On May 2 the board adopted "New and Revised Elementary
School Attendance Boundaries for the 1966–67 School Year."
These revised boundaries took into account the opening of the
new Hubert H. Bancroft School in the eastern part of the district
as well as the redistribution of pupils to implement the desegregation plan.

Redistribution of children in the black segregated schools was
accomplished by assigning geographic zones within existing attendance areas to other attendance areas in the general vicinity
of the sending schools. The American Legion attendance area
was subdivided into 11 small zones, for example, with all children in each of these zones assigned to a different school to
the north or northeast of American Legion. A "neutral zone"
between American Legion and Sierra was permanently assigned
to Sierra. Similarly, Argonaut was subdivided into four zones,
and kindergarten children in each of these zones were assigned
to four schools to the north and southwest of Argonaut. In

the Donner, Camellia, and Elder Creek attendance areas, where only a small number of children were to be reassigned to reduce overcrowding, one or two small zones were set up in each regular attendance area, and the children in these zones were permanently reassigned to adjacent or fairly nearby elementary schools. (See Figures 3 and 5.)

Altogether, an estimated 1,075 children were reassigned to 19 receiving schools. The largest number of children were moved from the American Legion School—815 in all. Only 51 kindergarten children were moved from Argonaut the first year. Donner was to lose 83 students; Camelia, 68; and Elder Creek, 58. Except for Argonaut, the children reassigned came from all elementary grade levels.

There was a great deal of variation in the numbers of children assigned to each receiving school. Caleb Greenwood in River Park received 143 American Legion children, more than any other school. Bear Flag, a newly opened school that serves a rapidly developing suburban area in southwest Sacramento, was assigned only eight children from the Argonaut school. Two other schools receiving American Legion children got 117 students each (Coloma and Newton Booth) and five schools in the north and northeast part of the city got from 52 to 77 American Legion children. Generally speaking, the more outlying schools in the southwest and south central suburbs got fewer children under the plan. None of the schools in the eastern suburban area outside the city limits were brought into the plan, although these schools had no black children or very low black enrollments. Available space and current enrollment of black students were the two factors officially considered in drawing up the new attendance zones. These two factors did not seem to be completely controlling, however. Several schools had to add one or two portable classrooms to accommodate the new students, and some schools that got large numbers of students already had more black students than some of the elementary schools that were not brought into the plan.

The specific reassignment plans adopted May 2 anticipated that all children would be bused, with three possible exceptions: the neutral zone between American Legion and Sierra, one of the American Legion zones reassigned to Newton Booth, and two American Legion zones reassigned to Coloma. The board recognized possible traffic hazards for the children transferred to Coloma and stated that transportation would be provided if the board concluded upon study that the route was "unsafe and impractical for pedestrian use." With children from these zones walking, the total number to be bused was projected at 875. The district already bused more than this number of pupils in special education programs and in outlying suburban areas where regular city transit service was not available.

Role of Federal Programs in Initiating Desegregation. In order to carry out the district's elementary desegregation project, soon known as Project Aspiration, several major changes in the compensatory education program were made.

The district's 1965–67 budget for funds received through Title I was revised to provide for busing, additional specialists in the receiving schools, and an expanded free lunch program. The district's 1966–67 total Title I allocation was a little over $1 million, and nearly $157,000 of this amount was set aside for free transportation for the bused Project Aspiration children. This figure provided for purchase of buses, maintenance and mileage, and the hiring of drivers and other personnel who operated the busing program. Four reading resource teachers and one elementary counselor were budgeted for the 19 receiving schools. The cost of these specialists, plus a research assistant and a programmer, an additional clerk in the ESEA Materials Center, study trips, instructional supplies, and other auxiliary staff, services, and equipment came to nearly $75,000. An additional $21,000 in ESEA money was earmarked for free lunches for Project Aspiration children whose families were on welfare or qualified otherwise because of limited incomes. These funds provided free lunches for a total of 447 bused Project Aspiration pupils the first year, but this aspect of the program was later cut back and limited to children on public assistance. Altogether, $253,000 of the district's 1966–67 Title I funds were specifically earmarked for Project Aspiration. The remainder was used in the existing compensatory program, which included both public and private schools.

Title I funds allocated to Project Aspiration increased annually as the program expanded. The 1967–68 Title I budget set aside $343,000 for Project Aspiraton, including bus transportation, six reading resource teachers, three elementary counselors, study trips, and the free lunch program. The total 1967–68 Title I program was also funded at a little over $1 million. By 1968–69, the Title I Project Aspiration budget had increased to about $415,000.

Both teachers and Project Aspiration children in the 19 receiving schools were eligible for and assisted by other Title I programs that cut across all schools in the compensatory education program. Children were eligible for audiometric services, for example, and teachers could use material from the ESEA Materials Center and call upon special resource and demonstration teachers who served all compensatory schools. Title I funds were also used to conduct in-service training programs, including some tailored for Project Aspiration personnel. About $72,500 in Title I funds was set aside for all in-service training in all of the compensatory programs during the 1966–67 school year. The in-service programs funded under Title I in 1966–67 included a bus matron's workshop and a summer workshop for teachers, counselors, and administrators in compensatory schools and Project Aspiration receiving schools.

In addition to Title I assistance, several supporting services for Project Aspiration were initially provided through Economic Opportunity Act funds. In 1966–67, Project Aspiration received about $47,000 from the Sacramento Area Economic Opportunity Council to provide two home visitors from the sending school areas, 14 bus matrons, and five walking matrons who escorted children who were not bused.

A 1966–67 grant under Title IV of the Civil Rights Act of 1964 was used to employ three advisors and three intergroup relations aides who assisted principals in identifying problems faced by minority groups and also worked with both the school and the community in the area of intergroup relations. The Title IV grant was used to sponsor a Teacher Training Class for Intergroup Relations that was broadcast on television in the spring of 1967 and a Workshop on Intergroup Relations in the summer of 1967. The television program, which concentrated on Project Aspiration, enrolled 150 teachers for credit. The Intergroup Relations Workshop was open to all schools in the district, with one teacher from each school chosen by the principal. This grant was renewed for the 1967–68 school year.

Preparation and Planning. Beginning early in May 1966, a three-phase program of disseminating information, detailed planning, and community orientation for Project Aspiration got under way.

The first phase of preparation, which extended through the end of the 1965–66 school year, concentrated on (1) getting basic information on the desegregation plan to principals, teachers, and parents and (2) introducing all parties involved through meetings in the sending and receiving schools, teachers visitations, and special joint school events for children, such as play days, track meets, lunches, and carnivals.

The second phase of preparation began at the end of the 1965–66 school year and extended to the opening of the 1966–67 school term. This phase focused on further orientation and completion of detailed planning for the opening of school. During this period there was, for example, a summer workshop on compensatory education for 150 teachers, counselors, and administrators.

Phase Three, projected for the 1966–67 school year, was to be a period for modification and evaluation of the initial desegregation program, with continuation of staff orientation and the development of long-range plans for desegregation.

As the opening day of school approached, both the Sacramento Area Council of Churches and the Catholic Diocese distributed information about Project Aspiration and called for support of desegregation. "Virtually all" of the churches talked about desegregation the Sunday before school opened. Although the City Council and the mayor had not been involved previously, just before the first day of school the mayor urged all citizens to put forth an effort to make the elementary desegregation plan succeed.

On the eve of school opening, some parents of Oak Park children assigned to the Coloma school were threatening a boycott to protest the fact that their children would have to walk a mile through a heavily traveled area and cross Stockton Boulevard, a major thoroughfare. These parents were initially told their children would be bused to their new school, but later found they would have to walk. A group had gone to the board in the summer to protest the change and to request busing, but the board ruled against their request. Teams of Alpha Phi Alpha members making door-to-door visits in Oak Park in August to promote desegregation found these mothers worried about the long and dangerous walk for kindergarten and first grade pupils, especially. They were not hostile to desegregation, but felt their children should be bused because of distance and traffic hazards.

Project Aspiration Begins.   On September 12, Project Aspiration was launched without the surfacing of any major racial problems or incidents. Many parents in the sending school areas—both mothers and fathers—waited with children at the bus stops and some parents took their children to school. Both black and white parents were somewhat apprehensive—for different reasons—and some Oak Park parents continued to take their children to school for several days. PTAs served coffee and cookies in some of the receiving schools on the first day of school and some principals set up a "buddy" or "big brother" system, assigning children in the receiving schools to orient the new Oak Park or Glen Elder children the day school started. There were some problems initially with bus schedules, missing buses, and children being left at the wrong stops.

On the opening day, district officials and the press were present at the schools they considered to be the potential trouble spots—Caleb Greenwood and Coloma. There were no overt incidents at either school, and the anticipated boycott of Coloma was limited to a small number of parents and children. At the last minute, parents of Oak Park pupils assigned to Newton Booth were also expected to boycott over the transportation issue. The Newton Booth situation was similar to the Coloma problem. In addition to distance and traffic hazards, Newton Booth parents were also concerned about their children walking through the construction of freeway interchanges. These parents demanded bus transportation along with Coloma parents, and were also unsuccessful in their plea. A few parents withheld their children from school initially, but the boycott was not large. Although the school board stationed a crossing guard at Stockton Boulevard and assigned a walking matron to the primary children assigned to Coloma, the Newton Booth children started out walking on their own.

There was, as a member of the school board described it, an initial period of "strangeness and adjustment" as school desegregation began. The daughter of this school board member, who attended John Cabrillo, approached an Argonaut child and asked if she might play jump rope with her. "We don't play with white trash," the black child replied. A black Oak Park leader said that their children got the feeling they were visitors in the schools, were called names, and got in trouble for picking flowers in the neighborhood. She also stated that teachers in Coloma, where the children were not under pressure to catch a bus, rushed the children out of school in the afternoon as soon as possible. She and another Oak Park leader were concerned about a situation in another school where the children were kept sitting in the buses until the school bell rang. They interpreted this as a measure designed to prevent black and white children from playing together and they went to the central administration to discuss the problem. This practice was eliminated after about three weeks.

Initial Impact of Project Aspiration. The district's fall 1966 racial and ethnic census showed that Project Aspiration had reduced the number of segregated elementary schools from seven to five. In addition to American Legion, Elder Creek also dropped off the segregated list, as the transfer of children from this attendance area reduced the black population from 56 to 41 percent. Camellia, Donner, and Argonaut maintained approximately the same ethnic distributions, although their 1966 populations were smaller and some children from these areas were moved out into desegregated situations. Argonaut was still 74 percent black in 1966; Camellia, 85 percent; and Donner, 64 percent. In spite of the fact that only two schools dropped off the segregated list, the proportion of black children in predominantly black schools was reduced by more than half. In 1965, 44 percent of the black elementary children in the district were attending predominantly black schools; in 1966, only 19 percent of all black children were in schools with a 50 percent or more black population. Although Project Aspiration greatly reduced the proportion of black children in black segregated schools, it left 55 percent of the black elementary children of the district in predominantly minority schools.

The impact of Project Aspiration on the racial and ethnic compositions of the receiving schools varied a great deal, depending on the previous ethnic makeup of the school and the numbers of black children brought in under the desegregation program. Several of the schools receiving the largest number of Oak Park children were in older, inner-city neighborhoods where the white population was aging and the number of white school children was declining. Minorities were already beginning to make up larger and larger proportions of the schools' enrollments. Marshall, for example, had only one black student prior to Project Aspiration, but one-third of its students were Mexicans, Orientals, and other nonwhites. The 117 Project Aspiration children assigned to Marshall in 1966 brought the total minority population up to 55 percent. Similarly, Newton Booth was 53 percent minority before Project Aspiration—9 percent black, 15 percent Mexican, 25 percent Oriental, and 4 percent other nonwhites. After Project Aspiration, the various minorities combined made up 61 percent of the Newton Booth enrollment. By contrast, Parkway, an elementary school in the south central suburbs, was 95 percent Caucasian before Project Aspiration, with no black students. Parkway received 29 Camellia children through Project Aspiration and was still overwhelmingly Caucasian (92 percent) after desegregation.

Receiving schools for the Argonaut kindergarten children were in sections of southwest Sacramento where there were sizable or growing Oriental populations and the basic racial breakdown was a Caucasian/Oriental split. Addition of 12 to 16 black children the first year did little to change the ethnic character of these schools. Sutterville, for example, was 42 percent minority before Project Aspiration; 39 percent of its pupils were Oriental, and 1 percent black. During the first year of Project Aspiration, Sutterville was 43 percent minority; the black population increased to 2 percent and the Oriental population decreased to 38 percent.

At least two of the older, inner-city schools receiving American Legion children were threatened with closing prior to Project Aspiration. Desegregation offered an opportunity to parents in these areas to keep these schools open. Coloma, for instance, had had a declining school enrollment for some time because of the changing character of the neighborhood. The white population was aging; there were fewer children, and a proposed freeway through the area, which took 80 percent of the school yard, was responsible for 125 children moving out in a period of seven weeks. According to the principal, Coloma had seven empty classrooms and the enrollment was down to 250 children at the end of the 1965–66 school year. The principal stated:

> We knew that we would be closed or change boundaries, that something would happen, as American Legion was growing and bursting at the walls. . . . We were aware of this before Project Aspiration was dreamed of.

Two years before Project Aspiration the board had considered closing Newton Booth because of the small number of children in that attendance area.

Coloma-Newton Booth "Walking" Problem. There were many problems to resolve during the first year of desegregation, but the one problem that became a full-blown public issue was the firm stand the school board took in refusing to bus Oak Park children assigned to Coloma and Newton Booth Schools. As mentioned earlier, all American Legion parents were told before the end of the 1965–66 school year that their children would be bused to other schools "with better teachers and facilities." Later, parents of children transferred to Coloma were told their children would walk as they were within "a reasonable walking distance." When these parents went to the board in June 1966 to protest, the board stood firm; the children would walk. Oak Park parents in the zone assigned to Newton Booth first went to the board in October 1966. They were supported by the Newton Booth principal and the Newton Booth PTA, but their request for busing was turned down. Instead, two walking matrons were assigned to escort the primary children.

After these initial attempts to secure busing, the two groups of parents joined forces and sought the help of the Oak Park Neighborhood Council, which set up a Parents Transportation Committee to work on the problem. Both black and Mexican parents were active in the Transportation Committee and parents' group. They secured the support of the Sacramento Area Economic Opportunity Council (SAEOC), the Mexican American Political Association, the local NAACP Branch, and the California state NAACP legislative representative, Mrs. Verna Canson. Early in the controversy, which continued throughout the school year, the SAEOC voted $22,744 from their funds to Project Aspiration with the condition that the funds would be withheld until the district reached a satisfactory agreement with the parents. The Sacramento County Grand Jury asked the district to liberalize its transportation policy so that fewer kindergarten and primary children would have to walk, in effect backing the parents.

There were numerous meetings and public hearings on the issue throughout the 1966–67 school year. Black and Mexican parents, walking matrons, and representatives of concerned organizations discussed traffic hazards, problems in keeping children together in groups, fatigue among small children, shoes wearing out, and colds and illness among the children from walking in rainy weather. A special review of district policy concerning the transportation of regular students was prepared by staff, and a three-member board committee was appointed to study the Coloma-Newton Booth issue. Both the staff and the special board committee declined to take a position on how the "walking" controversary should be resolved. In the course of the year, several important facts came to light:

(1) The district did not have a written definition of a "reasonable walking distance" for elementary children.

(2) Two years before, the board had refused to extend the Newton Booth boundaries to 36th Street in Oak Park, one block closer to Newton Booth than the new zone set up for desegregation, *because it was too far for elementary children to walk.*

(3) The state of California would reimburse the district for

transportation of kindergarten and primary children who lived over three-quarters of a mile from their school.

(4) Money for bus transportation was available but the board was concerned that other parents where children were walking the same distance would demand busing.

On May 1, 11 months after Oak Park parents first raised the issue, the board took a final vote of 5–2 turning down the parents' request for busing. The issue died publicly, but 'continued to be a sore spot with some Oak Park parents and leaders.

An Oak Park mother who was active in the effort to secure busing, for example, became quite disillusioned with the district and ultimately moved out of the neighborhood because of the school situation. While the children were still in Newton Booth, her family went into debt to buy a car to take their children to school. Since there were only two cars in her area among the children assigned to Newton Booth, a car pool was out of the question. In the winter, her car was jam-packed. She said that children not riding in the two cars had to walk under the construction of freeway overpasses, with wet cement dripping down. "They built five or six overpasses over the kids," she said.

After two years, she and her husband were able to buy a house and they moved. She stated that other Oak Park families who rented also moved out of the area because of the school situation, while homeowners could not afford to leave.

Other Problems with Project Aspiration. Other complaints about Project Aspiration came up in the Oak Park parents' efforts to mobilize support on the Coloma-Newton Booth transportation question. On June 29, following the board's final refusal to provide busing, the Education and Transportation Committees of the Oak Park Neighborhood Council called a meeting to discuss more "realistic" approaches to desegregation. One black and two Mexican women signed the letter announcing the meeting.

In preparation for the meeting, the Education Committee of the Oak Park Neighborhood Council distributed a 15-page packet of material on Project Aspiration, which raised the following problems related to the district's overall approach to desegregation:

(1) closing the neighborhood school had discouraged community efforts and accelerated the movement of parents from Oak Park;

(2) Project Aspiration children "feel inferior" when placed

with many middle class children who dress and eat better, have more spending money, and get better grades;

(3) teachers in the receiving schools are not adequately prepared to make the Project Aspiration children feel "worthy";

(4) federal compensatory funds earmarked for underprivileged children are being put into the "better schools," with every "two pennies" given the "poor child" being divided "with one penny for him and one penny for the rich child";

(5) instead of busing and bus matrons, Project Aspiration children need food and health services; and

(6) preaching democracy and making integration a one-way street is hypocritical, since the "deprived child" is the one who is uprooted and placed in a strange environment.[29]

Parents in other areas with segregated schools were warned their schools would be closed. They were urged to listen to the facts and work toward a constructive solution to these problems.

Argonaut School Closes. In the fall of 1967, the Argonaut School was phased out, and the remainder of the children from this school—approximately 240—were bused to the same schools that received the Argonaut kindergarten children the year before: Alice Birney, Bear Flag, John Cabrillo, and Sutterville. There was little publicity or fanfare as the second phase of Project Aspiration began.

Since more Argonaut children were involved in the 1967 shifts, the second year of desegregation had more of an impact on the racial and ethnic populations of receiving schools. Alice Birney, which received approximately 70 Argonaut children the second year, became 20 percent black. Alice Birney had had more black children than the other southwest receiving schools when Project Aspiration started. Bear Flag, which had had only two black pupils before desegregation, was 9 percent black by the fall of 1967. John Cabrillo's black student population increased to 12 percent, and Sutterville, which got the smallest number of Argonaut students, became 6 percent black the second year of desegregation. Sutterville, which had a substantial enrollment of Orientals before Project Aspiration, became 51 percent minority in 1967. John Cabrillo, which also had a sizable enrollment of Orientals before desegregation, became 48 percent minority in the second year of Project Aspiration.

Preparation for the second phase of Project Aspiration included completion of a special form by Argonaut teachers identifying each student's level in reading, mathematics, and spelling. These forms were sent to the receiving schools in April

1967, to provide the schools with data for placing the Argonaut children. Each receiving school invited parents from their zone in Argonaut to attend at least one PTA meeting before the end of the 1966–67 school year. District intergroup relations and community resource workers contacted parents in the Argonaut area door-to-door, identifying kindergarten children, discussing pre-registration dates, and encouraging parents to visit receiving schools and participate in PTA meetings. Each receiving school also invited the Argonaut transfer students to an orientation session before the end of the 1966–67 school year. Pupil orientation varied among the schools, but included such activities as a tour of the school, visiting classrooms, participation in May Day festivities, lunch at the receiving school, and meetings with the student body officers of the receiving school. Although Superintendent Lawson continually promised more community involvement in desegregation activities, there was considerably less community participation in the preparation of parents and students for the second year. More of the orientation programs took place in the receiving schools, in contrast to the first year, when there was more effort to have a mutual situation, with some meetings and activities centered in the black community and persons from the receiving schools coming into the sending areas.

The future of the Argonaut school was undecided in the fall of 1967, but Argonaut was ultimately utilized as an adult education and preschool center.

District Evaluation of Project Aspiration. The first phases of Project Aspiration, covering desegregation of the American Legion and Argonaut schools, were evaluated by the district at the end of the first year of desegregation and again at the end of the second year. In both evaluations, several different kinds of measures were used to assess the project's success. In addition to scores on standardized ability and achievement tests, the studies utilized attendance records, teacher assessments, and the opinions of principals, teachers, and parents. District officials were encouraged by the results, particularly by the findings of the second evaluation. Militant black and Mexican leaders, however, criticized the district's reports, especially the opinion surveys, and the fact that the district's research staff, rather than an independent outside agency, conducted the evaluations.

The 1967–68 evaluation which showed the most favorable results, was based primarily on data from 10 schools—the nine schools receiving Argonaut, Camellia, Elder Creek, and Donner children, plus one of the American Legion receiving schools. In order to assess the progress of children in desegregated versus segregated schools, bused children from Camellia, Elder Creek, and Donner were matched with similar children remaining in these schools. The test scores of both groups were compared. There were also comparisons of reading achievement scores of children bused in from the Argonaut area and resident pupils in the Argonaut receiving schools. Similarly, the reading achievement scores of Argonaut children in their first versus their second year of desegregation were studied. Since only a limited number of children completed all the tests, most of the evaluation of test scores was based on a relatively small number of children. This was another point criticized by militant community leadership.

Comparison of different test scores showed favorable progress trends on the part of children brought into desegregated schools but also pointed up a continuing gap between these children and the resident children in the receiving schools.

For example, children bused from Camellia, Donner, and Elder Creek and the pupils who remained behind in these schools were given a series of ability and achievement tests before and after desegregation, including the Stanford Reading Test (SAT), the California Test of Mental Maturity (CTMM), and the California Achievement Test (CAT). There was some variation in the testing, depending on grade level. Children who were bused out made higher scores than the children who remained in the segregated schools on all tests given after their transfer to desegregated schools. Where the same tests were repeated and score changes could be compared over a two-year period, the bused students also showed more improvement in their scores at the end of two years. While these results are encouraging, the children involved in the busing made higher scores than their matched peers on most but not all tests prior to the busing. The children had been matched on the basis of pre-desegregation reading achievement scores. As for the increases in test scores over the two years, with two exceptions the increases in the scores of the bused children were not sufficiently greater than those of the children who were not bused to be statistically significant. Thus, in most cases, the more favorable gains in the scores of the bused children could have been due to chance.

Reading achievement scores of two groups of children bused from the Argonaut area were studied to determine their rate of progress after one year of desegregation versus two years.

The Argonaut children were desegregated in a two-step plan. In the first phase of this evaluation, reading scores of 35 Argonaut children who transferred in the 1967–68 school year, the second year of desegregation, were compared with the reading scores of 221 resident pupils in the Argonaut receiving schools. Both groups were at the third grade placement level and both took the Stanford Reading Test (SAT) in the month of May in 1966, 1967, and 1968. The test scores showed that in their first year of desegregation, Argonaut transfer pupils doubled their earlier rate of progress, gaining the equivalent of nine-tenths of a year in test scores that year, as compared to two-fifths of a year the previous year. Their gains were the same as the resident pupils' during their first year of desegregation, but the resident pupils tested higher than the bused pupils both before and after desegregation.

A second comparison was made between the SAT reading achievement scores of the bused Argonaut pupils above, who had experienced one year of desegregation, and 56 Argonaut pupils who had been in desegregated schools two years. The two groups of students tested at the same reading level in 1966, prior to desegregation. At the end of the first year of desegregation, the pupils who were bused out tested slightly higher than those who remained in Argonaut. At the end of the second year, students who had been in desegregated schools two years tested slightly higher than those who had had only one year of desegregation. Both sets of students made the most gains in the second year of desegregation.

An examination of the attendance records of 412 Project Aspiration children in ten desegregated receiving schools showed overall gains during the 1966–67 school year, particularly among primary children in the four Argonaut receiving schools that were virtually in their first year of desegregation. Attendance records were already satisfactory, but the rate of attendance for primary children in the Argonaut receiving schools was higher than their old rate (95 percent, as compared with 93 percent) and increased more than the attendance rate of intermediate children also transferred to these schools. As a total group, the 412 Project Aspiration children whose attendance rates were checked were in school 95 percent of the time during the 1967–68 school year.

A mail survey of teachers in the 10 receiving schools indicated that the Project Aspiration children were improving in their attitudes, application, and interest in school; that their self-image was improving and their academic performance being raised; that they were being accepted by, and themselves accepted, resident pupils as friends, and that the parents of Project Aspiration children reacted favorably to the program. In most areas of concern, such as attitudes toward school, interest in learning, social adjustment, participation, and work habits, teachers felt that Project Aspiration had no effect on the resident children. Most teachers indicated they felt adequately prepared to work effectively with the children brought into their schools by Project Aspiration.

While the majority of teachers expressed the views listed above, a substantial minority felt that Project Aspiration had no effect on the desegregated children transferred to their schools in areas such as attitudes toward school, interest, work habits, self-confidence, and social adjustment. Depending on the question, from 30 to 49 percent of the teachers dissented from the majority as to improvement of the Project Aspiration children in particular areas. Two-fifths of the teachers also said that the least favorable aspect of the project was the limitation on pupil interaction outside the school setting. The teachers' survey was based on responses from 111 teachers in 10 receiving schools. A total of 184 teachers were sent questionnaires.

Principals in the receiving schools showed a broader range of opinion about Project Aspiration than teachers and, in a few instances, disagreed with the teachers in their assessment of the project. Principals of all 19 receiving schools were given a 15-point outline and asked to comment on each of the points. A total of 14 principals returned comments. The principals' statements indicated that the Project Aspiration pupils had generally developed positive relationships with the teachers and resident pupils, that they were making progress in social development, that the desegregation program had been well accepted by resident parents, and that participation of parents of Project Aspiration children in parent-teacher conferences was about the same as resident parents. The principals were less positive than the teachers about the academic growth of Project Aspiration children, however. Three-fourths of the teachers said that Project Aspiration had been successful in raising the academic performance of the minority children. Of the principals, 36 percent said that the Project Aspiration children had realized little academic growth; 29 percent felt that the primary children involved in Project Aspiration were progressing more rapidly than the children at the intermediate level; 36 percent indicated that the academic growth of the Project Aspiration children was comparable to that of the resident pupils. Principals and teachers also disagreed on acceptance of the program by sending parents. Of the teachers, 65 percent reported that the parents of sending Project Aspiration children reacted favorably to the program, but 38 percent of the principals felt that Project Aspiration was well accepted by sending parents. Of the principals, 61 percent said that parents of Project Aspiration children had mixed feelings about the program, and 85 percent also felt that the teachers needed in-service training regarding Project Aspiration. They said that teachers needed a program where they could become involved "rather than sitting and listening."[30] Sixty-one percent of the principals reported that there were positive relationships between resident parents and sending parents relative to school functions but that there were limited contacts outside school settings.

Parents of 557 Project Aspiration children in ten receiving schools were polled by mail as a part of the district's evaluation. A little over half of the parents responded (55 percent) and over two-thirds (69 percent) of those who replied indicated that their children were "getting a better education under Project Aspiration than before." More than half (55 percent) felt that their child was "more interested in learning this year than he/she was last year." Militants criticized the parents' survey because there were no direct questions asking parents about issues such as busing versus neighborhood schools, out-of-school contacts between parents and children in the sending and receiving schools, and possible negative effects on parent-child relationships. They also objected to questions that asked parents to compare the children's interest in school, participation, and habits of reading at home "this year" with "last year," as they felt a normal child would develop in these areas, regardless of his particular school. They claimed that the district was avoiding questions that would bring out negative reactions from the parents. Militants also noted that nearly half of the parents had failed to respond to the survey.

Other Evaluation of Project Aspiration. Mrs. Margaret M. Oakden, a second-grade teacher at American Legion school before desegregation, conducted a follow-up study of 24 children in her 1965–66 class one year after Project Aspiration began. The 24 children who were still in district schools when her report was made were transferred to nine different receiving schools at the beginning of the 1966–67 school year. Mrs. Oakden's research was done as a master's thesis at Sacramento State College, and she generally followed the approach used by the district in evaluating the effects of Project Aspiration on a particular group of children. She used reading scores from the Stanford Achievement Test, for example, attendance records, and modified versions of the questionnaires for parents and teachers used in the district's evaluations.

Mrs. Oakden's findings paralleled those of the district, except in the area of parents' reactions to Project Aspiration. She used a modified version of the district's questionnaire, but interviewed parents personally rather than mailing them a form. She talked to the parents of 23 of the 24 children in her study. Of the parents Mrs. Oakden interviewed, 48 percent felt their children were getting a better education under Project Aspiration than before, as opposed to 77 percent of the primary parents who responded by mail to the 1967–68 district survey. Only 43 percent of the parents Mrs. Oakden interviewed felt that their children were more interested in learning this year than the past year, compared with 57 percent of the primary parents in the 1967–68 district survey. Mrs. Oakden's research also indicated that 52 percent of the children were not taking part in student activities such as clubs, safety patrol, office helper, plays, or special programs. The district's 1967–68 evaluation reported that only 14 percent of the parents of primary children said their children had never participated in these kinds of school activities. As to reading at home, 52 percent of the parents in Mrs. Oakden's study said that their children read more at home than the year before, while over two-thirds of the primary parents in the district's 1967–68 evaluation reported their children were reading more at home. Her study was made after the first year, and her role as a former teacher could have colored some of the parents' responses. Mrs. Oakden concluded that one of the chief weaknesses of Project Aspiration is in communication with parents. She recommended more home-school communication, including "feeding back to the teachers the knowledge about parents and the culture of the parent community which the specialists and principals often possess."[31]

6.
Delays in Elementary Desegregation

Impact of Field Act on Desegregation. About the time the Sacramento City Unified School District was completing plans for the first phase of Project Aspiration, early in May 1966, the California State Attorney General issued an opinion in a completely different area that came to have an important influence on the progress and direction of desegregation.

In 1933, the California legislature passed a law known as the Field Act, which required school buildings to be resistant to earthquakes. All public school buildings constructed after 1933 had to meet certain specifications, and pre-1933 schools were to be rehabilitated to meet Field Act standards. Until 1966, local school districts largely ignored correction of buildings constructed prior to 1933. In May 1966, however, the California Attorney General ruled that school districts had a legal duty to inspect buildings constructed before 1933 and that failure to inspect these buildings could result in personal liability for board members in the event of an injury caused by a structural defect. Subsequent State legislation fixed 1970 as the date by which districts must inspect pre-1933 buildings and 1975 as the final date for local districts to repair or replace schools that do not conform to Field Act standards.

The Sacramento City Unified School District reacted immediately to the Attorney General's 1966 opinion and authorized a structural study of 20 buildings in the district constructed all or in part before passage of the Field Act. The 20 buildings surveyed included 16 elementary schools, three junior high schools and one senior high school. All of these buildings are in older parts of the city and many are located in inner-city neighborhoods with large and growing minority enrollments. Because of this, the board voted in January 1967 to delay long-range planning for desegregation until the results of the Field Act engineering survey were available.

When the Field Act survey was completed, it showed that no buildings would have to be abandoned immediately but that all 20 needed some rehabilitation to meet minimum requirements of the law. Estimates of the cost of renovating individual schools varied from $45,000 for Fruit Ridge Elementary School to $1,770,055 for the main building of Sacramento Senior High School. The total estimate for bringing 19 of the schools up to minimum Field Act requirements was $10,699,498. This figure did not include total replacement of Marshall Elementary, estimated at approximately $700,000, or the cost of replacing several wings of Newton Booth and Sacramento Senior High School. Nor did it include the cost of modernizing the buildings or providing them with new equipment. When costs of modernization were added to estimates for structural improvements, in many schools the total estimate approximated the cost of new construction. The central administration staff questioned the wisdom of spending money of this kind, particularly to rebuild or replace elementary schools in the older neighborhoods where school age populations were declining and minority populations were large and/or growing.

Further Study of Alternatives for Desegregation.   In the late spring of 1967, Superintendent Lawson began to study possible ways to meet both the Field Act and school segregation problems. His explorations were stimulated in part by a decision of the state to sell the old California State Fairgrounds, located between the Coloma and Donner schools. This site seemed to offer possibilities as a location for an educational center or park that would serve a large part of the older sections of the city. While the superintendent and top administrative staff had played an important role in defeating the cluster plan proposed by the Citizens Advisory Committee, which projected the idea of larger elementary attendance zones, they were gradually coming around to the point of view that the ultimate solution of Sacramento's segregation problems would be found in schools serving broad attendance areas. Dr. Lawson had recommended continuation of the neighborhood schools in 1965, but he was now willing to "put the educational center idea before the community" and say, "We should look at this." He was "for doing this if the community would support educational centers."

In June 1967, Dr. Lawson placed three alternative desegregation plans before the board, including a plan for organizing the entire district's enrollment by attendance areas based on the senior high school attendance zones or a series of large educational centers. Three educational centers were proposed: one at the fairgrounds site, which would serve central Sacramento, one in the eastern area, and one in the extreme southwest or "pocket" area. The board considered these proposals but took no action and asked Superintendent Lawson to continue studying the educational center proposal. The superintendent then recommended employing an outside consulting firm to examine all aspects of the district's Field Act and segregation problems and recommend a long-range master site and facilities plan. The board decided to do this and in January 1968 the district engaged Knight, Gladieux and Smith, a San Francisco firm to carry out the study. A 52-man Citizens Advisory Committee of district staff, citizens-at-large, teachers, representatives of community organizations, and city and county government was appointed to work with the consulting firm. Major action on desegregation was postponed, pending completion of the study.

Postponement of Camellia-Donner Desegregation. In spite of the decision to postpone long-range planning for desegregation, segregation in the Donner and Camellia schools continued to be an issue. About the time the master site study was arranged, in January, 1968, Dr. Jackson Faustman and Adolph Moskovitz, two board members, asked for a report on the possibility of desegregating Donner and Camellia schools. Dr. Faustman accused the staff of being "reluctant" to desegregate Camellia, stating, "It is inconsistent to have an 85 percent Negro enrollment in Camellia and not move on it."[32] Faustman had earlier suggested that the board change its definition of segregation if it could not live by it.

The follow-up staff report stressed the special problems that Camellia presents. Isolated in the Glen Elder subdivision at the extreme southeast corner of the city and school district, Camellia is too new to be abandoned, but is unsuitable for conversion to use for special education programs because of its inaccessible location. Camellia, the staff said, can be desegregated only by a two-way busing program in connection with a pairing plan, or by closing the school and busing all Camellia children out. The staff rejected a two-way busing plan "at the present time" but was also reluctant to close Camellia. The staff report favored closing Donner on a long-term basis, as it is one of the older schools not meeting Field Act requirements, but recommended delaying action on this school as well as on Camellia.

In February 1968, the board voted again to delay desegregation of the two schools. Although not stated, the district's reluctance to desegregate both Donner and Camellia apparently stemmed from the fact that eastern and south-central suburban schools, some outside the city limits, would be the logical receiving schools under any desegregation plan. Resistance to both busing and abandoning the neighborhood school was high in these areas in 1965 when the original cluster plan was proposed. District officials seemingly do not want to put large numbers of black children in these elementary schools or open up the

Pandora's box of two-way busing for fear of white reaction. All elementary desegregation plans and proposals have consistently avoided sending any black children to the eastern suburbs, and the south-central fringe areas have received comparatively small numbers of black pupils from Donner, Camellia and Elder Creek in connection with Project Aspiration. Within the city limits of Sacramento, however, many black children have been bused to schools where initial resistance to desegregation was strong.

7.

Washington School: Desegregation in the Mexican Community

ALTHOUGH desegregation came to a standstill in the black schools in 1967, the district moved ahead with desegregation of the Washington School, the district's one predominantly Mexican school.

When planning for Project Aspiration first got underway, some leaders in the Mexican community protested Mexicans being left out of the plan. Attorney Alfonzo A. Gonzales, a past president of the Mexican-American Education Association and the only Mexican on the Citizens Advisory Committee for Equal Educational Opportunity, was foremost in publicly raising the issue of desegregating the Washington School. In addition to prodding the district board, Gonzales wrote to the State Board of Education concerning Sacramento's failure to desegregate the Washington School in the first phase of Project Aspiration. District officials responded that students in the Washington School, the only segregated Mexican school, first required special language programs to help with bilingual problems. Superintendent Lawson has since said that he held off on the desegregation of Washington because "you can attack too much at once." He wanted to make a start with desegregation in the black community before he moved into what seemed to be a more complex problem in the Mexican community.

The central administration staff began laying the groundwork for Washington desegregation early in the fall of 1967. Superintendent Lawson felt that part of the problem was to "awaken people" in the Washington community to the need for desegregation. In September 1967, a Mexican-American Intergroup

Relations Aide was assigned to go door-to-door in the Washington attendance area, talking to parents about the advantages of integrated education, the importance of participation in school activities, and the need for children to develop good behavioral and study habits in school.

Washington Desegregation Proposals. In October, the Planning and Research Services Office of the district formulated five alternative plans for the desegregation of Washington. These plans were first presented to the board on October 16, 1967. The superintendent explained that desegregation should go ahead where there was no possible conflict with long-range plans the district might develop. Considering the declining school population in the Washington area, the increase in minorities in nearby schools, and the condition of the Washington building, the staff anticipated abandoning or converting the Washington School under any long-range plan that might evolve from the Field Act study. Washington is one of the older schools that does not conform to Field Act standards. An engineering survey subsequently estimated that structural rehabilitation to bring the school up to Field Act requirements would cost $864,888.

The staff's basic approach to the desegregation of Washington paralleled that used in Project Aspiration. Each of the five alternative plans projected reassignment of Mexican children to predominantly Anglo schools with smaller minority concentrations. Four of the plans provided for the closing of Washington as a regular elementary school in the near future and one proposed that both Lincoln Elementary and Washington be closed in two stages, busing out the primary children the first year and the upper elementary grades the second year. None of the plans explored bringing Anglo children into Washington or an exchange of pupils between Washington and other schools. Washington was 57 percent Mexican in the fall of 1967 when these considerations began.

Three of the alternative plans tied the desegregation of Washington to the building of the John Bigler Elementary School in the extreme southern part of the district. The John Bigler School was one of five new elementary schools projected for suburban areas in the district's last successful bond election; construction was scheduled to begin in the fall of 1968. Although little emphasis was placed on this aspect of the plan, three proposals for the desegregation of Washington suggested that state funds available to the district for the construction of classrooms for the pupil populations of Washington, Lincoln, or Earl Warren schools—all compensatory education schools with low-income populations—be applied to building John Bigler. The district was eligible for approximately $237,000 in classroom construction money for these schools, and recent amendments to state legislation made it possible to use such funds for classrooms at a location other than existing sites. The staff proposed that part of the state classroom funds be used for purchasing portables to provide temporary classroom space in receiving schools and that the rest be applied to the building of John Bigler. The staff also proposed allocating "some of the funds in the 1964 bond fund now earmarked for the renovation and improvement of older schools" to the construction of John Bigler.[33] The proposals to apply inner-city construction and renovation funds to the building of John Bigler became a bitter issue in the Mexican community, alienating many people and generating distrust and suspicion of the board.

The board scheduled several meetings to get public reactions to the Washington proposals, including a parents' meeting in the Washington school and a public hearing on December 1.

Public Hearing on Washington Desegregation. The December 1st public hearing pointed up the gap between Washington area parents and leaders of concerned community organizations, including some Mexican organizations. Most persons participating in the December hearing were from the Mexican community. The Mexican-American Political Association (MAPA) endorsed desegregation, including the closing of the Washington School. Ray Carrasco, a spokesman for Sacramento Concilio, also spoke in favor of desegregation. In 1967, Concilio was just beginning to operate as a full-time service agency in the Mexican community. The Mexican-American Education Association and its key leaders were already on record supporting desegregation.

The majority of parents from the Washington area who spoke at the hearing opposed the suggested plans for Washington desegregation. Mrs. Herbert Cortez, chairman of the district's newly reorganized Community Educational Advisory Committee on Compensatory Education (Title I) and an active proponent of bilingual and bicultural programs for Mexican children, presented a petition signed by 73 parents with approximately 123 children in the Washington School. The petition asked the board to: (1) develop a curriculum for Mexican students, utilizing teaching methods and materials recently demonstrated to Washington parents by district staff; (2) develop a language and

cultural center for children and adults that would emphasize
the value of cultural appreciation; and (3) institute an exchange
program for the upper elementary grades "with other students
of different parentage from other schools," to reduce the concentration of Mexican background students in the Washington
school.[34] The petition also opposed the closing of the Washington School, in the event that the board failed to accept the first
three recommendations. Mrs. Cortez said at the hearing that
the Mexican children "feel inferior already . . . and it would
make them more inferior to be with other children with better
things in life."[35] She had already written a long personal letter
to the board outlining the problems faced by Mexican children
in the district schools and the failure of the district to gear the
schools—including Washington—"to teach most of the Mexican-
American children." Mrs. Cortez questioned the advantages of
moving a child from a situation "where he at least feels comfortable and happy" to another "just as bad educationally."[36] Dr.
Leonard Cain, a sociologist from Sacramento State College, suggested that the motive behind integrating the Washington children into other schools was one of "attempting to change the
community to fit a monolithic culture."[37] Dr. Cain had supported dispersal of the Stanford Junior High students in 1963,
but had opposed the closing of American Legion School in 1966,
suggesting the busing of white children into Oak Park as an
alternative. Dr. Clark Taylor, an anthropologist at Sacramento
State College, proposed that Washington School be kept open
and that the board build the curriculum around the Mexican
culture. The majority speaking at the hearing were opposed
to the closing of the Washington School and the district's busing
proposals. The press reported that only two parents with children in Washington School supported the Superintendent's
desegregation proposals at the December 1 hearing. Opponents
of the various desegregation plans outnumbered supporters
14–6.

The December 1st hearing made it clear that the board faced
a different situation from that encountered in earlier phases of
desegregation. There was, for example, less interest on the part
of the larger community, among groups that had rallied to the
cause of black desegregation, as well as among those who had
opposed it. While white property owners did not come out to
protest, there was no overt support from groups that had backed
the desegregation of Oak Park schools in the face of opposition
from both the white and black communities.

The Spanish-speaking Washington parents themselves created a dilemma for the board, which was more conservative in makeup than in 1966 and still 100 percent Anglo, as well as 100 percent English-speaking. The District Intergroup Relations Service conducted a survey in the Washington attendance area during the months of November and December, for instance, and reported to the board that "by and large, the people are not in opposition to the integration plans of the district."[38] Mexican grass roots leadership immediately challenged this finding, pointing out that the survey form which each parent had signed was in English, and that the questions regarding desegregation were "loaded." The "favorable response" to desegregation quoted by Intergroup Relations officials was based on a "Yes" answer to this question:

> If the District would provide transportation for your child to another school where better learning opportunities and experience are available, would you favor such a program?

Mrs. Cortez, who contacted many of the Spanish-speaking Washington parents personally, stated that the district home workers who surveyed Washington "interpreted" as well as translated the question. Parents told her, for example, that the district surveyors said their child might be hurt in Washington by a brick falling on his head. The Washington parents group, however, circulated their petition and other material in English and Spanish. School officials' inability to speak Spanish continually complicated the Washington issue, as they were dependent on the translations and interpretations of bilingual Mexicans who represented different interests and points of view as to what was best for the children and the Washington School community.

Another significant difference was the alternative proposal for their school that the Washington parents put forth, with some backing from the larger community. As the controversy over Washington developed, the parents' demand for a solution that would be meaningful to them as well as to the Anglo community gained force and momentum.

Washington Plan Adopted. On February 5, 1967, the board unanimously adopted a desegregation plan for Washington that provided for a two-step phase-out of the school and for busing of Washington children to the southernmost part of the district. Washington children in grades K–3 were to be bused to Pony Express and Freeport schools in the fall of 1968, and the following year all grades were to be distributed between these schools and two new schools projected for the area, John Bigler and Carolyn Wenzel. (See Figure 6.) The plan involved setting up sub-attendance zones in the Washington area similar to those utilized for the first phase of Project Aspiration and the redrawing of attendance area boundaries for the receiving schools. Children were to be bused eight to 12 miles, depending on the receiving school to which they were assigned. Mexican community leaders who opposed the busing stated that district officials promised not to bus the children on freeways at first, but later backed down on this promise.

Auxiliary services that would follow the Washington children to the four receiving schools included a kindergarten resource teacher for language development problems and a counselor who would divide their time among the four schools; a half-time reading specialist in each receiving school; and a Spanish-speaking teaching assistant for roughly three-quarters of a day for each school. A full-time bilingual counselor was left in the Washington School. Children of families on public assistance were to receive lunch, transportation was provided for all children, and special materials were to be available to teachers through the ESEA library.

District officials estimated the cost of specialists, teachers' assistants, transportation, and other auxiliary programs and services at $126,803 for the first year and $156,356 for the second year. Since the district was already providing compensatory specialists in the Washington School, new funds needed for the first year were projected at $94,335. The cost of reading specialists and the resource teacher were to be met through state sources such as the Miller-Unruh Act and Senate Bill 28. The rest of the costs were to be financed through Title I.

The night the Washington plan was adopted, attorney Alfonzo Gonzales, Ted Neff, Chief of the Bureau of Intergroup Relations for the State Department of Education, and representatives of the Community Welfare Council and the School Dropout Committee urged the Board to adopt one of the proposed plans. Mrs. Herbert Cortez was the only person who spoke against the proposed plans. Mrs. Cortez supports two-way desegregation when mutual exchange is involved but believes the kind of one-way desegregation practiced in the district does more harm than good to the children.

Desegregation plans for Washington were reviewed and changed in March, when details of the proposed financing of the new John Bigler School were discussed. The administration

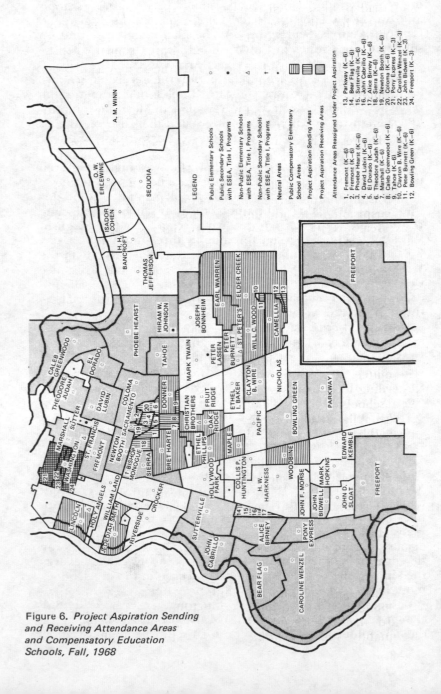

Figure 6. *Project Aspiration Sending
and Receiving Attendance Areas
and Compensatory Education
Schools, Fall, 1968*

staff had proposed that two-thirds of the cost of John Bigler be met with bond money voted in 1964 for the renovation of inner-city schools. The staff's reasoning was that the inner-city children were being moved to this school through the desegregation plan and would be served by the money. The board refused to make this transfer of funds, however, postponing the building of John Bigler and voting to desegregate Washington over a three-year period using existing schools. The revised plans utilized Carolyn Wenzel, Freeport, John Bidwell, and Pony Express as receiving schools. All are located in the outlying southwest sections of the city and the district. One board member accused the staff of having "downplayed" the financing of John Bigler when the board considered the first proposals for Washington desegregation.[39] As mentioned earlier, distrust and suspicion of the administration in the Mexican community was greatly increased by this staff proposal. Militant chicanos also accused the board of catering to vested commercial interests who wanted to hasten the deterioration of Washington as a residential community.

Opposition to Washington Desegregation Grows. Shortly after the board's decision to go ahead with the desegregation of Washington, without building John Bigler, the Community Educational Advisory Committee for the district went on record supporting two-way busing but opposing one-way busing. This committee, made up of approximately 38 persons chosen according to criteria specified under Title I, includes parents from schools receiving Title I funds, representatives of minority groups, religious and business leaders, delegates from community neighborhood councils, and district administration staff. Fifty percent of its membership was from low-income areas and in 1968 the committee included blacks and Mexicans who had been actively involved in earlier desegregation issues. This group had already discussed the need for more meaningful evaluation of desegregation with district officials and later declined to recommend that any new Title I money be used for the desegregation of Washington School. When members of this committee complained to the State Department of Education that their advice was being ignored, they were told it was not mandatory that the district accept their recommendations.

A Washington's People Committee was formed in the spring of 1968 to fight the closing of the Washington School and work toward "the best state-wide educational program in a school predominantly Mexican-American . . . ."[40] In cooperation with the

Federation of Neighborhood Councils, a unified board of local
poverty agencies, and the League of Women Voters, Washington area residents held an election on July 24 to determine
neighborhood sentiments on the school closing issue. Background material for and against closing Washington was distributed in English and Spanish and balloting was bilingual.
People in the area voted 560–15 against closing the school. Following this vote, the Sacramento Area Economic Opportunity
Council asked the board to reconsider its decision on Washington.

In August, the board held two public meetings to reconsider
the Washington desegregation. Louis Colmenarez, President of
the Washington Neighborhood Council, the anti-poverty
organization for the Washington community, asked the board
to rebuild the Washington School and implement two proposals
made by Washington residents in their November 1967 petition:
(1) development of a cultural enrichment program that would
use resource people from the area skilled in arts, crafts, folk
music, and dancing; and (2) initiation of an exchange of students
in the upper elementary grades to reduce the percentage of
Mexicans in the Washington School. Colmenarez stated,
"Parents of this area will not accept one-way busing." He also
said:

> We can no longer accept the usual procedures of constructing the
> school's educational program, teaching methods and evaluation
> techniques applicable to the English-speaking students as a valid
> educational approach for the Mexican-American.[41]

The demand for a new school in the Washington area was
endorsed by many speakers, and the Mexican-American Political
Association reversed its earlier stand and opposed the closing
of Washington School. George Choung, director of the Sacramento Congress of Young Adults, a militant anti-poverty
group attempting to work with young people of all races,
opposed the busing of Washington students from the area. In
spite of increased pressure from the grass roots, the Mexican-
American Education Association continued to support the phasing out of the Washington School.

On August 19, after hearing more speakers and redebating
the issue, the board voted 6–0 to go ahead with the desegregation of Washington. Several wavering board members had conferred privately a few days earlier with a Mexican-American
specialist in the school desegregation program of the Regional
Office of the U. S. Department of Health, Education and Wel-

fare, who advised them to carry out the Washington desegregation as planned. Following the August 19 board meeting, some board members still appeared to be uncertain, as they indicated that their decision was a temporary one for one year and they did not consider the issue closed permanently.

Preparation of pupils, parents, and teachers had already taken place in somewhat the same pattern as in earlier phases of Project Aspiration, except for the Spanish accent. There was a renewed effort to base some of the preparation in the sending community and for the first time, the district began communicating with the Washington parents in Spanish as well as in English. All invitations to meetings, explanations, and notices were translated and sent out in both languages. An orientation meeting for Washington parents was held in Washington School, and receiving school teachers were provided with released time to visit and observe in Washington. A Washington teacher and counselor participated in staff meetings to prepare the receiving school teachers. Washington students and parents were invited to receiving schools at the end of the 1968 school year with each school planning its own orientation.

Washington Desegregation Begins. In spite of a protest rally and parade in late August and a partially effective boycott during the first two weeks of school, phase one of the Washington School desegregation was accomplished in the fall of 1968. The district's projected enrollment figures indicated that approximately 239 children would be bused from Washington. On opening day, only 131 were collected by the buses. Poverty organizers working with the parents estimated that about 80 parents participated in the boycott and that most of them had more than one child affected by the busing. At the beginning of the second week, an estimated 40 to 50 children were still out of school. After the second week, the boycott gradually died out. The principal of Carolyn Wenzel, a receiving school for Washington, stated that only 45 Washington children attended his school the first day. A total of 78 children in grades K–3 were expected, based on March 1968 projections. The children dribbled in during the first week and enrollment gradually built up to 85 children. It remained at about that number throughout the 1968-69 school year. Washington Neighborhood Council workers charged the district with "intimidating" boycotting parents with threats of arrest.[42] They also said that neighborhood parents were told they would lose their welfare checks if they participated in the boycott. District officials replied that they acquainted parents with the state law on compulsory school attendance.

Final district enrollment figures showed that 227 K–3 children were transferred from Washington in the fall of 1968 with the desegregation program. Carolyn Wenzel received the largest number of Washington children and, because of special circumstances in the attendance area, Mexican children made up a larger proportion of the total enrollment in Carolyn Wenzel than they did in the other receiving schools. Carolyn Wenzel opened in the fall of 1968 in a suburban area with subdivisions still under construction and an under-capacity enrollment from the surrounding area. At the beginning of the year, the bused Washington children made up about half of the enrollment in the kindergarten and primary grades. As Caucasian families continued to move into the area, however, the balance of numbers shifted so that Caucasians were in the majority. When the district's fall racial and ethnic census was taken, Mexican children made up 24 percent of the total Carolyn Wenzel enrollment. While Carolyn Wenzel received about 85 Washington children, other schools got from 45 (John Bidwell) to 61 (Freeport) Washington pupils. Mexican enrollment in the receiving schools other than Carolyn Wenzel ranged from 3 to 10 percent. There were no other minorities present in large numbers in the schools to which Washington children were bused, and these schools remained from two-thirds to 70 percent Caucasian.

Community Pressure Continues.   Throughout the 1968-69 school year Washington residents and militant Mexicans continued to exert pressure on the board to keep a school in their community emphasizing new approaches to the needs of Mexican children. As the year went by, there were special meetings between school officials and Washington residents, rallies, parades, and protest meetings. Supporters for efforts to keep Washington open included the Anglo president of the Washington PTA and several predominantly Anglo groups, such as the Volunteers of the Unitarian Church, the United Friends of the Farm Workers, and a new citywide multiethnic group called Understanding Each Other. Concilio reversed its position and backed the drive to keep Washington School, and several new militant chicano groups in the Mexican community joined the fight, including Brown Berets, the Chicano Legal Defense Fund, and area chapters of the Mexican-American Youth Association (MAYA).

The board reconsidered its position on Washington on April

14, 1969, but finally voted to go back to its original plan to bus out all remaining children in the fall of 1969. The Washington building was to be discontinued as a regular school, but kept in use temporarily for classes for the orthopedically handicapped, preschool children, and adult education. The superintendent also proposed developing a preschool day-care center if financing could be found, and there was discussion of transferring some of the district's administrative staff to Washington. The night the board voted, community spokesmen opposed the Washington closing 4–1.

The board's final decision on Washington came on the heels of a district survey of Washington parents, released in March 1969, which indicated that a great many felt their children were making a favorable adjustment in the new schools. Parents of 213 children bused out of the Washington area received questionnaires by mail; 127, or 60 percent, returned the questionnaires. The overwhelming majority of the parents responding to the checklist questions answered that their children liked their new school (84 percent), were doing as well in school this year as they should be doing (80 percent), and had made many new friends (86 percent). Of parents turning in the survey form, 61 percent said that the new school program had helped to increase their child's interest in learning. Parents were also asked what they *disliked* most about their children's new schools. No checklist of answers was provided and their responses to this question documented the fact that there was strong sentiment against the busing. The most frequent comments of the 62 parents who responded to this question were categorized as follows: the receiving schools are too far away from home (30); the busing and related problems (21); everything is fine (7); and children should remain at Washington School (6).

The group trying to keep Washington open continued their campaign through the 1968-69 school year. Although they backed a two-way approach to desegregation, the overriding issue with many was an educational program tailored to meet the needs of Mexican children. And, for the first time, many Mexican parents and young chicano students who had come through the local school system publicly rejected what the schools had to offer. Ventura Lopez, co-chairman of the Chicano Legal Defense Fund, stated at a Save Washington School rally on April 27, 1969:

A business can't succeed without consumers. We are consumers in the business of Sacramento education. We are not pleased.[43]

The continuing Washington campaign attempted to provide ideas and opportunities for innovations in the education of Mexican children. In the fall of 1968, for example, Dr. Clark L. Taylor, an anthropologist at Sacramento State College, proposed a joint project with the district involving Washington area students "with special emphasis being directed toward the chicano student."[44] Dr. Taylor directed a federally financed Experienced Teachers Fellowship Program in Mexican-American Education at Sacramento State College. He had testified at public meetings on Washington in favor of keeping the school open and building the curriculum around the Mexican student. Dr. Taylor now proposed selecting 50 to 75 students in grades K–3 from the Washington attendance area, or the Washington area combined with another elementary school, concentrating on a special bicultural curriculum for one year, and comparing the results with the academic progress of the bused Washington children. The total program would involve in-service training for regular district teachers who would be released from teaching duties by Fellows in the Experienced Teachers Program. The proposal also suggested training bilingual teaching assistants drawn from the Neighborhood Youth Corps and community volunteers, and generally involving parents in the program. The 20 Fellows who would participate were already receiving a year's concentrated training in working with Mexican-background children, including participant observation in Mexican barrio areas and a study trip to Mexico carried out in cooperation with a Mexican university. Cost to the district would be minimal, as the sponsoring program was already funded. The proposal left the district the option of selecting a school other than Washington as a location for the project but specified that at least half the students involved must be from the Washington area and that a "substantial portion of the students must be of Mexican-American descent."[45] It asked that the district meet the cost of transportation if Washington children were bused to another area for the project.

Dr. Taylor's proposal received strong support from Washington community leaders but he was not able to work out a mutually satisfactory plan with the district. District officials maintained that the concentration on Washington children would constitute a reversal of the Board's decision to desegregate the school, and objected to possible costs involved. In addition, Dr. Taylor was pressured by an Office of Education official in Washington who accused him of being a segregationist and turning his project into a political activity. As a result, the Experi-

enced Teachers Program made arrangements with the North
Sacramento School District for a demonstration project in Dos
Rios School adjoining the Washington attendance area. Other
suggestions by Washington community leaders to utilize
resources available through the Experienced Teachers Program
and other services at Sacramento State College were also
rejected. Militant chicano leaders felt that the district would
have taken advantage of these resources and opportunities if
they were "really interested in the education of the Mexican
child."[46] Mrs. Cortez resigned publicly from the Title I Community Educational Advisory Committee over the district's
handling of the proposed Experienced Teachers Program project, blasting the district for ignoring community concern and
manipulating so-called community participation to support the
status quo in the schools. The Experienced Teachers Program
at Sacramento State College was then one of the few and best-
financed programs in the country training teachers to work with
Mexican children.

In the Washington Receiving Schools. In spite of continued
community protests and a threatened boycott in May, the
Washington children stayed in desegregated schools throughout
the 1968-69 school year. From the viewpoint of district officials,
the first year of Washington desegregation was successful. An
interview with the principals in two of the receiving schools,
Pony Express and Carolyn Wenzel, indicated that the year was
positive so far as desegregation was concerned and that, on the
whole, they felt that the Washington children were better off
in a desegregated setting.

The principal of Carolyn Wenzel had been principal of Bowling Green, a receiving school for Glen Elder children when
Project Aspiration began, and was able to compare the two situations. He said that a one-step program is easier, especially where
there is opposition. The Glen Elder parents, in contrast to many
of the Washington parents, had supported the busing and had
in some cases even given false addresses to be eligible for busing.
He said that the enrollment of Mexican children had fluctuated
more than black enrollment and he had had more instances
of children missing the bus from the Washington area than at
Bowling Green. This principal also stated that the Mexican children miss school more in mid-year as the fathers may move
with the farm crops or get their vacation during the school year.
He said some families go to Mexico in the middle of the year
for four to six weeks.

The Carolyn Wenzel principal stressed communicating with parents in Spanish and translated into Spanish all written material for parents, such as school newsletters, announcements, and year-end reports on children. Translators were also frequently used for telephone conversations, home visits, and parent-teacher conferences. There was one regular classroom teacher at Carolyn Wenzel who was fully bilingual and two others who were "moderately bilingual." Spanish-speaking staff brought in with the compensatory services accompanying desegregation included a three-fourths-time teaching assistant and a part-time counselor. The principal stated that he could also use a translator half-time or three-fourths time.

As far as the children were concerned, most of the Mexican children at Carolyn Wenzel spoke English, but their understanding was "superficial and limited." They had difficulty relating to unfamiliar objects and knowing the various meanings for the same word. His goal was to make it possible for the Mexican children to function in an English-speaking society without losing their Spanish. To facilitate teachers' communication with the pupils, District Intergroup Relations staff met with the Carolyn Wenzel faculty to teach them Spanish phrases, explain Mexican customs, and help the teachers develop ideas for working with the children. The teachers were taught phrases such as "It is now time to line up" and "You have a pretty new dress."

There were fewer Washington children and more staff who spoke Spanish at Pony Express. The principal said that about eight of the 55 Washington children had difficulty with English and that at least ten people in the school, including the custodian and the yard supervisor, spoke Spanish. He had one Mexican first-grade classroom teacher, and he put the youngsters with language problems in her class.

All district elementary schools had switched to a nongraded program by the time the Washington desegregation took place. The principals of both Pony Express and Carolyn Wenzel distributed the Washington children throughout the school for their regular classroom assignment. They took them out of the regular classroom, however, for work with the reading specialist and the English as a Second Language teacher. A bilingual teaching assistant also gave special help, under the direction of a teacher, to children having difficulty with English. The English as a Second Language teacher who worked with kindergarten children was to be eliminated in 1969-70 because of cuts in funds. The reading specialist was to continue, but the number of children bused would increase, making more demands on this teacher, who served four schools. Both principals feel that the supportive services are necessary for a successful program and that the nongraded structure helps by reducing competition and creating a pattern of flexible grouping and regrouping of children so that they can concentrate on particular skills. Both principals indicated that the Washington children were making progress and were changing in their attitudes toward school.

In an effort to recognize cultural differences and achievements, both Pony Express and Carolyn Wenzel planned special programs and activities through the year. Pony Express held a day-long celebration on May 5, Cinco de Mayo, one of Mexico's chief national holidays, with Mexican dances, songs, a mariachi band, a fashion show, and speeches by the Mexican consul in Sacramento and the governor's Mexican aide for community relations. The Sacramento police chief's Mexican community relations officer also attended. The Pony Express sixth graders, including the Anglo children, put on the dances. About 100 Washington parents, teachers, and children came as guests. The Pony Express Christmas program featured songs and dances of Mexico performed by the younger school children. Carolyn Wenzel also celebrated Cinco de Mayo and held a "Culture Week" in April in conjunction with John F. Kennedy High School. Each day a different "culture" was spotlighted, with emphasis on the particular group of people and their background. There was special food for lunch, with "soul food" one day, including chitterlings and collard greens, a sweet and sour Chinese dish on another day, and tacos on the day the Mexican culture was featured. Carolyn Wenzel also had a folk dance program to which parents were invited.

Militant chicano leadership maintained that the Washington children were socially isolated in the schools, but the principals of Carolyn Wenzel and Pony Express did not agree. They said that there was a tendency for some of the Washington children to play together at recess but that, as a whole, the Mexican children did not stand out from the other children. The principal of Pony Express challenged a TV reporter doing a special feature on the Washington issue to pick out the bused Mexican children at his school. The reporter selected an Oriental child and the son of the governor's Mexican aide, who was not involved in the busing. Participation in after-school activities such as Scouts was rare, however, and almost out of the question after a tightening up on the district's budget eliminated most after-school late buses. Children in only one Washington family at Carolyn Wenzel had stayed after school for Scouts and these children finally dropped out.

The poverty of many Washington families results in problems of health and nutrition among the bused children. The Pony Express principal said, for example, that both the school nurse and school health services were inadequate to meet the needs of the Washington children in the first phase of desegregation. This problem was new to his school, which is in a higher socioeconomic area. With budget cuts, both the free lunch program and existing health services were to be reduced with the 1969-70 school year, making these programs fall even more short of the need.

To help parents participate in school activities, bus transportation to the receiving schools was arranged for conferences and special events. The principal of Carolyn Wenzel also gave Washington parents the choice of meeting at either school for parent-teacher conferences. He found parents preferred conferences in the Washington School, and he planned to continue offering them the option of meeting with teachers in their own neighborhood area, using a community facility if Washington School was not available. Parent participation in receiving school activities was apparently uneven, depending on the school and the activity. Parent participation in Carolyn Wenzel's parent-teacher conferences was very high in the first year of desegregation.

Evaluations and Changes in Desegregation Plan.   At the end of the 1968-69 school year in August 1969, the district issued an evaluation of the academic progress of children in Project Aspiration that gave breakdowns on the achievement of bused and resident children in the Washington receiving schools. According to the tests administered, the first phase of the Washington desegregation had mixed educational results. When the rate of progress in reading achievement for the 1968-69 school year for bused children was compared to the rate of growth the year before, for example, the study found that Washington children at the second placement or grade level experienced "increased rates of reading achievement." Children at the third placement or grade level reassigned from Washington only "maintained their previous rate of growth in reading achievement," however. As for the resident pupils involved in Washington's desegregation, the report reached the overall conclusion that integration "generally had no apparent effect on the rates of achievement of the resident pupils." But resident children at the third placement or grade level in all four receiving schools demonstrated "a decrease in their mean rate of reading achievement during the 1968-69 school year"[47]

Non-academic aspects of the program were reported as favorable on balance, but also revealed some negative features of Project Aspiration. An assessment of the opinions of parents, teachers, and principals in *all* schools in the desegregation program, including those where blacks were bused:

> indicated that Project Aspiration was effective in promoting positive changes in pupil interests, attitudes and behavior and indicated a substantial degree of interaction between the integrated project [bused] and the resident pupils.

In addition to these positive opinions about pupil interests, attitudes, and behavior a "substantial minority" of the classroom teachers and principals surveyed "indicated discipline problems to be the major problem caused by Project Aspiration."[48] Of the teachers in Project Aspiration schools who had responded to a similar survey the previous year, 22 percent had said that the desegregation program had a negative effect on discipline among *resident* pupils. A much smaller proportion (9 percent) had reported discipline problems among the *bused* minority children as a negative aspect of the project. The 1968-69 evaluation concluded that a similar finding of discipline problems two years in a row "suggests that the receiving schools have not been effective in counteracting this negative aspect of the program."[49]

With the beginning of the 1969-70 school year, regular classes at Washington were discontinued and all children in the upper elementary grades were bused to the four schools receiving K–3 children in the first phase of desegregation. Special education and pre-kindergarten classes were housed in Washington during the 1970-71 school year, but were moved out by fall 1971 when new facilities for the physically handicapped were completed. Beginning in the fall of 1971 the Washington building was to be used temporarily for office space and adult education. The school board's long-range plans for the Washington site, a subject of much concern among opponents of Washington desegregation, were indicated in April 1970 when the board passed a resolution expressing its intention to sell the property to the city for a nominal sum. The sale was to be made at a later date with the stipulation that the Washington site be used for a multi-purpose neighborhood center.

As the result of several different kinds of pressures, the district revised its compensatory education program at the start of the

1970-71 school year, including the educational support services available to pupils in Project Aspiration. When field work for this study was carried out in 1969, minority community leaders were criticizing both the quality and quantity of special help for low income children under the federal Title I ESEA programs in desegregated as well as segregated schools. Complaints voiced by members or former members of the district's Title I community advisory committee included lack of teacher interest in black and Mexican children, continuation of traditional teaching methods that had already failed, and the spreading out of the services of specialists so thinly that their help was meaningless. Some principals and teachers noted the need for more specialists than were available in 1968-69. The next year, reading teachers, English as a second language specialists, and health services were spread out even more because of budget cuts and an increased number of children in the desegregation program. The district's 1969-70 evaluation of Project Aspiration admitted that the level of support services for the program was "inadequate" although the report concluded that existing services were "helpful" and "effective."[50] The most decisive factor in changing the Title I program, however, was a new policy from the State Board of Education in 1969 requiring local districts to give priority to elementary schools in allocating Title I monies and to concentrate funds on a saturation basis, spending at least $300 per child in the target schools.

In 1970-71, as a result of the factors discussed above, schools in the elementary desegregation project received: (1) more access to resource teachers, (2) more paid teacher aids, (3) student teacher aides from Sacramento State College, (4) an increased number of high school Neighborhood Youth Corps aides, (5) Harper and Row programmed tutoring for many pupils, (6) more reading specialists, and (7) increased counseling time. Compensatory education programs outside the Project Aspiration schools were concentrated in five public elementary schools only and the number of non-public schools receiving Title I aid was reduced. Public elementary schools continuing to receive compensatory education funds after fall 1970—Camellia, Donner, Elder Creek, Jedediah Smith, and Oak Ridge—were all at least 70 percent minority, and two, Donner and Camellia, were 64 and 85 percent black, respectively.

In the year following the changes described above, the district's annual analysis of the academic impact of Project Aspiration showed a more positive trend for both Mexican and black pupils in desegregated schools. The 1970-71 evaluation was based on two separate sub-studies: one was of the achievement gains of Mexican-background pupils bused from Washington, and the other was on black children from the Camellia, Donner, and Elder Creek attendance areas enrolled in segregated versus desegregated schools. Although more persuasive than some of the earlier studies, this report, like previous ones, showed only that minority children were "catching up" and made no claims that they were achieving at grade level or learning on a par with white children in the same schools.

In the sub-study of Mexican background pupils bused to the South Sacramento suburbs, elementary children from the Washington area in all placement or grade levels were given the California Achievement Test (CAT) in October 1970 and May 1971. Their scores in arithmetic and reading on the two sets of tests were then evaluated in terms of (1) project goals for the children, which were 7.5 months of growth for the 7-month period of instruction; and (2) the number of months of growth in achievement, as indicated by test scores, compared with actual months of instruction. In arithmetic, bused Mexican children at all placement levels progressed more than the project goal of 7.5 months of growth. Their gains ranged from eight months of progress for seven months of instruction at placement levels 2 and 6, to 16 months of growth at the fourth grade placement level. The Washington children did not do as well on the reading section of the test, however. Bused Mexican pupils in placement levels 3 and 4 did exceed project goals and gained more than 7.5 months of growth during the seven months of lessons. These children showed 10 and 11 months of growth from October to May. Children at placement levels 2 and 5 gained an even month of growth for each month of school, but in placement level 6, bused pupils scored only 6.5 months of progress for the seven-month period. There was no comparison of the pupils' rate of growth with that in the previous year, as in the 1970 study, nor was there any comparison of their achievement with that of Mexican-background pupils in other schools.

The evaluation of black pupil achievement was based on a direct comparison of test scores of children in segregated versus desegregated schools. This part of the research, especially, showed a somewhat stronger trend than earlier studies toward greater academic gains for black pupils in integrated schools. To assess the impact of desegregation on black children, pupils at placement levels 2–6 who were bused out of the Camellia, Elder Creek, and Donner attendance areas were tested in reading and arithmetic in the fall of 1970 and the spring of 1971. A total of 79 of these children took the California Achievement Test (CAT) reading section; 77 took the segment on arithmetic. A matched sample of black children at the same placement levels who lived in the same zones, but attended segregated schools, were given the same tests. This group of children was somewhat larger in size, with 197 taking the reading section of the California Achievement Test and 175 being tested in arithmetic. Children in the segregated schools also took the tests in the fall of 1970 and the spring of 1971.

Analysis of test results indicated that in arithmetic, the children who were bused to predominantly white schools scored higher than those remaining in segregated schools at all placement or grade levels. In reading, pupils in integrated settings tested higher in placement levels 2–4 and 6. Pupils in the segregated schools, however, made higher scores in reading in placement level 5. The difference between the arithmetic scores of the two sets of pupils were statistically significant at all placement levels—that is, the differences were sufficiently large enough that the higher scores could not be due to chance. The differences between the reading scores of desegregated and segregated pupils were statistically significant at placement levels 2–4 and 6, where children in the integrated schools made higher scores than those in segregated schools. It should be noted that children in both segregated and desegregated schools received the benefits of Title I compensatory education assistance.

Other conclusions of the 1970-71 evaluation of Project Aspiration were: "the concentration of compensatory programs had a positive impact on pupil interests, attitudes and attendance" and that bused children had, according to teacher ratings, gained in such areas as "respect for authority," "participation in activities," and "interaction with other pupils." The report also stated that staff in these schools evaluated the supplementary compensatory services as "good."[51] The presence of discipline problems in the receiving schools was not mentioned in the major conclusions of the 1971 study as in several years prior to 1971.

A fall 1971 district report summarized and reviewed the major findings of all past local studies of the academic and social impact of desegregation, dating back to the dispersal of Stanford junior high school students. Not all of the data highlighted in these evaluations was positive or conclusive, but district analysts came to the following conclusions, based on the total body of cumulative research:

(1) Minority pupils reassigned to desegregated schools tend

to perform better academically than do their peers in segregated schools.

(2) The academic achievement of resident pupils in schools that receive minority pupils because of desegregation is not adversely affected.

(3) Discipline problems in the elementary schools receiving minority pupils with desegregation dropped each year, to the point that only one in 20 teachers listed discipline as a problem by the end of the fourth year of Project Aspiration.

(4) Both staff and parents have indicated that a preponderance of positive effects have resulted from the reassignment of minority pupils.

Following presentation of the 1971 reports at a school board meeting on September 20, board member Adolph Moskovitz reacted enthusiastically to the implications for Sacramento and other school districts. Mr. Moskovitz, who has in the past advocated going ahead with more desegregation, stated:

> This is an issue on which the country is being torn apart. . . . In our district we have bused. We have put kids on buses and they've been taken outside their neighborhoods, and the results have been good—if we're to believe these statistics—it is good, educationally good. And if you read the comments of parents and teachers about how the kids behave, they've been good in other ways.
> And if busing does it, that awful word, then by golly use busing. And if it works here, let's extend it.[52]

8.
Other Equal Educational Opportunity Issues

WHILE protest and debate over the desegregation of Washington School was building up in the spring of 1968, a coalition of black and Mexican high school students raised a series of important demands in other areas as regards equal educational opportunity. The students' grievances, first articulated by Sacramento High School pupils in connection with a walkout demonstration, included: (1) the need for more counselors and principals who are members of racial minority groups; (2) discrimination and inequality in the treatment of blacks and Mexican pupils within the high schools; (3) failure of the schools to teach the roles and contributions of blacks, Mexicans, and other racial and ethnic minorities in U.S. and California history classes; and (4) the tracking of students into class groupings based on tests reflecting the values of white middle-class America. The students' complaints were sent to the superintendent in a letter on March 29 that was widely publicized, and in April and May a citywide coalition of high school minority students appeared at school board meetings to urge change in these areas in all the high schools. The students were backed by many adults in the community, including the black member of the City Council, the local NAACP Branch, the Congress of Young Adults, a militant anti-poverty group, and the former director of the Sacramento Area Economic Opportunity Council. The *Sacramento Bee,* which supported three of the minority students' four demands, called editorially for more minority counselors and administrators.

Minority Employment. In the area of employment, students accused the district of making only token efforts to recruit minority teachers, counselors, and principals. At the time the students went to the board, there was only one black principal in the district and one black assistant principal. The black principal of Sierra Elementary School was appointed principal of American Legion School in 1963 when it was a segregated school and was transferred to Sierra when Project Aspiration began and American Legion was discontinued as a regular school. He was only the second black principal in the city's history, the first dating back to the late 1800s and the early 1900s. The one black assistant principal in the district in 1968 was appointed to Will C. Wood Junior High School in the mid-1960s, following the desegregation of Stanford. There was only one top black administrator in the central office in 1968, Dr. Ervin Jackson, Assistant to the Superintendent for Intergroup Relations. Dr. Jackson was brought into the district in 1966 to help with planning for elementary desegregation. There were no Mexican-background principals, assistant principals, or administrators in 1968. Although there were several minority counselors working with adult education programs under the central administration during that school year, there were only two minority counselors in the regular schools. Both were at the secondary level, at Peter Lassen Junior High School and at Luther Burbank Senior High School.

Figures released by the district at the time of the student

demands indicated that in the 1967-68 school year there were 192 minority professional employees in the district, making up 8 percent of the total professional staff. This group included 98 blacks, 31 Mexicans, and 63 Asians and other nonwhites. In 1963, when the district first began keeping records of the racial and ethnic identification of minority staff, there had been only 40 blacks and 48 Orientals and other nonwhites out of a total of 2,051 professional employees. Mexican staff were not identified in the 1963 count, but there were 21 persons of Mexican background on the professional staff in 1966.

Superintendent Lawson defended the district's recruiting efforts, which included trips to predominantly black schools in the South, advertisements in Chicago and Detroit newspapers, contacts with southwestern colleges with concentrations of Mexican students, and a few recruiting trips to northern areas with large numbers of black students. California's high standards of certification, plus competition from other schools, business, industry, and government, limited Sacramento's ability to attract minority staff, according to the superintendent. He said that in the case of counselors and administrators, California's requirements make out-of-state recruiting almost impossible. He also maintained that many minority staff members did not want to be assigned to schools with large numbers of minority students. Active efforts to recruit minority staff began after the Citizens Advisory Committee report, which found in 1965 that the district was making no special effort to hire teachers of different ethnic backgrounds and that the personnel officer hesitated to hire minority teachers because of the reluctance of principals to have them on their staffs. Recruiting first emphasized black personnel, and here the most significant gains had been made.

Following a public hearing on the students' demands at which more than half the speakers were adults, the board agreed in May 1968 to hire a minority group member as dean of students at Sacramento High School and to gradually increase the number of minority counselors and administrators in the schools. Superintendent Lawson also announced a plan to place six minority student counseling assistants in the senior high schools for the fall of 1968. The local drive to gain more professional minority staff in the schools was reinforced by a new policy statement from the State Board of Education in June 1968. The state board identified the fact that "California schools employ a disproportionately low number of racial and ethnic minority teachers" and directed local districts to make "positive

and aggressive state and nationwide efforts . . . to seek out
and employ racial and ethnic minority teachers." The board
also asked local districts to upgrade and promote minority
teachers to "positions of added responsibility" and went on
record that it was "educationally sound" for both minority and
majority pupils to be exposed to minority teachers, counselors
and administrators.[53]

When the 1968–69 school year began, district officials stated
that the number of black professional employees had increased
to 115 and that the number of Mexicans on the professional
staff had increased to 35. There was a total of 217 minority professional employees in the district in the fall of 1968, making up
9 percent of the total staff. In addition to a new black dean of
students at Sacramento High School, the district had added five
minority principals and assistant principals and two new minority counselors. At the elementary level, Donner had a new black
principal and Washington, a Mexican principal. In the junior
high schools, a black assistant principal was put in Joaquin Miller
and a Mexican assistant principal in Peter Lassen and Sam Brannon. A black counselor was named for Sacramento Senior High
School. According to the State Department of Education's annual racial and ethnic census, 172 of the district's full-time
professional minority staff were actually working in the regular
schools in the fall of 1968 and all but 9 of these were classroom
teachers. (See Tables 3 and 4.)

Since 1968, the district's hiring and retention of minority staff
has been greatly affected by the failure of several successive
tax elections and by budget cuts in special programs such as
the federal Title I ESEA projects that have also caused staff
reductions. District officials stated in 1969 that they knew where
to find black teachers and could hire many more, if it were
not for cutbacks in the number of staff positions. A January
1969 report by the Assistant Superintendent, Personnel Services, commented, for example:

> Actually we could easily have more than doubled the Negro employ-
> ment for the 1968-69 school year had we had the vacancies we
> normally do for secondary teachers, since great effort was made
> to locate such candidates.[54]

District officials still maintained in 1969 that there were few
qualified Mexican background teachers available and that the
small supply accounted for poor progress in hiring. Mexican
leaders, however, pointed to the large number of Mexican-
background teachers who applied for the Experienced Teachers

Table 3—Full-Time Professional Instructional Staff in Regular Schools, by Race and Ethnic Identification, 1968 and 1970

School Level	Total Staff	Cau-casian	Black	Mexi-can	Asian	Total Minority
Elementary*						
1968	1,068	959	68	8	33	109
1970	1,151	1,019	73 ·	23	32	132
Junior High						
1968	532	487	23	6	16	45
1970	501	449	20	10	14	52
Senior High						
1968	462	444	10	5	3	18
1970	397	372	13	7	2	25
TOTAL						
1968	2,062	1,890	101	19	52	172
1970	2,049	1,840	106	40	48	209

*Nine schools did not report the racial and ethnic identification of staff members for Fall 1968. Fall 1967 reports were used where available.

Source: 1968, California State Department of Education, Bureau of Intergroup Relations; 1970, U.S. Department of Health, Education and Welfare, Office for Civil Rights, Washington, D.C.

Fellowship Program in Mexican-American Education at Sacramento State College and insisted that the district could find qualified Mexican teachers if it tried.

A decision to eliminate all non-tenured teachers in the spring of 1969 following the defeat of a tax override election affected newly employed minority teachers disproportionately, especially at the junior high school and high school levels where the cuts were greatest. Teacher reductions concentrated on the secondary level, since state policy regulates the pupil-teacher ratio in the elementary schools. Besides losing new minority teachers in the schools where the demand for them was greatest, some staff members were afraid that the cutbacks would have an unfavorable effect on future recruiting, as word got around that a job in Sacramento might not last very long.

In the fall of 1970, the U.S. Department of Health, Education and Welfare's survey of the racial and ethnic staff in local districts showed that the Sacramento City Unified District employed 209 members of minority groups in the regular

Table 4—Full-Time Professional Minority Instructional Staff in Regular
Schools, by Position in Schools and School Level, 1968 and 1970

School Level	Total Minority Staff	Princi-pal	Assist. Princi-pal	Class-room Teachers	Other Staff
Elementary*					
1968	109	3	0	106	0
1970	132	5	0	126	1
Junior High					
1968	45	0	3	41	1
1970	52	0	3	47	2
Senior High					
1968	18	0	0	16	2
1970	25	1	2	17	5
TOTAL					
1968	172	3	3	163	3
1970	209	6	5	190	8

*Nine schools did not report the racial and ethnic identification of staff members
for Fall 1968. Fall 1967 reports were used where available.

Source: 1968, California State Department of Education, Bureau of Intergroup
Relations; 1970, U.S. Department of Health, Education and Welfare, Office for
Civil Rights, Washington, D.C.

schools: 106 blacks, 40 Mexicans, 48 Asians, and 15 American
Indians. The largest number of minority staff were classroom
teachers at the elementary level, but by 1970 the district aso
had 6 minority principals and 5 minority assistant principals.
(See Tables 3 and 4.) In keeping with local, as well as state,
policy, minority principals and assistant principals were assigned
to both majority white and predominantly minority schools. At
the elementary level, for instance, there were black principals
in Sierra and Mark Hopkins, both predominantly white schools,
as well as in Camellia and Donner, both predominantly black
schools. Ethel Baker, an elementary school with a predominantly
Anglo enrollment, had a Mexican principal. At the senior high
school level, a black principal had been appointed to Sacramento
Senior High School, which had a 53 percent minority student
body in 1970 and which enrolled the largest number and percentage of blacks (24 percent) of any regular high school in
the district. McClatchy Senior High School, still predominantly

white but heavily minority (41 percent) had a black assistant principal. There was also a black assistant principal in Hiram Johnson Senior High School in 1970, which was three-fourths white according to the HEW survey. Black and Mexican assistant principals in the junior high schools were all assigned to schools with large minority populations: to Sutter, which was 51 percent minority; to Peter Lassen, 46 percent minority; and to Will C. Wood, 43 percent minority.

There have also been efforts to increase the employment of nonprofessional, as well as professional, minority staff in the Sacramento district. These efforts date back to the Citizens Advisory Committee report that found no black clerical personnel and only a few Asians on the clerical staff in 1964. The committee identified a total of only 18 noncertificated minority employees in 1964. Six of these were black and the rest Oriental and Filipino. By 1968, the number of all nonprofessional minority employees, including noncertificated staff and clerical positions, had increased to 201. The number of black nonprofessional staff members had grown to 92.

Inequality in Treatment of Minority Students. The minority high school students who approached the board in the spring of 1968 also complained that there was racial and ethnic discrimination in the high schools, stating:

> The counselors and administrators of our high schools must treat us as students rather than as Negroes or Mexicans for only then can we have a satisfactory student-teacher relationship with them.

They specifically mentioned the suspension of black and Mexican students without a hearing prior to suspension "when the same punishment is rarely given to white students." They also protested an armed guard on the campus at Sacramento High School, which then had a 51 percent minority enrollment, and a police patrol at four high schools "in an effort to monitor our every move and to intimidate us."[55]

Superintendent Lawson replied that it was clearly the district's policy that "there shall be equal treatment of all students regardless of race or ethnic origin." He reviewed the district's efforts to "create a better educational climate and a greater understanding among all racial and ethnic groups" through its in-service training program and the Intergroup Relations Service. He explained that all high schools had special, deputized uniformed law enforcement officers and that "the amount of police surveillance and the number of city police patrol cars assigned to any given area is the responsibility of the Sacramento Police Department."[56]

District activities in the area of in-service training of staff in intergroup relations and related fields have been numerous, as Dr. Lawson pointed out, and date back to the desegregation of Stanford.

In the early phases of the desegregation of Stanford, for example, principals in the junior high schools receiving black students met with central administration staff to help with planning and to hear from community leaders. These pre-desegregation meetings were followed by further in-service training for junior high school principals and teachers the next year. Recalling these 1964 and 1965 sessions, one principal stated, "We were all learning from one another." He said that creating an atmosphere where all students felt wanted was stressed. Another principal, who is critical of this early orientation, commented, "Nobody had any expertise at that time" and all were "groping," with much misinformation being spread.

When Project Aspiration began, the district stepped up its staff orientation program considerably with the help of two technical assistance grants under Title IV of the Civil Rights Act. Since 1966, the district has conducted compulsory meetings with principals involved in each phase of Project Aspiration and has instructed principals to set up informational meetings for their staff explaining the details and mechanics of the program. As part of the preparation for Project Aspiration, principals have also had the responsibility for setting up meetings between their staff and resource persons drawn from District Intergroup Relations staff, community leaders, and district specialists in related fields. All staff of the individual schools, including clerks, custodians, and cafeteria workers were included in these meetings. For several years, the district conducted separate orientation meetings for nonprofessional staff working with Project Aspiration, including bus drivers, bus matrons, and school clerks. As mentioned earlier, two related summer workshops for teachers were held for several summers, depending on the availability of funds—an Institute on Compensatory Education, which Project Aspiration teachers were encouraged to attend, and a Workshop for Intergroup Relations. The district also sponsored a seven-week television series on Teacher Training for Intergroup Relations for Project Aspiration staff, which was given for credit in 1967. Outside consultants and resource persons were used for all the teacher-training courses, which were attended on a voluntary basis, with a stipend for teachers who enrolled. In the spring of 1969 the district held a Seminar on Social Responsibility that was mandatory for all principals and administrators.

In addition to special training courses held on a districtwide basis, the Intergroup Relations Service has furnished speakers and resource persons for in-service programs conducted by individual principals. Staff members are available for consultation and special assistance with desegregation problems. The Intergroup Relations Service, which is now financed by the district's regular budget, also has films, records, and books available on loan to staff and notifies district schools and individual teachers of special holidays and events of interest to the different minorities.

In spite of the district's efforts at intergroup education, there were serious problems with regard to staff treatment of minority students and staff inability to relate to the interests and needs of black and Mexican students. This was a general problem that was not confined to the high schools or to the newly desegregated schools.

In 1968, shortly after the minority students' coalition made their demands public, parents of minority students at John F. Kennedy High School made a complaint to the State Superintendent of Education, Dr. Max Rafferty, which paralleled the students' complaints, including charges of a racist principal, selective enforcement of rules where black and Mexican students were concerned, and general inequality in the treatment of minority students in the district schools. This complaint was investigated by the Bureau of Intergroup Relations of the State Department of Education in the summer of 1968. The staff investigation found the same overall problems identified by the complaining parents and the minority high school students *at all school levels*. Specific examples of "school staff members' insensitivity, indifference, prejudice and discriminatory behavior toward pupils and students of racial and ethnic minority backgrounds" were cited. The report found "evidence of little and ineffective communication between the district's schools and the racial and ethnic students and parents" and noted that "community concern is increasing about the negative attitude of school staff to racial and ethnic minority students."[57]

What kinds of attitudes and behavior were parents and minority students concerned about? The following incidents and practices were reported by the State Bureau of Intergroup Relations' investigation and by persons interviewed for this study:

A black and white boy fought at one of the elementary schools after the white child burst the black child's balloon. The black youngster was suspended but the white child was not. When the parents inquired, the principal said he had not punished the white boy because he was new to the school. He suspended the black boy, not because of the fight, but because he did not like the boy's attitude—"he doesn't smile enough."

A remedial reading teacher who conducted summer classes for elementary children held back because of reading problems believes that most of the minority pupils she taught were not pupil learning problems but rather teacher problems. She cited a black boy who raised his reading test score by one year in the summer class and a Mexican student who was reading almost one year above placement at the end of the summer session. She said that too many times teachers are too quick to equate minority racial and ethnic background with little ability and little interest and thereby fail to inspire the youngsters and teach them to their fullest capacity.

A black junior high school student felt that the principal in his school was "pretty fair" most of the time, but did not feel that, as a whole, teachers and counselors understood the needs and problems of black students. He said "you have to try a little harder in everything you do" and pointed to one teacher, particularly, who is prejudiced and will give black students referral slips for looking "wrong" while he lets white kids "run all over you."

A Mexican girl who attended one of the junior high schools desegregated after the Stanford fire stated that she had only one "good teacher" who was "not prejudiced." This was the only class she "looked forward to." She said that the librarian was "down on dark Mexican girls" and would ask them for passes but would not ask the Anglo girls for passes.

A teacher at one of the junior high schools with a low minority enrollment deliberately called 15-year-old blacks "boy." The students got together and decided they would make a statement every time this happened. After they did, the teacher stopped.

A Chicano high school student said that his counselor wanted to give him typing and business courses and "didn't think I could make it in Spanish." He said that the counselors put the Mexican students "in the wood shop and typing to get them out of high school," while they "encourage white guys" and suggest that they take the college preparatory courses. His dad talked to the counselor and got him in classes that are junior college preparatory. Now that he has found out about the system, he is getting into college bound classes. He complained of a teacher who says "Ole" every time a Mexican student raises his hand for help and says that he has only one teacher he can talk to. He "feels comfortable" in only one class.

A former black high school student who worked in one of the school offices as part of her practice assignment was accused of taking material from the desk of a teacher who often made disparaging remarks about black students. The girl was removed from the practice assignment and sent to the library. There was never any evidence that the girl had taken anything and the teacher found that she had misplaced the item. As a result of parent insistence, the theft accusation was withdrawn and the teacher apologized. The girl missed three weeks of her placement during this period. She was bitter about having been wrongly labeled a thief.

A white principal interviewed for this study repeatedly said "nigra" in referring to blacks.

The investigation of racial and ethnic discrimination in Sacramento schools by the Bureau of Intergroup Relations concluded with the recommendation that the District establish a mandatory intergroup education program reaching all schools "so that there will be a level of awareness and sensitivity to the needs and feelings of the minority student population." Some individual staff members interviewed also felt that a compulsory program was necessary, as the teachers who need the training the most will not participate on a voluntary basis. One teacher in a school with a heavy minority enrollment thought that teachers who are not happy in schools with many low income black and Mexican students should be transferred to other schools where they would fit in better. She said that there were teachers in her school who had been trying unsuccessfully to transfer since the school was desegregated. Others pointed out that something has to be done about the older, tenured teachers who cannot adjust. There is also criticism and resentment among militant minority group members of the Intergroup Relations Service, which, they say, serves the interests of the central administration rather than helping with the problems of minorities. They feel that their grievances are not heard when they conflict with plans that the district wishes to implement.

Ethnic History Courses and Teaching Materials. Other demands of the minority high school students in the spring of 1968 were for separate courses in black and Mexican history and an assurance from the board that "all classes in history include adequate instruction and materials dealing with the contributions made by minority citizens to the history of our state, country, and world." The students said that they needed "historical images to identify with, just as white America needs them" and they pointed out that there would be more respect for minorities if all students were exposed to the contributions of all Americans.[58]

The board did not go along with the students' demand for separate history courses but responded to the issue in several ways: (1) a course outline for an elective eleventh-grade course in "Ethnic Relations and Contributions" was organized by the District Curriculum Development Services during the summer, and the curriculum center assisted high schools in setting up courses in ethnic history and relations in the fall of 1968; (2) resource guides on blacks and Mexicans in the United States were made available to fifth- and eighth-grade social science and history teachers during the 1968-69 school year; (3) a "Bibliography on Mexican-Americans" was prepared and distributed to all schools; and (4) $5,000 was budgeted for the development of the high school ethnic studies courses and for the distribution of resource materials on minority history to teachers and students at the secondary level.

Most emphasis was placed on the high school level, where district staff admitted "textbooks now available do not provide an adequate treatment of the role of the Negro in American history."[59] Ethnic relations or ethnic history courses were instituted in all regular high schools, plus American Legion, in the fall of 1968. These classes were taught during the regular school day for credit and were open to all students. According to a district staff member, about 50 percent of the enrollment was Caucasian. More students signed up for the courses the second semester than did for the first. The "Ethnic Relations and Contributions" course guide prepared by the district used the paperback McGraw-Hill *Americans All* series as the basic text and had major sections devoted to blacks in America, the Oriental, and the Mexican-American. Two in-service training courses for teachers were offered during each semester of the 1968-69 school year—one on black history and one on Mexican-American history. About 40 teachers registered for each of these courses. High school teachers conducting ethnic relations classes were furnished with a set of reference materials for their own use, and reading material for students was placed in the library or the social science department of the various schools. The Curriculum Development Services recommended that sociology teachers be selected for the ethnic studies courses and that they stress contemporary problems. "The students demanded black history," a staff member of the Curriculum Development Services stated:

but youngsters are more interested in contemporary problems and respond better to discussion of current problems than to the African historical background.

There were no further confrontations over minority history during the 1968–69 school year, but in the fall of 1969 a group of about 250 chicano students representing four of the city's high schools boycotted classes and presented 11 demands to the school board, including development of an ethnic studies program "that can relate to minorities."[60] There were other indications that at least some students were not satisfied with the way the ethnic studies program was being conducted. In the spring of 1970, Alan Watahara, a Sacramento High School pupil, stated in a roundtable discussion on student government that the president of his student body was in a "big hassle" with the administration over issues such as trying to improve the ethnic studies programs and bringing in outside minority speakers not approved by the administration, such as a Black Panther. Another Sacramento high school pupil on the same panel said that John F. Kennedy High School had let a John Bircher come in to speak, but would not allow a Panther to address the student body.

At the junior high school level, the district reprinted and distributed to eighth grade teachers of American history two supplementary resource units developed by other California districts: (1) "Resource Units on Mexican-American History in the United States," initially prepared by the San Diego City Schools; and (2) "Resource Guide on Negro History in the United States," developed by the Stockton Unified School District. In addition, junior high schools were sent copies of the 1968 edition of *Negro American Heritage* by Arna Bontemps, Paul Lawrence, and others. This book, published by Century Communications, Inc. of San Francisco, is on the California state adoption list as a supplementary text for eighth grade United States history. The two resource units on blacks and Mexicans which were developed by different districts, utilize a basically different approach. The "Resource Guide on Negro History in the United States," for example, is organized chapter by chapter as a supplement to the basal text, *Land of the Free*. The "Resource Units on Mexican-American History in the United States," however, digests the history of Mexico and Mexican-United States relations, Mexican immigration to the United States, and the characteristics of the Mexican-American community in the United States. Neither ties in local Sacramento ethnic history and resources in the area, since both were developed for other districts.

At the elementary level, the district reprinted a "Resource Guide on the Negro in America," prepared by the Berkeley Unified School District for fifth grade social science teachers. This guide includes several African folk songs and recent freedom songs, and stories illustrating problems of prejudice and discrimination. Activities for the children and teacher approaches to discussion are suggested. This was the only resource material sent to social studies teachers at the fifth grade level.

The State Education Code, Sections 8553 and 8576, provides that instruction in the social sciences at elementary and secondary grade levels:

> shall include . . . a study of the role and contributions of American Negroes, American Indians, Mexicans and other ethnic groups to the economic, political and social development of California and the United States of America.[61]

The special courses and supplementary materials initiated by the district, following student protests, were viewed as a means of carrying out state policy in this area, pending improvements in the regular textbooks.

New Textbooks and Minorities.   Recent improvements in the portrayal and inclusion of minority groups in district textbooks have come as a result of changes in state adoptions and the pressure of California state policy on publishers.

In 1964, following expressions of concern from a number of sources, including civil rights organizations, the state Senate, and a statewide group of social studies curriculum experts, the State Curriculum Commission adopted a new set of guidelines on the treatment of minority groups in textbooks to be used in California. The 1964 "Guidelines for Reference to Ethnic and Cultural Minorities in Textbooks," the first major step toward change in this area, stated:

> Textbooks must be free of bias and prejudice and, in fulfillment of this aim, must accurately portray the participation of minority groups in American life.[62]

The guidelines also maintained that textbooks for older pupils should "treat with particular accuracy and frankness those situations in our history in which people have not supported our enduring ideals." The Commission argued, "Only when they are in possession of historical truth can citizens now and in the future offer the kind of enlightened criticism that is necessary for our democracy to endure."[63] A year following the adoption of these guidelines, in 1965, the state legislature adopted laws requiring the teaching of the role and contributions of blacks and other ethnic groups in social science courses at both the elementary and secondary level. At the same time, the legislature passed companion legislation specifying that the State Board of Education and local districts could adopt only those history and civics textbooks which

> correctly portray the role and contribution of the American Negroes and members of other ethnic groups in the total development of the United States and the State of California.[64]

The statutes providing for the teaching of the role and contribution of minority groups in social science courses were amended in 1967 to stipulate that the contributions of American Indians and Mexicans, as well as American Negroes must be taught.

Actual change in the treatment of minorities in textbooks in use in California has been slow, in spite of the policy guidelines and new laws, particularly as far as minorities other than blacks are concerned. *Land of the Free*, a United States history for eighth grade students, written especially to conform with the 1964 State Curriculum Commission guidelines, was adopted by the State Board of Education in 1967 after nearly two years of study, restudy, evaluation by experts, and revisions of the text to make the book "even more explicit in its denunciation of Communism."[65] The most unbiased general history textbook available at the time of its adoption, *Land of the Free* represented a major break with the past in its treatment of the American Negro. Partly because of its inclusion and portrayal of American blacks and its discussion of historic discrimination against blacks and other minorities, *Land of the Free* generated controversy throughout the state. Opponents have charged that the book "overemphasizes" the role of blacks in America's past and portrays America as a "land of prejudice."[66] Although *Land of the Free* is a decided improvement over traditional textbooks, it is considerably weaker in its utilization of material on minorities other than blacks and has been criticized for its more limited coverage of blacks after the Reconstruction period. There is scanty coverage of the role and contributions of Mexicans in the development of the southwest and discussions of some of the key events in United States-Mexican history fail to give a balanced picture. The Treaty of Guadalupe Hidalgo, for example, is discussed without reference to the important provisions for citizenship and protection of the political and property rights of Mexicans in the territory ceded to the United States. China in the 19th century is described as a "backward" nation[67] and the achievements and problems of contemporary Chinese, Japanese, Mexicans, and American Indians are hardly mentioned. *Land of the Free* is currently used at the junior high school level in Sacramento and other California districts.

Following adoption of *Land of the Free,* the second major change in California textbooks took place in 1969, with approval at the state level of an ungraded or "continuous progress" reading program for grades K–6. The new reading series includes the Bank Street Readers, developed by Bank Street College in New York for urban children, with stories depicting social, economic, and racial diversity in a city setting. The total reading series also contains new editions of other textbook series with pictures of black as well as white children. Like *Land of the Free,* the inclusion of minorities in the "continuous progress" series focuses on blacks rather than all racial and ethnic groups. Another shortcoming of the proposed program is that it recommends readers such as the Bank Street series for "culturally disadvantaged pupils" instead of all pupils. If teachers follow the suggested outline, only poorer readers judged "culturally deprived" will be exposed to the Bank Street Readers.

By 1971, a statewide drive to reform the treatment of all minorities in textbooks began to pick up more steam. The State Board of Education refused to adopt a K–4 elementary social science series in 1970 recommended by then Superintendent of Public Instruction Max Rafferty over the advice of the State Curriculum Commission. A black board member, Dr. John R. Ford opposed the series as "entirely undesirable." Dr. Ford said the "racial intonations and innuendos were extremely insulting."[68] In 1971, when public hearings were held on proposed adoptions for basic social science texts and supplementary texts for grades 5–8, much of the criticism centered on the treatment of minorities other than blacks, especially the distortion or omission of adequate material on Americans of Mexican, Indian, and Asian background. At a hearing on September 9, 1971, educators, school board members, and administrators made the following complaints about the books that were being considered: (1) most of the texts distort the history of the relationship between the United States and Mexico; several contain "outright lies"; (2) the role of Mexicans in the history of California and the southwest is ignored and the history written almost entirely from the Anglo perspective; (3) a 10,000-year history of the American Indian is dismissed with a single sentence in one book, suggesting United States history began with the arrival of Europeans; (4) Asian Americans are virtually ignored, fostering a presumption that Asian Americans are "foreign"; and (5) one book declares China was a backward nation, fostering the impression that all progress came from Europe. After hearing such statements from educators and the public at large, the state board voted to postpone action on any of the books and appointed a 13-member interracial task force to evaluate the textbooks and suggest needed changes to bring the books into compliance with the provisions of state law.

The task force, made up mostly of educators and headed by Kenneth Washington, an assistant superintendent in the Los Angeles school district, reported to the board in December 1971 that the books were "written chiefly from the Anglo point of view" and

> generally reflect an absence of intellectual rigor, a superabundance of factual errors, a pervasive ethnocentrism in both framework and content and an insensitivity to people of various ethnic groups and, at times, intellectual dishonesty.[69]

Specific faults and weaknesses pointed out by the task force paralleled those made at public hearings. The task force noted, for instance, that one book "includes native Americans only as they constitute a problem for the Anglo-American society" and that a second book, *The Nation Expands to the West,* implies that Texas was not settled until the whites arrived, although Indians and Mexicans had been there for many years.[70] Modern black leaders were not mentioned in one basic U.S. history text under consideration and the slavery issue was "sugar coated." In another book, the history of the United States-Mexican War was distorted and there was no reference to present-day Indians, their current status, and the Indian rights movement. None of the proposed basic texts and only some of the supplementary texts were judged to meet the requirements of the state education code. Finally, members of the task force asked that their group be kept alive to review other textbooks in the fields of reading, music, art, and the humanities.

After studying the task force's report, the State Board of Education voted on January 4, 1972 to continue using current adoptions, while the State Department of Education and the State Curriculum Commission made specific recommendations for revisions and ascertained whether the publishers were willing to make the changes needed to bring the books in line with state law. Black board member John Ford was pessimistic regarding the possibility of revisions after the September hearing. "It is utterly impossible to make adequate changes in some of them without major, substantive improvements," he said.[71] The state board stated after its September meeting that it would start again with a new set of proposed adoptions if the books proved to be beyond redemption.

9.
Future Desegregation: When and How?

SINCE 1966, when Sacramento's first partial elementary desegregation project was proposed, the district has been considering various alternative plans to end segregation in the rest of its elementary schools. All of these plans have been rejected or withdrawn by the board and/or the superintendent or defeated at the polls. A major cause of delay is the degree to which the board has linked further desegregation to long-term, costly building plans. Meanwhile, new state policy on desegregation and racial balance and new state and federal court decisions, more demanding than those in force in the mid-1960s, have made some plans the district has considered obsolete. The Sacramento board is officially committed to further desegregation, but when and how will it take place?

Community Elementary Schools Proposal. In October 1969, after 20 months of study, the San Francisco consulting firm engaged to develop a "Long Range Sites and Facilities Plan" for the district presented its report. In addition to resolving the question of what to do about the 20 inner-city schools that do not meet earthquake standards, Knight, Gladieux and Smith were also to "point the way toward elimination of de facto segregation and relieving of ethnic imbalance."[72]

The major recommendation of Knight, Gladieux and Smith was the establishment of four new "community elementary schools" in attendance areas served by the 15 neighborhood inner-city schools that are structurally unsafe, as far as earthquake standards are concerned, plus two other elementary schools in the vicinity that are structurally sound. The report suggested two new attendance areas to replace the old attendance zones served by the 17 schools, with one primary (K–3) and one intermediate (4–6) school in each attendance area. The primary schools would enroll approximately 1,800 pupils each and the intermediate schools, about 1,400 pupils. An estimated 4,000 pupils living more than one mile from their school would be bused to community schools under this plan.

Knight, Gladieux and Smith proposed that the Sierra School site be used for the new primary school in Area 1 and that the William Land site be used for the intermediate school. The Theodore Judah site was proposed for the new primary elementary school in Area 2 and it was suggested that the intermediate school in this area be built at the site of the old California State Fairgrounds, where a new central administration building would also be built. The present administration offices must be moved because of expansion of the State Capitol building.

Replacing the old attendance lines of the 17 schools with two broader attendance areas would result in the following racial and ethnic distribution for this part of the District:

Racial and Ethnic Distribution

Area	Total Enrollment	Caucasian (%)	Black (%)	Mexican (%)	Oriental (%)	Other Nonwhite (%)
1	3,088	44	18	19	17	2
2	3,077	53	22	21	2	2

As for school segregation problems outside the inner-city area, the report proposed: (1) continuation of the Argonaut busing program "at least for the immediate future";[73] and (2) a new desegregation plan for Camellia and Elder Creek, such as pairing these two schools with nearby, predominantly Caucasian schools, or closing the schools and assigning the pupils to other schools with predominantly majority enrollments. Specifically Knight, Gladieux and Smith suggested pairing Camellia and Elder Creek with the adjacent Nicholas and Clayton B. Wire Schools. Both are outside the Sacramento city limits, but within the school district's boundaries. Pairing these schools, plus the Argonaut busing, would mean that the district would bus about 700 children in those areas.

At the secondary level, the report recommended rehabilitating and modernizing Kit Carson and California Junior High Schools; rehabilitating Crocker Elementary, adjacent to California Junior High School and converting it to an annex to California; and rehabilitating and modernizing Sacramento Senior High School. The report recognized no problems of racial and ethnic imbalance at the junior and senior high school level although both California and Sutter Junior High Schools and Sacramento Senior High School were over 50 percent minority by 1969. Several other junior high schools were then approaching a 50 percent minority enrollment.

A total of 10 existing elementary schools and one existing junior high school would be permanently closed under the plan recommended. This number included Washington and Lincoln schools, already abandoned by the district as regular schools by the time the study was completed. The report proposed that four other elementary schools, including American Legion, be brought up to minimum structural standards and used for adult education, continuation schools, and special education facilities. One of the results of the recommended plan would be the closing or converting of all the city's elementary schools that had previously had predominantly minority enrollments. (See Table 5.)

As to future building, the report stated that two junior high schools and one senior high school should be constructed in the outlying eastern and south Sacramento suburbs by 1978. The report did not explicitly call for the building of new elementary schools in suburban areas, but projected the need for 10 new elementary schools in the eastern and southwestern suburbs by 1985. Costs for building these schools, already part of earlier master plans developed by the district, were included in the "package price" for the report's recommendations.

The total cost of all sites and facilities recommended up to 1985 was estimated at $43.3 million, with an added $5.1 million allowance for escalation in new construction costs. The complete "package" included a new special education building for the orthopedically handicapped, the replacing of 100 portable classrooms currently owned by the district, new offices for the central administration, and the new schools recommended for suburban areas. Approximately $19 million of the total figure would be used for converting and replacing the pre-1933 schools; $2.7 million for new administrative facilities and new portable classrooms; and a little over $21 million would be spent for new schools in suburban areas. In addition, the annual cost of busing children to the community elementary schools, plus continuation of current desegregation busing from Argonaut, Camellia, and Elder Creek, was estimated at $250,000. Approximately $50,000 of the projected busing costs appeared to be reimbursable by

Table 5—Recommendations for Schools in Inner-City Area Under Long-Range Sites and Facilities Plan

	Close	Rehabilitate	New Facility	Converted Use
Structurally Unsafe Schools				
Elementary				
Bret Harte	√			
Coloma	√			
Crocker		√		Junior High
David Lubin	√			
Donner	√			
El Dorado		√		Adult Education
Fremont	√			
Lincoln	√			
Marshall	√			
Newton Booth	√			
Riverside		√		Special Education
Sierra			√	
Tahoe		√		Continuation H.S.
Washington	√			
William Land			√	
Secondary				
California Junior		√		
Kit Carson Junior		√		
Lincoln Junior	√			
Sacramento Senior		√		
American Legion		√		Adult Education
Structurally Safe Schools				
Jedediah Smith	√			
Theodore Judah			√	

Source: Knight, Gladieux and Smith, Inc., *Long-Range Sites and Facilities Plan. Sacramento City Unified School District, Sacramento, California* (San Francisco: Knight, Gladieux and Smith, Oct. 6, 1969), f. v. 75.

the state, setting the estimated cost to the district at about $200,000.

Knight, Gladieux and Smith offered two alternative plans for the Field Act segregation problems based on more extensive one-way busing or two-way busing between existing schools. They warned, however:

> continuation of one-way busing out of minority group neighborhoods will probably be opposed by a significant proportion of minority group parents; but on the other hand, extensive two-way busing between minority and majority group neighborhoods will be opposed by a considerable proportion of majority group parents.[74]

In effect, the "Long Range Sites and Facilities Plan" proposed two essentially different approaches to elementary education for the district: the development of large educational parks for the inner city with enrollments including a substantial number of minority students, and continuation of the smaller, predominantly Caucasian neighborhood schools for most of the outlying areas.

New Desegregation Plans Debated. In February and March 1970, the school board held a series of five public hearings on the proposed plan for community elementary schools. The hearings took place in different parts of the city and were attended on each night by about 100 to 200 people. Statements presented to the board bore out Knight, Gladieux and Smith's prediction that "there is no 'right' plan" as far as community acceptance is concerned; that there would be "considerable support for, as well as opposition to almost any plan."[75] The *Sacramento Union* reported, for example, that testimony at the first hearing "clearly supported continuation of the neighborhood schools," with 15 of the 18 speakers flatly opposing the idea of community schools.[76] Most of the opinion expressed at the second hearing was also described as negative, but the bulk of the 18 persons testifying at the third hearing were generally favorable to the proposed plan.

Much of the opposition at the hearings focused on busing and preserving the neighborhood school and in this respect the dialogue was reminiscent of public reaction to the cluster plan in 1965. Press reports indicated the recurrence of themes such as, "I want the neighborhood school," busing is bewildering to small children, one-way (minority) busing is adequate, and "I don't want my children bused."[77] There was also opposition to the prospect of a bond proposal to implement the plan and some speakers denied the need for rehabilitating the schools to withstand earthquakes. There appeared to be less intensity and less panic on the part of citizens who were against the community school plan, as compared with the cluster plan, however.

The central administration, including the superintendent, backed the proposed plan and several members of the board were known to favor it. At least two board members chided the opposition at the hearings for being narrow and unrealistic as far as busing and the neighborhood school issue were concerned. Board member Hugh F. Melvin, Jr., who supported the community school plan, asked toward the end of the first hearing if it were "fair that only [some] minorities are bused and people with white skin or yellow skin aren't?" He added, "Don't stand there and tell me, 'I like the neighborhood school.' That doesn't help a damn bit. Tell us how you feel, but listen to the problem." Elaborating further, Mr. Melvin stated:

> These problems aren't going away just because we don't want to face them. Let's not kid ourselves. These laws are there, and the trial courts are going to put them into effect.[78]

A new board member, William G. Rutland, the first black man and the first minority member on the board, said on the night of the second hearing that discussion of the proposed community schools had "gotten hung up in a bus." "Nobody or very few who have talked to us have seemed very concerned about what's best for all the children of the district." Rutland pointed out that the goal of community schools is to get away from racial isolation that "is not good for your child and is not good for mine."[79] Rutland was elected to the board in November 1969 and took office on January 1, 1970.

Backers of the community school idea included Harold Blomberg, a former school board president, who testified favorably at one of the hearings. Blomberg, former superintendent of schools, Dr. F. Melvyn Lawson, and two other former board members, Mrs. Alba Kuchman and Milton Schwartz, joined 63 other persons in signing a statement endorsing "some form of community elementary school" as part of the solution to the problems of Sacramento's 20 oldest schools.[80] This group offered the board their support and cooperation and called for meeting the challenge of urban decay in the inner city. Some parents spoke in favor of community elementary schools at the hearings, denying that busing is harmful, opposing the idea of minorities only being bused, and stressing the educational and social benefits possible with the kind of schools under consideration. One mother said she thought the schools would "broaden their [the children's] viewpoint."[81] Another stated that community schools offer the promise of "quality" education "which could never come from books alone."[82] At a hearing where a Pony Express parent objected to busing low income children into that area, another resident mother said that she felt that she represented 95 percent of the school's parents in saying that their children were "enriched beyond measure" by their contact with minority children. A student from John F. Kennedy Senior High School who spoke in favor of the community schools at the same hearing said that he found the opposition's attitude of "what applies to me need not apply to you," "shocking." Another high school pupil testifying at this hearing pointed to the basic lack of tolerance among many people who had been heard that night. She said, "To me, these parents are postponing the inevitable."[83]

In addition to the Knight, Gladieux and Smith community school plan, two other desegregation proposals were being discussed during the winter and early spring of 1970. Board member Dr. Jackson Faustman suggested an alternative for the Knight, Gladieux and Smith plan that involved closing only six inner-city schools violating the Field Act and developing "neighborhood elementary complexes" that were smaller and required less busing than the community school plan. Dr. Faustman proposed four such complexes on the sites of schools not meeting earthquake standards, enrolling 800 to 1,000 pupils from two or three adjacent elementary attendance zones. His plan also called for the repair of four other pre-1933 elementary schools. These schools would be kept open with their current enrollments, along with a fifth school, Coloma, which would be repaired on its present site or replaced with a new building on the old state fairgrounds. Dr. Faustman's proposal would bus about 2,700 white and minority pupils at an estimated annual cost of $100,000. One-way busing out of Oak Park would continue. The neighborhood complexes Dr. Faustman outlined would range from 50 to 73 percent minority but none would violate the district's segregation policy since no single minority group in any of the schools would exceed 39 percent of the school's enrollment.

Two different plans to desegregate Camellia were also under consideration while the community school proposal was being debated. The Knight, Gladieux and Smith study did not say much about how Camellia should be desegregated, although it suggested pairing Camellia and Elder Creek with two nearby, predominantly Caucasian schools, or closing Camellia and Elder Creek and busing pupils out. The board was already well aware of these alternatives, having discussed and temporarily rejected both in the past.

In March 1970, then-Superintendent Paul Salmon stated that he was developing a new plan for a magnet school at Camellia which would attract elementary pupils from the total city. A board vote on this proposal was scheduled and then postponed. Before a decision was made, Superintendent Salmon dropped the magnet school idea, claiming funds were not available. Salmon then suggested combining the attendance areas of Elder Creek, Peter Burnett, and Camellia in a modified Princeton plan arrangement where children in the combined attendance area would be enrolled in Camellia K-1, Elder Creek 2-3, and Peter Burnett 4-6. A vote on this proposal was scheduled and then postponed until after a decision on the community school plan. The modified Princeton plan idea did not receive community support and was never formally presented to the board for action.

On April 6, 1970 the board voted 4-1 in favor of a slightly altered version of the Knight, Gladieux and Smith proposal for community elementary schools. Board member William G. Rutland was out of town at the time the vote took place and Dr. Faustman abstained. There was no vote on Dr. Faustman's proposal. The lone dissenting vote on the community school plan was cast by Mrs. J. F. Didion, a board member of many years tenure and a vocal advocate of maintaining neighborhood schools in all parts of the district. Mrs. Didion voted against Project Aspiration in 1966 and also voted against the closing of the Lincoln school in 1969. The modified version of the Knight, Gladieux and Smith plan adopted by the board shifted the projected site for one of the community schools from Theodore Judah to David Lubin.

Defeat of Community School Proposal. In the final analysis, the proposed community school plan was defeated by district voters at the polls. In November 1970, voters in the Sacramento City Unified School District were asked to approve $43.7 million in bond and loan measures to implement the total Knight, Gladieux and Smith building sites plan. The proposal was divided into two separate items on the ballot: (1) a $25 million bond issue to build the four community elementary schools and rehabilitate other pre-1933 junior and senior high schools; and (2) an $18.6 million state loan request to meet subdivision growth needs in the eastern and southwestern sections of the district;

this money would construct two new junior high schools, a senior high school, and various elementary schools. A third bond issue measure was also on the November 1970 ballot—a $16.5 million bond issue to modernize older schools not affected by the Field Act, including McClatchy Senior High School, Joaquin Miller Junior High School, and 19 elementary schools.

All three bond and loan proposals were approved by a majority of the voters in November 1970, with 55 and 56 percent of those casting ballots endorsing each individual measure. The election was ultimately invalidated by a U.S. Supreme Court ruling, however, when the court decided in June 1971 to uphold a provision of the California constitution requiring a two-thirds vote on bond issues. The two-thirds provision had been overturned by the California State Supreme Court in June 1970 in a decision finding that a majority vote was sufficient to pass a bond issue. This ruling was under appeal at the time the community school proposal passed and action on the building program was delayed, pending the outcome of the appeal.

It is difficult to assess the degree to which November 1970 voters were reacting to increased school taxes, the earthquake safety issue, the closing of neighborhood schools, and/or the two-way busing measure built into the community school plan. The last three proposals to increase the rate of school taxes in the district had failed and, as noted earlier, sentiment against spending money to meet the state's new earthquake safety standards was expressed at public hearings. A debate over the whole issue of the new pressure from the state to make schools earthquake resistant was, in fact, running parallel to the controversy over two-way desegregation. In both cases, the opposition sounded somewhat the same note of disbelief that people in the district might have to do things they did not want to do in order to solve specific problems.

Letters to the editor published in the *Sacramento Union*, for example, tended to reject the necessity of the district's meeting state earthquake safety requirements. A total of 12 letters to the editor from Sacramento residents on the community school proposal and school desegregation in general were published in the *Union* between February 16, 1970, the day of the first hearing on the Knight, Gladieux and Smith plan, and May 15, 1970. Only one supported busing for desegregation purposes and 11 were against the community school plan. Seven of the 11 negative letters based their opposition on some aspect of the earthquake safety issue, a main theme being that "scare tactics" were being used to force the taxpayers to spend large amounts of money on schools that have been proven safe by virtue of the fact that they have been standing for so many years. Two of the letters stressed the improbability of danger from earthquakes in the Sacramento area and two challenged Sacramento's politicians and lawmakers to work for a variation in state law that would allow for different earthquake requirements in different parts of the state. The four other letters unfavorable to the community school plan concentrated on themes such as busing, keeping the neighborhood school, and forced desegregation.

Factual information on the earthquake issue, including the requirements of state law, was publicized during the hearings and prior to the school board's vote on the Knight, Gladieux and Smith plan. The *Sacramento Union* printed a detailed, school-by-school report of the findings of the engineering survey of older buildings—for example, listing the structural problems, repairs needed to meet state standards, and the projected cost of rehabilitating and modernizing each of the schools. A special television program broadcast in the Sacramento area in late March 1970 featured seismologist Charles F. Richter, an authority on earthquakes and a professor at the California Institute of Technology, Pasadena. Richter appeared on a panel with Sacramento's Superintendent of Schools, the president of the school board, and the district's consulting engineer. The Superintendent of Schools from Stockton, California also participated in the program. Richter stated that the last two earthquakes in Sacramento took place in 1892, but that "given time," a moderate to heavy earthquake in Sacramento is "a near certainty."[84] Richter supported the structural changes in schools required by the Field Act, based on other districts' experiences with earthquakes in 1940 and 1952. He said a moderate to heavy earthquake in Sacramento would possibly cause partial collapse of the older schools. Many people in the Sacramento district apparently remained unconvinced, however.

New State Policy on Desegregation. Before another proposal for Field Act-desegregation problems was fully approved by the board, a new set of controversial state regulations making more demands on public schools to establish racial and ethnic balance was passed by the California legislature. California state policy on desegregation was relatively weak when Sacramento's desegregation began, particularly in crucial areas such as defining segregation, setting a goal of racial balance for local districts, and effective procedures to enforce desegregation where districts failed to end segregation voluntarily. In the absence of any real standards, and a policy on the part of the board of "assisting" districts rather than insisting on desegregation, progress at the local level was largely dependent on court suits and whatever pressure citizens of a community could bring to bear. Leadership from the State Department of Education was limited and declining in the face of growing opposition to busing. The state Office of Compensatory Education had used the leverage of federal funds to help pressure Sacramento into starting to desegregate its elementary schools, in 1966, for instance, but had not continued to use this same leverage to move the district toward a comprehensive desegregation plan. While then-State Superintendent of Public Instruction Max Rafferty gave formal lip service to existing regulations on desegregation and equal opportunity in education, he openly opposed "compulsory busing" and staunchly defended a parent's "right to send his own children to school in his own neighborhood."[85]

The State Board of Education strengthened its guidelines on desegregation effective March 1969, amending Section 2011, Title 5, California Administrative Code, to require local districts to submit statistics on the racial composition of schools and "study and consider possible alternative plans when the percentage of pupils of one or more racial or ethnic groups differs significantly from the districtwide percentage." A more precise definition of racial and ethnic imbalance was also inserted in the regulations and it was this provision that touched off the most opposition. Specifically, the new racial balance formula provided that:

> . . . racial or ethnic imbalance is indicated in a school if the percentage of pupils of one or more racial or ethnic groups differs by more than 15 percentage points from that in all schools of the district.

In addition to these amendments, the old Section 2010 of Title 5 was changed to instruct districts to give "high priority" to the "prevention and elimination of racial and ethnic imbalance . . . in all decisions relating to school sites, school attendance areas and school attendance practices."[86] The new regulations were followed by an evaluation of the status of racial and ethnic imbalance in each school district, based on a survey covering the 1968–69 school year. A total of 197 California districts with schools violating the ethnic balance guidelines were then asked to submit a progress report by June 1, 1970, showing evidence of planning to correct racial balance.

Sacramento had 33 schools that were out of balance under the new regulations in 1968–69, but the guidelines were not taken seriously by top school district leadership. The new racial balance formula was not incorporated into the proposal developed by Knight, Gladieux and Smith, for instance, although their final report was completed eight months after the new regulations were published. Sacramento's Board of Education and Superintendent F. Melvyn Lawson had opposed the racial balance definition publicly in 1967, when it was first under consideration, stating it was "too strong and too strict" and placed an "unrealistic" burden on school systems.[87] When asked about implementing the new guidelines in the late spring of 1969, school officials responded that the Sacramento district was well ahead of many other California school systems in eliminating segregation, that the new guidelines had not been tested in the courts, and that the district had recently been cited by the State Department of Education as one of ten outstanding districts in California, based on its use of federal Elementary and Secondary Education Act funds. There were no indications at that time that any attempt would be made to comply with the new formula. The community school proposal was based on the district's rather than the state's definition of segregation and would have established racial balance, according to the new state definition, in only one of the two large inner-city attendance areas created. A total of 21 existing schools would still fail to meet the new state policy had the Knight, Gladieux and Smith plan been implemented, and most of the new schools they proposed would also be classified as imbalanced by the new state regulations, since they were located in predominantly white neighborhoods.

From early 1970 until January 1971, while the board and public in Sacramento were considering the community school proposal, the new state guidelines were in a state of flux, with the outcome uncertain. In March 1970, following citation of the regulations in a February 11 ruling on the Los Angeles schools by Superor Court Judge Alfred E. Gitelson, the state board repealed the guidelines without notice or a hearing in a so-called "emergency" meeting. Judge Gitelson had said that the constitution and the state board's regulations imposed an "absolute" duty to desegregate and integrate schools on a districtwide basis and that the Los Angeles board was in error in thinking that the state board's rules

only "seem to require each district continually to strive, insofar as seems feasible" to [the] board "to achieve this ideal racial and ethnic balance."[88]

Los Angeles school officials were ordered to prepare a plan
that distributed pupils in accordance with the regulations, which
meant that large-scale busing would be necessary. At the same
time, as the ethnic balance guidelines were repealed, the board
passed a resolution making known its "disfavor" of the regulations being used in support of mass busing. The board also
went on record "as favoring the achievement of ethnic balance
in California public schools by means other than compulsory
busing." Howard Day, president of the State Board of Education,
defended repeal of the new regulations on the ground that the
board's "good intentions" had been "distorted" by the courts
in recent decisions. "It was never the intention of the State Board
of Education as it existed in 1969 to have judges use our advisory
guidelines as ironclad rules of law," Mr. Day stated.[89] The 1969
regulations had also figured in a recent case in Pasadena, where
a U.S. district judge ordered full-scale desegregation.

The board's decision to rescind the 1969 guidelines was
blocked in May 1970 by a court suit filed in the Sacramento
County Superior Court by Nathaniel S. Colley, a black Sacramento attorney who was formerly a member of the State Board
of Education. An NAACP national board member, Colley had
drafted the original guidelines on school segregation for the
State Board of Education. He based his challenge to the board's
repeal on the failure of the board to make a proper finding
of an emergency that would justify their hasty action. Colley's
suit was filed on behalf of his son, a student in Sam Brannon
Junior High School, and on behalf of all similarly situated pupils
in the Sacramento district. Following reinstatement of the regulations under court order on May 26, 1970, the state board
appointed an ad hoc committee to study and recommend a set
of substitute regulations. Protests from organizations, agencies,
and school districts at public hearings discouraged the board
from continuing in this attempt. Meanwhile, state Superintendent of Public Instruction Max Rafferty, who had suggested
the repeal to help the Los Angeles board in its appeal of the
Gitelson decision, was defeated at the polls in the fall of 1970.
Rafferty was replaced by Dr. Wilson Riles, formerly a consultant
in the Bureau of Intergroup Relations, State Department of
Education, which administers school desegregation policy. Riles
was the director of the Office of Compensatory Education
immediately prior to his election as State Superintendent. Soon
after taking office on January 27, 1971, Dr. Riles issued a direc-
tive to all school districts and superintendents of schools informing them of the reinstatement of the ethnic balance regulations.

The Bureau of Intergroup Relations had continued to implement the guidelines during the controversy.

New legislation passed by the California legislature during its 1971 session incorporated most of the provisions of the 1969 revised guidelines into state law as Sections 5002 and 5003 of the Education Code. Assemblyman William T. Bagley (R-Marin County), who introduced the bill, also sponsored a second successful bill which instructed the State Department of Education to spend an estimated $2 million in federal funds to improve racial integration in the California schools. The new Section 5002 of the Education Code is stronger in one respect than the revised 1969 regulations, since it states that persons or agencies responsible for pupil assignments or school attendance centers *"shall prevent and eliminate* racial and ethnic imbalance in pupil enrollment." (Emphasis added.) Section 5003 defines racial or ethnic imbalance in more general terms than the 1969 regulations, providing that

> racial or ethnic imbalance is indicated in a school if the percentage of pupils of one or more racial or ethnic groups differs significantly from the district-wide percentage.[90]

The Bagley bill gives the Department of Education the authority to require desegregation plans where racial imbalance exists, to determine the adequacy of a district's plans and schedules to accomplish desegregation, and to adopt rules and regulations to carry out the intent of the legislation. The final authority for compelling desegregation is left with the State Board of Education, however. No time limit for achieving racial balance in the districts is set and no penalties for non-compliance are outlined. The Bagley bill became effective in March 1972 and new Board of Education regulations to implement it were not expected for at least several months after the law went into effect.

Desegregated Middle Schools? Shortly before the state legislature passed the new laws on racial and ethnic balance, district officials tentatively adopted a second major plan to correct Field Act and segregation problems. This plan was still being evaluated and revised early in 1972.

District administrators began to restudy alternatives for a building program to meet earthquake, desegregation, and long-range growth needs immediately after the June 1971 court decision invalidated the bond issue on community schools. A report from staff submitted to the board on June 28 recommended dropping the overall plan developed by Knight, Gladieux and Smith and instead considering the possibility of a building proposal based on a change to middle schools. Knight, Gladieux and Smith had investigated the prospects of converting to middle schools in 1968 and 1969 but did not recommend this, since it would cost more than other alternatives and they did not believe it was then economically feasible. By mid-1971, however, with new state funds available for rehabilitating or replacing pre-1933 schools and a change in the availability of state loans, the district's Research and Development Services Office felt that a building program linked to middle schools could be financed. At the suggestion of state Assemblyman Leroy Green, chairman of the Assembly Education Committee, the district also began investigating the idea of operating schools on a year-round basis, as a means of reducing future building needs.

On November 29, 1971, the board approved "in concept" an overall sites and facilities plan that was based on a middle school, or K–5, 6–8, 9–12, grade organization pattern. This proposal, which was to be developed in detail for the board's further consideration in February 1972, abandoned the idea of large community elementary schools, offering new K–5 schools that would enroll an optimum of about 600 pupils. The new middle schools, which would replace existing junior high schools, were each to have about 900 students. In another key strategy area, the November 1971 plan tried to straddle the issue of adhering to the state guidelines on racial and ethnic balance. One "basic assumption" of the proposal was that the plan would follow the district's 1965 policy on desegregation—that is, that it would alleviate or eliminate the adverse effects of segregation in schools where one minority makes up more than 50 percent of the enrollment. Another "general provision" said, however, "Each senior high school attendance area would serve as a basic unit for providing ethnic balance K–12."[91] This language implied that the guidelines would be met, but there was no specific commitment to do so and no discussion in the staff's written statement as to the impact of the proposal on the racial and ethnic composition of individual schools or the broader senior high school attendance areas suggested. As one of many California districts with segregated and imbalanced schools, the board was due to submit a progress report on its plans for eliminating racial imbalance to the State Department of Education in January 1972. The November 1971 proposal, which suggested compliance without specifically committing the board or spelling out the ways and means by which concentrations of minorities were to be reduced, was forwarded to the Bureau of Intergroup Relations, State Department of Education, in January 1972.

The November 1971 plan outlined a rather drastic approach to Field Act problems in the pre-1933 inner-city elementary schools and it was this part of the proposal that was put aside temporarily on February 8, 1972. This segment of the plan provided for abandoning all of the older schools in the heart of the downtown area, where most schools have a heavily minority enrollment. Specifically, Lincoln and Washington, already discontinued as regular schools, would be torn down and razed along with William Land, Newton Booth, Fremont, and Marshall. Staff pointed out that several of these schools were currently kept open by Project Aspiration busing from Oak Park. A few elementary schools in the next tier of residential areas surrounding the core of the city were also to be leveled and replaced by semi-permanent structures with a life expectancy of 25 years. The rest of the pre-1933 grade schools in this vicinity were to be converted to special purpose schools or abandoned. David Lubin, El Dorado, and Sierra were the three elementary schools tentatively selected to be replaced as regular elementary schools with temporary units. A third group of schools in the next circle of residential areas, including Caleb Greenwood, Phoebe A. Hearst, Tahoe, and Theodore Judah, were to be enlarged by placing one or more semi-permanent structures on the sites. These schools would presumably receive more bused children from inner-city neighborhoods losing their own schools. Donner was among the pre-1933 schools to be permanently closed and Camellia was to be converted to a middle school. No specific proposal for housing Camellia's elementary enrollment was discussed, but it was recognized that alternative facilities would have to be provided with Camellia's conversion.

Beyond the elementary level, middle schools enrolling pupils in grades 6–8 were to be set up, primarily in the district's existing junior high schools. Nine junior high schools built since 1933 were to be converted to middle schools along with Camellia, and the November proposal also projected two new middle schools, one to be built in the eastern suburbs and another in the southwest corner of the district. In addition, the November plan recommended rebuilding or rehabilitating California Junior High School on its present site and utilizing this school as a middle school in combination with Crocker elementary, located adjacent to the California plant and also in need of repair to meet earthquake standards. Two middle schools were to serve each senior high school attendance area, with new high school zones providing the basis for better racial balance at the middle school level.

The middle school proposal was tentatively revised in February 1972 to substitute the conversion of Bear Flag elementary to a middle school, eliminating the need for construction of a new school for grades 6–8 in the southwest "pocket" section. The revised February plan also considered remodelling Joaquin Miller Junior High School as a middle school, instead of California, and abandoning California in 1975 when state law prohibits further use of schools not meeting earthquake requirements. The board postponed firm agreement on which of these two schools would be converted to a middle school at the end of February, as it was also examining the possibility of remodelling Joaquin Miller as an adult education facility. How Bear Flag and Camellia elementary children would be reassigned was also undetermined by the February 22 meeting. Another possibility under discussion was the rehabilitation of Kit Carson Junior High School, also a pre-1933 school, as a continuation high school. If this were done, Kit Carson would absorb the continuation school located at American Legion, the formerly black elementary school, converted to a special purpose facility as a part of Project Aspiration.

At the high school level, major features of the November 1971 proposal included rebuilding Sacramento Senior High School on a "neutral" site, constructing a new senior high school in the eastern suburbs, and revising high school attendance areas to balance school enrollments and the ethnic composition of students. No definite site for the new Sacramento High School building was named when the board adopted the "concept" of the November plan, but on February 8, 1972, the staff proposed relocating Sacramento High in East Sacramento on the grounds of Kit Carson Junior High School. This site would transplant Sacramento High School from Oak Park to a predominantly white residential section. Grant Bennett, a board member who supported this move when it was first introduced, stated that he "hoped it would result in reattracting East Sacramento students to Sacramento High."[92] Bennett said that many East Sacramento residents have taken their children from the public schools and placed them in private or parochial schools in recent years, in response to racial incidents in Sacramento High. In addition to rebuilding Sacramento High School and constructing a new high school in the eastern suburbs, the plan recommended the remodelling of McClatchy Senior High School to modernize it. McClatchy is structurally sound, but lacks some of the features of more recently built schools such as a swimming pool, tennis courts, air conditioning, and up-to-date gymnasium, labs, and shops.

Exactly how the senior high schools would be balanced under the November 1971 proposal was not spelled out, but possible new attendance boundaries, based on six senior high schools, were outlined on a map presented with the overall plan. This map showed attendance lines from Sacramento High School extending eastward to include some of the new, predominantly white subdivisions. Similarly, the heavily black and minority Glen Elder section in the southeast corner of the district was in a zone that also took in other predominantly white suburbs to the east.

The November 1971 plan also suggested instituting a pilot program of year-round schools at the John F. Kennedy Senior High School and all of its feeder schools, on the condition that residents of the area would support such a project. Year-round high schools throughout the system were to be considered later, depending on the success of the Kennedy project. Rehabilitating Riverside elementary as a secondary continuation school, to house the program currently located at Lincoln, was another provision of the proposal affecting the district's high schools.

By the end of February 1972, the board had acted on several facets of the general plan adopted in November 1971 and had agreed to work out the final details of two major segments by April, so that the necessary bond and loan election items could be placed on the June 1972 primary ballot. The board decided on February 22, 1972, after hearing new recommendations from staff, to concentrate on the middle school and high school sections of the November plan, postponing resolution of the elementary Field Act-segregation problems until the fall of 1972. Staff stated at a special meeting on the proposed plan on Feburary 8, 1972 that enrollments in the inner city were dropping rapidly, but, more important, that

> after a study of many alternatives at the elementary level it was clear that public involvement and understanding over a period of time would be required before a final plan could be suggested.[93]

There was time, the staff noted, even with this delay, to correct earthquake violations before the 1975 deadline. In addition to these factors, uncertainty as to the future of busing for racial balance, high estimates of the cost of busing to establish racial balance at the elementary level, and a reluctance on the part of the board to adopt a two-way busing proposal were also behind the board's decision to put off action on the elementary schools. Discussion of the November 1971 proposal coincided with an upsurge of political attacks on busing at the national level generated by the Richmond, Virginia decision and the 1972 Presidential campaign. Debate over continued use of federal funds, especially Title I funds, for busing also contributed to the board's hesitation to commit the district to a more extensive busing program.

At the high school level, the board agreed on February 22 to accept the basic concept of six attendance areas for the district and also adopted a slightly modified version of the senior high school attendance zones proposed by staff in November 1971. The new attendance areas, according to Dr. Donald Hall, Assistant Superintendent, Research and Development Services Office, will give the district the capability of establishing racial balance at the senior high school and middle school levels. Present enrollment patterns indicate that with the new zones, the district could meet the state racial balance guidelines at the high school level in all schools except McClatchy, which would enroll more Asian students than allowed under the state racial balance formula. The board had not yet adopted a definite policy stand that it would conform with the state guidelines, however.

A firm commitment to rebuild Sacramento High School on its present site was also voted on February 22, 1972, and the board agreed to submit a request for $35 million in local bonds and state loans on the June 1972 ballot. The staff's February 8th report had estimated that the various changes and new building recommended at the middle school and high school levels could be financed with $27 million in local bonds and $8 million in state loans. The basic approach to middle schools outlined in the November proposal was also approved, with the provision that Bear Flag and Camellia would both be converted to middle schools. Plans for reassigning Camellia and Bear Flag elementary children were still open and several other specifics of the middle school and high school proposal were undecided. The board agreed to work out all details of the middle school and high school segments of the plan by April 1972, keeping costs within a $35 million bond and loan request.

Future Desegregation—When and How? In early 1972, as the board considered new building plans related to desegregation and ethnic balance, three elementary schools were officially identified as segregated by local policy—Camellia and Donner, discussed many times already, and William Land, which became

51 percent Asian in 1969 when it merged with nearby Lincoln elementary, which was closed without a desegregation plan. Camellia was 85 percent black and 96 percent minority during the 1970–71 school year; Donner, 64 percent black and 79 percent minority; and William Land, already overwhelmingly minority before its population merged with Lincoln's, was 51 percent Asian and 86 percent minority in 1970–71. Riverside elementary, which was 51 percent Asian in 1963 when the district's first racial census was taken, had dropped off the district's list of segregated schools in 1967. The increased proportion of whites in Riverside was the result of two factors—a steady decline in the Asian population, a trend that is still continuing, and a temporary increase in Caucasian pupils resulting from a gifted students program housed in Riverside in 1967–68. By 1970–71, Caucasians made up 52 percent of Riverside's students; Mexicans, 6 percent, and blacks, 3 percent. The school's total enrollment was down 89 pupils from the number attending in 1963 and the percentage of Asian children had gone down to 38 percent.

In addition to the three elementary schools identified as segregated by local policy, schools dominated by several minorities and other schools with ethnic concentrations high enough to violate the state regulations on racial and ethnic balance are now the most serious situation facing the district. Sacramento had 34 racially and ethnically imbalanced schools according to the state guidelines in the fall of 1971. A total of 16 of these are regular schools where over half the student enrollment is made up of one or more racial minority groups; there are 13 such elementary schools, two junior high schools, and one senior high school. In addition, three special schools—continuation schools at the junior and senior high school levels—are out of balance because the student body has too high a concentration of one or more minorities. Two more regular elementary schools currently have too high a proportion of Asian children and another has too high a percentage of Mexican pupils. Besides these schools, ten more elementary schools and two more junior high schools are imbalanced because they have too many Caucasians in their student populations. Under the state formula now in force, a school in Sacramento is racially imbalanced if it is more than 30 percent black, 27 percent Mexican, 23 percent Asian, or 16 percent Indian. A school is also classified as imbalanced by the state if a combination of two or more minorities make up more than 50 percent of its enrollment, or if it has a minority student population of less than 21 percent.

While the district's desegregation policy has been aimed at schools dominated by single minorities and has reduced the percentage of black and Mexican pupils attending this kind of segregated school, it has left substantial numbers of racial and ethnic minority pupils in multi-minority schools, especially at the elementary level. The number of such schools has not been substantially reduced and the percentage of Asian children in multiminority schools is actually growing, as the figures below show:

Year	Number of Schools with Minority Enrollments of 50% or More	Enrollment of Minority Students in Predominantly Minority Elementary Schools		
		Black %	Mexican %	Asian %
1965–66	14	71	50	21
1968–69	17	46	46	36
1970–71	13	39	32	32

The situation currently facing the district is far different from what it was in 1963 when the question of junior high school and elementary segregation was first raised. Beginning in March 1972, new state policy on racial and ethnic balance, which the district has been loath to accept, has the force of state law. The new legislation requires local districts to prevent as well as eliminate racial imbalance. State Board of Education leadership in enforcing the new law is open to question, but the current direction of the California state and U.S. district courts in California is clear. Recent rulings have not only upheld the right and duty of school districts and the courts to establish racial balance, but have also required boards to put the state racial balance guidelines into effect through comprehensive, districtwide desegregation plans that must be implemented in fairly short order. At least two U.S. district courts, in cases involving San Francisco and Oxnard, California schools, have banned one-way busing or busing of minority pupils only to bring about desegregation. The San Francisco decision called that district to task for building programs that reinforced separation, for failure to recruit and upgrade minority teachers, and for in-school discrimination stemming from the tracking of students. Furthermore, a California State Supreme Court decision in January 1971 neutralized the impact of a state anti-busing law passed in 1970 to thwart busing in connection with desegregation plans.[94]

The Sacramento district has continuously discussed desegregation of the Camellia and Donner schools since the mid-1960s
and has reviewed and debated other, broader desegregation
plans. But when and how will more desegregation take place?
The current plan, based on middle schools, was still undefined
in many crucial respects in early 1972 when this report was
completed. While this plan is more comprehensive than any
other considered to date, in that it covers all school levels and
has the capability for providing racial balance at all levels, it
will require (1) at least two bond issues, (2) coordination with
the state guidelines on racial and ethnic balance, and (3) extensive
busing and/or two-way desegregation at the elementary level,
if the state racial balance regulations are to be met. A specific
plan for reassigning Camellia elementary children, the stumbling
block in all plans considered to date, a policy decision to meet
the state guidelines at all school levels, and a definite plan for
assigning children at the elementary level were still open at the
time this report was finished. Given that these problems are
resolved, there is also the question of public support for financing
the plan at the polls.

Clearly, further desegregation, especially comprehensive desegregation, requires a great deal of committed and wholehearted leadership from the board, the kind of leadership it
has been reluctant to assume on the issue of desegregation for
some time. In view of the increasing alientation of the district's
minority groups because of school closings and differential
treatment in desegregation plans, a third basic question is
whether blacks and Mexicans, especially, would support the
November 1971 elementary proposal as it now stands. To be
acceptable to minority groups, the elementary segment of the
proposal will probably have to be revised to keep some formerly
minority schools open on a desegregated basis and to insure
that whites, blacks, Mexicans, and other minorities will be bused
on an equal basis.

In early 1972 the board had several new assets to aid in desegregation. In addition to a new state law requiring racial and
ethnic balance, beginning January 1972 the board had its first
black president, William Rutland, and also seated a new Asian
member elected in November 1971. With the force of state law
behind it and better minority representation, the district would
be wise to go ahead with the broadest kind of desegregation
plan possible, before its problems become more acute. This will
require leadership, an educational campaign, greater involvement of minorities in shaping decisions and interpreting their

needs to the majority community, and political risks on the part
of the board and administration. Establishing complete desegregation and racial balance would also involve gains, and one
gain should be the lessening of a great deal of racial unrest
and tension that has troubled many people.

10.
Summary and Conclusions

Urban Renewal, Housing Policy and School Segregation.
Racial segregation and ethnic imbalance in the Sacramento
schools became an acute problem in the early 1960s largely because of the buildup of black and other minority concentrations
in several residential areas of the city. The development of
separate, heavily black, Mexican, and Asian sections, a relatively
new phenomenon in Sacramento, resulted partly from the city's
urban renewal program, which destroyed older, multi-minority
neighborhoods without providing replacement housing on a
non-segregated basis, and partly from housing discrimination,
which is aimed at blacks more than at other minority groups.
The city's failure to provide adequate community services and
facilities to a new, interracial community in the southeast corner
of the city and school district helped to make that subdivision
a predominantly black and minority area. In the absence of any
action on the part of the Board of Education to plan new
schools, adjust boundaries or assign students to prevent and reduce minority concentrations, school segregation developed in
these newly emerged racially segregated residential areas.

**Building Program Intensifies Inner City/Suburban Dif-
ferences.** City and school district annexations of large parcels
of suburban land, some not yet developed, plus the merger of
the Sacramento City Unified School District with some suburban
elementary districts outside the city, more than doubled the size
of the school district in the late 1950s and set the stage for
a second kind of discrimination against minorities in the inner

city. Active neighborhood school building in these outlying subdivisions, coupled with little money spent in the heart of the
city, intensified the contrast between older, heavily minority
schools in the inner city and the newer, Caucasian schools in
suburban areas. The differential in building plans and programs
for the inner city versus the white suburbs has carried over
into recent sites and facilities proposals involving desegregation.
Minority leaders are aware of gaps in spending, school plants,
and school closing in their neighborhoods as opposed to the
white suburbs, and the continuation of this kind of double discrimination has compounded the district's racial and ethnic
problems.

Status of Minority Achievement in Segregated Schools.
Eighth grade test scores prior to desegregation were lower in
the two junior high schools with the heaviest concentrations of
minorities, and evaluations of the achievement and ability test
scores of junior high school and elementary pupils since desegregation have generally indicated that minority pupils in segregated schools do not progress quite as well academically as
their counterparts in desegregated schools. While district officials did not admit a correlation between segregation and
achievement in the early 1960s, when pressure to desegregate
the junior high schools was first mounted, they have since concluded that minority pupils remaining in segregated schools do
not perform as well academically as their peers in integrated
schools. This has placed an additional pressure on the district
to carry out further desegregation, since the whole rationale
for integrating schools has been to reduce the unfavorable
educational effects of segregation.

Importance of State Policy to Desegregation. State policy
encouraging districts to avoid and eliminate segregation, and
State Board of Education regulations requiring the consideration of racial and ethnic factors in establishing school attendance
boundaries, were important influences in Sacramento's first
major desegregation, which took place under court order at
the junior high school level. Later, state board policy and State
Department of Education guidelines concerning the use of compensatory education funds were key factors in bringing about
Sacramento's initial elementary desegregation project. Although
the potential for state action to insist that local districts desegregate has increased, with new State Board of Education regulations and new state legislation on racial and ethnic balance, Sac-

ramento has recently enjoyed a kind of moratorium from state pressure, partly because the district has undertaken some voluntary desegregation and has proposed additional integration plans.

The positive impact of state policy on Sacramento's desegregation in the early and mid-1960s illustrates the effectiveness of state regulations and guidelines, provided they are actively enforced at the local level. With the passage of a new state law requiring districts to prevent and eliminate racial and ethnic imbalance effective in March 1972, the State Board of Education and the State Department of Education have a basis for exerting considerably more influence and authority over the planning and pace of local desegregation. New state regulations to implement this legislation should not only set a time limit for compliance, but should also provide for sanctions such as the withholding of state funds where districts fail to establish racial balance. Once more stringent regulations are written, persistent enforcement is necessary to make the new law and guidelines meaningful.

Federal Policy and Desegregation. Title VI of the Civil Rights Act of 1964 was also important to the beginning of Sacramento's elementary desegregation, since state policy and guidelines on the use of federal Title I ESEA funds not only prohibited discrimination, but also linked eligibility to affirmative efforts on the part of local districts to reduce high concentrations of minority pupils. Interest in qualifying for these and other federal funds, coupled with local community demands for desegregation, helped bring about the district's first partial desegregation project in the elementary schools. With financial problems in the district becoming more serious in the past few years, continued ability to receive federal funds has become more important; further partial desegregation projects have been launched and discussed. Pressure to conform with Title VI has been indirect rather than direct, since Sacramento was not involved in a federal complaint of segregation or discrimination nor in any direct confrontation with HEW over problems of segregation and racial imbalance.

Sacramento's situation, in fact, illustrates the shortcomings in HEW's enforcement of Title VI in northern school systems. With no clear definition of "segregation" or "desegregation" in northern systems, no deadline for ending racial concentrations in predominantly minority schools, and no complaints of segregation from the local level, Sacramento can probably go on indefinitely receiving federal funds for partial desegregation projects while failing to end segregation in other, overwhelmingly minority schools. This kind of situation has existed since passage of the Civil Rights Act and should be remedied by new, realistic HEW guidelines and regulations for school desegregation that can be applied effectively to the north as well as to the south.

Evolution of Desegregation Leadership and Support.
Black-led civil rights organizations were responsible for the initial challenge to segregation in Sacramento's schools and for mobilizing the pressures that resulted in the district's first desegregation efforts in predominantly black schools in the early and mid-1960s. Liberal whites and a few key leaders from other ethnic communities joined blacks in these early desegregation campaigns, but broad community support and involvement had waned by the late 1960s when the district began desegregation in the one Mexican-dominated school in the city. Leadership for desegregation had by this time shifted to district administrators and board members, who alienated a large segment of the Mexican community by refusing to give serious consideration to their demand for an integrated school in their area that would bus in whites and offer a bilingual, bicultural educational program tailored to meet the needs of the Mexican community.

The district has not only made desegregation more difficult by postponing much of it past the time when key minority and majority leaders and groups were organized and active around desegregation goals; it has also courted the dissatisfaction of minority groups by proposing plans that rely heavily on school closings in their neighborhoods. With organized support for desegregation generally on the decline, plans that make more equitable demands on all segments of the community would strengthen the board's support among members of minority groups, who are in the best position to make a case for integration to the white public. Support for the future is extremely important, since the board is now considering a desegregation plan linked to a building program requiring a bond issue.

Adoption of Local Desegregation Policy. The Sacramento district's written policy on school desegregation, adopted in the mid-1960s, put the board on record as to its responsibilities and committed the district to a course of action. While this policy was an important step in beginning elementary desegregation and has continued to act as a pressure on the board, it has several major weaknesses and is now outdated in light of the provisions of subsequent State Board of Education regulations and new state legislation requiring districts to prevent and eliminate racial and ethnic imbalance in the schools. If Sacramento is to work realistically within the framework of state policy, its present board statement on desegregation should be revised to bring it in line with new state requirements.

Need for New Definition of Segregation. One of the chief shortcomings of Sacramento's present policy on school desegregation is that it ignores schools where several different minorities combine to make up a substantial proportion or over half of the total enrollment. Multi-minority-dominated schools not only present many of the same problems characteristic of schools where a single minority prevails, but are now classified as racially and ethnically imbalanced by state law and policy. New state legislation and policy also considers the all-white and overwhelmingly Caucasian schools to be segregated, another kind of racial concentration overlooked by local school district policy. Sacramento needs to identify both multi-minority and overwhelmingly white schools as segregated and to make a commitment to reduce racial concentrations in these schools, along with others enrolling higher proportions of minority pupils than permitted by current state policy.

Need for Consistent Desegregation Policy and Practices. The third weakness of the district's present policy that should be corrected is the board's resolution to deal with the adverse effects of school segregation, rather than with the existence of segregation itself. This position has permitted different treatment of the various minority grups, particularly of Asians, who do not seem to suffer the same drastic academic hardships in segregated schools in Sacramento as do blacks and Mexicans. Because of its commitment to remedy the effects of segregation only, the board has overlooked segregation in predominantly Asian schools and assumed that Asian children do not need desegregation while the other minorities do. This inconsistency vis-à-vis the different minorities is not only unfair to Asian children, who benefited most academically from junior high school desegregation, but puts the board in a position of having different policies for different minority groups. A policy dealing directly with segregation would affect all elements of the population equally and insure all children the social benefits of desegregation that were widely acknowledged in interviews with school personnel, community leaders, and parents in the district.

Local Race and Ethnic Census. The annual race and ethnic census of schools, conducted by the district since 1963, has been a valuable tool in planning and implementing desegregation, helping district officials as well as community groups who wish to monitor desegregation progress. Although a similar census is now conducted by the Bureau of Intergroup Relations, State Department of Education, the local census is tabulated and published much more quickly and results are available in mid-year, in time to be used as a basis for the next year's planning. This kind of regular ethnic count is important to keeping schools desegregated.

Minority Representation in Decision-Making and Planning. With no representation on the Board of Education and almost no minority group members in top administrative positions, until recently the basic desegregation plans of the district were formed by Caucasians and then presented to the public, including minority groups, for reaction and acceptance. Since plans were already made before minority spokesmen were heard, minorities were always put in the position of being against what the administration was for, where a difference of opinion existed. Advisory committees in connection with major desegregation and compensatory education programs seemed to lead only to more frustration and conflict, since advice was frequently not accepted. In addition, the district's Intergroup Relations Service, created to assist with desegregation and racial tensions, has had no power and has tended to interpret and persuade compliance with existing policy, rather than to protect or advocate minority rights.

Recent election of two minority members to the Board of Education should help remedy the lack of representation in decision-making. In addition, other new official structures maximizing minority representation and participation should probably be created, such as the School Ombudsman proposed by Understanding Each Other in 1968 and the Community Review Board requested by Mexican high school students in 1969. Minority ombudsmen or advocates or a Community Review Board would improve the situation only if they have specific powers and functions, have the confidence of the community, and are not subservient to the interests of existing district policy.

Overall Desegregation Strategy. While the Stanford junior high school desegregation plan had several major weaknesses, including the concentration of large numbers of minority students in two of the receiving schools and failure to provide transportation, it had the virtue of settling the junior high school issue quickly so that it was over and done with. The students were dispersed, the school was gone, and there was no institution left with which students could be identified.

The board's approach to elementary desegregation, however, has been gradual and piecemeal, permitting progress but leaving some schools segregated, allowing high concentrations of minorities to build up in others, and postponing what were thought to be the more difficult problems. Practices such as maintaining the sending elementary attendance areas for junior high school assignment and keeping the same names for schools in the sending areas converted to other uses have helped create a tentative atmosphere about the program and to maintain the children's sending area identification. The board's long period of wavering and reconsideration of the desegregation of Washington School gave rise to false hopes and encouraged opposition. More recently, tieing further desegregation to lengthy studies and costly building plans has stymied progress. The net effect of all these factors has been to drag out the issue in the community and to involve district personnel in a continual process of formulating and defending plans and making preparations for future desegregation. Meanwhile, minority children continue to attend segregated schools.

In the long run, a comprehensive systemwide desegregation plan implemented in one stage and carried out with firmness seems to be fairer and easier. An effective desegregation plan should also eliminate identity with the old school or sending area and create a bond with the new school. Where busing is necessary, every effort should be made to see that children are fully associated with their new receiving school, rather than maintaining ties to the old sending area. Techniques such as changing the names of schools in the sending areas that are converted to other uses might help.

Administration of Desegregation Projects. In carrying out its various desegregation projects, especially elementary desegregation, the central administration has planned all steps carefully and, in most instances, has made a comprehensive effort to inform principals, parents, teachers, and pupils of how the plan will affect them. The notable exception to good administrative planning was, of course, the case where parents of Oak Park pupils were misinformed concerning busing of their children to Coloma and Newton Booth. The general pattern of detailed planning in advance and providing information at all levels, however, has usually resulted in a smooth working out of the mechanics of desegregation plans. Good planning and administration of desegregation eases the process and makes it much more acceptable to many people.

Pupil Orientation. Introduction of pupils to their new schools has been handled well in the district's elementary desegregation program and has assisted in the children's initial adjustment to the receiving schools. Preliminary visits to receiving schools, featuring joint activities such as sports, lunches, and festivals, have helped the children get acquainted. Informal activities such as picnics and outings in the first phase of Project Aspiration were particularly effective in helping children to know each other and in lessening the strangeness of the receiving school.

Academic and Social Gains with Desegregation. Evaluations of the academic achievement of desegregated minority children in the period since desegregation have been encouraging on the whole, indicating that these pupils are catching up and achieving at higher levels than their peers in segregated schools. Based on standardized tests, these studies have shown a generally favorable trend, rather than dramatic or conclusive results. Evaluations have also indicated that, for the most part, resident white children continue to achieve at higher levels than the bused minority pupils. Apart from the question of what the tests measure and what they reveal, many people in the district, including school staff, stress the importance of the social gains of desegregation—children learning to live together, making the schools more representative of the population, and taking children "out of the little glass boxes." It appears that the academic gains accompanying desegregation will be slow, unless the schools improve their ability to teach minority children. But the social gains are also vastly important and are recognized as such by many people.

Success of Busing. The district's busing program has worked reasonably well in the sense that the children have caught the buses, attendance has been good, busing has not interfered with the regular school program, and the schools have been able to cope with the special situations created by busing. The one-way aspects of busing are resented by parents in minority neighborhoods, however, and it apparently has been much harder for the Mexican than for the black parent to accept busing, partly because of the tradition of Mexican mothers keeping their children close to them. The Mexican mothers also seem to have more fears for the physical safety of their children on the buses. Another problem connected with busing in 1969 was the limited number of children eligible for the free lunch program in the receiving schools. With cutbacks in funds, many pupils whose families could not really afford to pay were no longer eligible for free lunches at schools. Many of these children could eat at home in a neighborhood school setting.

A two-way busing program would even out the inconveniences and limitations inherent in a busing situation and would be fairer to all concerned. An extensive free lunch program accompanying busing would remove some of the financial strain on low income families with children participating in the busing.

Proliferation of Title I Program. The district's elementary school desegregation program, financed largely by Title I ESEA funds, attempted to transfer compensatory educational services offered in the sending schools to the many receiving schools involved in desegregation. The compensatory services that followed the children were minimal, however, since they were spread out over 23 desegregated receiving schools, as well as over 22 other public and parochial schools not participating in desegregation projects. Title I funds were also used in these schools for field trips and cultural events for children from the target areas and to furnish special books and materials to teachers. Spreading out the Title I program over so many schools and services was criticized by community leaders and ultimately curtailed by state policy requiring the concentration of funds in fewer schools, with an emphasis on elementary schools. Concentration of specialists and special help on a limited number of children, to a degree that promises substantial progress, is the intent of the Title I legislation. This approach is also more effective than thinly spread services, in light of Sacramento's experiences.

Separation Within the Schools. There is also some question as to how much special programs that take the minority child out of the regular classroom and school situation counteract the desired effects of desegregation. If many special compensatory activities and services are carried out independently of the regular school program they tend to make a distinction between resident and sending school children. Where a compensatory program is combined with desegregation, it should not single out, stigmatize or separate the sending area children from the mainstream of the classroom and school life.

Innovation in Compensatory Programs. Both community people in the district and a special study of educational programs carried out by an outside consultant criticized the district's total compensatory education program for failing to introduce real innovations. The district's reading program, which absorbed a substantial proportion of Title I funds in the first few years, brought little improvement in reading scores in the compensatory schools, for instance. Giving children more of traditional approaches that have already proven unsuccessful defeats the purpose of compensatory education in both segregated and desegregated settings. Much more willingness to try different approaches and eliminate teacher barriers to educating minority children are needed. The consultant's report recommended bringing in new personnel from outside the system as a means of introducing new ideas.

Desegregation and "The Culturally Deprived Child." Another weakness of the district's desegregation program is that it has tended to confuse racial and ethnic identification with educational and other handicaps, with minority children involved in desegregation being frequently labelled as "culturally deprived." The many references to "the culturally deprived child" in the district's announcements and discussions of desegregation have caused resentment and humiliation among both blacks and Mexicans and have particularly handicapped the district in approaching the Mexican community. Proud of their own background and heritage, Mexicans have resented the inference that their culture is inferior and they must be remade in the image of the middle class white Anglo Saxon Protestant. Official use of labels such as "the culturally deprived child" has undoubtedly contributed to paternalistic attitudes toward children from the sending areas among some teachers and principals. Humiliating labels and stereotypes should be avoided in developing shorthand phrases to identify problem areas or target populations.

Variation in Approach to Minority Communities. Mexicans in the district have also complained that thinking and planning on minority problems focuses on the black/white issue, either ignoring the problems of the Mexican community or attempting to solve them with approaches used in the black community. Overall policy affecting desegregation, such as the definition of a segregated or imbalanced school should be consistent, but a district should consider each group's own special needs and concerns. Special attention to language. cultural interests, and customs in planning for the desegregation of different minority communities should not be regarded as compromising or reversing policy.

The "Language Problem." The district's approach to Spanish-speaking and Chinese students has been to concentrate on teaching English to those whose knowledge of the language is so limited that they are incapable or almost incapable of functioning in school. These pupils make up only a small minority among both the Mexican and Chinese enrollments, however. More often students with a Mexican background, for instance, have some knowledge of both English and Spanish, but may not be competent in either. There should be programs to help develop English skills among these English-handicapped pupils, as well as among those whose primary language is Spanish or Chinese. Early bilingual programs that would involve other ethnic groups could be combined with desegregation and would probably be welcomed by many Caucasian parents.

Bilingual Staff and Teaching Aids. Staff who speak languages other than English are needed for good teaching and communication in a district such as Sacramento where there are students in the public schools with Spanish, Chinese, and other language backgrounds than English. One of the criticisms of the "English as a Second Language" program is that teachers have too little knowledge of Spanish and other languages to be able to communicate with the children in teaching. The schools could also make use of more initiative and ingenuity in developing language teaching aids in the absence of bilingual teachers. Mathematics teachers in Sacramento High School, for instance, found that by taping several beginning units of basic math in Spanish, Mexican students could "catch on" and then go ahead with the regular students. Such aids need to be developed and used on a wider basis, although they would not be a substitute for teachers speaking the students' primary language.

Some Mexican parents who speak English, moreover, are more comfortable with Spanish, especially in discussing a problem.

More staff with the ability to converse in Spanish would make these parents feel more at ease and would create a bond that would assist in working with parents.

Staff Selection. In addition to the district's special need for bilingual teachers, there is also a need for more minority staff in the regular schools, particularly for staff with a Mexican background, and for more teachers in schools with large minority populations who are unbiased, flexible, and adaptable. Although the district has made progress in increasing the number of black and Mexican teachers, more than token representation of minority staff at administrative levels and in counselor's positions is a top priority need. Minority staff are doubly important in newly desegregated situations so that minority students will have persons with whom they can identify and will have more confidence in their own ability to succeed.

Compulsory In-Service Training. Compulsory in-service training for total staff is needed in a desegregation program; teachers must have a willingness to identify, discuss, and resolve racial problems. While top district officials admitted there were many racial problems in the schools and had conducted mandatory in-service training for principals and nonprofessional staff, teacher training was carried out on a voluntary basis through the 1960s. An effective, compulsory program for teachers in the first stages of desegregation would reach the teachers who need it most and should help modify attitudes and practices that hinder the learning process and contribute to racial problems in the schools.

Curriculum Changes and Teaching Aids. As the schools become desegregated there is a more obvious and pressing need for recognition of the dignity of each child and for accurate facts about all peoples. The district's experience indicates that it is important to provide supplementary books, pictures and references on minorities for student and teacher use in individual schools. New courses, curriculum changes, and in-service training on the history and contribution of racial and ethnic groups should be planned and implemented on a districtwide basis, however. In-service training for teachers in black and Mexican history, the literature of different minority groups, and other appropriate subject areas should be carried out on a mandatory basis.

Because of the dependence of the schools on textbooks, it

is crucial that the state of California enforce its existing laws and policies requiring inclusion and correct portrayal of the role and contributions of ethnic and racial minorities in history and other social studies courses. Particular attention should be paid to reforming the presentation of the history and role of Mexican, Asian, and Indian Americans, since these minorities are often overlooked in books and materials prepared in other parts of the country where the black/white situation prevails. Textbooks that ignore, stereotype, or distort the history and present status of the various minority groups should be banned. If necessary, the writing of acceptable textbooks should be commissioned by the state.

Opportunity as Well as Obligation. Because of its particular local history, Sacramento has a unique opportunity to take advantage of an extremely rich and varied mixture of people from different countries, cultures, and racial and ethnic backgrounds. A mutual exchange of languages, history, customs, and experiences, carried out in such a way that the dignity and humanity of each group is respected, would provide the schools with learning possibilities not present in many areas of the country. Full and complete desegregation should be looked upon as an opportunity as well as an obligation.

NOTES

1. Christian L. Larsen, James R. Bell, Leonard D. Cain, Jr., Lyman A. Glenny, William H. Hickman, and Irl A. Irwin, *Metropolitan Action Studies, No. 4* (Bloomington, Indiana: Indiana University Press), 1965, p. 17.
2. *Ibid.*, p. 8.
3. "Mexican" is substituted for the official U. S. Census category "White with Spanish Surname," since those included in this category in Sacramento are primarily Mexican and identify themselves as such.
4. "Caucasian" and "white" are used to refer to the non-minority white population.
5. "Asian" is substituted for the U. S. Census category "Other Races," since Chinese and Japanese people constitute most of this category in Sacramento. The "Other Races" category of the Census also includes Filipinos and American Indians; both are present in small numbers in Sacramento.

6. *Sacramento Bee*, Sept. 16, 1971, p. C-1.
7. *Ibid.*, Sept. 17, 1971, p. B-1.
8. *Ibid.*, Editorial, June 5, 1969.
9. *Ibid.*, Editorial, June 21, 1969, p. A-13.
10. *Ibid.*, May 25, 1969, p. C-2.
11. In 1966 the district began using the category "White of Spanish Surname" to conform with this classification in ethnic surveys conducted by the State Department of Education. This change enlarged the district's classification of Spanish-background students, which had previously been restricted to children of Mexican background. The number of Caucasians decreased correspondingly, as some pupils who were previously counted as Caucasians were shifted into the "White of Spanish Surname" category. Data for both Caucasians and Mexicans in this section are based on figures adjusted for the change in definition.
12. The history of the initial phases of desegregation of Stanford Junior High School draws heavily on Edward B. Fort's "Decision Making in the Sacramento De Facto Segregation Crisis," in *School Desegregation in the North: The Challenge and the Experience*, edited by T. Bentley Edwards and Frederick M. Wirt (San Francisco: Chandler Publishing Company, 1967), pages 77—115. For a fuller account, see Edward B. Fort, *A Case Study of the Struggle to Secure an Administration Plan for Eliminating De Facto Segregation in the Junior High Schools of Sacramento, California* (unpublished Ph.D. dissertation, University of California, Berkeley, 1964).
13. Edward B. Fort, "Decision Making in the Sacramento De Facto Segregation Crisis," in *School Desegregation in the North: The Challenge and the Experience*, T. Bentley Chandler and Frederick M. Wirt, eds. (San Francisco: Chandler Publishing Company), 1967, p. 92.
14. *Ibid.*, p. 94.
15. *Keller vs. Sacramento City Unified School District*, No. 146525, Supreme Court of the State of California, Sacramento County, Oct. 8, 1963, p. 4.
16. *Ibid.*
17. Sections 2010 and 2011, Title 5, California Administrative Code, were amended in March 1969 and were renumbered as Sections 14020 and 14021. Most of the provisions of Sections 14020 and 14021 were incorporated into state law in the regular session of the 1971 California Legislature and now appear in the state Education Code as Sections 5002 and 5003.
18. *Sacramento Union*, Feb. 26, 1967.
19. "We the undersigned residents of River Park . . . ," June 28, 1965.
20. "Recommendations of Special Study Group of David Lubin PTA," no date.
21. *Sacramento Union*, Oct. 3, 1966.
22. *Ibid.*
23. Sacramento City Unified School District, *Statement of Policy on Providing Equal Educational Opportunity in the Sacramento City Unified School District*, Oct. 4, 1965, pp. 1—5.

24. *Sacramento Union,* Mar. 22, 1966.
25. *Sacramento Bee,* Apr. 12, 1966.
26. *Ibid.*
27. *Ibid.,* Apr. 26, 1966.
28. *Ibid.*
29. Mimeographed letter signed by Mrs. Eva Flores, Chairman of the Education Committee of the Oak Park Neighborhood Council, Sacramento, California, no date.
30. Sacramento City Unified School District, *Programs and Services Provided Under the Elementary and Secondary Education Act of 1965,* A Board of Education Report to the California State Department of Education (Sacramento, California), Aug. 1, 1968, p. 172.
31. Margaret M. Oakden, *Selected Case Studies of Former Second Grade Pupils of American Legion Elementary School as Participants in "Project Aspiration" of the Sacramento City Unified School District* (unpublished Master's thesis, Sacramento State College), Dec. 13, 1967, p. 69.
32. *Sacramento Bee,* Jan. 23, 1968.
33. Sacramento City Unified School District, *Possible Plans for the Alleviation or Elimination of the Adverse Effects of De Facto Segregation at the Washington Elementary School (Including Cost Estimates for Each Plan)* (Sacramento, California), Nov. 3, 1967, p. 9.
34. Petition to the Sacramento City Unified School District, "We the people, residents of the Washington area . . . ," Nov. 28, 1967, p. 2.
35. Sacramento City Unified School District, Minutes of the Board of Education, Special Meeting on the Washington Elementary School, Dec. 1, 1967.
36. Letter from Mrs. Herbert Cortez to the Board of Education, Sacramento City Unified School District, Nov. 27, 1967, pp. 1–2.
37. Sacramento City Unified School District, Minutes of the Board of Education, Special Meeting on the Washington Elementary School, Dec. 1, 1967.
38. *Sacramento Union,* Nov. 30, 1967, p. C-1.
39. *Sacramento Bee,* Mar. 5, 1968.
40. Washington's People Committee, Statement sent to members of the Board of Education, Sacramento City Unified School District, Apr. 4, 1968.
41. Statement to Board of Education, Sacramento City Unified School District, Aug. 8, 1968, pp. 4–5.
42. *Sacramento Bee,* Sept. 10, 1968, p. 31.
43. *Ibid.,* Apr. 28, 1968, p. B-1.
44. "An Innovative Approach to the Education of the Culturally Disadvantaged," no date, p. 1.
45. *Ibid.*
46. Mary Cortez, "Who Is to Blame," in *El Hispanoamericano,* Jan. 14, 1969, p. 7.
47. Sacramento City Unified School District, *A Summary of Assessments of the District's Integration Programs, 1964–1971,* Research Report No. 9,

Series 1971–72, Sept. 28, 1971, p. 8.
48. *Ibid.*
49. *Ibid.*
50. *Ibid.* p. 9.
51. *Ibid.*, p. 10.
52. *Sacramento Bee*, Sept. 21, 1971, p. B-1.
53. California State Department of Education, *California Laws and Policies Relating to Equal Opportunities in Education* (Sacramento, California: The Department), 1969, p. 9.
54. Sacramento City Unified School District, "Annual Report to the Board of Education on Certificated Personnel," (Sacramento, California), Jan. 20, 1969, p. 44.
55. Letter from Miss Sharon Pinkney for the Minority Students of the High Schools of the City of Sacramento, to Mr. F. Melvyn Lawson, City Superintendent of Schools, Sacramento, California, Mar. 29, 1968, p. 2.
56. Letter from F. Melvyn Lawson, City Superintendent of Schools to Miss Sharon Pinkney, Sacramento, California, Apr. 15, 1968, p. 7.
57. Memorandum from Mr. Ples A. Griffin, Bureau of Intergroup Relations, California State Department of Education, to Mr. Ted Neff, Bureau of Intergroup Relations, California State Department of Education, Aug. 30, 1968, pp. 2, 4.
58. Letter from Miss Sharon Pinkney, *op. cit.*, p. 2.
59. Memorandum from Mr. Richard D. Whinnery, Program Specialist, Social Science, to Dr. Agnes S. Robinson, Assistant Superintendent, Curriculum Services Department, Sacramento City Unified School District, Apr. 24, 1968, p. 2.
60. *El Hispano*, Sept. 30, 1969, p. 6.
61. California State Department of Education, *op. cit.*, pp. 22–23.
62. *Ibid.*, pp. 24–25.
63. *Ibid.*, p. 25.
64. *Ibid.*, pp. 23, 24.
65. California Teachers Association, *Land of the Free and Its Critics* (Burlingame, California: California Teachers Association), 1967, p. 9.
66. *Ibid.*, pp. 18–24, 29–32.
67. John W. Caughley, John Hope Franklin, and Ernest R. May, *Land of the Free. A History of the United States* (New York: Benziger Brothers, Inc.), 1969, p. 516.
68. *Sacramento Union*, Mar. 13, 1970, p. 3.
69. *Sacramento Bee*, Jan. 5, 1972, p. A-4.
70. *Ibid.*, Dec. 9, 1971, p. A-6.
71. *Ibid.*, Sept. 10, 1971, p. A-3.
72. Knight, Gladieux and Smith, Inc., *Long-Range Sites and Facilities Plan. Sacramento City Unified School District, Sacramento, California* (San Francisco: Knight, Gladieux and Smith), Oct. 6, 1969, p. 6.
73. *Ibid.*, p. 83.
74. *Ibid.*, p. 68.
75. *Ibid.*
76. *Sacramento Union*, Feb. 17, 1970, p. 1.

77. *Ibid.*
78. *Ibid.*
79. *Ibid.*, Feb. 27, 1970, p. 9.
80. *Ibid.*, Mar. 18, 1970, p. 3.
81. *Ibid.*, Feb. 17, 1970, p. 1.
82. *Ibid.*, Mar. 3, 1970, p. 5.
83. *Ibid.*, Mar. 17, 1970, p. 6.
84. *Ibid.*, Apr. 1, 1970, p. 3.
85. Max Rafferty, *Max Rafferty on Education* (New York: The Devin-Adair Co.), 1968, pp. 37–38.
86. California State Department of Education, *op. cit.*, pp. 2–3.
87. *Sacramento Bee*, Oct. 14, 1967.
88. Alfred E. Gitelson, "The Power and the Duty to Integrate," in *Integrated Education: Race and Schools*, Vol. 8, No. 3 (May–June 1970), p. 13.
89. *Sacramento Union*, Mar. 12, 1970, p. 1.
90. Assembly Bill No. 724, Amended in Senate on August 3, 1971; Amended in Assembly on April 2, 1971. California Legislature – 1971 Regular Session, pp. 2–3.
91. Sacramento City Unified School District, *A Conceptual Plan for Meeting the Long-Range Site and Facility Needs of the District*, Nov. 17, 1971, p. 4.
92. *Sacramento Bee*, Feb. 9, 1972, p. C-1.
93. *Sacramento Union*, Feb. 5, 1972, p. A-8.
94. Gitelson, *op. cit.*, pp. 10–15; Stanley A. Weigl, "Supreme Court Ruling Applied in California," in *Integrated Education: Race and Schools*, Vol. 9, No. 4 (July–August 1971), pp. 29–32; and Stanley A. Weigl, "Chronicle of Race and Schools, April–May, 1971," in *Integrated Education: Race and Schools*, Vol. 9, No. 4 (July–August 1971), p. 55.

schools used successfully in these districts indicates there is no one way or model way to desegregate and that desegregation can generally be carried out within the framework of existing space, provided that all buildings are used. Nearly all desegregation in these districts took place without waiting on the completion of new buildings, sometimes by combining different approaches to school or grade reorganization. Specific techniques of desegregation that worked at some point in the districts' desegregation histories include: the realignment of attendance boundaries to get a better racial mix; a modified version of school pairing combining the attendance areas of three contiguous schools; the creation of model schools to attract and hold whites; a one-grade citywide center; reorganization of high school feeder patterns on a racial basis; mandatory reassignment of both white and minority children to nearby and distant schools; closing minority schools or converting them to special use; assignment of black children to previously white schools; assignment of white pupils to formerly black schools; and short- and long-distance busing of some children for desegregation purposes.

It appears that even small school districts will have to combine several different methods or techniques to achieve complete desegregation and that total desegregation cannot be accomplished without reassigning both white and minority children.

4. *All school policies and practices that contribute to segregation should be abandoned.*

There was a tendency in these districts, usually in the earlier phases of desegregation, to focus on pupil assignments or school reorganization needed to implement some desegregation, while continuing other policies and practices that caused or continued segregation in other segments of the school population. Transfer policies, new building, other school reorganization, and auxiliary moves to free space for desegregation sometimes increased segregation in schools not involved in the desegregation program.

Total desegregation cannot be achieved or maintained unless all policies and practices that foster separation are reversed or abandoned.

5. *Procedures for reviewing and revising desegregation plans should be established.*

With new schools opening and old schools closing, records of population and enrollment shifts, periodic racial censuses of the schools, and records of classroom assignments by race were important aids in monitoring the progress of desegregation projects. In the two larger districts, appointment of an intergroup relations officer and an equal educational opportunity officer

Summary and Conclusions: Implications for Future Desegregation

The three school districts covered in this report made substantial gains in pupil desegregation in the 1960s and into the 1970s, particularly after passage of the 1964 Civil Rights Act. Two of the school systems, Charlottesville, Virginia, and Providence, Rhode Island, implemented desegregation plans that covered all grade levels and eliminated all predominantly black regular elementary, middle, junior high, and senior high schools. Charlottesville no longer operates any all-white schools and Providence has made progress in this area. In addition to accomplished major pupil desegregation, the three school districts also began to recognize and address themselves in some way to what might be called the "second front" of desegregation—the problems of bias, discrimination, and inequality within schools and the task of reorienting school staffs and programs to the new educational situation resulting from desegregation. In another significant gain, school officials in these systems were beginning to revise and extend desegregation plans without the full-scale community campaigns required to start the desegregation process at an earlier stage. By the time this study ended, it appeared that school boards and administrators in these districts had accepted, at least at some level, that the task of maintaining desegregated schools was one of their on-going responsibilities.

While progress in these districts was very real, their experiences point up some of the major weaknesses in the process of school desegregation at the local district level, as it has existed to date. First, desegregation in these districts proceeded entirely too slowly, taking place in a halting and piecemeal way, through a series of partial plans spaced out over a period of time. There were sometimes one to three years between major desegregation efforts. In the most extreme of the cases studied—Charlottesville, Virginia—it was 12 years—one whole generation of school children—between the time the first suit was filed and full desegregation of all grades. Second, the desegregation process was unequal. With some notable exceptions, the bulk of the desegregation carried out in these districts was designed so that the minority community made most of the changes and sacrifices necessary to bring about racially mixed school populations. Schools in minority neighborhoods were generally closed or converted to special use, and blacks and Mexicans were usually reassigned long distances from home, requiring busing, while whites, if transferred at all, were generally close enough to their new schools to walk. This was done not because it was the only way or the best way the schools could be desegregated, but because of fears that whites would not tolerate their children being assigned to ghetto and barrio schools and would not accept the inconvenience of busing.

Third, an important problem illustrated by these case studies is the reluctance of school administrators to come to grips with racial and race-related educational problems in the schools. Racism on the part of teachers and principals, inadequate minority staff, discrimination against blacks and Mexicans at administrative levels, and the biased nature of the curriculum were among the other racial and equal-education problems that came to a head in these districts with desegregation. Finally, in spite of the 1954 Supreme Court decision outlawing school segregation, the 1964 Civil Rights Act, and state policy calling for an end to segregation and racial imbalance in Providence and Sacramento, too little action to bring about desegregation was initiated at the federal and state levels. Local leaders, mainly in the black community, were instrumental in bringing federal and state anti-discrimination policy to bear in these districts, but very little federal and state pressure originated with the responsible governmental agencies. If concerned citizens had waited on appropriate federal and state officials to enforce desegregation on their own, or had depended on them to do most of the prodding, these districts would probably still be segregated.

What can we learn from these three school districts' experiences as far as future desegregation is concerned? How can local districts accomplish desegregation more quickly, on a more comprehensive basis, and with more fairness to minority groups? How can districts better cope with school racial and educational problems after desegregation? How can federal and state policy be more effective in bringing about desegregation at the local level? The following summary of the most important findings of the study focuses on these and other key questions.

PLANNING COMPREHENSIVE DESEGREGATIO

1. *Desegregation should be defined in terms of racial* *a desired ratio of blacks to whites in each school.*

The decision to approach desegregation by establishi balance in each school was one of the most important ments furthering broad-scale desegregation in these Definitions of racial balance vary, but they usually set a mi and maximum percentage of minorities that can be as to any one school. The ratio of black or minority stude white students that is incorporated in such a formula frequ approximates the black/white or minority/white proportio the total school enrollment. A racial balance formula of kind has the following advantages: (a) it emphasizes districtv desegregation, since the ratio applies equally to all schools; it eliminates the all-white and overwhelmingly white school, well as the all-black or predominantly minority school; (c) closes off white "escape" areas within a district, since all schoo are desegregated and (d) it establishes a clear, positive standar for desegregation.

Similarly, racial balance goals applied at the classroom level avoid segregated learning situations within desegregated schools. A racial balance classroom approach can also prevent the isolation of one or two black children by fixing a minimum number of minority children that can be assigned to any one class.

2. *Desegregation should be implemented in all schools at once, rather than gradually in successive stages.*

The partial and piecemeal approach to desegregation in these districts tended to drag out the issue in the community, keep school officials and community leaders tied up with desegregation plans over a period of years, delay building programs and other planning, and keep some minority pupils enrolled in segregated schools. Postponing desegregation did not make it easier, nor did successful experience with one phase of desegregation necessarily prevent confrontations over extending integration to other segments of the school population.

By contrast, an all-inclusive, districtwide plan, implemented in one step, would resolve the issue quickly, give both white and minority children the benefits of a desegregated education, and permit the school district to go ahead with solutions to other pressing problems.

3. *Districts should desegregate with currently available facilities, rather than wait for the completion of elaborate building programs.*

The variety of methods of reassigning pupils and reorganizing

fixed responsibility for changes in pupil assignments, for new desegregation planning, for development of teacher training programs, and for trouble-shooting on problems related to current desegregation. It is important that such an equal educational opportunity or intergroup relations officer serve as an advocate for minorities, rather than as an interpreter or apologist for district policy. Establishing a community review board is another possibility for evaluating and updating a desegregation plan.

EQUALIZING THE DESEGREGATION PROCESS

6. *All segments of the minority community should have adequate representation in the formulation of policy and plans for desegregation.*

Whites and elite-type members of the minority communities dominated most of the desegregation planning and policy-making in the three districts, especially in the early stages of desegregation. Top school administrators involved in developing desegregation plans in the first stages of major desegregation were white and none of the school systems had any minority school board members when desegregation efforts first began. In each district, at some stage of desegregation, lack of sufficient minority representation, including the absence of "grass roots" and the most militant minority leaders, contributed to the development of plans and approaches that were unacceptable to a large part of the minority community.

Bringing knowledgeable and representative members of minority groups into the decision-making process is a "must" if biracial and multiracial school districts are to solve their problems. Participation on only an advisory level seems to increase frustration where advice is not accepted and translated into policy.

7. *Policy and planning for desegregation should be based on the premise that desegregation is a two-way process involving a mutual adjustment between whites and minorities.*

As mentioned earlier, most of the desegregation plans in these districts were "one-way," sending blacks and Mexicans to white schools, closing or converting schools in minority neighborhoods only and assigning minorities most of the travel associated with desegregation. This one-way approach generated opposition to desegregation plans among minority groups and reinforced a rather limited point of view among many whites that desegregation is an opportunity for blacks and other minorities to "come over and be white." Desegregation worked successfully, however, in the few instances where plans involving more equitable adjust-

ments were tried—where whites were assigned to formerly black
schools and bused along with blacks to achieve racial balance
and where black principals were put in charge of formerly white
schools.

If desegregation is public policy, then it cannot be framed
in terms of the wishes of the white public only. If segregated
schools are a community problem then the total community
should share equally in the solution.

8. *If busing is used in connection with desegregation plans, both
white and minority children should be bused.*

The long-term problem connected with busing in these districts
was the double standard as to who was bused. There were minor,
recurring problems associated with schedules, discipline on the
buses, and the impact of busing on after-school activities and
punishment, but these could be overcome. Busing was successful
otherwise, in the sense that the children caught the buses,
attendance of bused children was satisfactory, and busing was
organized so that it did not interfere with the normal school
routine. Blacks and Mexicans were increasingly resentful of the
fact that their children bore the brunt of busing, however, and
were beginning to see the bus as another symbol of discrimination.

Busing itself is not the real issue, rather it is the question
of whose children will be reassigned where, what schools will
be closed or converted to special use, and whether there is equity
in the sacrifices made to accomplish desegregation. When the
broader issues associated with busing are resolved, busing is,
after all, only a means of transportation.

MULTIETHNIC AND MULTILINGUAL SCHOOL DISTRICTS

9. *The multi-minority school in multiracial districts should be desegregated along with schools dominated by a single minority group.*

Sacramento's experiences indicate that multiracial and multi-
ethnic school districts experience two kinds of segregation: (1)
schools dominated by a single racial or ethnic group, the pattern,
familiar in the east, of black/white segregation and (2) multi-
minority segregated schools where no one racial or ethnic minority prevails, but where over half of the school population is made
up of a combination of different racial and ethnic minorities.
In Sacramento, the schools dominated by several minorities evi-
denced many of the same educational and social problems found
in schools with a preponderance of a single racial or ethnic group.

These schools were not considered "segregated," however, and were not touched by desegregation plans.

Multiethnic school districts should identify the multi-minority school as a segregated school and adopt policies that will end the concentration of minorities in these schools, along with those dominated by a single racial group.

10. *Overall policy affecting the desegregation of different racial and ethnic groups in multiracial districts should be consistent, but should also consider each group's special interests, needs and problems.*

The Sacramento district's approach to desegregating its one Mexican school, patterned largely after the desegregation plan and strategy used with black schools, alienated many Mexicans who saw their problems as different from those of blacks, warranting a different solution. Grass roots chicano leaders, especially, fought the district's desegregation plan and attempted—unsuccessfully—to secure an alternative approach, tailored to meet the special needs of Mexican children and the surrounding adult Mexican community.

Flexibility in approaching and planning the desegregation of schools in different minority communities should be possible within a framework of a common definition of segregation and common goals for desegregation or racial balance. Variation in specific desegregation planning should not be regarded as compromising or reversing policy.

11. *Special language programs for English-handicapped pupils in multilingual districts are needed to guarantee equal educational opportunity.*

Apart from issues of segregation and desegregation, many pupils in multiracial and multilingual districts are handicapped by the lack of teachers who speak languages other than English. The schools have also failed in many instances to give sufficient attention to the language difficulties of children who speak English along with another language, such as Spanish or Chinese, but who need special help in developing their skills in English if they are to be successful in school. A common complaint in the Sacramento district, for example, was that Mexican background children without adequate ability to function in English were frequently put in "slow" or mentally retarded classes or did so poorly in school they dropped out at an early age.

The multilingual district should hire more teachers who speak languages other than English and should plan programs for the child who is partly bilingual and has special English problems, as well as for the child who enters school speaking no English at all. Early bilingual or multilingual programs involving both majority and minority students could be combined with desegregation and would be of benefit to all concerned.

GAINING ACCEPTANCE FOR DESEGREGATION

12. *White acceptance of desegregation can be encouraged by a districtwide plan with a racial balance formula.*

Even though all schools might not receive the same number of minority children, the idea that desegregation is districtwide, applying to all schools or almost all schools, seems to neutralize and homogenize white opposition. Wider dispersal of blacks in two of the districts evolved largely from the pressures of whites. Whites, rather than blacks, were mainly responsible for a decision in Charlottesville to bus black children to establish better racial balance and integrate the district's last remaining all-white school. When the *fact* of desegregation is established, whites seem to prefer a plan that evens out the distribution of black pupils and sets up a formal or informal control over the proportion of blacks that can be placed in any school.

13. *Two-way desegregation is now a condition of minority acceptance of desegregation plans.*

As suggested earlier, black and Mexican opposition to neighborhood school closings and one-way pupil transfers in these districts became a key point. Minority acceptance of desegregation was advanced by keeping at least some schools in the minority community open on a desegregated basis and by implementing at least some two-way pupil exchanges to bring white children into formerly all-black or high-black enrollment schools.

Since minority resistance to one-way plans will certainly increase, future desegregation plans will have to desegregate both minority and white schools, bus and transfer majority and minority pupils, and otherwise even out any of the inconveniences or hardships accompanying desegregation. On a long-term basis, minorities will oppose one-way desegregation plans as another form of discrimination.

14. *Opposition to desegregation should be met with firm, positive, and unified leadership.*

Organized opposition to desegregation, present in some form in all three districts, has recently centered on specific aspects of proposed desegregation plans or approaches, rather than on desegregation itself. Both whites and minorities usually concentrate on the effects of a particular plan on their children or their neighborhood schools and both groups frequently propose alternatives. Whatever the source or motivation for opposition, resistance is encouraged by the failure of school officials to vigorously defend proposed plans, by vacillation in the face of opposition, by wide splits within the ranks of top school and community officials, and by desegregation plans that make widely different demands on different segments of the population without any real justification for these differences.

Firm, positive, unified leadership from the school superintendent, school board members, and local civic officials; active support from as many community leaders and organizations as possible; and a willingness to alter plans where there are legitimate grievances related to major inequities in the plans, help to check opposition and build community acceptance of desegregation.

ADJUSTING THE SCHOOLS TO DESEGREGATION

15. *A well-established pattern of token desegregation will not necessarily pave the way for an easy adjustment to full desegregation.*

In several schools in these districts, the transition from token to full desegregation seemed to be as difficult for many white teachers, students, and parents as a change from an all-white to a desegregated school. Several schools experiencing some of the greatest problems after major desegregation had previously enrolled small numbers of minority students and had, in some cases, made what appeared to be a fairly successful adaptation to token desegregation. The token situation, in which a few blacks tend to blend in with the dominant white structure, seems to have little or no relationship to absorbing larger numbers of black students. Several factors seem to be at work. The minority stuudent who comes in with full desegregation is more likely to be average, rather than highly qualified and highly motivated, and may present challenges that the teachers and the school are not prepared to face. Class differences as well as differences in educational background are likely to be greater with full desegregation, and minority students and parents also seem more likely to protest unfair treatment. Minorities who make increased demands with major desegregation may be viewed as troublemakers by some whites, who may feel they have already made all the necessary adjustments to desegregation.

16. *School districts beginning desegregation need to take aggressive steps to prevent staff racism and to insure that the school and classroom climate will be receptive to minority children.*

The failure of white staff to accept and understand minority children and otherwise adjust positively to desegregation was a major problem in some schools in all three districts. In two districts, shortly after desegregation began, staff racism provoked major community confrontations between parents and students on the one side and the school administration on the other. There were community confrontations over school racial practices in the third district as well, but this development was not directly related to recent desegregation.

These districts' experiences suggest that there is a need for a strong school board policy prohibiting all discriminatory and racist behavior on the part of staff. This policy should specifically ban common forms of in-school discrimination and unequal treatment, such as the use of racial slurs and labels and harsher disciplinary measures against minority students, and should be adopted before desegregation begins. A districtwide grievance procedure for complaints against staff discrimination and racism should also be established, with provisions for transfer, reassignment, or dismissal of staff who persist in treating majority and minority children unequally. Staff should be oriented to the provisions of the policy and the importance of acceptance and equal treatment of all children, and top administrative staff and the board must be willing to deal firmly with both principals and teachers who are unwilling or unable to cope with the demands of a desegregated school. Tenure and seniority in the school system should not insulate teachers and administrators from policy related to racial justice in the schools.

17. *Principals capable of giving positive and sensitive leadership on racial issues are a key factor in successful school desegregation.*

Acute and overt problems in adjusting to desegregation, found to some degree in all three districts, seemed to cluster in schools where a weak, inept or hostile principal's administration was accompanied by prolonged antagonism on the part of many white parents, by panic on the part of white parents over a possible decline in the school's academic standards, or by widespread teacher resistance to desegregation. A practice of ignoring or dismissing legitimate concerns and complaints of parents and students and letting the situation "drift" usually preceded major outbursts and confrontations on racial issues.

Careful selection and orientation of principals, strong leadership from principals in providing a program that is as positive and relevant as possible for the school's total population, principals' ability to work with members of minority groups as well as with whites, and prompt action to resolve valid complaints seem to aid in developing a good climate and preventing racial crises. School district leadership also has to face the fact that some principals who functioned adequately in all-white schools will have to be transferred, retired, or otherwise removed from new school situations they cannot handle.

18. *The academic gap between white and minority children will not be bridged quickly or easily, unless the schools improve their ability to teach children with ghetto and barrio backgrounds.*

Evaluations of the academic achievement of white and minority pupils involved in desegregation were carried out on a systematic basis in one district only, Sacramento. Minority children's test scores were encouraging, but the children did not show dramatic or conclusive gains on a short-term basis. Tests of comparable white children and interviews with teachers indicated that deseg-regation had no negative effects on the academic progress of resident children in schools that were desegrated and that these children continued to achieve at a higher level than minority children.

There was concern in all three districts as to how well prepared the schools were to teach minority children, regardless of deseg-regation. These was no general desire to go back to segregation, where the educational level of minority schools was below that of white schools, but rather a growing awareness that the children might be similarly handicapped in desegregated schools if the schools and the teachers remained the same or were negative toward minority children. Teachers and the educational pro-grams in the desegregated schools were major points of com-munity concern.

19. *Preparation of staff for newly desegregated schools should be compulsory and geared to real problems.*

The need to prepare the schools' predominantly white teachers and principals for desegregation was recognized in all three dis-tricts, but staff training was not always carried out in an effective way. Early in-service teacher training programs, especially, were attended on a voluntary basis and often consisted of university-type courses on subjects such as intergroup relations or the educa-tion of the "culturally deprived child." The most effective efforts at in-service education, rather, were small and compulsory work-shop sessions for individual schools or for a select group, such as principals. The sessions took place over a period of weeks and dealt with concrete issues and problems. Community input into in-service training was important in two areas: in sensitizing teachers and principals to the needs and problems of minority pupils; and in acquainting principals, counselors, and community liaison staff with resources available to the schools.

A range of different kinds of staff preparation is probably needed in most schools—required sessions to sensitize all staff to the similarities and differences between white and black Americans and to common problems in newly integrated schools; workshops for principals, counselors, and teachers related to special problem areas, such as the handling of discipline; and compulsory courses in the history and literature of minority groups for social studies and language arts teachers.

20. *Special personnel and resources introduced along with desegregation seem to be most effective when combined with total school reorganization or a "model school" approach.*

Widely scattered special personnel spread thinly over many schools, continued use of traditional teaching methods in supplementary educational programs, and extra help for minority pupils carried out without teacher interest and understanding of the students were weaknesses of some of the special education programs introduced to bridge the gaps between black, Mexican, and white pupils in newly desegregated schools. The most favorable school situations, by contrast, were those where the use of special resources was a part of a broad reform effort that included both a change in the school's overall philosophy and approach and a concerted effort to increase community participation and involvement in the school.

School districts planning to introduce special personnel and resources in connection with desegregation programs would apparently do well to limit the number of schools receiving special education services, giving first priority to those schools where the need is greatest; to make sure that the schools involved have effective principals capable of working with minority as well as majority parents and children; and to encourage principals and teachers in the schools to reevaluate the school's total organization and program, reorienting it to the new situation and involving the community as widely as possible in meeting the challenges of desegregation.

21. *A school's total program should be reexamined and possibly restructured with desegregation so that the minority student is not always "out" where the white student is "in."*

Thoughtful principals, teachers, and students in these districts were becoming increasingly aware of the need to make special efforts to prevent racial separation within the desegregated schools. Even with a policy of nondiscrimination covering all school activities, many factors contributed to separation, such as the use of ability grouping to organize classes; the tracking of students into college preparatory, general, or vocational education courses; grade requirements for extracurricular activities; the gearing of extracurricular activities to the interests of whites; and the fact that in most instances minority pupils came into a school where the life of the school was already dominated and controlled by whites.

Many facets of school life may need to be reoriented or reorganized to insure mixed contact between the students, to increase the participation of minority students in the full range of school activities, and to reflect the interests and heritages of all groups in the school's program. In the area of student activities, it is important to reach both the average and the outstanding minority pupil; to hold sustained activities that appeal to minority students, rather than one-time affairs; and to help students come together in a genuine spirit of acceptance. Paternalistic attitudes and a vivid contrast between in-school and out-of-school behavior on the part of whites were common barriers to good in-school relations.

22. *Open channels of communication within individual schools and the school district are needed so that student grievances can be aired and resolved.*

The main thrust of minority students' organized protests in these districts was aimed at basic school racial problems that adults had failed to solve, such as the teaching of black and chicano history, more black and Mexican staff, prejudiced treatment from teachers, harsher discipline for minority students, and the need for remedial courses to help weak students improve their academic backgrounds. Even major disruptive outbursts on the part of black students in mixed schools seemed to stem from the frustration of living in the enemy's camp, as it were, without any real hope of change. Many of the student protests and outbursts came after major desegregation campaigns, when adult community activity on school racial issues was on the wane. Students not only *wanted* to act on their own; the prospect of their parents or other adults resolving these grievances seemed unlikely.

A basic problem was that there were no channels within the schools that students could use to effect major change. Hearings before the school board, serious negotiations with principals or school superintendents, and the organization of student-principal or student-community "rap" sessions came *after* boycotts, walkouts, and demonstrations. In the first stages of desegregation, especially, there is a need for school districts to find ways to hear and respond to serious student grievances concerning racial problems in the schools. Some permanent channels, such as student representation on school boards, an advisory student school board, or a special community review

board with minority representation should be established to fulfill this function.

OTHER EQUAL EDUCATION ISSUES

23. *More minority staff serving in key leadership positions in
individual schools, as well as in the central administration, are essential
in solving schools' racial problems.*

The desegregation of schools intensified the demand on the
part of both students and community groups in these districts
for more minority staff and the upgrading of blacks and Mexicans to key leadership and decision-making positions within
individual schools. The presence of minority principals, vice principals, and guidance counselors seemed imperative, in view of
the many problems centering around discipline.

More than token minority staff are necessary if the schools
are to relate to minority children, maintain fair discipline, provide adult figures with whom black and Mexican children can
identify, and convince the students that the schools are not racist
institutions. It is also important that minority staff be accepted
on a full professional basis, so that they feel free to contribute
ideas, take initiative, and otherwise participate in shaping the
direction of the schools.

24. *Minority school board members are needed to formulate and implement sound policy on school racial issues.*

Black school board members were appointed in two of these
districts as desegregation was underway and the schools faced
many racial problems. These board members not only provided
a link to the black community, but also those with leadership
ability were effective in developing more understanding of racial
problems in the larger community and played important roles
in troubleshooting on racial issues.

School boards should have more than token minority representation and, where board members are appointed, those selected
should have stature in their own communities and the ability
to give independent leadership on racial issues. Minority board
members who are able to relate to black and chicano students
and student movements are especially needed. "Uncle Tom"
and "Tio Taco" minority board members will probably be
rejected by a large number of adults as well as by students in
the minority communities.

25. *Serious and sustained efforts to root out the white bias in textbooks
and curricula must be made.*

Deficiencies in teachers' knowledge of minority history and

culture and the basic dependence of the schools on teaching from textbooks—which continue to be biased—were two immediate stumbling blocks to implementing the demand in these districts for curriculum reform in black and Mexican history. The districts did take steps to introduce new black history and ethnic studies courses, to provide teachers with more information and source material on minority history, and in some instances, to suggest ways in which teachers could integrate aspects of minority history and culture into their classes. Making changes in the material presented in key courses was left largely up to the teachers, however, and the districts failed to require teachers to take courses in minority studies to get a basic foundation in the subject matter they were to introduce to students.

Social studies, English, and history teachers should be required to complete courses in minority studies to qualify for continued employment. There also needs to be comprehensive, districtwide revision of course outlines in these fields and a reevaluation of supplementary materials provided for classroom use, of classroom projects, and of places visited on field trips, to widen the scope of teaching beyond the limits of the white Western world. Abandoning textbooks in some subjects is probably the best solution to the textbook problem, at least for the present.

MORE EFFECTIVE STATE POLICY

26. *More state leadership is crucial to the development of textbooks that are historically accurate and that include adequate material on all racial and ethnic groups.*

Because of the role of state adoption lists in the selection of textbooks at the district level, it is critical for states to ban the use of biased textbooks and stipulate definite criteria concerning the treatment of ethnic and racial minorities for texts to be approved for use in the state. California has already moved in this direction through the state curriculum commission's "Guidelines for References to Ethnic and Cultural Minorities in Textbooks" and through provisions of the state Education Code requiring inclusion and correct portrayal of the role and contributions of racial and ethnic minorities in history, civics, and social studies courses.

Other states need to adopt policies of this nature and California needs to do more to implement the code it has already set, particularly with regard to the treatment of minorities other than blacks. Most reform to date has concentrated on the portrayal of the American Negro. Refusing to place texts that do

not meet positive standards set by the state on adoption lists
is one of the keys to textbook change.

27. *States need to develop effective policy and compliance procedures
to end school segregation in the local districts.*

The most important leadership role the states must perform
is that of beginning and speeding up the process of desegregation
at the local district level.

State policy on desegregation and racial balance, backed by
specific guidelines and regulations, was one of the key pressures
for desegregation in the two northern districts. Local leadership
had to enforce this policy, but a major factor in Sacramento's
elementary desegregation, for example, was a state Department
of Education regulation declaring school districts ineligible for
federal Title I ESEA funds unless affirmative action was being
taken to reduce high concentrations of ethnic minorities.

To be most effective, state policy should: (1) establish a concrete
definition of segregation and racial imbalance that is appropriate
to the situation within the state; (2) fix responsibility for enforcement in a specific office or department that can also provide
technical assistance and otherwise support local districts undertaking desegregation; (3) develop workable compliance procedures, including an annual racial census of all local districts;
(4) set a deadline for compliance with state policy where violations
exist; and (5) impose economic sanctions where districts fail to
meet desegregation regulations. Providing special funds to help
meet the costs of desegregation is another positive role the states
can play.

State policy and leadership to set the process of desegregation
in motion in local districts *within a specified time period* are crucial.
The Rhode Island State Board of Education's 1970 policy statement on equal educational opportunities included a time
schedule for districts to eliminate racial imbalance and also provided for action by the state Commissioner of Education to
guarantee racial balance if a district does not come into compliance in the stipulated time. California's state guidelines on
racial and ethnic imbalance, which are considerably weaker, do
not include a deadline for ending segregation and depend largely
on leadership from the State Department of Education for their
effectiveness. A decline in pressure from the State Department
of Education has rendered the guidelines almost ineffective in
Sacramento at the time field work for this study was done.
Neither Rhode Island nor California state policy provides
explicitly for withholding state funds where districts continue
segregation, although California sometimes cuts back state funds

in other instances where local districts fail to comply with a new policy within a specified period of time.

IMPROVED FEDERAL POLICY AND PRACTICES

The most pressing need for major change to generate more desegregation at a faster pace is at the federal level, where there should be a realistic drive to end segregation on a national basis. In order to do this, the federal government would have to assume increased responsibility for both initiating and enforcing desegregation.

28. *A single national policy on desegregation is needed, ending false distinctions between "de jure" and "de facto"—southern and northern —school segregation.*

Differences in the problems of desegregating Charlottesville and the two northern school districts began to wash away with the defeat of "massive resistance" and were fairly well eliminated by the passage of the 1964 Civil Rights Act. There was hardly any difference in the methods and techniques used to segregate and desegregate children in these three districts after about 1963, when the federal courts struck down all of the blatantly discriminatory features of Charlottesville's voluntary pupil transfer plan and Charlottesville began segregating in a "northern" fashion, by continuing to operate schools in the black residential area and zoning elementary schools according to racial neighborhoods. Charlottesville's experiences suggest that a different federal policy for ending northern and southern school segregation is no longer appropriate and may be postponing a national solution to what is truly a national problem.

29. *Enforcement procedures under Title VI of the Civil Rights Act that will better identify and schedule an end to racial segregation in schools receiving federal monies must be developed and implemented.*

Basic weaknesses in the U.S. Department of Health, Education and Welfare's enforcement of Title VI illustrated by these case studies include: (1) lack of a clearcut definition of segregation which districts must follow; (2) failure to set a general deadline or a timetable for ending segregation in all districts receiving federal funds; (3) inadequate followup on citizens' complaints of segregation; (4) a policy of refusing to act on complaints of racial discrimination in school districts that are or have been under court orders to desegregate; and (5) failure to initiate action to end segregated schools in northern and southern school districts such as those studied. Where federal funds are received, the official policy is one of nondiscrimination, but the majority of the children at some grade levels are enrolled in racially separate schools.

To improve its enforcement practices, HEW should: (1) abandon its fairly routine acceptance of statements of compliance with Title VI by most northern districts and by southern districts that have been under court order to desegregate; (2) use a single, concrete definition of a segregated school that can be applied to all districts in the nation, such as an enrollment of minority pupils that makes up more than 50 percent of a school's population; (3) begin systematic reviews of compliance in all districts where there are indications that segregation exists, including the many southern districts under court orders to desegregate that are now virtually immune from further pressure to desegregate; (4) act promptly to investigate and follow up on all citizen complaints of segregation; (5) speed up the process of investigating and negotiating plans for ending segregation, especially in northern districts; (6) use the sanctions available under Title VI more frequently to stop the flow of federal funds into districts that maintain segregated schools and fail to come into compliance within a specified time; and (7) require states distributing federal funds to local districts under programs such as Title I of the Elementary and Secondary Education Act to be responsible for strict compliance with federal nondiscrimination policies.

A more realistic approach in the north and HEW's taking the initiative to end segregation at the local district level are the two major needs. In the past, blacks and other minorities have carried most of the enforcement burden for federal policies. With less and less willingness on the part of minority groups to lead the kind of community campaigns that brought about desegregation in these districts, future desegregation will have to depend more on the actions of the responsible governmental agencies.

30. *The economic sanctions and incentives provided by Title VI of the Civil Rights Act sould be used more frequently and strategically to end segregation and discrimination in the schools.*

The experiences of these districts point to the potential of Title VI for bringing about desegregation, provided that enforcement is sufficiently vigorous to convince local districts that their funding will be affected by continued segregation. The passage of Title VI marked a turning point in the desegregation of schools in all three districts, with maximum progress taking place from about 1965 to 1967, when federal regulations to enforce Title VI were beginning to penetrate at the state and local level and new funds were available to local districts through the Elementary and Secondary Education Act. The districts not only expected to lose federal funds if they continued to segregate, but also believed the federal government would "smile more favorably" on desegregated districts in the future in awarding new funds.

While much of the early "fallout" effect of Title VI has now dissipated with cutbacks in enforcement and the continued flow of federal monies into districts that maintain racially separate schools, this trend could be reversed. Title VI should be used positively to channel funds into districts with the best records in desegregation, as well as to cut off funds from districts practicing segregation.

A FEW FINAL WORDS

It should be said, in conclusion, that there was a feeling of accomplishment and a better comprehension of racial problems in education among most people who had become involved in the desegregation process. Many—but not all—who had struggled with the issue felt that desegregation was a necessary step and that only through mixed schools could the districts begin to meet their responsibilities to all children. There was no sense that the job of providing equal educational opportunity was done, but, rather, a feeling of satisfaction among many that it had begun. Both whites and blacks also saw the schools performing a vital long-range role in preparing children of different racial groups to live together in a multiracial society. There was understanding in depth among some, at least, of the real urgency and relevance of this aspect of integration.

From the vantage point of these districts, pupil desegregation appears to be a minimum first step toward equal educational opportunity, providing a framework for further changes that must come if all children are to be fully accepted, learn according to their ability, and develop a balanced knowledge and understanding of society, based on facts and scholarship rather than on the myths of the white man's world.

Although the mood of minorities has changed and many members of minority groups have become increasingly disenchanted with the kind of desegregation they are experiencing in the schools, most minority leaders in these communities were still amenable to the *right kind* of desegregated schools. Most of the newer, more "militant" demands—upgrading and desegregation of ghetto and barrio schools, two-way pupil exchanges, the busing of both whites and blacks, black and chicano history courses,

more minority staff—represent attempts to equalize the desegregation process and improve racial conditions in the schools
and are in no way hostile to desegregation. Willingness on the
part of school districts and communities to meet these demands,
to correct existing racial problems in the schools, and to fully
incorporate minorities into the intellectual and social life of the
schools offers the best and probably the only hope of offsetting
further disillusionment and a stronger movement in the direction
of separatism. Not just desegregation, but desegregation and
racial balance combined with racial justice must be the goal for
the public schools.

Sources

The following sources were used throughout Part 1.

Charlottesville-Albemarle Tribune (Charlottesville, Virginia). January 1969—November 1969.

Charlottesville Public Schools. Minutes of Meetings of the School Board of the City of Charlottesville: Board Conferences, November 13, 1967 and May 17, 1968. Executive Sessions, January 19, February 2, April 20, July 20, and August 14, 1967. Informal Session of School Board and City Council, March 12, 1968. Regular Meetings, March 18, 1965; July 14, and December 15, 1966; September 21, October 21, and December 21, 1967; May 22, June 20, and November 21, 1968. Special Meetings, February 22, and June 30, 1965; July 27, September 27 and 28, and October 5, 1967; February 28 and June 3, 1968. School Board and City Council Workshop November 26, 1968.

Charlottesville, Virginia Public Schools. A Survey Report. (Nashville, Tennessee: Division of Surveys and Field Services, George Peabody College for Teachers), 1967.

Daily Progress (Charlottesville, Virginia). January 13, 1969—September 30, 1969.

Gaston, Paul M., and Hammond, Thomas T. "Public School Desegregation: Charlottesville, Virginia, 1955—1962." A report presented to the Nashville Conference, "The South: The Ethical Demands of Integration," December 28, 1962 (mimeo).

Personal interviews with 46 community leaders, parents, public school students, former students, members of the School Board, and staff of the Charlottesville Public Schools. These interviews were conducted by a biracial team of the Center for Urban Education, December 15—21, 1968, and January 13—24, 1969.

In addition, the following sources were used for individual chapters.

Chapter 1.

Barksdale, James W. *A Comparative Study of Contemporary White and Negro Standards in Health, Education and Welfare. Charlottesville, Virginia.* Phelps Stokes Fellowship Papers, No. 20. Charlottesville, Virginia: University of Virginia, 1949.

Jefferson's County. Charlottesville-Albemarle County, Virginia. (Charlottesville, Virginia: Charlottesville and Albemarle County Chamber of Commerce), no date.

"Jefferson's County . . . Charlottesville and Albemarle County," Charlottesville and Albemarle County Chamber of Commerce, Charlottesville, Virginia [1967?]

The Newcomer's Guide to Charlottesville and Albemarle County. Charlottesville, Virginia: National Bank and Trust Company, no date.

U. S. Bureau of the Census. U. S. Census of Housing: 1960. Vol. I:

"States and Small Areas;" Part 8: "Texas-Wyoming." Washington, D.C.: U.S. Government Printing Office, 1963.

U.S. Bureau of the Census. *U.S. Census of Population: 1960; Vol. I:* "Characteristics of the Population"; Part 48: "Virginia." Washington, D.C.: U.S. Government Printing Office, 1963.

U. S. Bureau of the Census. *U. S. Census of Population: 1970.* "Advance Report"; PC(VI)-48: "Virginia." Final Population Counts. Washington, D.C.: U.S. Department of Commerce, December 1970.

U. S. Bureau of the Census. *U. S. Census of Population: 1970.* "Advance Report"; PC(V2)-48: "Virginia." General Population Characteristics. Washington, D.C.: U.S. Department of Commerce, February 1971.

Virginia Writer's Program. *Jefferson's Albemarle. A Guide to Albemarle County and the City of Charlottesville, Virginia.* American Guide Series, Works Projects Administration, 1941.

Chapter 2.

Barksdale, James W. *A Comparative Study of Contemporary White and Negro Standards in Health, Education and Welfare. Charlottesville, Virginia.* Phelps Stokes Fellowship Papers, No. 20. Charlottesville, Virginia: University of Virginia, 1949.

New Dimensions, 1969. A Look at the Charlottesville Public Schools. Charlottesville, Virignia: Charlottesville Public Schools, 1969.

Virginia Writer's Program. *Jefferson's Albemarle. A Guide to Albemarle County and the City of Charlottesville, Virginia.* American Guide Series, Works Projects Administration, 1941.

Chapter 3.

Charlottesville Public Schools. "Outline of Charlottesville School Integration Case," December 2, 1963 (typewritten).

Mearns, Edward A. Jr., "Virginia," in U. S. Commission on Civil Rights, *Civil Rights U.S.A. Public Schools. Southern States, 1962.* Washington, D.C.: U.S. Government Printing Office, 1962.

Muse, Benjamin. *Virginia's Massive Resistance.* Bloomington, Indiana: Indiana University Press, 1961.

Richmond [Virginia] Times Dispatch. July 13 and August 28, 1956; July 27, 1957.

Southern School News (Nashville, Tennessee). November, 1955; August, December 1956; January, August 1957; August—October 1958; January—February 1959.

"Virginia versus the Court," *The Economist* (December 10, 1955), p. 942.

Wakefield, Dan. "Charlottesville Battle. Symbol of the Divided South," *Nation,* Vol. 183, No. 11 (September 15, 1956), pp. 210—213.

Chapter 4.

Allen vs. School Board of the City of Charlottesville, Virginia. Civil

Action No. 51, U. S. District Court for the Western District of Virginia, Charlottesville. Opinion by the Court, December 18, 1961 (mimeographed copy).

Boyle, Sarah Patton. *The Desegregated Heart. A Virginian's Stand in a Time of Transition.* New York: William Morrow and Company, 1962.

Charlottesville Public Schools, "Brief Account of Admission of Negro Pupils to Lane High School and Venable Elementary School in Charlottesville, September 9, 1958—June 20, 1961," June 20, 1961 (typewritten).

Charlottesville Public Schools, "Outline of Charlottesville School Integration Case," December 2, 1963 (typewritten).

Charlottesville Public Schools. Report on Pupil Scholarship Program: December 10, 1959; June 30, 1961; June 30, 1962. First Installment Payments, 1962-63, undated; January 21, 1964. Second Installment Payments, 1963-64, undated; May 11, 1965; November 28, 1968.

Dillard et al. *vs. School Board of the City of Charlottesville,* U. S. Court of Appeals for the Fourth Circuit. Opinion of the court, September 17, 1962 (mimeographed copy).

Ellis, Fendall R., Superintendent of Schools, Charlottesville, Virginia. Statement *in* U. S. Commission on Civil Rights, *Conference before the U. S. Commission on Civil Rights. Second Annual Conference on Problems of Schools in Transition from the Educator's Viewpoint,* March 21—22, 1960, Gatlinburg, Tenn. Washington, D.C.: U. S. Government Printing Office, 1960.

Washington Post. February 21, 1969.

Chapter 5.

Babcock, Chester R., Chairman, Charlottesville School Board. Letter to Henry A. Haden, Chairman, Community Relations Committee, Charlottesville, Virginia, October 25, 1964.

Bash, James H. *Effective Teaching in the Desegregated School. A Guidebook.* Bloomington, Indiana: Phi Delta Kappa, 1966.

Brown, Drewary, President, NAACP, Charlottesville Branch. Letter to the School Board and Office of the Superintendent of Schools, Charlottesville, Virginia, September 8, 1965.

Charlottesville Public Schools. "Elementary and Secondary School Report for the School Year, 1967-68," August 17, 1967.

Charlottesville Public Schools. "Selection of Students for Greenbrier Elementary School from the Venable School District," September 20, 1967.

Daily Progress (Charlottesville, Virginia). February 19 and 23, May 21, and July 1, 1965; August 18 and October 13 and 17, 1967; April 16, 1968.

Haden, H. A., Chairman, Community Relations Committee. Letter to Chester R. Babcock, Chairman, Charlottesville School Board, October 22, 1964.

Harris et al. *vs. Charlottesville City School Board.* Civil Action No.

68-C-25-C, U. S. District Court for the Western District of Virginia, Charlottesville Division, Answer, November 30, 1968.

Harris et al. *vs. Charlottesville Redevelopment and Housing Authority and the School Board of the City of Charlottesville.* Civil Action No. 68-C-25-C, U. S. District Court for the Western District of Virginia, Charlottesville Division, Complaint, November 4, 1968.

National Association for the Advancement of Colored People, Executive Board, Charlottesville Branch. "The 1963 Revolution Comes to Charlottesville. A Statement of Grievances and Recommendations." A text prepared for the Charlottesville Community Relations Committee, September 11, 1963.

National Education Association, PR&R Committee on Civil and Human Rights of Educators. "Faculty Desegregation," Spring 1966 Conferences. Washington, D.C.: National Education Association, PR&R Committee, 1966.

Richmond [Virginia] News Leader. June 19, 1963.

Richmond [Virginia] Times Dispatch. December 14 and 19, 1962.

Rudy, Edith H., Chairman, School Board of the City of Charlottesville. Letter to Drewary Brown, President, NAACP, Charlottesville, Virginia, September 9, 1965.

School Board of the City of Charlottesville. "Statement of Policies and Plans for Compliance under Title VI of the Civil Rights Act of 1964," May 20, 1965.

Townsend, Mrs. Thelma J., President, Charlottesville Branch NAACP. Letter to Chester R. Babcock, Chairman, Charlottesville School Board, December 1, 1964.

U.S. Department of Health, Education and Welfare. Equal Educational Opportunities Program. File on Charlottesville, Virginia. Washington, D.C.

U.S. Department of Health, Education and Welfare, Office of Education. "General Statement of Policies under Title VI of the Civil Rights Act of 1964 Respecting Desegregation of Elementary and Secondary Schools." Washington, D.C.: U.S. Government Printing Office, April 1965.

Venable Elementary School. *Venable Building Policy.* Charlottesville, Virginia, [1966?] (ditto).

Venable Elementary School. *Venable School Handbook for Teachers.* Charlottesville, Virginia [1967-68].

Chapter 6.

Bradner, N. P., Executive Secretary, Virginia Committee, the Commission on Secondary Schools of the Southern Association of Colleges and Schools, Richmond, Virginia. Letter to P. H. Cale, Superintendent, Albemarle County Public Schools; Dr. E. W. Rushton, Superintendent, Charlottesville Public Schools; and A. L. Scott, Principal, Jackson P. Burley High School, November 4, 1966.

Bradner, N. P., Executive Secretary, Virginia Committee, the Commission on Secondary Schools of the Southern Association of Colleges and Schools, Richmond, Virginia. Letter to DeWitt T. Miller, Assistant Superintendent, Albemarle County Public Schools, November 17, 1966.

Charlottesville parent. Letter to Dr. Edward W. Rushton, Superintendent, Charlottesville Public Schools, May 17, 1968.

Charlottesville Public Schools. "Cost Comparisons of Pupils at Burley and Lane," September 8, 1965.

Charlottesville Public Schools. "Language Arts Guide," 1969 (mimeo).

Charlottesville Public Schools. Statement of Superintendent in Response to Lane Student Demands, May 21, 1968.

Consultative Resource Center. "Report to the Faculty, Lane High School." Charlottesville, Virginia: University of Virginia, 1968 (mimeo).

Daily Progress (Charlottesville, Virginia). December 7, 1966; April 10, May 13–15, 17, and 22, June 4, October 24, November 4, 5, 7, 9, 24, and 27, 1968.

Nickels, W. I., Jr., Principal, Lane High School. Letter to Dr. Edward W. Rushton, Superintendent, Charlottesville Public Schools, April 18, 1968.

Richmond [Virginia] Times Dispatch. May 14 and 23, 1968.

Robinson, Willard A., Chairman, Jackson P. Burley High School Faculty. Letter to Dr. Edward W. Rushton, Superintendent, Charlottesville Public Schools, February 27, 1967.

Scott, A. L., Principal, Burley High School. Letter to George C. Tramontin, Superintendent, Charlottesville Public Schools, February 16, 1966.

Scott, A. L., "Where the Faculty Went," *The Burley Bulletin,* November 1966.

Tramontin, George C., Superintendent, Charlottesville Public Schools. Letter to Paul H. Cale, Superintendent, Albemarle County Public Schools, November 15, 1965.

U.S. Department of Health, Education and Welfare, Office for Civil Rights, Region III. "Resume. Inquiry into Complaint against Lane High School." Charlottesville, Virginia, 1969.

Chapter 7.

Heller, Landis R., Jr., and Potter, Norris W. *One Nation Indivisible.* Columbus, Ohio: Charles E. Merrill Books, Inc., 1966.

Hemphill, William Edwin; Schlegel, Marvin; and Engelberg, Sadie Ethel. *Cavalier Commonwealth. History and Government of Virginia.* (Rev. Ed.) St. Louis: Webster Division, McGraw-Hill Book Company, 1963.

School Board of the City of Charlottesville. "Advisory Specialist Program to Promote Desegregation in the City Schools, Especially Lane High School," September 1, 1968–June 30, 1969 (mimeo).

School Board of the City of Charlottesville, Statement, November 20, 1969 (mimeo).

The Virginian-Pilot. October 26—28, 1965.
Washington Post. October 19, 1969.

Epilogue.

Telephone interviews, March 26, 1970; November 24 and 28, 1971.
Varner, Thomas, Director of Secondary Education, Charlottesville
Public Schools. Letter to author, March 10, 1970.
Washington Post. January 29 and February 19, 1972.

The following sources were used throughout Part 2.

Bakst, M. Charles, *Providence Journal-Bulletin.* Education Writer.
Selected newspaper reports on desegregation and related Providence
school issues.
Department of Public Schools, Providence, Rhode Island. Adminis-
trative Office. Newspaper clipping file, June, 1966 — March, 1969.
Gibson, Reverend Raymond E., Chairman, Rhode Island State
Advisory Committee to the U.S. Commission on Civil Rights. Newspaper
clipping file, 1966-1967.
League of Women Voters of Providence, Rhode Island. Files on
school desegregation and reorganization of school committee, 1966-
1968.
Personal interviews with 39 community leaders, parents, members of
the Providence School Committee, staff of the Department of Public
Schools, and the state Commissioner of Education. These interviews
were conducted by a bi-racial team of the Center for Urban Education
March 21 — April 11, 1969.
Pfautz, Harold W. "Providence, Rhode Island: The Politics of School
Desegregation." Unpublished paper, Providence, Rhode Island [1968].
Providence Evening Bulletin. March 20 — October 18, 1969.
U.S. Commission on Civil Rights. Xerox newspaper clipping file on
Providence, Rhode Island from Southern Education Reporting Service.
April 13 — October 8, 1967.
Urban League of Rhode Island, Providence, Rhode Island. News-
paper clipping file on school desegregation, 1966-1968.
Young, Carol J. *Providence Journal-Bulletin.* Education Writer.
Selected newspaper reports on desegregation and related Providence
school issues.

In addition, the sources listed below were used for individual chapters.

Chapter 1.

Bakst, M. Charles. "The School Board Acts Daringly on Desegregation." *Providence Sunday Journal,* March 14, 1971, p. N-39.

Durant, Charles H.; Moore, Soraya; Kiven, Arline R.; and· Swan, Bradford F. "The Negro in Rhode Island from Slavery to Community" in "Our Black Heritage." *Providence Sunday Journal Magazine*, October 12, 1969, pp. 16—23.

Gabriel, Richard A. "Ethnic Voting in Primary Elections: the Irish and Italians of Providence, Rhode Island," Research Series Number 12, Bureau of Government Research, University of Rhode Island, Kingston, Rhode Island, 1969.

Gabriel, Richard A. "The Political Machine Is Still Alive and Well in Rhode Island" in *The Rhode Islander, Providence Sunday Journal*, March 21, 1971, p. 18.

Mayer, Kurt B. *Economic Development and Population Growth in Rhode Island.* Brown University Papers No. 28. Providence, Rhode Island, 1953.

Pfautz, Harold W. "The Power Structure of the Negro Sub-Community, A Case Study and a Comparative View." *Phylon*, V. 23 (No. 2, Summer, 1962), pp. 156—166.

"Providence." *Encyclopaedia Britannica*. 1970. Vol. 18.

"Providence." *The Encyclopedia Americana*. 1969. Vol. 22.

"Providence." *Collier's Encyclopedia*. 1970. Vol. 19.

Providence Journal. June 6, 10, October 16, 1970; May 5, July 3, 1971.

Providence Sunday Journal. September 26, 1971.

"Rhode Island." *Encyclopaedia Britannica*. 1970. Vol. 19.

Rhode Island Department of Employment Security. *Employment Security. State of Rhode Island 1967-1968*. Providence, Rhode Island: The Department, no date.

U.S. Bureau of the Census. *County and City Data Book. 1967*. Washington, D.C.: U.S. Government Printing Office, 1967.

U.S. Bureau of the Census. Current Population Reports. *Special Census of Rhode Island, October 1, 1965*. Series P-28, No. 1393. Washington, D.C.: U.S. Department of Commerce, January 24, 1966.

U.S. Bureau of the Census. *U.S. Census of Population: 1950*. Vol. II. Characteristics of the Population, Part 39, Rhode Island. Washington, D.C.: U.S. Government Printing Office, 1952.

U.S. Bureau of the Census. *U.S. Census of Population: 1950*. Vol. III. Census Tract Statistics, Chapter 44. Washington, D.C.: U.S. Government Printing Office, 1952.

U.S. Bureau of the Census. *U.S. Census of Population: 1960*. Vol. I. Characteristics of the Population, Part 41, Rhode Island. Washington, D.C.: U.S. Government Printing Office, 1963.

U.S. Bureau of the Census. *U.S. Census of Population: 1970*. Advance Report PC (V2)-41. General Population Characteristics, Rhode Island. Washington, D.C.: U.S. Department of Commerce.

U.S. Bureau of the Census. *U.S. Census of Population: 1970*. General Social and Economic Characteristics. Final Report. PC(1)-C41. Rhode Island. Washington, D.C.: U.S. Government Printing Office, 1972.

U.S. Bureau of the Census. *1970 Census of Population and Housing*.

General Demographic Trends for Metropolitan Areas, 1960 to 1970. Final Report. PHC(2)-41. Rhode Island. Washington, D.C.: U.S. Department of Commerce. July, 1972.

Urban League of Rhode Island. "The Non-White In Providence." Providence, Rhode Island (1966).

Chapter 2.

Archambault, Reginald D. and others. *A Plan for the Re-Organization of Providence Schools.* Project C.O.P.E. (Cooperative Planning for Excellence). Brown University, Providence, Rhode Island, July 1967.

Department of Public Schools. Pupil Accounting Office. "Final Enrollment — February 14, 1969." Providence, Rhode Island, February 19, 1969.

General Assembly of Rhode Island. S 888A (1968). An Act in Amendment of Chapter 680 of the Public Laws of 1925 Entitled, "An Act Relating to the Management and Support of the Public Schools of the City of Providence," as Amended, and Providing a Referendum on the Manner of Selecting the School Committee of Said City.

Lieberman, Myron. "The City's Schools After Decades of Indifference," *Providence Sunday Journal.* August 17, 1969. pp. N-41, N-45.

Peat, Marwick, Mitchell & Company, Certified Public Accountants. Letter to Providence School Committee, Providence, Rhode Island, February 12, 1969.

Rhode Island School of Design. *Survey and Recommendations: Physical Plant. Public Schools of the City of Providence.* Project C.O.P.E. (Cooperative Planning for Excellence). Providence, Rhode Island, June 1967.

Rollins, Sidney P. *Survey of Curriculum and Instruction in the Providence Public Schools.* Project C.O.P.E. (Cooperative Planning for Excellence). Rhode Island College, Providence, Rhode Island, June 1967.

U.S. Department of Health, Education and Welfare. Elementary and Secondary Public School Survey. Fall, 1970. Print-out, Providence, Rhode Island.

U.S. Department of Health, Education and Welfare. "School System Report — Fall, 1968 Elementary and Secondary School Survey." Public Schools of the City of Providence, Rhode Island. January 23, 1969.

Wilkins, Ralph W. Department of Public Schools, Providence, Rhode Island. Letter to Mr. William L. Taylor, United States Commission on Civil Rights, Washington, D.C., June 17, 1966.

Chapter 3.

City Plan Commission. *Master Plan for Public Schools.* Providence, Rhode Island: City Plan Commission, November 1966.

Complaints of Discrimination in John Howland School and Summit Avenue School. Hearing before Charles A. O'Connor, Superintendent of Schools, City of Providence, April 4-5, 1968. Providence, Rhode Island.

Curwood, Sarah Thomas. *A Report on Lippitt Hill, Providence, Rhode Island.* A report to William Gaige, President, Rhode Island College. Providence, Rhode Island, August 31, 1963.

Department of Public Schools. *Integration Plan. Citywide.* Providence, Rhode Island, 1967.

Department of Public Schools. *Providence Schools 1965 — 1968. Report on Federal Programs in the Providence School Department.* Providence, Rhode Island.

Durant, Charles H.; Moore, Soraya; Kiven, Arline R.; and Swan, Bradford F. "The Negro in Rhode Island from Slavery to Community" in "Our Black Heritage." *Providence Sunday Journal Magazine,* October 12, 1969, pp. 16–23.

"The Lippitt Hill School." Providence, Rhode Island. December 10, 1967.

Rhode Island School of Design. *Survey and Recommendations: Physical Plant. Public Schools of the City of Providence.* Project C.O.P.E. (Cooperative Planning for Excellence). Providence, Rhode Island, June, 1967.

Rhode Island State Advisory Committee to the U.S. Commission on Civil Rights. *A Comparative Study of Three Elementary Schools in Providence.* Providence, Rhode Island, May 4, 1965.

Wilkins, Ralph W., Department of Public Schools, Providence, Rhode Island. Letter to Mr. William L. Taylor, United States Commission on Civil Rights, Washington, D.C., June 17, 1966.

Chapter 4.

City Plan Commission. *Master Plan for Public Schools.* Providence, Rhode Island: City Plan Commission, November, 1966.

Curwood, Sarah Thomas. *A Report on Lippitt Hill, Providence, Rhode Island.* A report to William Gaige, President, Rhode Island College. Providence, Rhode Island, August 31, 1963.

"The Lippitt Hill School." Providence, Rhode Island. December 10, 1967.

Martin Luther King, Jr. Elementary School (Lippitt Hill). School Scrapbook. Providence, Rhode Island.

O'Connor, Charles A., Jr. "Position Paper of the Superintendent on the Integration of the Providence Public Schools." Providence, Rhode Island, July 28, 1966 (mimeo).

U.S. Department of Health, Education and Welfare. Equal Educational Opportunities Program. File, Providence, Rhode Island. Washington, D.C.

Chapter 5.

Department of Public Schools. *Providence Schools 1965 — 1968. Report on Federal Programs in the Providence School Department.* Providence, Rhode Island.
Department of Public Schools. *A Proposal for Quality Education in Providence.* Providence, Rhode Island [1967].
Department of Public Schools. *Integration Plan. Citywide.* Providence, Rhode Island, 1967.
Hazeltine, Mrs. Barrett. President, League of Women Voters of Providence. Letter to Honorable Joseph A. Doorley, March 9, 1967.
State Board of Education. Minutes of the Meeting, April 13, 1967.
"Summary of Conclusions Reached by Mayor Doorley's Subcommittee on De Facto Segregation. Meeting of April 4, 1967." Providence, Rhode Island.

Chapter 6.

Department of Public Schools. *Integration Plan. Citywide.* Providence, Rhode Island, 1967.
Department of Public Schools. Tables outlining detailed plans for desegregation. Providence, Rhode Island [1967] (mimeo).
Flynn Model School Steering Committee. "Edmun W. Flynn Model School Rationale." Providence, Rhode Island [1967].

Chapter 7.

The Committee to Eliminate Racism in the Public Schools. Leaflet explaining committee and its program. Providence, Rhode Island, March 1967. (mimeo).

Chapter 8.

Department of Public Schools. "Black and White Pupil Distribution." Providence, Rhode Island, May 16, 1969.
Department of Public Schools. Pupil Accounting Office. "Final Enrollment — February 14, 1969." Providence, Rhode Island, February 19, 1969.
Complaints of Discrimination in John Howland School and Summit Avenue School. Hearing before Charles O'Connor, Superintendent of Schools, City of Providence, April 4-5, 1968. Providence, Rhode Island.

General Assembly of Rhode Island. S 888A (1968). An Act in Amendment of Chapter 680 of the Public Laws of 1925 Entitled, "An Act Relating to the Management and Support of the Public Schools of the City of Providence," as Amended, and Providing a Referendum on the Manner of Selecting the School Committee of Said City.

Kramer, Louis I., Acting Superintendent, Providence, Public Schools. Letter to Mr. Kenneth Williams, Human Relations Commission, Providence, Rhode Island, February 24, 1969.

Rhode Island Special Commission to Study the Entire Field of Education. *Education in Rhode Island: A Plan for the Future.* Final Report to the General Assembly. Providence, Rhode Island: The Commission, June 1968.

Some Proposals for the Improvement of Education in the Providence Public Schools Through the Development of New Relationships among the Citizens, Mayor, City Council, and School Committee. Report of the Mayor's Advisory Committee to Study Possible Revision of the Strayer Act. Providence, Rhode Island, September 1, 1967.

Tomassi, Fred, Principal, Esek Hopkins Junior High School. Memorandum to the Parents and Students at Esek Hopkins Junior High School, March 6, 1969 (mimeo).

Chapter 9.

Durant, Charles H. "Proposed Providence Plan for Desegregation of Senior High Schools. Alternate Proposals for September, 1971-72." Providence, Rhode Island, February 25, 1971.

Providence Journal. March 3, May 4, June 1 — July 31, September 1 — October 22, 1970; March 1 — May 15, June 15 — July 28, September 1 — October 10, 1971.

Telephone interviews, November 16 and 21, 1971.

U.S. Department of Health, Education and Welfare. Equal Education Opportunities Program. File, Providence, Rhode Island. Washington, D.C.

U.S. Department of Health, Education and Welfare. Elementary and Secondary Public School Survey. Fall, 1970. Print-out, Providence, Rhode Island.

The following sources were used throughout Part 3.

California State Department of Education. *California Laws and Policies Relating to Equal Opportunities in Education.* Sacramento, California: The Department, 1969.

Cortez, Mrs. Herbert, former Chairman, Community Education Advisory Committee on Compensatory Education, Sacramento City Unified School District. Personal files.

El Hispano (formerly *El Hispanoamericano*). Sacramento, California: Available back files, December 29, 1967 — May, 1969; July, 1969 — September, 1969.

Personal interviews with 46 community leaders, parents, students, members of the Board of Education, and Sacramento City Unified School District staff. These interviews were carried out by a biracial team of the Center for Urban Education, May 16 — June 6, 1969.

Sacramento (California) *Bee.* June, 1969 — September, 1969; September 1-30, December 1-31, 1971; January 1-7, 9, February 1-10, 20-23, 1972.

Sacramento City Unified School District. *Actions toward Equal Educational Opportunity Taken by the Sacramento City Unified School District, 1963-1968.* Sacramento, California, February 20, 1968.

———. *The Ethnic Composition of the Pupil Population of the Sacramento City Unified School District.* Research Report No. 5, Series 1964-65 (December 10, 1964); Research Report No. 7, Series 1965-66 (December 16, 1965); Research Report No. 8, Series 1966-67 (January 18, 1967); Research Report No. 9, Series 1967-68 (January 2, 1968); and Research Report No. 8, Series 1968-69 (November 20, 1968). Sacramento, California.

———. Newspaper clipping file, Administration Office. September, 1965 — May, 1969. This clipping file includes articles from the *Sacramento Bee, The Sacramento Union* and other area papers.

———. *Programs and Services Provided Under the Elementary and Secondary Education Act of 1965 and SB 482, McAteer Act of 1965.* A Board of Education Report to the California State Department of Education. Sacramento, California, August 1, 1968.

Sacramento (California) *Union.* February 16 — May 15, September 1-15, November 1-15, 1970; September 1-30, November 1-30, 1971; February 1-10, 20-23, 1972.

In addition, the sources listed are used for individual chapters.

Chapter 1.

"Black, Brown, and White." A Special Report, *The Sacramento Bee.* Sacramento, California, September 28, 1969.

Gillespie, Alger C. "The Human Element of an Area Selected for Redevelopment." Unpublished Master's thesis, Sacramento State College, August, 1964.

Industrial Development, ed. *California Site Selection Handbook.* Conway Research, 1967.

Larsen, Christian L.; Bell, James R.; Cain, Leonard D., Jr.; Glenny, Lyman A.; Hickman, William H.; and Irwin, Irl A. *Growth and Govern-*

ment in Sacramento. Metropolitan Action Studies, No. 4. Bloomington: Indiana University Press, 1965.

McGowan, Joseph A. *The Sacramento Valley. A Students' Guide to Localized History.* New York: Teachers College, Columbia University, 1967.

Public Administration Service. *The 'Government of Metropolitan Sacramento.* Chicago: Public Administration Service, 1957.

"Sacramento." *Collier's Encyclopedia.* 1968. Vol. 20.

———. *Encyclopaedia Britannica.* 1968. Vol. 19.

———. *The Encyclopedia Americana. International Edition.* 1967. Vol. 24.

U.S. Bureau of the Census. *County and City Data Book, 1967. A Statistical Abstract Supplement.* Washington, D.C.: U.S. Government Printing Office, 1967.

———. Current Population Reports. *Special Census of North Sacramento and Sacramento, California. November 9, 1964.* Series P-28, No. 1386. Washington, D.C.: U.S. Department of Commerce, April 19, 1965.

———. *U.S. Census of Population: 1950.* Vol. III. Census Tracts Statistics, Chapter 46. Washington, D.C.: U.S. Government Printing Office, 1952.

———. *U.S. Census of Population and Housing: 1960.* Census Tracts. Final Report PHC (1)-129. Washington, D.C.: U.S. Government Printing Office, 1962.

U.S. Bureau of the Census. *U.S. Census of Population: 1970.* General Population Characteristics. Final Report PC (1) 36. California. Washington, D.C.: U.S. Government Printing Office, 1971.

White, Willie R. "A Descriptive Study of a Disadvantaged Community." Unpublished Master's thesis, Sacramento State College, May 24, 1968.

Chapter 2.

Fort, Edward B. "Decision Making in the Sacramento De Facto Segregation Crisis" in Edwards, T. Bentley, and Wirt, Frederick M. *School Desegregation in the North. The Challenge and the Experience.* San Francisco: Chandler Publishing Company, 1967.

Larsen, Christian L.; Bell, James R.; Cain, Leonard D., Jr.; Glenny, Lyman A.; Hickman, William H.; and Irwin, Irl A. *Growth and Government in Sacramento.* Metropolitan Action Studies, No. 4. Bloomington, Indiana University Press, 1965.

Public Administration Service. *The Government of Metropolitan Sacramento.* Chicago: Public Administration Service, 1957.

Sacramento City Unified School District. *Report on 1964 Building Fund.* Sacramento, California, March 8, 1968.

———. "School Construction Since School Year 1949-50." Sacramento, California, no date. (typewritten)

U.S. Bureau of the Census. *Special Census of North Sacramento and Sacramento, California: November 9, 1964.* Series P-28, No. 1386. Washington, D.C.: U.S. Department of Commerce, April 19, 1965.

Chapter 3.

Fort, Edward B. "Decision Making in the Sacramento De Facto Segregation Crisis" in Edwards, T. Bentley, and Wirt, Frederick M. *School Desegregation in the North. The Challenge and the Experience.* San Francisco: Chandler Publishing Company, 1967.

Keller vs. Sacramento City Unified School District, No. 146525, Superior Court of the State of California, Sacramento County. Opinion by the Court, October 8, 1963 (xerox copy).

Sacramento City Unified School District. *Follow-Up Study of Former Stanford Junior High School Pupils.* Research Report No. 7, Series 1966-67. Sacramento, California, January 16, 1967.

————. *Low Enrollment Schools.* Research Report No. 15, Series 1968-69. Sacramento, California, April 3, 1969.

————. *New and Revised Junior High School Attendance Boundaries for the 1966-67 School Year.* Research Report No. 5, Series 1965-66. Sacramento, California, November 19, 1965.

————. *Preliminary Report on the Ethnic Composition of the Pupil Population of the Sacramento City Unified School District.* Research Report No. 3, Series 1963-64. Sacramento, California, September 25, 1963.

————. *Revised Junior High School Attendance Boundaries.* Research Report No. 2, Series 1963-64. Sacramento, California. November 4, 1963.

Chapter 4.

Citizens Advisory Committee on Equal Educational Opportunity. *Equal Educational Opportunity in the Sacramento City Unified School District.* A Report to the Board of Education, Sacramento City Unified School District. Sacramento, California, May 22, 1965.

Moskovitz, Adolph. Xerox file of communications to Sacramento City Unified School District concerning report of Citizens Advisory Committee on Equal Educational Opportunity, June — July, 1965.

Sacramento City Unified School District. Minutes of Special Meetings of the Board of Education, May 27, June 21 and June 30, 1965.

————. *Statement of Policy on Providing Equal Educational Opportunity in the Sacramento City Unified School District.* Sacramento, California, October 4, 1965.

Chapter 5.

Cain, Leonard D., Jr. "Cultural Deprivation and the Emerging Generation." An address presented before one of the sections of the annual conference of the National Federation of Settlements and Neighborhood Centers, Chicago, May 27, 1966 (mimeo).

Committee for Project Aspiration. *Project Aspiration.* Sacramento, California: The Committee [1966].

Community Educational Advisory Committee of the Sacramento City Unified School District. Minutes of January 25, 1968 Meeting. March 4, 1968. (typewritten)

Oak Park Neighborhood Council. Education Committee. "Project Aspiration — Success or Failure?" and other materials. Sacramento, California, June 24, 1967. (Mimeo and Xerox packet)

Oakden, Margaret M. "Selected Case Studies of Former Second Grade Pupils of American Legion Elementary School as Participants in 'Project Aspiration' of the Sacramento City Unified School District." Unpublished Master's thesis, Sacramento State College, December 13, 1967.

Sacramento City Unified School District. *In-Service Training Program for the Alleviation of the Adverse Effects of De Facto Segregation.* Administrative Bulletin No. 151, Series 1965-66. Sacramento, California, June 3, 1966.

_____. Minutes of Meeting of Board of Education, March 21, 1966.

_____. *New and Revised Elementary School Attendance Boundaries for the 1966-67 School Year.* Research Report No. 13, Series 1965-66. Sacramento, California, April 26, 1966.

_____. *Possible Plans for Meeting the 1966-67 Classroom Needs in Elementary Schools which by Board Definition Are De Facto Segregated.* Sacramento, California, March 16, 1966.

_____. *A Program for the Educationally Deprived Under the Elementary and Secondary Education Act of 1965, Public Law 89-10 Title I.* Sacramento, California, 1968-69, no date.

_____. *Study of District Policy in Regard to the Transportation of Regular Students.* Sacramento, California, February 6, 1967.

_____. *Summary of Evaluation Reports Regarding E. S. E. A. and E. O. A. Program of 1966-67.* Research Report No. 2, Series 1967-68. Sacramento, California, July 27, 1967.

Chapter 6.

Sacramento City Unified School District. *Current Status of Efforts to Alleviate or Eliminate the Adverse Effects of De Facto Segregation at the Camellia and Donner Elementary Schools.* Sacramento, California, January 30, 1968.

_____. Minutes of Meeting of the Board of Education, February 5, 1968.

_____. *A Program for the Educationally Deprived Under the Elementary and Secondary Education Act of 1965, Public Law 89-10 Title I.* Sacramento, California, 1969-69, no date.

_____. *Progress Report on Implications of Attorney General's Opinion 65/324 Relating to Pre-Field Act School Buildings.* Sacramento, California, June 27, 1966.

Chapter 7.

Community Educational Advisory Committee of the Sacramento City Unified School District. Minutes of the March 21, 1968 Meeting. April 15, 1968. (typewritten)

Cortez, Mrs. Herbert. Letter to the Board of Education, Sacramento City Unified School District, November 27, 1967.

Sacramento City Unified School District. *A Summary of the Assessments of the District's Integration Programs, 1964-1971.* Research Report No. 9, Series 1971-72. Sacramento, California, September 28, 1971.

Sacramento City Unified School District. Minutes of Regular and Special Meetings of the Board of Education, October 16, 1967; November 13, 1967; December 1, 1967; February 5, 1968; March 18, 1968; August 16, 1968; and February 10, 1969.

_____. *New and Revised Elementary School Attendance Boundaries for the 1968-69 School Year.* Research Report No. 13, Series 1967-68. Sacramento, California, March 26, 1968.

_____. *Possible Alternate Plans for the Alleviation or Elimination of the Adverse Effects of De Facto Segregation at the Washington Elementary School (Including Cost Estimates for Each Plan).* Sacramento, California, November 3, 1967.

_____. *Summary of Questionnaire Responses Received from Parents of Pupils Transferred from the Washington Elementary School in the Fall of 1968.* Sacramento, California, March 18, 1969.

U.S. Department of Health, Education and Welfare. Equal Educational Opportunities Program. Sacramento City Unified School District File. Washington, D.C.

Washington People's Committee. Statement to Members of the Board of Education, Sacramento City Unified School District, April 4, 1968.

_____. Handbills and other mimeographed material on Washington School desegregation issue.

Chapter 8.

Bontemps, Arna; Lawrence, Paul and others. *Negro American Heritage.* San Francisco: Century Communications, Inc., 1968.

California State Department of Education. Bureau of Intergroup Relations. "Individual School Report. Fall, 1968 Elementary and Secondary School Survey. U.S. Department of Health, Education and Welfare." Survey forms for Sacramento City Unified School District collected by State Department of Education, October 4, 1968. (Xerox)

_____. "Racial and Ethnic Distribution of Employees." Survey forms, Sacramento City Unified School District, December 22, 1967. (Xerox)

California Teachers Association. *Land of the Free and Its Critics.* Burlingame, California: The Association, 1967.

Caughey, John W.; Franklin, John Hope; and May, Ernest R. Revised 1966. *Land of the Free. A History of the United States.* New York: Benziger Brothers, Inc., 1969.

Dymally, Mervyn M. "The Struggle for the Inclusion of Negro History in Our Textbooks . . . A California Experience," *Negro History Bulletin,* Vol. 33 (December, 1970), 188-191.

Griffin, Ples A., Bureau of Intergroup Relations, California State Department of Education. Memorandum to Mr. Ted Neff, Bureau of Intergroup Relations, California State Department of Education, August 30, 1968 (typewritten).

Lawson, F. Melvyn, Superintendent, Sacramento City Unified School District. Letter to Miss Sharon Pinkney (?), Sacramento, California, April 15, 1968.

Pinkney (?), Miss Sharon. Letter to F. Melvyn Lawson, City Superintendent of Schools, Sacramento City Unified School District, March 29, 1968, for the Minority Students of the High Schools of the City of Sacramento.

Sacramento City Unified School District. *An Application for a School Board Grant Program on School Desegregation Problems under Title IV, Section 405, Civil Rights Acts of 1964.* Board of Education. Sacramento, California, April, 1967.

————. *Annual Report to the Board of Education on Certificated Personnel.* Sacramento, California, January 20, 1969.

————. *Bibliography on Mexican-Americans.* Sacramento, California, 1968.

————. *Ethnic Relations and Contributions 11.* A Course of Study. Senior High School Segment. Trial. Sacramento, California, 1968.

————. *Resource Guide on Negro History in the United States. Grade Eight.* Junior High Segment. Trial. Sacramento, California, 1969.

————. *Resource Guide on the Negro in America.* Intermediate Segment. Trial, Sacramento, California, 1968.

————. *Resource Units on Mexican-American History in the United States.* Junior High Segment. Trial. Sacramento, California, 1969.

U.S. Department of Health, Education and Welfare. "Individual School Report. Fall 1970 Elementary and Secondary School Civil Rights Survey." Survey forms, Sacramento City Unified School District. Office for Civil Rights, Washington, D.C.

Whinnery, Richard D., Program Specialist, Social Science, Curriculum Development Services, Sacramento City Unified School District. Memorandum to Dr. Agnes S. Robinson, Assistant Superintendent, Curriculum Development Services, Sacramento City Unified School District, April 24, 1968.

Chapter 9.

Assembly Bill No. 724, Amended in Senate August 3, 1971; Amended in Assembly April 2, 1971, California Legislature — 1971 Regular Session.

California State Department of Education. Bureau of Intergroup Relations. *A Proposal for a Technical Assistance Program on Problems of School Desegregation in California under the Provisions of the Civil Rights Act of 1964, Public Law 88-352, Title IV, Section 403.* Duration July 1, 1971 — June 30, 1972. The Department, Sacramento, California, March 23, 1971.

California State Department of Education. Bureau of Intergroup Relations. "Measuring Racial or Ethnic Imbalance in the Pupil Enrollment of a School." Report CE-IR-149. Sacramento, California, November 29, 1968.

"Chronicle of Race and Schools, December, 1970 — January, 1971," *Integrated Education: Race and Schools,* Vol. 9, No. 2 (March — April, 1971), pp. 50-60.

"Chronicle of Race and Schools, April — May, 1971," *Integrated Education: Race and Schools,* Vol. 9, No. 4 (July — August, 1971), pp. 50-66.

Gitelson, Alfred E. "The Power and Duty to Integrate," *Integrated Education: Race and Schools,* Vol. 8, No. 3 (May — June, 1970), pp. 10-15.

Griffin, Ples A., Bureau of Intergroup Relations, California State Department of Education. Memorandum to the author, June 23, 1970. (typewritten)

Knight, Gladieux & Smith, Inc. *Long Range Sites and Facilities Plan. Sacramento City Unified School District, Sacramento, California,* San Francisco, California, October 6, 1969.

Rafferty, Max. *Max Rafferty on Education.* New York: The Devin-Adair Co., 1968.

Sacramento City Unified School District. *A Conceptual Plan for Meeting the Long-Range Site and Facility Needs of the District.* Sacramento, California, November 17, 1971.

Sacramento City Unified School District. *A Time Phased Plan for Meeting the Long-Range Site and Facility Needs of the District.* Sacramento, California, February 4, 1972.

Telephone interviews with staff of Sacramento City Unified School District and Bureau of Intergroup Relations, California State Department of Education, January 12, February 19 and 25, 1972.

U.S. Department of Health, Education and Welfare. "Individual School Report. Fall 1970 Elementary and Secondary School Civil Rights Survey." Survey forms, Sacramento City Unified School District. Office for Civil Rights, Washington, D.C.

Weigel, Stanley A. "Supreme Court Ruling Applied in California," *Integrated Education: Race and Schools,* Vol. 9, No. 4 (July — August, 1971), pp. 29-33.

Index

Summary and Conclusions: Implications for Future Desegregation

The three school districts covered in this report made substantial gains in pupil desegregation in the 1960s and into the 1970s, particularly after passage of the 1964 Civil Rights Act. Two of the school systems, Charlottesville, Virginia, and Providence, Rhode Island, implemented desegregation plans that covered all grade levels and eliminated all predominantly black regular elementary, middle, junior high, and senior high schools. Charlottesville no longer operates any all-white schools and Providence has made progress in this area. In addition to accomplished major pupil desegregation, the three school districts also began to recognize and address themselves in some way to what might be called the "second front" of desegregation—the problems of bias, discrimination, and inequality within schools and the task of reorienting school staffs and programs to the new educational situation resulting from desegregation. In another significant gain, school officials in these systems were beginning to revise and extend desegregation plans without the full-scale community campaigns required to start the desegregation process at an earlier stage. By the time this study ended, it appeared that school boards and administrators in these districts had accepted, at least at some level, that the task of maintaining desegregated schools was one of their on-going responsibilities.

While progress in these districts was very real, their experiences point up some of the major weaknesses in the process of school desegregation at the local district level, as it has existed to date. First, desegregation in these districts proceeded entirely too slowly, taking place in a halting and piecemeal way, through a series of partial plans spaced out over a period of time. There were sometimes one to three years between major desegregation efforts. In the most extreme of the cases studied—Charlottesville, Virginia—it was 12 years—one whole generation of school chil-

dren—between the time the first suit was filed and full desegregation of all grades. Second, the desegregation process was unequal.
With some notable exceptions, the bulk of the desegregation
carried out in these districts was designed so that the minority
community made most of the changes and sacrifices necessary
to bring about racially mixed school populations. Schools in
minority neighborhoods were generally closed or converted to
special use, and blacks and Mexicans were usually reassigned
long distances from home, requiring busing, while whites, if
transferred at all, were generally close enough to their new
schools to walk. This was done not because it was the only way
or the best way the schools could be desegregated, but because
of fears that whites would not tolerate their children being
assigned to ghetto and barrio schools and would not accept the
inconvenience of busing.

Third, an important problem illustrated by these case studies
is the reluctance of school administrators to come to grips with
racial and race-related educational problems in the schools.
Racism on the part of teachers and principals, inadequate minority staff, discrimination against blacks and Mexicans at administrative levels, and the biased nature of the curriculum were
among the other racial and equal-education problems that came
to a head in these districts with desegregation. Finally, in spite
of the 1954 Supreme Court decision outlawing school segregation, the 1964 Civil Rights Act, and state policy calling for
an end to segregation and racial imbalance in Providence and
Sacramento, too little action to bring about desegregation was
initiated at the federal and state levels. Local leaders, mainly
in the black community, were instrumental in bringing federal
and state anti-discrimination policy to bear in these districts,
but very little federal and state pressure originated with the
responsible governmental agencies. If concerned citizens had
waited on appropriate federal and state officials to enforce desegregation on their own, or had depended on them to do most
of the prodding, these districts would probably still be segregated.

What can we learn from these three school districts' experiences as far as future desegregation is concerned? How can
local districts accomplish desegregation more quickly, on a more
comprehensive basis, and with more fairness to minority groups?
How can districts better cope with school racial and educational
problems after desegregation? How can federal and state policy
be more effective in bringing about desegregation at the local
level? The following summary of the most important findings
of the study focuses on these and other key questions.

PLANNING COMPREHENSIVE DESEGREGATION

1. *Desegregation should be defined in terms of racial balance, or a desired ratio of blacks to whites in each school.*

The decision to approach desegregation by establishing racial balance in each school was one of the most important developments furthering broad-scale desegregation in these districts. Definitions of racial balance vary, but they usually set a minimum and maximum percentage of minorities that can be assigned to any one school. The ratio of black or minority students to white students that is incorporated in such a formula frequently approximates the black/white or minority/white proportions in the total school enrollment. A racial balance formula of this kind has the following advantages: (a) it emphasizes districtwide desegregation, since the ratio applies equally to all schools; (b) it eliminates the all-white and overwhelmingly white school, as well as the all-black or predominantly minority school; (c) it closes off white "escape" areas within a district, since all schools are desegregated and (d) it establishes a clear, positive standard for desegregation.

Similarly, racial balance goals applied at the classroom level avoid segregated learning situations within desegregated schools. A racial balance classroom approach can also prevent the isolation of one or two black children by fixing a minimum number of minority children that can be assigned to any one class.

2. *Desegregation should be implemented in all schools at once, rather than gradually in successive stages.*

The partial and piecemeal approach to desegregation in these districts tended to drag out the issue in the community, keep school officials and community leaders tied up with desegregation plans over a period of years, delay building programs and other planning, and keep some minority pupils enrolled in segregated schools. Postponing desegregation did not make it easier, nor did successful experience with one phase of desegregation necessarily prevent confrontations over extending integration to other segments of the school population.

By contrast, an all-inclusive, districtwide plan, implemented in one step, would resolve the issue quickly, give both white and minority children the benefits of a desegregated education, and permit the school district to go ahead with solutions to other pressing problems.

3. *Districts should desegregate with currently available facilities, rather than wait for the completion of elaborate building programs.*

The variety of methods of reassigning pupils and reorganizing schools used successfully in these districts indicates there is no one way or model way to desegregate and that desegregation can generally be carried out within the framework of existing space, provided that all buildings are used. Nearly all desegregation in these districts took place without waiting on the completion of new buildings, sometimes by combining different approaches to school or grade reorganization. Specific techniques of desegregation that worked at some point in the districts' desegregation histories include: the realignment of attendance boundaries to get a better racial mix; a modified version of school pairing combining the attendance areas of three contiguous schools; the creation of model schools to attract and hold whites; a one-grade citywide center; reorganization of high school feeder patterns on a racial basis; mandatory reassignment of both white and minority children to nearby and distant schools; closing minority schools or converting them to special use; assignment of black children to previously white schools; assignment of white pupils to formerly black schools; and short- and long-distance busing of some children for desegregation purposes.

It appears that even small school districts will have to combine several different methods or techniques to achieve complete desegregation and that total desegregation cannot be accomplished without reassigning both white and minority children.

4. *All school policies and practices that contribute to segregation should be abandoned.*

There was a tendency in these districts, usually in the earlier phases of desegregation, to focus on pupil assignments or school reorganization needed to implement some desegregation, while continuing other policies and practices that caused or continued segregation in other segments of the school population. Transfer policies, new building, other school reorganization, and auxiliary moves to free space for desegregation sometimes increased segregation in schools not involved in the desegregation program.

Total desegregation cannot be achieved or maintained unless all policies and practices that foster separation are reversed or abandoned.

5. *Procedures for reviewing and revising desegregation plans should be established.*

With new schools opening and old schools closing, records of population and enrollment shifts, periodic racial censuses of the schools, and records of classroom assignments by race were important aids in monitoring the progress of desegregation projects. In the two larger districts, appointment of an intergroup relations officer and an equal educational opportunity officer